The Sydney Morning Herald

good food
guide 2001

terry durack & jill dupleix

with Country Editor Bruce Elder

ANNE O'DONOVAN

Sixteenth edition, August 2000

Published by Anne O'Donovan Pty Ltd
171 La Trobe Street, Melbourne 3000

First published in 1984
Fully revised and reset for this edition

Edited by Foong Ling Kong
Indexed by Ev Beissbarth
Cover design by Cheryl Collins
Cover photograph by Alan Weekes, taken at Otto
Text design by Ruth Grüner
Hat design by David Band
Typeset by Ruth Grüner and J&M Typesetting
Maps by Country Cartographics
Printed in Australia by McPherson's
Distributed by Penguin Books Australia Ltd
Advertising sales (02) 9282 2833

National Library of Australia
Cataloguing-in-Publication entry:

The Sydney Morning Herald good food guide.
16th ed.
Includes index.
ISBN 1 876026 34 0.
1. Restaurants – New South Wales – Sydney region –
Directories. I. Dupleix, Jill. II. Durack, Terry. III. Title:
Good food guide.
647.959441

Copyright in photographs: George Fetting (pp. iii, vii,viii,
xii, 1, 20, 43, 64, 86, 108 and 131); Jill Dupleix (pp. 153,
154 and 218).

Every effort has been made to ensure that the
information in this book is accurate and up to date.
The editors and publisher welcome advice of any
changes or corrections for the next edition.

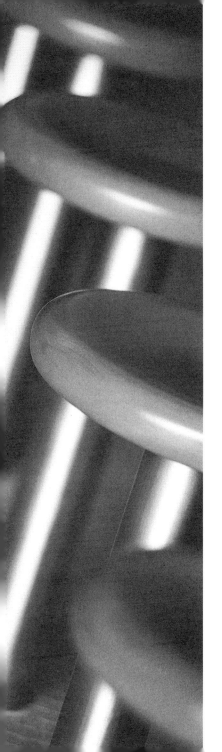

contents

2001: the future is here

Some cities live for the past, and some for the present. Sydney lives for the future, which is why dining here is unlike dining anywhere else in the world.

Spruced up in time for our big coming-out party, otherwise known as the Olympic Games, Sydney is now ready to share its good fortune. There are probably more great restaurants, bars and cafés than four million people have a right to enjoy all to themselves anyway.

What is Sydney food? It's smart, casual and solar-powered. It's a quick grill and a glass of sunny wine, a platter of seafood by the sea, and some French-based finesse and Italian-based hospitality when you need it. It's rice noodles in a designer teahouse and Grange Hermitage by the glass in a sparkling city eyrie. You will see a lot of Asian ingredients and techniques used cleverly and authentically, and you'll find widespread acceptance of simple Mediterranean flavours. These diverse dining experiences are not fused into some global mish-mash, but simply re-presented, in true Sydney style. Sydney takes what it likes from global trends, and fits them into its own sense of itself.

Tracking the trends of the last year leads directly to the water. The completion of East Circular Quay and The Wharf Woolloomooloo have raised the standards of harbourside eating to way beyond tourist fodder. The second biggest trend is the Smart Casual bistro: small and streetside, with great food, low prices, a no-nonsense licence, no bookings and no fuss.

The introduction of a goods and services tax (GST) and the probability of new smoking bans (detailed in the following pages) will also affect dining habits.

Sydney-siders love eating out, and take advantage of the climate to do so in every sunny corner. They love being tourists in their own town – and their own state – and this attitude has led to a bright, sunny, casual form of dining that most cities would kill for.

This, the sixteenth edition of *The Sydney Morning Herald Good Food Guide*, contains more restaurants than any other edition. What is especially pleasing is the groundswell of consistently enjoyable restaurants at the lower end of the scale. The extraordinary thing about the recent restaurant boom is that most of it is about quality rather than quantity, reflected in the number of restaurants winning the coveted chef hats' awards. This means Sydney dining is getting better from the ground up – a healthy thing for the future of democratic dining.

There are serpents in Paradise, however. We would like to see the end of foiled butter portions, overfilled wine glasses, bland background music, wine lists without vintages, restaurant names ripped off from overseas, gratuitous garnishing, food in bowls (other than soup), fluffy bread, fish knives, sticky toffee pudding in summer, having to ask for a glass of water and paying precocious prices in junior establishments.

Even so, the *New York Times* has been moved to compare Sydney to Paris, London and New York, calling it 'the home port of the good life'. But we think Paris, London and New York still have a fair way to go.

TERRY DURACK & JILL DUPLEIX

gst: its initial impact

On 1 July 2000, all food served in Australian restaurants and cafés became subject to a new 10 per cent GST (Goods and Services Tax). We have taken this into account when calculating the costs of meals. However, these costs are estimates only, and should be used only as an approximate guide. It's worth pointing out that the cost of eating out in Sydney still compares more than favourably with just about any other major city in the world.

the smoke clears

By the time you read this, a Bill will have been put before State Parliament banning smoking inside restaurants or cafés in New South Wales. In the event of its being passed, the smoking policy listed in each review will be redundant. We include it only because at the time of going to press, it was not clear when the new law would be coming into force. The best advice would be to ask when booking.

the olympic thing

For three weeks in September 2000, Sydney will be like a foreign city to its residents, and will indeed be a foreign city to over a million visitors. The Olympics will place more strain on our resources than any single event in this city's history.

The rule is: don't assume anything. Don't assume you can get a table at any restaurant you want just by booking a week or so ahead. Several of our top restaurants are booked out by corporate or international bodies for the duration. But don't assume you can't get in, either. The timing of Olympic events means that Olympic visitors will often be dining in the late afternoon and late evening. So you may be able to get a table after all.

It is the perfect time to explore the dining scene away from the city centre, but give yourself plenty of time to get anywhere you're going, as frustrations are inevitable.

The hospitality industry will be stretched to its utmost, in supplying young and often quickly trained staff to cope with the demand. As a diner, your patience may be required.

Another unknown quantity is the effect hugely inflated demand on restaurants and cafés during the Olympics will have on prices. Top-quality food supplies are not inexhaustible, and prices may well suffer a temporary increase before things get back to normal. If things ever do get back to normal.

thanks

Anyone can go out to dinner, but it takes a special mix of talents to be able to convey an entire dining experience with wit, knowledge and informed judgement.

The editors would like to thank the following for their dedication to the usually enjoyable, but sometimes challenging, task of eating their way around Sydney: Jane Adams, Maggie Alderson, Keith Austin, David Dale, George Epaminondas, Matthew Evans, Carolyn Garner, Guy Griffin, Dennis Hearfield, Kendall Hill, Rosemary Lobban, Les Luxford, Jannine Mezrani, Lyndey Milan, Lynne Mullins, Philip Putnam, Alan Saunders and Kim Terakes.

It takes even more fortitude, not to mention fuel, to eat your way around the whole state, as well as Canberra. Thanks go to country editor Bruce Elder, as well as Matthew Evans, Molly Foskett, Lynne Mullins, John Pegrum, Philip Putnam, Rosemary Stanton and Simon Thomsen.

Gratitude also goes to editor Foong Ling Kong, publishing administrator Marg Slessar and publisher Anne O'Donovan for yet another as-perfect-as-possible edition.

Thanks, too, to our indispensable administrator Donna Maiolo and coordinator Sue McGuinn for their ceaseless efforts, and to designers Cheryl Collins (for the cover) and Ruth Grüner (for everything else).

Finally, thanks to the team at Otto for the cover photography, to George Fetting for the interior photography, and to all our readers for their feedback and support. You're the ones we do it for, after all.

policy statement

This is the most up-to-date, honest and helpful guide humanly possible, given the dynamism of the Sydney dining scene. Every restaurant is revisited, rejudged and rescored each year by an experienced member of our reviewing team. Reviewers visit in anonymity, and pay in full. This year, the budget has been extended to allow a minimum of two visits by different reviewers for all three-hat contenders and any contentious two-hat contenders.

This is not a restaurant guide written for restaurateurs, nor to amuse a small dining elite. It is for everyone who eats out – whether it be twice a year or twice a week. It should help you choose the right restaurant for the occasion, and get better value for your money.

The editors welcome your feedback, care of The Sydney Morning Herald, 201 Sussex Street, Sydney, or email tdurack@ozemail.com.au or jdupleix@ozemail.com.au

need to know

The new review format makes it easier to see the important stuff at a glance. At the top of each entry, symbols will denote any special awards, good value (under $60 for two) and good wine lists. (See key to symbols on page *xii*.)

The digest of relevant information is now at the base of the page. The term BYO means you can bring your own bottled wine, which will generally incur a small corkage charge per head or per bottle (corkage of more than $5 is not considered hospitable enough to be given the BYO symbol). Wine by the glass is listed only if we consider the choices substantial enough.

The cost quoted is for *two courses* each, for two people, without drinks.

If you have special concerns, the information at the bottom of each review should give you the answers. If not, always ring the restaurant to check the things that are crucial to your enjoyment.

the scores

We score restaurants out of 20 because we believe it to be the fairest way for us to judge and the easiest way for you to understand where a restaurant sits among its peers.

Of the 20 points, 10 points are for food (quality, value, technique, philosophy, commitment etc.), 5 points for the people (service, greeting, timing etc.), 3 points for the place itself (atmosphere, comfort, style, noise levels etc.) and the final 2 points are for what our experience and instinct tell us is true.

1–9	Not good enough
10–11	Needs work, can improve
12	Satisfactory, without being special
13	Pleasant, agreeable dining
14	Good food, service and atmosphere (exceptional cases will be awarded one hat)
15	♟ Really good food, service and atmosphere
16	♟♟ Really, really good food service and atmosphere
17	♟♟ Great food, service and atmosphere
18	♟♟♟ Excellent food, service and atmosphere
19	♟♟♟ A uniquely wonderful dining experience
20	♟♟♟ The very best of food, service and atmosphere

awards

🍷🍷🍷 Banc | Claudes | MG Garage | Rockpool | Tetsuya's

🍷🍷 Aria | Bathers' Pavilion | bel mondo | Bistro Moncur | Boathouse on Blackwattle Bay | Buon Ricordo | Catalina Rose Bay | Cicada | Forty One | Golden Century | Longrain | Lucio's | Marque | Paramount | Pier | Sailors Thai | Salt | Wockpool

🍷 Ampersand | Aqua Luna | Arakawa | Arena | bonne femme | Darling Mills | De Beers Whale Beach | Eleni's | Elio | Fuel | Galileo | Grace | Grappa | harbour kitchen & bar | Hugo's | International | The Jersey Cow | Kam Fook | Lothar's on Pymble Hill | Mezzaluna | Milsons | The Mixing Pot | Oh! Calcutta! | Otto | Pavilion on the Park | Post | Prime | Pruniers | Ristorante Riva | Sean's Panaroma | Unkai | Ying's Seafood Restaurant

country

🍷🍷 Cleopatra | Fins | Selkirks

🍷 Atlantic | Caffe Bassano | Cellar Restaurant | Darley's | Juniperberry at the NGA | Lynwood Café | Ottoman Cuisine Ristorante Due Mezzi | Scott Street Restaurant | Silk's Brasserie | Vulcans

restaurant of the year
Banc

best new restaurant
Longrain

best country restaurant
Fins (Byron Bay)

best café Latteria

best bar International

special categories

best chinese Golden Century
best french Claudes
best indian Oh! Calcutta!
best japanese Unkai
best malaysian Temasek
best seafood Pier
best steak Prime
best thai Longrain
best turkish Ottoman Cuisine (Canberra)
best vegetarian Bodhi Vegetarian
best yum cha Kam Fook

the sydney morning herald award for professional excellence

DAVID THOMPSON for the integrity and scholarly passion he brought to Thai food, raising the standards of all Sydney dining by showing what is possible within a single cuisine.

the vittoria coffee silver service award

JENNICE KERSH of Edna's Table, for years of service to the fine art of hospitality, and for making celebrities feel like regulars and regulars feel like celebrities.

the josephine pignolet award

KYLIE SIMPSON of Lynwood Café, a young chef with a passion for good food linked with a philosophy of tradition. She receives a return flight to London courtesy of QANTAS, and a set of Furi Australian-designed professional knives from Furitechnics.

$ good value

CITY

2 ENTRÉES AND 2 MAINS FOR $60 AND UNDER

Abhi's | Alhambra | An Restaurant | Andy's | Azteca's | BBQ King | bills | bills 2 | Bodhi Vegetarian | Bombay Heritage | Caffé Agostinis | Casa Asturiana | Chinta Ria Temple of Love | Corinthian | Dakhni | Domo Sushi Kitchen | Dragonfly | Emperor's Garden BBQ | Epoque | Fez Cafe | Fifi's | Fishface | Flavour of India Edgecliff | Flavour of India Glebe | Flavours of Peking | Fu-Manchu | Fu-Manchu Bondi | Harry's Fish Cafe | Iku | Il Baretto | Indian Palace | Ju-Ju | Kokum – Taste of Goa | La Disfida | Malabar | Malaya on George | Masuya | Minh | Obar | Ocean King House | Odeon | Onde | Original Peking VIP | Out of Africa | Paddington Inn | Prasit's Northside Thai Takeaway | Radio Cairo | Raw Bar | Sam Won Garden | Scoozi Trattoria | Shimbashi Soba | Sosumi Sushi Bar | Summerland | Szechuan Garden | Taqsim | Temasek | Thanh Binh | Tsukasa | Uchi Lounge | U-Turn | Yulla

COUNTRY

2 ENTRÉES AND 2 MAINS FOR $60 AND UNDER

Abell's Kopi Tiam | Bianca's | Caffe Bassano | Civic Theatre Brasserie | Doncaster Inn | Echidna Cafe | The Elephant Bean | Elton's Cafe | Inland Cafe | Loaves and the Dishes | Georgie's Cafe | Jameson's on the Pier | The Little Snail | Pacific Hotel Bistro | The Post Office Restaurant | The Rimbolin | Silo Bakery | The Silos | Station Street | The Sturt Café | Tasuke | That Noodle Place | Timmy's Kitchen | Victory Theatre Cafe | Viva Zapata | The Wheelhouse

⚱ good wine lists

CITY

Ampersand | Arena | Aria | Banc | Banjo Paterson Cottage | Bathers' Pavilion | Bathers' Pavilion Café | Bayswater Brasserie | bel mondo | Beppi's | The Boathouse on Blackwattle Bay | Bocca | Bohem | Buon Ricordo | Catalina Rose Bay | Cicada | Claudes | Coast | Cottage Point Inn | Courtney's Brasserie | Darling Mills | Dolphin on Crown | Edna's Table | Forty One | Gekko | Grace | Grand National | Grappa | harbour kitchen & bar | International | Jaspers | Kable's | Kingsleys Steakhouse | Kök (shirk) | La Grillade | Lennons | Longrain | Lothar's on Pymble Hill | Manta Ray | Marque | Mezzaluna | MG Garage | Milsons | Mosaic | Nelsons Brasserie | Niche Dining House | Otto | Paramount | Pavilion on the Park | Pier | Post | Prime | Pruniers | Quay | Rockpool | Royal Hotel Restaurant | Salt | San Francisco Grill | Slip Inn | Tetsuya's | Two Chefs on Stanley | Vault | Watermark | Wine Banc | Wockpool | Zaaffran

COUNTRY

Cafe Albion | Cellar Restaurant | The Chairman & Yip | Chez Pok | Credo Restaurant | Darley's | Feast | Fins | Juniperberry at the NGA | Merrett's at Peppers Anchorage | The Old George and Dragon | Roberts at Pepper Tree | Silk's Brasserie | Willowvale Mill

watch this space

arte e cucina

2 SHORT STREET, DOUBLE BAY
PHONE 9328 0880 | Lucio Galletto of Lucio's
combines art and cooking in a neo-Tuscan
trattoria tucked away in a Double Bay site
that many will remember as the old Zigolini's.
Opens August 2000.

biba

155 VICTORIA STREET, POTTS POINT
PHONE 9357 6060 | Chef Jimmy Tsimikas
moves into the old Star Bar & Grill/Rocket/
Arthur's site with a wood-burning grill, two
bars and casual southern French, Northern
Italian food, seven days a week. Now open.

celsius

66 PITT STREET, SYDNEY PHONE 8214 0496 |
Cicada's Peter Doyle moves into a sleek city
eatery to do contemporary French food for
lunch and dinner. Opens August 2000.

establishment

252 GEORGE STREET, SYDNEY
PHONE 9240 3000 | Justin Hemmes heads up
the Hemmes family's most ambitious project
yet. Housed within Heritage-listed skin, it
includes a sushi bar, three bars, Tank nightclub,
a small luxury hotel, two ball rooms, and est,
a restaurant headed by ex-CBD chef Matthew
Fleming. Opens August 2000.

hugo's lounge

33 BAYSWATER ROAD, KINGS CROSS
PHONE 9357 4411 | It's been a long time
between cocktails for the much-loved Hugo's
team from Bondi, as they put together a
restaurant, bar, private dining rooms and
lounge, open from 6pm for cocktails until late.
Opens September 2000.

kingsleys steak & crab house

9 THE WHARF WOOLLOOMOOLOO,
6 COWPER WHARF ROAD, WOOLLOOMOOLOO
PHONE 9331 7788 | Turf meets surf as
Sydney's pubby, clubby steak specialist goes
harbourside, adding clam chowder and crab
cocktails to aged Angus rumps. Now open.

laurent boulangerie pâtisserie

3 THE WHARF WOOLLOOMOOLOO,
6 COWPER WHARF ROAD, WOOLLOOMOOLOO
PHONE 9380 4718 | Highly decorated
French cakes, freshly baked breads, ice-creams,
confectionery and coffee run from 7am to
7pm in Laurent Boillon's smart bakery café.
Now open.

quay

OVERSEAS PASSENGER TERMINAL,
CIRCULAR QUAY PHONE 9251 5600 | While
Quay was the winner of three hats last year, as
we go to press, the future of its star chef
Guillaume Brahimi is in doubt, so this year's
experience must remain unscored (see review).

tetsuya's

529 KENT STREET, SYDNEY PHONE 9267 2900 |
Tetsuya Wakuda, Sydney's most original
chef, finally makes the move from his much-
acclaimed Tetsuya's (see review) to a large city
space that once housed the Suntory Japanese
restaurant. Opens October 2000.

symbols

 Award-winning restaurants

 Restaurant of the year

 Best new restaurant

 Best country restaurant

 Best café

 Best bar

 Best special-category restaurant

§ Good value

𝒴 Good wine list

 Non-smoking policy or area

AE   American Express

BC   Bankcard

DC   Diners Club

MC   Mastercard

V   Visa

city 2001

$

abhi's

163 CONCORD ROAD, NORTH STRATHFIELD
PHONE 9743 3061   MAP 6

INDIAN

Abhi's is as bright as a button; which isn't
bad going for a restaurant nine years in
the same place, and with only a minor
renovation a couple of years ago. The cosy
downstairs room fills up fast, and the
upstairs dining room is in constant demand
to absorb the overflow – if overflow can run
upstairs, that is. The views back to the city
lights are satisfying rather than spectacular,
and the same must be said about the food.
Alu tikki had wonderful flavours but
featured cold potato patties and a chickpea
masala of soggy pulses. Better was the
palak patta chaat, a street-food staple of
crisp spinach leaves in lentil batter rather
overwhelmed by a saucy combination of
date, tamarind, chilli and mint. Beef ishtew,
from the southern state of Kerala, was just a
beef stew, with added interest coming from
some excellent, house-made pickles (the
green chilli is wonderful). Be prepared for
the odd wait when it's busy – and it's
always busy.

licensed & byo
lunch Mon–Fri & Sun noon–3pm
dinner Daily 6–10pm
cards AE BC DC MC V   Bookings essential
seats 180; private room; wheelchair access;
no smoking ☒
owner Kumar Mahadevan
chefs Kumar Mahadevan & Gopal Kochak
cost Around $60 for two, plus drinks
plus Hot pickles   **minus** Arctic air-con
score 12/20

$

alhambra

SHOP 1, 54 WEST ESPLANADE, MANLY
PHONE 9976 2975   MAP 7

MOROCCAN/SPANISH

Even toned knights in fireproof armour find
it hard to compete when there's a sprightly
tagine of chicken and preserved lemon on
the table. There was a fire in the serviced
apartments above the Alhambra the night
we were there, but such is the draw of the
food that the local firemen were paid only
cursory attention. While much of the menu
is Spanish – chorizo and sardines for tapas,
paella to share – there are plenty of North
African touches, too. The couscous is
gossamer light, steamed not twice, but
three times. There are Moroccan beef
meatballs, fragrant in a succulent tomato
sauce and even a rosewater-scented burnt
cream (like a crème brûlée, with a soft
rather than crisp top). Noise levels soar as
numbers increase, and the service can be
very backpackerish. At these prices,
however, it would be mean-spirited to
complain, so we won't.

licensed & byo
lunch Mon–Fri noon–3pm; Sat–Sun noon–5pm
dinner Daily 6–10.30pm
cards AE BC DC MC V   Bookings recommended,
essential weekends
seats 124; outdoor area; wheelchair access;
non-smoking area ☒
owner/chef Aziz Bakalla
cost Around $52 for two, plus drinks
plus Aromatic spicing   **minus** Trainee staff
score 13/20

alio

5 BAPTIST STREET, SURRY HILLS
PHONE 8394 9368   MAP 3B

ITALIAN

In a year when every second new Sydney restaurant seems to sport an East Circular Quay address and property-developer views, Alio comes as something of a change. For a start, it has Redfern at its front and Surry Hills at its back, and the view is of jasmine creeping over uninspired cream brick. Nevertheless, it is an attractive, spacious bar and dining room, with its Mary Quant cutout panels, long banquette seating and sleek, dark jarrah chairs. While its young owners may not be household names yet, give them time. Chef Ashley Hughes cooked at London's River Café, and it shows in a menu that includes spaghetti vongole cooked bravely al dente with no shortage of sweet baby clams. Fig and prosciutto salad is freshness on a plate, and a bollito misto of mixed boiled meats has bounce and flavour. It's not an *Italian* Italian restaurant, but it is a good modern Italianish restaurant.

licensed; wine by the glass
lunch Tues–Sat noon–3pm
dinner Mon–Sat 6–10.30pm
cards AE BC DC MC V   Bookings recommended
seats 90; wheelchair access; no smoking ♿
owners Ashley Hughes, Tracey Hughes & Ciaran Carmichael
chef Ashley Hughes
cost Around $86 for two, plus drinks
plus Finesse with pasta   **minus** Alio should be aglio (garlic in Italian)
score 14/20

al ponte

LEVEL 2, HARBOURSIDE, 461 DARLING HARBOUR
PHONE 9212 6001   MAP 5B

ITALIAN

The waiter seemed quite thrilled that we liked the linguine with clams. 'And do you know,' he beamed, 'that the chef isn't even Italian – he's German, like me.' We have no problem with the notion of Germans cooking and serving Italian food, but wondered if this explained the conservatism of the menu. 'Breaded veal escalopes' with cheese, roast chicken and onions, beef carpaccio, baked eggplant, seafood risotto and tiramisu were all pleasantly made, but reminiscent of the kind of dishes we were eating in Leichhardt ten years ago. When the chef tried to be more ambitious, it didn't quite come off. The meat component of the vitello tonnato seemed dry, and the tuna sauce was not altogether together. If you're in the Darling Harbour neighbourhood at lunchtime, however, you can still do quite well at Al Ponte. Enjoy the water views and the cheerful service, but stick to simple things such as the linguine with clams.

licensed
lunch Mon–Fri & Sun noon–2.30pm
dinner Daily 6.30–10.30pm; Saturday from 6.30pm
cards AE BC DC MC V   No bookings
seats 300; private room; outdoor area; wheelchair access; non-smoking area ♿
owner Domenic Moio
chef Azmi Jamar
cost Around $86 for two, plus drinks
plus Cockle Bay views   **minus** Conservative food
score 11/20

ampersand

LEVEL 2, THE ROOF TERRACE,
COCKLE BAY WHARF, DARLING PARK,
201 SUSSEX STREET, SYDNEY
PHONE 9264 6666   MAP 1

MODERN AUSTRALIAN

Ampersand burst flamboyantly onto the
Sydney scene two years ago with its creator,
Tony Bilson, boldly predicting that it would
soon be listed among the ten greatest
restaurants of the world. With time, Bilson
has wound back his ambitions somewhat.
The wine list, along with lunch prices, seem
more pared back than before. The haute
cuisine has become simpler, and the waiters
more relaxed. The plush couches and
sparkling view of Darling Harbour, however,
remain the same. Ampersand has now
settled into the middle ranks of Sydney fine
dining, with well-crafted French food and
the odd Japanese touch. Bilson spends more
time in the kitchen than before, generating
classics such as zucchini flowers stuffed
with lobster mousseline, duck terrine with
foie gras, and peppered chocolate tarte.

licensed; wine by the glass
lunch Mon–Fri noon–3pm
dinner Mon–Sat 6–10.30pm
cards AE BC DC MC V   Bookings recommended
seats 250; private room; outdoor area;
wheelchair access; non-smoking area
owners Tony Bilson & Company
chefs Tony Bilson & Haru Inukai
fixed price lunch $49.50 p.p. for two courses;
dinner around $135 for two, plus drinks
plus Graceful comfort   **minus** Narrow walkways
score 15/20

an restaurant

29–31 GREENFIELD PARADE, BANKSTOWN
PHONE 9796 7826   MAP 6

VIETNAMESE

So much for all our jokes about Vietnamese
pho soup being the fast food of the future.
An is now run as if it's a modern burger
joint, complete with a computer-coded
ordering system that goes straight to the
kitchen, and the dreaded but practical
plakky bowls colour-coordinated to the
jungle-green décor. All the good bits are still
there, however: the hustle-and-bustle
shared tables, the babies and grandmas, the
young coconut juice, the bowls of freshly
chopped chilli and the boutique range of
eight different pho soups. An still does the
best pho ga in town, with its fragrant
chicken broth, tender slices of chicken,
greens and bean shoots, and a great pho
dac biet, of beefy bits. Ask for the smoky
chilli oil as an extra, tuck in, then go
shopping in the great Asian food stores
of Bankstown for your next meal.

unlicensed
hours Daily 7am–9pm
cards None   No bookings
seats 135; wheelchair access;
non-smoking area
owner Phantran Pty Ltd
chef Xuan Doan Phan
cost Around $22 for two, plus drinks
plus Great stocks
minus Shame about the plastic
score 12/20

andy's

658 BOURKE STREET, REDFERN
PHONE 9319 6616   MAP 3B

MALAYSIAN INDIAN

Some restaurants are made for going out to,
while others are more for dropping in to, on
the way home from the office, or on the
way out. This neighbourly Indian/Malaysian,
with its low-key takeaway-counter ambience
and friendly, honest ways, definitely falls
into the latter category. Locals barely give
the menu a second glance, for they already
know they'll be having the rich and spicy
beef rendang, or the lamb biryani of electric
yellow rice with its little booby traps of star
anise. Or maybe the murtabak – a moreish
Malaysian bread stuffed with minced meat,
onions and eggs. Cheap and cheerful is the
catch-cry here. The staff couldn't be nicer if
they tried, and the prices are, well, quaint.
The great thing about the weekend lunches
is the dosai: delicious, crisp riceflour
pancakes. And we've found the Malay
equivalent of bill's ricotta hot cakes with
banana – Andy's roti pisang of roti bread
stuffed with sweet bananas.

byo
lunch Sat–Sun noon–3pm
dinner Tues–Sun 6–11pm
cards AE BC DC MC V   Bookings recommended
seats 60
owners Andy Mohamed, Raj Palany
& Christina Ganaesan
chef Christina Ganaesan
cost Around $30 for two, plus drinks
plus Weekend dosai   **minus** Bain-marie
score 12/20

aqua luna

NO. 2, SHOP 18, OPERA QUAYS,
EAST CIRCULAR QUAY
PHONE 9251 0311   MAP 1

ITALIAN/MEDITERRANEAN

What a likeable restaurant to have right on
the harbour at East Circular Quay. Once you
find the entrance (up the grand staircase
and to your right) walk past an array of
market-fresh vegetables awaiting the chef's
chopper. Prime position is a comfy dark
chocolate booth from which you can survey
the long stretch of diners along the
windows. The menu is a love affair with
Italian dishes from beautiful vegetable and
seafood salads to classics such as a
20-minute risotto (that means it's done
properly, from scratch). Chef Darren Simpson
is on assisted passage from Conran's
Sartoria restaurant, and is a great enthusiast
for rich, full-bodied Italian flavour. His food
runs a fine line between gusto (risotto with
rabbit) and finesse (oven-roasted fish), and
prices are gently sloping rather than steep.
The menu changes often – just when you
want that seafood salad again, it's deep-
fried sweetbreads with zucchini flowers.

licensed; wine by the glass
lunch Mon–Fri noon–2.30pm
dinner Mon–Sat 6–11pm
cards AE BC DC MC V   Bookings recommended
seats 140; wheelchair access; non-smoking
area ⚒
owner Leigh Moulds
chef Darren Simpson
cost Around $103 for two, plus drinks
plus Big windows   **minus** Low ceilings
score 15/20

arakawa

LEVEL 1, CHIFLEY PLAZA,
2 CHIFLEY SQUARE, SYDNEY
PHONE 9229 0191 MAP 1

JAPANESE

Is this Sydney's most restless restaurant?
It started life five years ago as Matsukaze,
the city's first specialist tempura bar.
Then the tempura turned into sushi, and
the menu ran the full gamut of Japanese
cooking. Now reborn as Arakawa, the dining
room has been redefined into a sleek non-
denominational space of grained woods,
chocolate carpets and recessed spotlights.
The idea, we're told, is to make it more
acceptable to a non-Japanese audience.
The menu does your thinking for you, with
a series of set-price lunchbox menus by day
and set-price kaiseki menus at night. The
skills of talented Takaaki Nakoji shine in
dishes such as his clever combination of
chilled fried eggplant and warm grilled eel,
and a delicate salad of okra, prawn, sea
urchin and wakame seaweed jelly, but we're
a little worried by fusion curiosities such as
grilled oysters with blue cheese and miso,
which were no better than oysters mornay.

licensed
lunch Mon–Fri from noon
dinner Mon–Sat from 6pm
cards AE BC DC MC V   Bookings essential
seats 80; private rooms; wheelchair access;
non-smoking area ⊱✘
owner MID Sydney Pty Ltd
chef Takaaki Nakoji
cost Around $140 for two, plus drinks
plus Bento boxes   **minus** Fusion flavours
score 14/20

arena

LEVEL 1, 212 BENT STREET, FOX STUDIOS
AUSTRALIA, MOORE PARK
PHONE 9361 3833 (GROUND FLOOR: ARENA
BAR AND BISTRO 9361 3930)   MAP 4B

MODERN AUSTRALIAN

While the eating outlets at Fox Studios have
met with mixed reviews, Arena stands out
like a high-powered light beam at a movie
premiere. Housed in a futuristic glasshouse,
it attracts a fair mix of destination diners
and pre- and post-showgoers. Downstairs is
a buzzy bar and a feed-'em-fast bistro, while
upstairs is a linger-longer restaurant flanked
by what looks like the world's longest red
sofa, and walls of serious wine racks. In the
see-through kitchen you can watch chef
Dean Sammut and his team go through
their paces. Sammut's classic training shows
in a show-stopping salad of crisped pigs'
cheeks with kipfler potatoes, and a mini-me
poule au pot of baby chicken, cocktail
boudin noir and liver dumpling with a
just-baked baby brioche. Prices are highish,
but you get lots of little extras on the side,
and the loos are gorgeous.

licensed; wine by the glass
dinner Tues–Sat 6–10.30pm
cards AE BC DC MC V   Bookings recommended
seats 120; private room; outdoor area;
wheelchair access; non-smoking area ⊱✘
owner Paul Dawson
chef Dean Sammut
cost Around $110 for two, plus drinks
plus The red banquette
minus The too-formal bar
score 15/20

aria

1 MACQUARIE STREET, EAST CIRCULAR QUAY
PHONE 9252 2555   MAP 1

MODERN AUSTRALIAN

Welcome to the big league, Matthew Moran. After carving out a cosy niche for himself among Potts Point's inner urbanites, this popular, high-profile chef and his team have gone decidedly upmarket, with a modern, ageless harbourside restaurant that's pulling in power Sydney in droves. See the Opera House, thrill to the bridge, gasp at the ferries. With its dullish, clubby bar, deluxe livery and well-honed service team, it's about as grown-up as Sydney gets. Can Moran grow into it? We think so. A tiny amuse-gueule tart of avocado, tuna and wasabi is so perfect, you want to amuse your gueule all night. Fish is a highlight, especially fleshy pan-fried snapper with prawn colcannon, while a perfect cylinder of roasted milk-fed veal rack with foie gras and potato galette is relaxed and refined. You can see in the detail and the quality where you are spending your money, but do the prices have to be quite so high? We don't think so.

licensed; wine by the glass
lunch Mon–Fri noon–2.30pm
dinner Mon–Sat 5.30–7pm pre-theatre; 7–11.30pm à la carte; Sun 6.30–10pm
cards AE BC DC MC V   Bookings recommended
seats 190; private room; wheelchair access
owners Peter Sullivan & Matthew Moran
chef Matthew Moran
cost Around $155 for two, plus drinks
plus The Opera House   **minus** Clichéd music
score 16/20

armstrongs manly

SHOP 213, MANLY WHARF, MANLY
PHONE 9976 3835   MAP 7

MODERN AUSTRALIAN

What can be nicer than to fall off the Manly ferry and straight into the arms of a bottle of James Squire amber ale or a classy glass of fruity cab merlot, and crisply battered fish and chips? Simplicity is the watchword here. An entrée of barbecued prawns is accompanied by a delicate mango and chilli dip, and for those who prefer turf to surf, the main course of spiced lamb loin is a more than adequate alternative. Service is super friendly, if occasionally erratic, and children are positively welcomed with a kids' meal that comprises chicken nuggets and smashing chips, pink lemonade (or, as we call it, Chef's Blood), and an ice-cream dessert. Not to be outdone, a semifreddo with espresso ice-cream is a chocolate mousse concoction that makes it a sin not to lick the plate. Since last year, Armstrongs has also acquired one of those shiny new licences that allow you to wander in for a drink without eating.

licensed; wine by the glass
hours Daily noon–11pm
cards AE BC DC MC V   Bookings recommended
seats 150; outdoor area; wheelchair access; no smoking inside until 3pm & 10pm
owner Tony Kalajzich
chef Tracy Braithwaite
cost Around $86 for two, plus drinks
plus High on location   **minus** Low on character
score 12/20

the asian kitchen

LEVEL 1, 220–888 BENT STREET,
FOX STUDIOS AUSTRALIA, MOORE PARK
PHONE 9358 4488   MAP 4B

CHINESE/ASIAN

When the Golden Century group first opened Asian Kitchen, it sported a fashionable but head-spinning pan-Asian menu that cavorted from China to Japan, to Thailand, to India. Later, the group decided to concentrate on doing what it does best, and installed a Golden Century chef and a mainly classical Cantonese and seafood menu. While you can still order the Japanese-influenced Unkai duck and a curious green tea fried rice, the real highlights are the Chinese classics. Try a steamed whole fish with soy, ginger and spring onions, simply cooked gai laan cabbage with ginger sauce (so much nicer than oyster sauce), and noodle dishes such as a suppertime favourite of silky, fresh rice noodles (hor fun) with beef. Attractively designed, with its open kitchen and clean, almost Scandinavian lines, the Asian Kitchen may well become the top-class Chinese the eastern suburbs has been missing.

licensed & byo
lunch Daily 11.30am–5pm
dinner Mon–Thurs 5–11pm; Fri–Sun 5–11.30pm
cards AE BC DC MC V   Bookings recommended
seats 200; wheelchair access;
non-smoking area ⃠
owners Eric & Linda Wong & Kevin Kam
chef Feng Wei Gang
cost Around $76 for two, plus drinks
plus Modern space   **minus** Noisy neighbours
score 13/20

awaba

67 THE ESPLANADE, BALMORAL
PHONE 9969 2104   MAP 7

MODERN AUSTRALIAN

Even a drizzly Sunday commands a respectable crowd at this white airy haven overlooking Sydney's most charming beach. What you read is what you get here. Uncomplicated and fresh, a penne salad with spinach, roast pumpkin, green bean and blue cheese succeeds in its simplicity. Awaba also passes the fish-and-chip test beautifully when a lovely, light, crisp batter coating perfectly cooked white flesh arrives – and the chips don't fare too badly either. There's corned beef on potatoey mash with mustard sauce, which is comforting and warm. The same can be said of the service – comforting and warm, that is, not potatoey or mustardy. We also like the way serving temperatures of dishes are listed where confusion may occur. What Awaba does, it does exceedingly well, but we wish we could see some desserts that rise above the cakey café variety. Especially on a drizzly Sunday.

licensed & byo
breakfast Daily 7.30–11.15am
lunch Mon–Sat noon–3pm; Sun noon–4pm
dinner Wed–Sat 6–10pm
cards AE BC MC V   No bookings
seats 60; outdoor area; no smoking ⃠
owners Peter & Fiona Rose & Jenny Jackson
chef Darren Farr
cost Around $65 for two, plus drinks
plus Cool beachside ambience
minus Few dessert options
score 13/20

azteca's

140 AVOCA STREET, RANDWICK
PHONE 9398 1020   MAP 9

MEXICAN

Now in its brand-new home just over the
road from its original location, Azteca's
continues to pull in the Randwick faithful.
Tacos, chilli con carne, ponchos, a pile of
sombreros ominously waiting for tequila-
sodden customers to dance in or on
may not seem encouraging. But a closer
look reveals that this is a real Mexican
restaurant: no inverted commas, no swampy
plates of mincemeat and melted cheddar.
There are few Mexican restaurants in
Sydney that offer even a relatively familiar
delicacy like ceviche and still fewer that
rise to provincial specialities like pozole
blanco, a soup of puffed white corn and
pork from the state of Guerrero. Above all,
chicken served with mole poblano – not,
as we're sometimes told, a chocolate sauce,
but a sauce in which chocolate and chilli
are equal partners among the spices –
emerges not as a novelty but as the classic
dish it truly is. Jose Cruz is a charming,
knowledgeable and patriotic host. Musical,
too: ask him to play you his CD.

licensed & byo
dinner Tues–Sun 6pm–late
cards AE BC MC V   Bookings essential weekends
seats 75; wheelchair access
owners Jose Cruz & Anne Leeson
chef Anne Leeson
cost Around $54 for two, plus drinks
plus Chilli & chocolate   **minus** Hoons & tequila
score 12/20

azuma

32 FALCON STREET, CROWS NEST
PHONE 9436 4066   MAP 5A

JAPANESE

In a Sydney of production-line sashimi and
railway-line sushi it's reassuring to walk into
Azuma and see the man himself flashing
smile and knives behind the bar in a simply
decorated room. It means your fish will
be of exemplary quality, freshness, texture
and flavour, so have the sashimi (sorry, no
sushi). But then comes the surprise: a
carefully translated menu with sections for
fish, wild duck, beef, chicken and pork.
A flounder dish has plump nubbins of flesh
in a gentle stew of vegetables, with the
bones deep-fried to the satisfying crispness
of a large corn chip. Unagi yanagawa is eel
in a rich soup of soy and mirin (rice wine),
with egg and the twig-like gobo (burdock).
And among the sake and beer are vintage
Australian wines. There are also two
different kaiseki banquets and a new
vegetarian tasting menu of Japanese
temple dishes, Shojin ryori. This is different,
interesting yet highly approachable food
in a pleasant setting.

licensed; wine by the glass
dinner Daily 6–11pm
cards AE BC DC MC V   Bookings essential
seats 50; private room
owner/chef Kimitaka Azuma
cost Around $108 for two, plus drinks
plus The freshness   **minus** The music
score 14/20

bambini trust cafe

185 ELIZABETH STREET, SYDNEY
PHONE 9283 7098   MAP 1

MEDITERRANEAN

It may be called Bambini but its food is very grown up. With its city location, small menu and serious wood panelling, it's a bit like entering a private club in which you're immediately made to feel a member. Italy reigns on the menu, with starters including linguine with herbs and olives, spaghettini with Atlantic salmon and rocket and classic spaghetti vongole. The twice-cooked duck salad features a perfectly cooked, crisp-skinned duck leg sitting on mixed leaves, with a dressing that doesn't fight the good ducky flavour. Daily specials may include roast quail with basil mash or risotto with swordfish, scampi and clams, which, while correctly al dente, felt just a little unbalanced. A classic plate of tuna Niçoise is close to flawless, and a rocket salad has an appealing, lively, almost wild taste. Start with good ingredients, treat them with respect, and it's hard to go wrong.

licensed; wine by the glass
breakfast Mon–Fri 7–11.30am
lunch Mon–Fri noon–3pm
dinner Mon–Fri 5–10pm
cards AE BC DC MC V   Bookings recommended
seats 55; outdoor area; wheelchair access; non-smoking area ⊁
owners Angela Ioannides & Michael Potts
chef Wayne Rowe
cost Around $76 for two, plus drinks
plus Top produce   **minus** Awkward banquettes
score 14/20

banc

53 MARTIN PLACE, SYDNEY
PHONE 9233 5300   MAP 1

MODERN FRENCH

Banc is full of surprises. The crowd, for one. It's a regular Sydney mix-and-match affair, not the button-down lot you may expect in such a stately, serious CBD dining room. Chefs Liam Tomlin and Matthew Kemp may offer some fine old European standards, including a flavour-rich version of fillet of beef Rossini, but the menu is also studded with surprisingly refined and contemporary fare. From the first sip of a complimentary, smooth-as-silk sweetcorn and basil soup, you can't help but be startled by the breathtaking balance of flavours. Two scallop-filled tortellini rub shoulders with grilled scampi tails, only to be covered with a steaming lobster bisque at the table. Roast barramundi has a wonderfully crisp skin protecting flesh full of flavoursome juices, and is served in a rich red wine-based sauce Matelote. This is food that is bold, but always in harmony, representing some of the most refined and defined French/British cooking you'll find anywhere.

licensed; wine by the glass
lunch Mon–Fri noon–2.30pm
dinner Mon–Sat 6.30–10pm
cards AE BC DC MC V   Bookings essential
seats 90; private room; no smoking until 2.30pm & 10.30pm ⊁
owners Stan Sarris & Rodney Adler
chefs Liam Tomlin & Matthew Kemp
cost Around $140 for two, plus drinks
plus Sweetcorn soup   **minus** Slippery-dip cutlery
score 18/20

banjo paterson cottage

'IN THE PARK',
END OF PUNT ROAD, GLADESVILLE
PHONE 9816 3611   MAP 7

MODERN AUSTRALIAN

They won't let you forget that poet
A. B. ('Banjo') Paterson once lived in this
sandstone cottage. Even the lavatories are
labelled 'Matildas' and 'Clancys' (the latter,
fortunately, without overflow). You almost
expect jumbuck tuckerbag steak washed
down with billy tea. Actually, a continuation
into the kitchen of the colonial heritage
theme would at least give unity to the
food. As it is, the laminated menu rivals
that of many an international hotel in its
combination of eclecticism and caution.
There's regulation obeisance to Asia (spicy
beef salad Thai-style), to North Africa (mild
chilli harissa with the kangaroo fillets) and
to Italy (polenta cake under the lamb), but
no very strong flavours anywhere. A beef
and vegetable pie, which promised an old-
world depth of flavour, seemed bland. The
view, though, is very charming.

licensed; wine by the glass
lunch Tues–Fri & Sun noon–2.30pm
dinner Tues–Sat 6.30–9.30pm
cards AE BC DC MC V   Bookings essential
seats 120; private room; summer outdoor area;
no smoking ✣
owner Ross Pitts
chef Marcel Widmer
cost Around $92 for two, plus drinks
plus Blinding views   **minus** Bland flavours
score 12/20

bathers' pavilion

4 THE ESPLANADE, BALMORAL
PHONE 9969 5050   MAP 7

MODERN AUSTRALIAN

It's always been a charming spot, and now,
after years of legal battles and million-dollar
renovations, the Bathers' Pavilion is
magnificent testimony to its owners'
passionate persistence. Stretched out
languidly along one of Sydney's prettiest
harbourside beaches, it's all silk, leather,
artfully arranged cushions, high-tech
kitchens and very twenty-first-century
dining, with a fixed-price approach that
makes dining a commitment. You may miss
the raffish casualness of the old Bathers',
but get over it. The food of ex-Regent
Sydney chef Serge Dansereau is very good,
and not as finicky as the menu might
suggest. 'Oxtail gow gee, scallops, crunchy
broccoli, crisp potato, soy-ginger sauce', for
example, means quite delightful dumplings
with a few textural garnishes. This is brave
food (abalone matched with crisped pig's
ear), although a doughy scallop dumpling
showed that it's sometimes pushed too far.

licensed; wine by the glass
lunch Mon–Sat from noon; Sun 2 sittings
dinner Daily from 6.30pm   Bookings essential
cards AE BC DC MC V
seats 78; private room; wheelchair access;
no smoking ✣
owners Victoria Alexander & Serge Dansereau
chef Serge Dansereau
fixed price $95 p.p. for dinner and Sat–Sun
lunch (less for weekday lunch), plus drinks
plus The lush new fitout   **minus** Getting in
score 16/20

bathers' pavilion café

4 THE ESPLANADE, BALMORAL
PHONE 9969 5050   MAP 7

MODERN AUSTRALIAN

Half the long, lean line of the Bathers' Pavilion is now taken up by a bright and colourful up-market café, one of the best beachside experiences in Sydney. Serge Dansereau's spectacular seasonal menu makes all right with the world. Breakfast, lunch and dinner menus dish up as little or as much as your appetite demands, and we love that every wine is available by the glass. There's a big busy bustle here, but a small relaxed room to the side provides an oasis and, once mesmerised by the waves, you may never leave. A delightful prawn salad is all freshness and generosity with – count them – ten prawns, and a nicely frothy avocado soup. Seafood risotto is a little dry but again, is generous in its seafood offerings, as is a pool of hearty, if a little overcooked, fish stew. Woodfired pizzas are popular. So are the divine desserts, and you can choose from five different types of water if you so wish. A beachside breakfast here is the new North Shore institution.

licensed; wine by the glass
hours Daily 7am–midnight   No bookings
cards AE BC DC MC V
seats 80; private room; outdoor area; wheelchair access; no smoking ⅍
owners Victoria Alexander & Serge Dansereau
chef Serge Dansereau
cost Around $76 for two, plus drinks
plus The kids' loo   **minus** No bookings
score 14/20

bay road bistro

146 BURNS BAY ROAD, LANE COVE
PHONE 9427 1778   MAP 7

MODERN AUSTRALIAN

Although long-time owner/chef Richard Bullock has moved on, Bay Road has barely skipped a beat. Munch on sweet potato and parsnip chips while listening to Whitney Houston as you browse through the menu of this still very popular suburban eatery. But when booking, ask for a table downstairs, which has a genuinely happy buzz. Upstairs lacks atmosphere, although the service is still attentive. The food? Tender smoked breast of chicken and capsicum salad is complemented by a tangy pear and blueberry chutney, and wok-tossed prawns with coconut and coriander have just enough chilli to spike the dish. This would be a real stunner served on a pile of fresh rice noodles instead of pappardelle pasta. The Manning Valley double rack of lamb with parsnip mash, crunchy spring onions and port wine jus is a perfectly balanced dish, the sauce evidence of chef Weiler's training. For dessert, a trio of ice-creams with Vienna biscuits is as pretty as a picture.

byo
dinner Tues–Sat from 6pm
cards AE BC DC MC V   Bookings essential
seats 65; private room; no smoking ⅍
owners Erich & Colleen Weiler
chef Erich Weiler
cost Around $80 for two, plus drinks
plus Good sauces   **minus** No ice buckets
score 14/20

DEVELOP
A TASTE FOR
HISTORY.

WYNDHAM ESTATE
ESTABLISHED 1828
HUNTER VALLEY

AUSTRALIAN WINE MAKING HISTORY.

bayswater brasserie

32 BAYSWATER ROAD, KINGS CROSS
PHONE 9357 2177   MAP 2

MODERN AUSTRALIAN

The Bayz, as it is known, tries for the allure of a great Paris bistro, and largely succeeds. A happening bar, plenty of charmingly odd characters, a wine list full of gems, and fresh, opened-to-order regional oysters served on a high-legged platter are straight out of the Boulevard St Germain. The menu, however, makes a culinary tour of the globe, and not all the touchdowns are successful. Certainly, house-cured anchovies with celery and parmesan formed a well-balanced entrée, and veal shank was expertly boned and nicely cooked. On the downside, salmon fishcakes arrived almost cold. In trying to be all things to all people, the kitchen appears to have lost a little of its focus. It's still the Bayz, but with a little less buzz. Service can be brisk and robotic, although this is likely to become turbo-charged under new co-owner Nigel Lacy.

licensed; wine by the glass
hours Daily noon–midnight
cards AE BC DC MC V   Bookings recommended
seats 150; private rooms; outdoor area;
non-smoking area
owners Nigel Lacy, Robert Smallbone &
Tony Papas
chef Michael Klausen
cost Around $92 for two, plus drinks
plus Great bistro feel   **minus** Food lacks focus
score 13/20

bbq king

18–20 GOULBURN STREET, SYDNEY
PHONE 9267 2433   MAP 3A

CHINESE

More than just another cheapie Chinese restaurant, BBQ King is a Sydney institution where our most highly lauded chefs take their late-night suppers, where the noodle soups can cure hangovers and the roast duck mends broken hearts. No matter that the décor looks like the People's Republic roadside diner circa 1950, all rather tired Formica, vinyl and lino. That's part of the charm, along with the famous 'Harro mate!' greeting from the cheery pink-cheeked owner when you walk in. The menu is as long as the Shanghai phonebook, but most regulars have their own little repertoire of favourites, from the wonderfully fragrant and luscious roast duck, and the wickedly crackling suckling pig, to the melting steamed chicken with its piquant dipping sauce and the greenest greens in town, served with oyster sauce. Lone diners feel very comfortable at any time of day or night, especially at the big, round communal table with the other solo supperers. Either way, you've got your duck for company.

licensed & byo
hours Daily 11.30am–2am
cards AE BC DC MC V   Bookings recommended
seats 200; private room
owners Yuen Cheung, Robert Ho & Philip Chau
chefs Hop Chai Wong & Hui Hung Wong
cost Around $55 for two, plus drinks
plus Because it's there   **minus** The upstairs room
score 13/20

bel mondo

LEVEL 3, THE ARGYLE STORES,
18–24 ARGYLE STREET, THE ROCKS
PHONE 9241 3700   MAP 1

ITALIAN

Sydney isn't blessed with many great Italian restaurants but the Manfredi family's flagship tucked away in the back of The Rocks in the revitalised Argyle wool stores is still one of the best. Peak produce, an exceptional, heavily Italianate wine list, Teflon-smooth service, and Luigi Rosselli's theatrical open kitchen will set you in perfect holistic balance. Passionate poet–sommelier Franck Crouvezier will have you ready to relish the right glass with such well-executed rarities as succulent roast Murray cod with Ligurian olive salsa; Barossa-bred venison with white asparagus; or a broad bean salad with Basque ewe's milk cheese. Accepting that such premium ingredients and specialist wines come at a price, one still has to bring a platinum mentality to Manfredi's table. Or graze the seasonal six-course dégustation menu and make a night of it.

licensed; wine by the glass
lunch Mon–Fri noon–2.30pm
dinner Daily from 6.30pm
cards AE BC DC MC V   Bookings recommended
seats 150; outdoor area; no smoking until 2.30pm & 10.30pm
owners Franca Manfredi, Julie Manfredi-Hughes, Stefano Manfredi & Franck Crouvezier
chefs Stefano Manfredi & Franca Manfredi
cost Around $162 for two, plus drinks
plus Franca's gnocchi   **minus** The bill
score 17/20

bel mondo antibar

LEVEL 3, THE ARGYLE STORES,
18–24 ARGYLE STREET, THE ROCKS
PHONE 9241 3700   MAP 1

ITALIAN

The Manfredi operation isn't the first to launch a diffusion range – a less expensive, more accessible version of the top-dollar main game – but it takes confidence to put the cheaper label right next to the couture original. The question is: can you eat in the bar without casting too many longing glances at the vaulted spaces of the main dining room? Yes, you can, easily, in part because the bar area, though narrow, has a vibe of its own and partly because the food can stand the comparison. First, there is the antipasto itself, available in countless permutations, depending on how many of you there are, and whether you're after meat or veg. Then there are mains such as tagliatelle with chorizo, and pan-fried silver dory fillet with peperonata – serious dishes in their own right and quite enough if you feel called to the bar for a whole evening.

licensed; wine by the glass
hours Mon–Fri noon–11pm; Sat 6.30–11pm; Sun 6.30–10pm
cards AE BC DC MC V   Bookings recommended
seats 30
owners Franca Manfredi, Julie Manfredi-Hughes, Stefano Manfredi & Franck Crouvezier
chefs Stefano Manfredi & Franca Manfredi
cost Around $80 for two, plus drinks
plus A taste of bel mondo
minus Hard-to-read menus
score 13/20

bennelong

SYDNEY OPERA HOUSE,
BENNELONG POINT, SYDNEY
PHONE 9250 7548   MAP 1

MODERN AUSTRALIAN

You need a libretto to keep up with the
rapidly changing performances and cast at
Bennelong. The kitchen door has revolved
again, leaving former Bathers' Pavilion chef
Xavier Mouche at the helm of the iconic site
that hasn't found its stride since Janni
Kyritsis opted for a new life. Sydney's
visitors and local concert-goers should
expect a short, safe, uninspiring menu
executed by a team that could do with
more rehearsals, and an adequate but
xenophobic wine list. It's a pity, because
Utzon's soaring sails deserve better. Pass
up the whole grilled baby snapper, corn-fed
chicken with tagliatelle, lamb racks, smoked
salmon and prawn bisque and play it raw
with a selection from the mezzanine-level
crustacea bar. Super-fresh plump prawns,
glistening Pacific oysters, Balmain bugs,
blue swimmers and lobster will all
appreciate a good Australian bubbly. Then
pop upstairs for any further artistic
sustenance you may need.

licensed; wine by the glass
dinner Mon–Sat 5.30pm–midnight
cards AE BC DC MC V   Bookings essential
seats 120; private room; smoking allowed in
bar area only
owner Sodexho Australia
chef Xavier Mouche
cost Around $130 for two, plus drinks
plus Crustacea bar   **minus** Unmet expectations
score 12/20

♀ beppi's

CNR YURONG & STANLEY STREETS,
EAST SYDNEY
PHONE 9360 4558   MAP 2

ITALIAN

It takes a well-honed sense of hospitality to
know when your customers are on edge. So
it is with Beppi Polese, one of Sydney's best
hosts since 1956, a man who reads his
guests the way most of us read the *Sydney
Morning Herald*. One minute you're sitting
next to a table of noise-makers, the next
he's moved you to a safer (and quieter)
seat. Most of the floor staff have been there
for twenty years, too. The food is good, solid
Italian, without trying to be too smart. You
can lap up a porcini-laden risotto with its
meaty wild mushrooms, and the saltimbocca
is so traditional, it's as salty as you'd find in
Rome. A creamy zabaglione is all foam and
fragrance. They even keep the kitchen open
until 11.30pm for late-night moves. Beppi's
is loved by older business types, but you'll
also see younger business types and
occasional couples in non-corporate
hideaway corners.

licensed
lunch Mon–Fri noon–3pm
dinner Mon–Sat from 6pm
supper Mon–Sat until late
cards AE BC DC MC V   Bookings recommended
seats 130; private room; wheelchair access
owners Beppi, Norma & Marc Polese
chefs Tony Biondi & Didi Douadi
cost Around $97 for two, plus drinks
plus The host   **minus** Can get noisy
score 13/20

bills

433 LIVERPOOL STREET, DARLINGHURST
PHONE 9360 9631   MAP 2

MODERN AUSTRALIAN

Many people don't get bills. What's the fuss, they ask, as they queue for a spot at the big, blond communal table, or they get the odd piece of burnt toast or slow coffee. But those who go regularly are hooked on this sunny little corner café, where a tiny kitchen with little storage means the food comes in fresh each day. Staff are as sweet as sugarpie, the muffins are from the land of the giants, and the giant blackboard menu is a roll-call of what is now Sydney's favourite food. That means ricotta hot cakes or ludicrously creamy scrambled eggs for breakfast, and coriander noodles with salmon or a chicken club roll for lunch. It's time, however, to review the door-stopper-sized toast now that Sydney has more than one fine bakery, and shake things up a bit on the menu at lunch. But only at lunch. Change the ricotta hot cakes, Bill, and even such a nice-looking crowd as this could get ugly.

byo
breakfast Mon–Fri 7.30am–noon;
Sat 7.30am–3pm
lunch Mon–Sat noon–3pm
cards AE BC MC V   No bookings
seats 45; no smoking
owner Bill Granger
chef Daniel Gale
cost Around $43 for two, plus drinks
plus The crowd   **minus** The crowds
score 14/20

bills 2

359 CROWN STREET, SURRY HILLS
PHONE 9360 4762   MAP 3B

MODERN AUSTRALIAN

Brother restaurant of breakfast emporium bills in Darlinghurst, this chic, simple eatery attracts all types, from grey-power tourists to Helmut Lang-wearing locals, from parents with babes to inner-city muscle boys who think they are babes. Bills 2 offers mouthwatering breakfast and lunch options like its Darlinghurst sibling, but also serves dinner. It fills up rapidly most evenings, with excess diners waiting at the Dolphin Hotel across the road, desperate for their mobile phones to ring with news of a table. Some dishes – a wholesome parmesan veal schnitzel with creamed potatoes or a zingy prawn, rocket and chilli linguine – have been perfected over the years. Others, such as a warm quail salad with borlotti beans and radish, have been added more recently. Try to resist the giddy ginger ice-cream with chocolate sauce, or the urge to scream 'Go girl!' as you watch the Surry Hillbillies sashay past your window.

byo
hours Mon–Fri 7am–3pm, 6–10pm;
Sat 7am–10pm; Sun 7am–3pm
cards AE BC MC V   No bookings
seats 40; wheelchair access; no smoking
owner Bill Granger
chef Katherine Townsend
cost Around $54 for two, plus drinks
plus Buzzy feel   **minus** Fuzzy service
score 14/20

billy kwong

3/355 CROWN STREET, SURRY HILLS
PHONE 9332 3300   MAP 3B

CHINESE

When a chef renowned for her take on
Modern Asian flavours joins up with the big
Sydney cafémeister, expect the unexpected.
Kylie Kwong and Bill Granger deliver, in the
shape of a new eatery that takes the feel of
a Shanghai teahouse, shakes it up a little
and dishes out one of Sydney's most
exciting new dining experiences. With its
dark wooden trim, designery giant hanging
lantern and three-legged (beware) moulded
stools, Billy Kwong would be the new corner
Chinese except it's not on a corner, and the
food is full of flavour and craft. Traditional
Chinese favourites are revisited for a young
and savvy crowd who thinks it's all new.
We love the pippis in XO sauce – spicy, yet
balanced – and the tang of dried mandarin
in an overly sweet oxtail braise. Must-haves
include a bouncy prawn, mushroom and
garlic chive omelette, and slippery rice
noodles stir-fried with soy sauce and bean
shoots, the ideal supper dish.

byo
dinner Mon–Sat 6–10pm
cards AE BC MC V   No bookings
seats 50; no smoking; wheelchair access ⛄
owners Bill Granger & Kylie Kwong
chef Kylie Kwong
cost Around $65 for two, plus drinks
plus Giant lantern   **minus** Very squeezy
score 14/20

bistro moncur

THE WOOLLAHRA HOTEL,
116 QUEEN STREET, WOOLLAHRA
PHONE 9363 2519   MAP 4B

MODERN FRENCH

There are some things without which
Sydney would be a far poorer city. The
bridge, of course; the Opera House, perhaps;
but more importantly, Damien Pignolet's
French bistro food. It is simply built on the
integrity of ingredients, so duck, braised
with green olives, is masterful. The way
fontina-glazed beets are matched with
frisée, hazelnuts and beans is worthy of a
few gasps, and the sultry, house-made pure
pork Lyonnaise sausages are legendary. The
room is graced with a Michael Fitzjames
wall-length mural. Professional staff flit
hither, but can let down the fluid nature of
the bistro. We admire Pignolet's insistence
on no bookings to make Moncur accessible,
but it does make life difficult when you're
meeting up with friends. Go early, go late or
go on a quiet night, and hope you get a
table without too long a wait at the bar.

licensed; wine by the glass
lunch Tues–Sun noon–3pm
dinner Daily 6–10.30pm
cards AE BC DC MC V   No bookings
seats 100; outdoor area; no smoking until
2pm & 10pm ⛄
owners Damien Pignolet & Dr Ron White
chefs Damien Pignolet & Jason Roberts
cost Around $90 for two, plus drinks
plus Long flavours   **minus** Pub loos
score 16/20

blue elephant

38 WILLOUGHBY ROAD, CROWS NEST
PHONE 9439 3468   MAP 5A

MODERN SRI LANKAN

Innovative town planning has dramatically changed the Willoughby Road dining scene – it's now a veritable UN eat street strip. China, Japan, India, Thailand, Greece and Italy are all represented, as is the tiny jewel island of Sri Lanka. Look carefully for the discreet doorway to the immensely popular Elephant, an incongruous tropical-island-themed basement where Friday nights mean good moody jazz, a sleeves-up, equatorial blue swimmer crab curry and chilled beer. Charming hostess Theonie Best and her almost all-girl team know just how to make the regulars relax over tried, true and trad dishes such as tamarind goat curry; paripoo, a spicy red lentil dahl; and pol roti made with coconut. Stick to the authentic Sri Lankan dishes cheerily explained by the knowledgeable staff. Leave room for wattalappan, the lip-smackingly delicious jaggery-sweet custard, and finish with cups of orange pekoe from Kandy, the tea capital.

licensed & byo; wine by the glass
lunch Mon–Fri noon–3pm
dinner Mon–Sat 6.30pm until late
cards AE BC DC MC V   Bookings essential
seats 80; no smoking until 10pm
owner/chef Theonie Best
cost Around $65 for two, plus drinks
plus Wattalappan   **minus** Desert-island décor
score 13/20

the boathouse on blackwattle bay

END OF FERRY ROAD, GLEBE
PHONE 9518 9011   MAP 5B

SEAFOOD

To not start with oysters at The Boathouse would be silly indeed, as there is a dedicated list of up to six different varieties, opened to order and correctly presented. Situated on the first floor of the University of Sydney boathouse, this shipshape statement to Sydney comes complete with a view of the Fish Markets, Anzac Bridge and flip-side Sydney skyline. It's a great place to bring visitors for a bit of showing-off, as you point out the local celebs drawn from the arthouse and academic villas of Glebe and Balmain. Chef Yvan Meunier has a delicate, formal touch with seafood: big, fleshy sea scallops topped with little cubes of foie gras sit on a moss-green lettuce sea, and skin-on jewfish is teamed with an almost rustic bed of beans. Prices can sometimes be high for very little (yabby, cress and truffle entrée) and sometimes low for a lot (the signature fish pie).

licensed; wine by the glass
lunch Tues–Sun noon–2.30pm
dinner Tues–Sun 6.30–10.30pm
cards AE BC DC MC V   Bookings recommended
seats 120; wheelchair access; no smoking until 10.30pm
owners Robert Smallbone & Tony Papas
chefs Michael Klausen & Yvan Meunier
cost Around $108 for two, plus drinks
plus The bridge   **minus** The back room
score 16/20

bocca

5/84 CAMPBELL PARADE, BONDI
PHONE 9130 8611   MAP 9

MEDITERRANEAN

In the heartland of the kebab and the great hangover breakfast, it's surprising to find Bocca. Bondi tends to offer variety at the expense of quality when it comes to restaurants, but the strip does seem to be on the up. To prove it, here's this tiny French restaurant serving honest, delicious Mediterranean cooking with a wine list showing a great Bandol, a very respectable burgundy and some good French country wines. Begin with a complimentary demitasse (in Bondi!) of watercress and crème fraîche soup; then choose from a cute menu that might feature corn-fed chicken and pistou terrine with a gribiche vinaigrette; goat's cheese and rosemary ravioli; or braised snapper with kipfler potatoes, zucchini and tapenade. A vanilla custard crème with madeleines is sheer comfort food. Chef Olivier Rossi knows how to dress a green salad, too. Let's hope the locals rumble to this promising newcomer.

licensed
brunch Sat–Sun 10am–2pm
dinner Daily from 6.30pm
cards AE BC DC MC V   Bookings recommended
seats 40; no smoking
owners Juliet Vladimir & Bosko Vujovic
chef Olivier Rossi
cost Around $97 for two, plus drinks
plus The ocean   **minus** The cars
score 13/20

bodhi vegetarian

SHOP 10, GROUND FLOOR, CAPITOL SQUARE,
730–42 GEORGE STREET, SYDNEY
PHONE 9281 6162, 9212 2828   MAP 3A

CHINESE/VEGAN

Last year Bodhi moved from its character-laden Hay Street premises to a modern, streamlined space in nearby Capitol Square, complete with designer seating, groovy young staff in black T-shirts and a wine list. What makes this place special is not that it's a very good vegan restaurant, but that it's a very good yum cha restaurant. Here, freshly made dim sum comes by the tray, to be wolfed down by an eclectic young city crowd. The only difference is that instead of prawns in the prawn dumplings it's minced water chestnuts; instead of pork in pork buns, it's cabbage and beancurd; and instead of snowpea sprouts, it's – well, it's still snowpea sprouts, actually. About 150 different types of yum cha are made here, and you can even order them at night, along with more full-on dishes such as vegetarian 'fish' with sambal sauce and vegetarian Peking duck.

licensed & byo
hours Daily 9am–midnight
cards None   Bookings essential
seats 150; outdoor area; wheelchair access; no smoking
owner Lee Leng Whong
chef Pei Wang
cost Around $38 for two, plus drinks
plus The yum cha   **minus** Scatty service
score 13/20

Breakfast (till 12 ...
...ist drink of orange ...all day...
...uit & yoghurt. sm 3.50 ...
...sonal fruit bowl with...

* Fresh fruit pla...

coconut toast + m...

slices of wholeme...

marmalade, jams...

maple por...

bre

lightly toasted by the sun

bathers' pavilion café Curl up in a booth for a classy breakfast of blueberry pancakes with warm maple syrup on Balmoral Beach. 7am–noon, 7 days. 4 THE ESPLANADE, BALMORAL BEACH 9969 5050

yulla North African baked eggs or an Israeli omelette with goat's curd within eyeshot of the Bondi surf – ain't Sydney grand? LEVEL 1, 38 CAMPBELL PARADE, BONDI BEACH 9365 1788

bourbon & beefsteak bar Sydney's great yuppie-free hangover cure is the famous Ranch breakfast, available 24 hours a day, every day. 24 DARLINGHURST ROAD, KINGS CROSS 9358 1144

the bower A magic spot by the Fairy Bower rockpool for a beachside breakfast of spiced pancakes and home-made muesli. 7 MARINE PARADE, MANLY 9977 5451

canteen Balmainliners goss over fruit and coffee inside and out this fresh, simple café. SHOP 1, 332 DARLING STREET, BALMAIN 9818 1521

fuel Fuel up in style on champagne sausages with oysters, or coddled eggs with salmon caviar. 8am–noon; brunch–3pm, Sat–Sun. 476 CROWN STREET, SURRY HILLS 9383 9388

bills and bills 2 *(left)* Join the queue to worship at the shrine of those famous ricotta hot cakes and scrambled eggs. BILLS 433 LIVERPOOL STREET, DARLINGHURST 9360 9631; BILLS 2, 359 CROWN STREET, SURRY HILLS 9360 4762

lunch A fresh sunny little courtyard with save-your-life warm banana bread and ricotta cakes with crisp café bacon. 5/100 EDINBURGH ROAD, CASTLECRAG 9958 8441

swell Breakfast by the beach with sweet spiced ricotta, Hanks jams and a local, free-range crowd that's lightly toasted by the sun. 465 BRONTE ROAD, BRONTE 9386 5001

watermark Raise a toast to the waves over an elegant eggs benedict in the sun on famous Balmoral Beach. Such civilisation so early in the day. 2A THE ESPLANADE, BALMORAL BEACH 9968 3433

akfast

bohem

467 PITT STREET, HAYMARKET
PHONE 9211 8777   MAP 3A

FRENCH/MEDITERRANEAN

The grand old Australia Gas Light building has been transformed into a glamorous date restaurant. The dining room is a dazzling space that is part Roman temple, part Manhattan, part Melbourne and all Sydney. At one end sits a huge open kitchen housed under a metallic Ottoman empire canopy, while at the other is a gloriously long wooden bar. After a semi-successful attempt at French-ish–Moroccan cooking, the kitchen has now gone a little more mainstream with widely travelled chef-about-town Ken Gomes. There is more than a touch of Sydney bistro in his fettuccine with mushrooms and poached egg, goat's cheese salad with walnuts and olives, and tomato and roast pumpkin risotto. Those still looking for a little North African mystique can always try the duck tagine with green olives and preserved lemon.

licensed; wine by the glass
dinner Tues–Sat 6.30–11.30pm
cards AE BC DC MC V   Bookings essential
seats 150; wheelchair access;
non-smoking area
owners Ian Spicer, Sean Finlay & Barry Wain
chef Ken Gomes
cost Around $130 for two, plus drinks
plus The space   **minus** Cool – take a wrap
score 13/20

bombay heritage

82 WILLOUGHBY ROAD, CROWS NEST
PHONE 9906 5596   MAP 5A

INDIAN

Among the mishmash of restaurants lining Willoughby Road at Crows Nest, Bombay Heritage is a local favourite. The rosy pink glow of the dim lighting and formal table settings promise a comfortable evening, although the service can be, shall we say, aloof. Upmarket Indian cuisine is prepared by Taj-trained chef Sandeep Chatterjee and comprises a balanced selection of northern and southern Indian dishes, with the tandoor oven producing meltingly tender boneless chicken tikka and trimmed lamb cutlets served with coriander yoghurt. The Parsi speciality of fish with mint chutney will always remain on the menu, judging by the orders emerging from the kitchen. Try the baigan ka salam from Hyderabad, a spicy vegetarian dish of eggplant cooked with tomato, tamarind and cashew. Follow with a refreshing kulfi for dessert, a homemade non-aerated Indian ice in flavours of mango, almond and pistachio.

licensed & byo
lunch Tues–Fri noon–2.30pm
dinner Daily 6–11pm
cards AE BC DC MC V   Bookings recommended, essential weekends
seats 60; outdoor area; wheelchair access;
no smoking inside
owners Sandeep Chatterjee & Tirandaz Kermani
chef Sandeep Chatterjee
cost Around $54 for two, plus drinks
plus Good value   **minus** The wine glasses
score 13/20

bond

111 PHILLIP STREET, SYDNEY
PHONE 9223 9332   MAP 1

MODERN AUSTRALIAN

Considering the hectic development of the city dining scene in the past twelve months, this smart, minimalist eatery feels like something of a veteran, even though it only opened in mid-1999. The settled, solid feel is due largely to the skills of chef Christopher Whitehead and the on-site dedication of Matthew Monahan, who also finds time to run a vineyard. Whitehead's food is pure Sydney with its scattering of Mediterranean, Asian and classic French influences, plus that icon of Australian cuisine – seared kangaroo fillet with beetroot. Bizlunchers who love their steak can have it with onion marmalade, spinach and mushrooms, while more adventurous diners should take advantage of Whitehead's ways with offal, especially the crumbed tripe with sauce rémoulade and stuffed pork hock with savoy cabbage. Lighter eaters may find the going a little rich.

licensed; wine by the glass
breakfast Mon–Fri 7–11am
lunch Mon–Fri noon–3.30pm
dinner Thurs–Fri 6pm–midnight
cards AE BC DC MC V   Bookings recommended
seats 120; outdoor area; wheelchair access; non-smoking area ⅔✗
owners Matthew Monahan & Christopher Keenan
chef Christopher Whitehead
cost Around $86 for two, plus drinks
plus Crumbed veal tripe   **minus** Signage
score 14/20

bonne femme

191 PALMER STREET, EAST SYDNEY
PHONE 9331 4455 MAP 2

MODERN AUSTRALIAN

The original 'bonne femme', Genevieve Copland, has moved on. But new chef and owner, bon homme Andy Turner, has filled this unobtrusive inner city restaurant with his own brand of bonhomie. Having honed his cooking style with London's Marco Pierre White, Turner has put together a British–French menu that perfectly matches the mood of designer Neil Bradford's cool, coffee-chocolate makeover. Softly spoken, sensitively groomed inner urbanites tuck into Turner's nicely balanced mussel, garlic and parsley soup, and fresh, tangy celeriac rémoulade served with rocket leaves and wilted forest mushrooms. Relaxed, fall-apart braised pork cheeks come with an irresistible sage and roast carrot purée (worth a visit in its own right), while a pan-fried barramundi fillet is a lesson in getting your textures right without interfering with the integrity of your produce. If Turner gets the right breaks, and if we can find a parking spot, this could be a very important Sydney restaurant.

licensed; wine by the glass
lunch Fri noon–3pm
dinner Daily 6–11pm
cards AE BC DC MC V   Bookings recommended
seats 60; private room; no smoking ⅔✗
owner/chef Andy Turner
cost Around $76 for two, plus drinks
plus Roast carrot purée   **minus** Parking
score 15/20

brazil

46 NORTH STEYNE, MANLY
PHONE 9977 3825   MAP 7

MODERN AUSTRALIAN

The view through the louvred windows on the first floor of Brazil is worthy of a glossy mag – Norfolk pines in the foreground and the sparkling Pacific behind. So serene, so simple, so seductive. But even if you're downstairs in the café-style space, there's much to like about this light, bright, buzzy place. From the modern, béchamel-coloured chairs to the flavours on the plate, Brazil has a distinctly eastern suburbs feel, with a touch of beach thrown in for good measure. Chef Peter Gong's dinner menu runs the Mod Oz line, with offerings such as a mezze platter with olives, feta and pide, and a succulent, well-crafted Japanese crab omelette with ponzu. The place is open all day for one of Manly's best post-swim coffees or cocktails. This is the kind of food you love to eat, and very much the kind of modern café which you love to eat it in.

licensed & byo; wine by the glass
hours Daily 8am–10pm
cards AE BC DC MC V   Bookings recommended, essential weekends
seats 100; private room; outdoor area; non-smoking area ✖
owners Rod McDonald, Jim Buda, Kate Lester & Alexandra Riddig
chef Peter Gong
cost Around $80 for two, plus drinks
plus The view from upstairs   **minus** The noise
score 13/20

brooklyn hotel

CNR GEORGE & GROSVENOR STREETS, SYDNEY
PHONE 9247 6744   MAP 1

MODERN AUSTRALIAN

From the Brooklyn's restaurant, you can look one way through plate glass into the austerity of a Harry Seidler skyscraper foyer, or the other way into the smoke of a renovated old pub frequented by city suits. Best to turn your eyes to what's on your plate, where the view is much more encouraging. New chef Damien Monley is energising inner city bistro food, taking risks that usually pay off, and has the craft to coax maximum flavour out of old favourites. The ravioli stuffed with salt cod seems ideally matched with tarragon sauce; a duck salad with walnuts and spiced apple is an operetta of flavour and texture; and roast mahi mahi with avocado, corn and zucchini is the perfect Sydney summer dish. The poached peach with buttermilk bavarois needs a stronger adjective than luscious. Those who work down the Quay end of the CBD will be desperate to keep this discovery from the tourists.

licensed; wine by the glass
lunch Mon–Fri noon–3pm
cards AE BC DC MC V   Bookings recommended
seats 100; private room; non-smoking area ✖
owner The Brooklyn Group
chef Damien Monley
cost Around $86 for two, plus drinks
plus Smart, lively food   **minus** The pokies
score 14/20

browns

SHOP 2–4, LEVEL 2, QUEEN VICTORIA
BUILDING, 455 GEORGE STREET, SYDNEY
PHONE 9269 0080   MAP 1

MODERN ITALIAN

Browns combines modern Milanese chic
with QVB's ageless Victorian charm to
dramatic effect. Mark Landini's classy
makeover runs from a look-at-me marble
and glossy white bar to sueded chairs and
feature wall, giving the place a feel that is
at once stark and luxe. Starched tablecloths
and elegant tableware may all seem over
the top for what is basically a lunch
restaurant, yet the serious intent is echoed
by the equally smart and purposeful menu.
Chef Danny Russo (ex-Martini) has a
designer's hand when it comes to
composing a plate. Pea-filled ravioli in a
frothy, seedy, vanilla sauce is all soft creams
and pastels, and the trio of Muscovy duck
(duck neck sausage, double-cooked leg and
pink breast) is framed by the plate as if it's
a still life. Flavours can occasionally feel
strained and intense. Nonetheless, Browns is
the ideal place in which to recover from the
rigours of serious shopping.

licensed; wine by the glass
lunch Mon–Fri noon–3pm
dinner Thurs 6–10pm
cards AE BC DC MC V   Bookings recommended
seats 35
owners Manuel Spinola & John Ubakli
chef Danny Russo
cost Around $103 for two, plus drinks
plus Plush feel   **minus** Shopping arcade
score 13/20

bukhara double bay

55 BAY STREET, DOUBLE BAY
PHONE 9363 5510   MAP 4A

INDIAN/MAURITIAN

Rattan chairs, swanky fellow diners, elegant
palms and a pre-dinner cocktail conjure up
the British Raj at Bukhara, but the finest
pedigree here is Mauritian. While the menu
features many subcontinental standards (it
does a very good marinated tandoori fish)
the stand-outs are all Mauritian. Tandoor-
baked five-spice garlic prawns, for example,
are lovely; but prawn à la Mauritian, though
oddly named, is sensational. The hot spices
literally jump in the mouth. The only real
downfall foodwise was a mixed side plate
of condiments that featured a limp dice of
tomato and onion. This upstairs eatery is
spacious and relaxed and, while some may
be content to gaze out over exclusive
Double Bay boutiques, the best view is
through the glassed kitchen at the rear,
watching Vijay & co. cook up a storm.
Bukhara also features an affordable,
attractive wine list, and fans of India's
Kingfisher lager ('Most Thrilling Chilled!')
will find that here too, at a price.

licensed & byo; wine by the glass
lunch Thurs–Fri noon–2.30pm
dinner Daily 5.30–11pm
cards AE BC DC MC V   Bookings essential
seats 90; non-smoking area
owner Vijay Baboo
chefs Vijay Baboo & Shylash Ramah
cost Around $70 for two, plus drinks
plus Mauritian prawns
minus Hard rattan chairs
score 14/20

buon ricordo

108 BOUNDARY STREET, PADDINGTON
PHONE 9360 6729   MAP 2

ITALIAN

Here is a joyous, seamless Italian dining
experience that builds to a climax, relaxes,
and lingers in the gustatory memory long
after Gemma Cunningham has gracefully
bid you goodnight. Is there a better starter
than the crisp, one-bite baby harbour
prawns? Figs more voluptuous than those
reclining in a gorgonzola sauce? A dish
more ingratiatingly moreish than the
fettuccine with cream and parmesan,
draped with a truffle-infused fried egg?
Carpaccio of beef with shiitake mushrooms
is baby-tender, and the mille mele dessert,
a painstaking 'thousand leaves' of apple
caramelised into a pudding, melts in the
mouth. All the floor staff seem concerned
for your comfort, and Peter Surtenich knows
the stimulating wine list well enough to
be truly helpful. With a brand new kitchen
and new dishes, Buon Ricordo is a bright
new experience, overseen by a new, mellow
Armando Percuoco.

licensed; wine by the glass
lunch Fri–Sat noon–2.30pm
dinner Tues–Sat 6.30–10.30pm
cards AE BC DC MC V   Bookings essential
seats 100; private room;
no smoking until 10pm
owner/chef Armando Percuoco
cost Around $113 for two, plus drinks
plus The signature dishes
minus When they're not on
score 17/20

cafe sel et poivre

263 VICTORIA STREET, DARLINGHURST
PHONE 9361 6530   MAP 2

FRENCH

To be met and greeted by the inestimable
Daniel Perchey is to be swept up in a warm
and enthusiastic wave of Gallic charm. The
standard menu of this cheerful, casual café
is a carnivore's delight, with just the one
vegetarian pasta dish fighting it out with a
magical mix of expertly prepared fish and
meat dishes. Pork and duck rillettes with
cornichon have quite rightly achieved
legendary entrée status among habitués, as
has the crisp galette of fresh swimmer crab
and leeks with a beurre blanc sauce. Pair
these with a freshly baked baguette and a
bottle of the smooth and fruity Côtes du
Rhône Gentilhomme France 1997 at a very
reasonable price and you will begin to think
that God is indeed a Frenchman. After a
main course of sensuously soft braised beef
cheeks with burgundy sauce and potato
purée, and a blackboard special of rabbit
casserole, you may not need the profiterole
mountain for dessert, but really, when has
need had anything to do with it?

licensed; wine by the glass
hours Daily 7am–10.30pm
cards AE BC DC MC V   Bookings recommended
seats 95; outdoor area; wheelchair access
owners Daniel Perchey & Laurent Deslandes
chef Laurent Deslandes
cost Around $80 for two, plus drinks
plus Relaxing and fun   **minus** Paper serviettes
score 12/20

cafe sydney

LEVEL 5, CUSTOMS HOUSE,
31 ALFRED STREET, CIRCULAR QUAY
PHONE 9251 8683   MAP 1

MODERN AUSTRALIAN

Position, position, position may well be the real-estate mantra, but if there isn't food, food, food to match then it doesn't work for us diners. Sydney is full of stunning locations but there are few as memorable as this, with its glorious views, day or night, of the harbour, bridge and Opera House. While the staff are well-schooled, professional and friendly, they, too, are let down by a menu that has changed little in the last year. Asparagus was tough and stringy, its bitterness emphasised by a tomato sauce flecked with fresh tomato that also dressed the freshly shucked oysters. Tuna was much better, rare as ordered, and finished with wasabi aïoli. Spit-roasted duck was chewy, smoky and lacking flavour. Garlic naan bread from the tandoor remains a popular signature item. Desserts tended to be overdressed, with a pleasant enough peach tart confused by raspberries, syrup, raspberry sorbet and fresh peaches.

licensed; wine by the glass
hours Mon–Sat noon–11pm; Sun noon–5pm
cards AE BC DC MC V   Bookings recommended
seats 250; private room; outdoor area;
wheelchair access; non-smoking area
owner Customs House Cafe Pty Ltd
chef Lars Svensson
cost Around $84 for two, plus drinks
plus The terrace   **minus** Flavour clashes
score 12/20

caffé agostinis

SHOP 5, 118 QUEEN STREET, WOOLLAHRA
PHONE 9328 6140   MAP 4B

MEDITERRANEAN

Should you wish to experience it, this is quintessential Woollahra. At any given moment of night or day, there is enough gold jewellery and haute couture present to ransom a small African country. Not that you'd find too many Africans, for this is Wasp territory, where Woollahra comes to gossip and to show off its pearls among the fashionable courtyard shops. It's better than the zoo, and cheaper. Reasonable prices mean anyone who's no-one can while away an hour or so with a steak sandwich, salmon fillet or the very popular scrambled eggs and not break the bank that the other customers probably own. Excellent fun for breakfast, brunch or lunch on a beautiful day, Agostinis also delights as a cosy, chatty spot at night. Whatever you order, do NOT leave without asking for a fork each and attempting the huge, moist and rightly famous orange cake.

byo
breakfast Mon–Fri 8–11.30am;
Sat–Sun 8–11.45am
lunch Mon–Fri noon–3.30pm;
Sat–Sun noon–4pm
dinner Mon–Sat 6–10pm
cards AE BC MC V   No bookings
seats 80; outdoor area; non-smoking area
owner/chef Margie Agostini
cost Around $54 for two, plus drinks
plus Cosy courtyard   **minus** Too-safe menu
score 12/20

cala luna

235 SPIT ROAD, MOSMAN
PHONE 9968 2426   MAP 7

ITALIAN

Even though it's at the Spit, this cosy, noisy
Italian eatery is pointing the wrong way for
big-time water views. Regulars, however,
content themselves with big, close-up views
of the delicious spaghetti alla bottarga,
dusted with shavings of dried and salted
fish roe. Sardinian-born Giovanni Pilu and
co-chef Tony Nelson specialise in big-
hearted Sardinian food that is generous,
honest and, at times, sensational. People
who can't live without garlic bread or
spaghetti bolognese won't have to, but
they'd be missing out on something special.
Why order veal scaloppine when you can
order crisp, golden suckling pig roasted
Sardinian style, or a lush, tomatoey
Sardinian fisherman's soup? Even the bread
here is a revelation – a shatteringly crisp
double-baked flat bread known as carta
di musica, as big as sheet music. Service is,
well, different. Unless, of course, you're
used to having your wine brought to you
balanced on your waiter's head.

byo
lunch Tues, Wed & Fri noon–2.30pm
dinner Tues–Sat 6–9.30pm
cards AE BC DC MC V   Bookings essential
seats 85; private room; outdoor area; wheelchair
access; non-smoking area ⋈
owners/chefs Tony W. Nelson & Giovanni Pilu
cost Around $70 for two, plus drinks
plus Sardinian specialities   **minus** No water
score 13/20

campari

111 ELIZABETH STREET, SYDNEY
PHONE 9231 5707 MAP 1

MODERN AUSTRALIAN/ITALIAN

At first glance, this busy split-level eatery
may look suspiciously like every other CBD
churn-'em-over lunch spot. Yet, it is actually
capable of turning out good, generous
meals to a mainly mid-executive crowd.
The Campari theme runs from the canvas
barriers outside and a dedicated cocktail
list – a negroni, vespa and the beautiful
bicicletta – to fluorescently carmine interior
walls that give everybody a rosy post-
Campari glow. The menu covers the usual
gamut of carpaccio and risotto as well as
a good range of salads and seafood dishes.
A daily special of Moreton Bay bugs had
height but no depth. Ah, but gnocchi with
a meat ragù was a stunner, the gnocchi
light, and the sauce hearty. The most
popular dish in the place – justifiably so –
is a well-balanced combination of snapper
fillets propped on top of a spinach and
lemon risotto.

licensed; wine by the glass
breakfast Mon–Sat 7am–noon
lunch Mon–Sat noon–3pm
dinner Tues–Sat 6–11pm
cards AE BC DC MC V   Bookings essential
seats 110; outdoor area; wheelchair access;
non-smoking area ⋈
owner Leon Matt
chef Franco Berlusconi
cost Around $65 for two, plus drinks
plus Campari cocktails   **minus** Butter roses
score 13/20

casa asturiana

77 LIVERPOOL STREET, SYDNEY
PHONE 9264 1010   MAP 3A

SPANISH

There's an elderly man playing guitar like a demon. There are couples clutching, families arguing, waiters dodging traffic, and you may, if you're lucky, hear yourself ordering a glass of Rioja. Welcome to a busy night at the Casa. Everything about this popular Spanish town favourite conspires to make you feel as if you are in one of those older, atmospheric bars in Madrid. Think of gloriously rustic chairs, ornate iron light fittings and a backdrop of rendered white walls stained with smoke. There are even white display dishes of albóndigas (meatballs), anchovies and artichokes. From the menu there's a local version of jamon; a superb chorizo simply grilled; splendid, garlicky mushrooms or good versions of the Spanish classic paella. The food tastes of Iberia and is honest without being too coarse. While it may be on the other side of the world, it's a fun place from which to continue your love affair with Spain.

licensed & byo
lunch Tues–Fri & Sun noon–3pm
dinner Daily 5.30–11pm
cards AE BC DC MC V   Bookings recommended, essential weekends
seats 170; private room; wheelchair access
owners The Garcia-Villada family
chef Lorenzo Garcia-Villada
cost Around $54 for two, plus drinks
plus The energy   **minus** The elbow room
score 12/20

catalina rose bay

1 SUNDERLAND AVENUE,
LYNE PARK, ROSE BAY
PHONE 9371 0555   MAP 9

MODERN AUSTRALIAN

Catalina is the restaurant that has everything – great views, soothing minimalist décor, the kind of food that makes you glad to be living in Sydney, and the sort of clientele who also have everything, including a booking. It all feels very Frank Lloyd Wright – the big, airy whitewashed building plonked in the harbour with its long deck for sundowner drinks and Sunday lunches. As befits the location, the menu leans toward the marine, with the sushi menu very popular with those looking for low fat/high glamour dining options. Oysters were as good as they should be in this location, and come with a shot of iced vodka if you wish, a suitably decadent notion. More serious grazers can go modly Mediterranean with Angel Fernandez's always popular snapper fillet with potato and garlic purée, or a fleshy steamed groper with braised silverbeet, arbequiña olives and truffled penne. If you're not known, service can be on the slow side.

licensed; wine by the glass
hours Daily noon–midnight
cards AE BC DC MC V   Bookings recommended
seats 170; outdoor area; no smoking 🚭
owners Judy & Michael McMahon
chef Angel Fernandez
cost Around $173 for two, plus drinks
plus The deck   **minus** The air-kissing
score 16/20

cbd restaurant

75 YORK STREET (CNR KING STREET),
SYDNEY
PHONE 9299 8911   MAP 1

MODERN ITALIAN

It's not your usual smart restaurant that has
a heaving, suit-packed pub to greet you
when you step off the street. Head straight
upstairs to the more sedate, timber-floored
dining room where the hubbub is replaced
by the restrained energy of the young staff.
The opening of the owners' new
establishment, The Establishment, means a
move for Matthew Fleming's modern British
food, with Slip Inn chef Adrian Way slipping
into the CBD with his Italian-influenced
smart casual cooking. It's too early for us
to score the restaurant, but we suspect Way
will take his conservative city clientele into
adventureland with food that is at once
popular and a bit edgy. Expect dishes such
as rare seared beef with gorgonzola,
mascarpone and horseradish, or risotto with
king prawns and apple balsamic. Service is
smooth and business-friendly.

licensed; wine by the glass
lunch Mon–Fri noon–3pm
dinner Mon–Fri 6–10pm
cards AE BC DC MC V   Bookings recommended
sears 85; wheelchair access;
non-smoking area ♨✘
owners John & Merivale Hemmes
chef Adrian Way
cost Around $86 for two, plus drinks
plus The room   **minus** Bum seats
score unscored

chequers

LEVEL 2, MANDARIN CENTRE,
65 ALBERT AVENUE, CHATSWOOD
PHONE 9904 8388   MAP 7

CHINESE/SEAFOOD

You could be in Hong Kong or Singapore.
There's Asia-pop music coming at you from
tinny speakers in the carpark. And in the lift.
And as you step onto the second floor.
Entering Chequers completes the illusion –
the fish tanks, the red-paper 'specials' on
the walls and the mail-order Chinese décor.
Service is very friendly with helpful advice
always on hand. Choose from the well-
thumbed paperback Chinese menu rather
than the ritzy-looking one. Complimentary
pickled cabbage with chilli is a tasty tease,
and the velvet corn soup with crabmeat is
just that – velvet. Abalone with oyster
sauce, julienned ginger, celery and bamboo
shoots is perfectly tender, and spicy salt-
and-pepper prawns plump and juicy. Try the
Swatow chilli steak, Chinese ham and
sausage with snowpeas and celery, or the
special hotpots. It's all as good as you'd
get in Chinatown, if not better.

licensed & byo; wine by the glass
lunch Mon–Fri 11am–3pm; Sat–Sun 10am–3pm
dinner Mon–Sat 5.30–11pm; Sun 5.30–10pm
cards AE BC DC MC V   Bookings recommended
seats 250; private room; wheelchair access;
non-smoking area ♨✘
owners Winkie Chan, Johnson Wong, Norman Tai
& Tong Lau
chef Sum Chow
cost Around $80 for two, plus drinks
plus Chinatown quality   **minus** Piped music
score 14/20

chicane

1A BURTON STREET, DARLINGHURST
PHONE 9380 2121   MAP 2

MODERN EUROPEAN

One day we'll have to produce ID at places like Chicane to prove that we're young and gorgeous enough to enter. It would be a shame to spoil such a chic, modern setting with fat people in bad suits. A dramatic wrought-iron Addams Family staircase spills down to a poured concrete bar. Cushy booths line the wall of the atmospherically moody (read: dark) dining room. Pray that you are booth-worthy. If not, console yourself with Jeffrey Schroeter's chubby duck livers served with a delicious mess of wild mushrooms, or crisp seared red emperor with a seaweed and broad bean stew. Spring lamb Dijonnaise is a well-trimmed, rare-cooked mustard-crusted treat, although a parcel of King George whiting fillets and witlof cooked in crisped rice paper tended toward soggy. As the night goes on, the bar menu comes into force, with smart, helpful food such as steak frites.

licensed; wine by the glass
dinner Daily 6–11pm
supper Sun–Wed 11pm–1am;
Thurs–Sat 11pm–2am
cards AE BC DC MC V   Bookings essential
seats 124; outdoor area; wheelchair access;
non-smoking area ✠
owners Ian Davidson & Galeb Kilzi
chef Jeffrey Schroeter
cost Around $108 for two, plus drinks
plus The booths   **minus** The dark
score 14/20

chinta ria
temple of love

LEVEL 2, THE ROOF TERRACE,
COCKLE BAY WHARF, DARLING PARK,
201 SUSSEX STREET, SYDNEY
PHONE 9264 3211   MAP 1

MALAYSIAN

An irrepressible fusion of food, jazz and great feng shui, Chinta Ria is much too deft to be simply labelled a theme restaurant. Melbourne restaurateur Simon Goh shares his passion for modern jazz and traditional Malaysian street food at one of Sydney's buzziest harbourside dining venues. Good, homely Malay, Indian and Chinese dishes are served all day from the busy open kitchen. If it's lunchtime and you're thinking quick and cheap, there's fried kueh teow, Indian-style mee goreng, curry laksa or the delicious Chinta soup, a real revitaliser of pure chicken stock, tung chai (Chinese preserved vegetable), Hokkien noodles, fishcake, crisp-fried shallots and spring onions. At night, try specials such as assam fish or fresh king prawns sautéed with a spiced red sauce.

licensed & byo; wine by the glass
lunch Daily noon–2.30pm
dinner Mon–Sat 6–11pm; Sun 6–10.30pm
cards AE BC DC MC V   Bookings for lunch only
seats 160; outdoor area; wheelchair access;
no smoking inside ✠
owner Simon Goh
chef Donny Pang
cost Around $54 for two, plus drinks
plus The energy   **minus** Vague service
score 13/20

cicada

29 CHALLIS AVENUE, POTTS POINT
PHONE 9358 1255   MAP 2

MODERN AUSTRALIAN

Cicada now has a new makeover (including a Schiaparelli pink wall) courtesy of designer Iain Halliday, and an approachable menu in which entrées, mains, salads and sides sit cheek to cheek. To be honest, the changes are marginal. Prices are a touch lower, and the dishes a smidge less formal, but hardly what you'd call bistro simple. Flavours and textures contrast in a salad of endive, mâche, pear, gorgonzola and pecans; tiny tendrils of spicy salted squid hide in a tumble of bitter greens; and swordfish nestles on a bed of red capsicum, artichokes, chickpeas and baby leeks. Black potato gnocchi may not be the lightest but the old Trianon soufflé is a masterful confection of nectarine and peach schnapps served with passionfruit sorbet. Doyle promises his new city bistro Celsius will not affect Cicada to any great degree.

licensed; wine by the glass
lunch Thurs–Fri noon–2.30pm
dinner Mon–Sat from 6.30pm
cards AE BC DC MC V   Bookings recommended
seats 140; private room; no smoking until 10.30pm ⅹ
owners Beverley & Peter Doyle
chef Peter Doyle
cost Around $86 for two, plus drinks; daily menu $27.50 for 3 courses p.p. at lunch and from 6.30–7.15pm
plus Pink wall   **minus** Bland bar
score 16/20

civic dining

388 PITT STREET, SYDNEY
PHONE 8267 3183   MAP 3A

MODERN AUSTRALIAN

As chef at the much-loved Burdekin, Tony Barlow pioneered the revival of great pub food, and the revolution continues in the comfortable Art Deco dining room of the Civic. Actually, this is more a first-rate contemporary restaurant than a pub dining room. The cooking is adventurous and assured, starting with oysters shucked to order, Civic's home-smoked ocean trout, steak tartare or a perfectly clear consommé of beef shin with sherry and shiitake mushroom ravioli. It's difficult to categorise the style beyond a good version of Sydney modern, but European and Middle Eastern influences (rather than Asian) dominate mains, with hearty dishes such as a rich and lush crab bisque risotto, and roast duck on cannellini beans that ooze with the duck's hearty cooking juices. The dessert menu is loaded with puddings, trifles, panna cotta and cheese. This is modern, well-crafted cuisine with lots of presence – just what this end of town needs.

licensed; wine by the glass
lunch Tues–Fri noon–2.30pm
dinner Tues–Sat 6.30–10.30pm
cards AE BC DC MC V   Bookings recommended
seats 150; private room; outdoor area; non-smoking area ⅹ
owners James & John Kospetas
chef Tony Barlow
cost Around $97 for two, plus drinks
plus The big bar   **minus** Skid-row location
score 14/20

clareville kiosk

27 DELECTA AVENUE, CLAREVILLE BEACH
PHONE 9918 2727   MAP 7

MODERN AUSTRALIAN

If cooked fish with simple fresh flavours is
your idea of a good time, proceed directly
to the Clareville Kiosk. This popular
unpretentious restaurant with its ceiling
fans and louvred windows used to be the
general store and post office, but now
concentrates on delivering good food to a
steady stream of locals and visitors. Grilled
Streaky Bay scallops sit happily in a tangy
lemon and caper sauce while the chunky
vegetable terrine of eggplant, pumpkin,
capsicum and olives is complemented by
a vibrant beetroot juice dressing. Don't go
past the fish for mains. Rainbow trout and
spicy mango relish marries well, and the
whole baby snapper with oven-baked red
and yellow tomatoes, fresh dill and whole
mint leaves is simple but stunning. Leave
room for a refreshing finale of boysenberry
parfait with praline and pashtak (Iranian
spun sugar). Very pleasant, reasonably
priced dining in a relaxed holiday
atmosphere.

byo
lunch Sat–Sun noon–3pm
dinner Tues–Sat 6–10pm
cards AE BC DC MC V   Bookings recommended
seats 70; outdoor area; no smoking inside ✳
owners Helen & Joe Gracie
chefs Joe Gracie & Nicole Day
cost Around $92 for two, plus drinks
plus Attentive service   **minus** Parking
score 14/20

claudes

10 OXFORD STREET, WOOLLAHRA
PHONE 9331 2325   MAP 4B

FRENCH

We'll continue to bitch about those chairs
but it's impossible to ignore the other
bottom line: glorious food executed with
artistry. Tim Pak Poy is indeed the god of
small things that hug your palate memory.
An exquisite cockle custard which, although
merely a support act to abalone, is an
apotheosis for a humble mollusc; the
haunting fragrance of a currant and almond
milk sauce for a breast of quail; an
exhilarating pink gin jelly tart; the simple
addition of sweet, cooked cherries to rare,
peppered venison; a perfect cinnamon
soufflé. Claudes' wine list is short but highly
individualistic. Alongside a few fine old
Bordeaux, top-flight Rhône and New World
wines are seldom seen entries such as a
brilliant Jurançon dessert wine. Service isn't
as starchy these days, but we'd love to see
more interaction between the shy one and
his admiring customers. It's a pleasure to
restore Claudes to three-hat status this year.

licensed & byo
dinner Tues–Sat from 7.30pm
cards AE BC DC MC V   Bookings essential
seats 40; private room; no smoking ✳
owner/chef Tim Pak Poy
fixed price Three-course menu $110 p.p., plus
wine, Mon–Fri; dégustation menu also available
plus Small and intimate   **minus** You know what
score 18/20

claudine's

GALLERY LEVEL, CHATSWOOD CHASE,
345 VICTORIA AVENUE, ARCHER STREET
ENTRANCE, CHATSWOOD
PHONE 9411 1688   MAP 7

MODERN FRENCH

Shopping-mall snacks and sushi wouldn't do
for the well-heeled retail therapy-seekers in
Chatswood. That's why this serious
restaurant, tucked away on the first level,
has a loyal following. Newly installed Brit
chef Stephen Gill has the career credits and
apparent skill to deliver contemporary,
complex French dishes. Savour his perfectly
cooked scallop 'pie', opaque fat molluscs
sheathed in fly-away pastry; nutmeg-glazed
plump duck; or adventurous surf-and-turf
variations such as stuffed pig's trotter with
scampi. Attentive service, upholstered chairs
and a comprehensive wine list add to the
occasion. Only the impersonal hotel-style,
mirrored room and the intrusive overhead
music detract.

licensed (byo Mon & Tues); wine by the glass
lunch Mon–Sat noon–3pm
dinner Mon–Sat 6–9.30pm
cards AE BC DC MC V   Bookings essential
seats 140; private room; outdoor area;
wheelchair access; no smoking ⇻
owner Claudine Dalco
chef Stephen Gill
cost Around $110 for two, plus drinks
plus Set menus   **minus** BYO limits
score 14/20

clock hotel restaurant

470 CROWN STREET, SURRY HILLS
PHONE 9331 5333   MAP 3B

MODERN AUSTRALIAN

Old-timers who remember the original Clock
Hotel restaurant may be surprised by the
comfort of the first-floor dining room, with
tables available on the enclosed balcony
overlooking the very English Shannon
Reserve. They would certainly be taken
aback by the ocean trout carpaccio, lamb's
brains with sorrel, zucchini flowers stuffed
with ricotta, and squid ink pasta. That's just
for starters, with mains featuring seared
kangaroo, Asian spiced duck, poached
salmon and daily specials. For all the
modern hype, the cooking remains solidly
basic, with the best choices being grills like
the octopus or the steak, or a simple roast
turkey with stuffing and two veg. Some of
the dishes are clearly too sophisticated for
the kitchen, which tends to cram conflicting
flavours on the plate. Great sherry trifle,
friendly service and a good choice of wines
go a long way toward making this one of
the better pub restaurants, especially when
they keep it simple.

licensed; wine by the glass
hours Mon–Sat noon–11pm; Sun noon–9pm
cards AE BC DC MC V   Bookings recommended
seats 140; outdoor area; non-smoking area ⇻
owners Maurice Green, Tony Green, John Tierney
& Anders Ousback
chef Sebastian Tyson
cost Around $86 for two, plus drinks
plus The balcony   **minus** The bar downstairs
score 14/20

coast

THE ROOF TERRACE, COCKLE BAY WHARF,
DARLING PARK, 201 SUSSEX STREET, SYDNEY
PHONE 9267 6700   MAP 1

MEDITERRANEAN

Coast became very hot very quickly, and
early fans worried that it might collapse
under the weight of its success. Amazingly,
it has never wavered in the smoothness of
its service and the liveliness of its food since
its strong start. Even a standard Sydney
entrée such as fried calamari is enlivened by
a light crisp batter and a generous serve of
aïoli for dipping, but there are many more
imaginative choices than that. The gnocchi,
seasonally changing risotto and linguine
with clams are reliable favourites. Each
day's chargrilled fish arrives crisp on the
outside and moist on the inside, while the
corporate crowd value the fat veal chop
served with pea risotto. The range of veggie
side orders is one of the biggest in town,
and if the dessert array doesn't quite come
up to standard, you're inclined to be
forgiving by then. The watchful, speedy staff
actually seem to know their wines, too – a
rarity in Sydney restaurants.

licensed; wine by the glass
lunch Mon–Sat noon–2.30pm; Sun noon–9pm
dinner Mon–Sat 6–10.30pm; Sun 6–9pm
cards AE BC DC MC V   Bookings recommended
seats 220; private room; outdoor area;
wheelchair access; no smoking 🚭
owners Tim Connell & Frank Wilden
chef Adam Birtles
cost Around $92 for two, plus drinks
plus Consistency   minus Hard to get in for lunch
score 14/20

the coonanbarra cafe

64 COONANBARRA ROAD, WAHROONGA
PHONE 9489 0980   MAP 6

MODERN AUSTRALIAN

Mercedes saloons line the street and mums
line the pavement at this suburban café,
where it's more fashionable to be outside
than in. The restored Federation building is
furnished with period pieces while the
popular outdoor area comes complete with
heaters for winter. Waitresses in joggers
provide swift, smiling service but we'd like
to see some more surprises on the menu.
For lunch, compatible flavours include
rocket, parmesan and avocado salad with
balsamic dressing. A basil and tomato
bruschetta was made with good bread but
scarce on aromatic basil. A puff pastry
tartlet of eggplant, goat's cheese and
marinated peppers topped with a good
dollop of pesto is simple but effective. At
dinner, try the whole roasted quails served
with glazed peaches or maybe beef fillet
with ratatouille and red wine sauce.
Chocolate bread and butter pudding, mixed
berry crumble and pecan pie all come with
moreish home-churned ice-cream.

byo
breakfast Sat–Sun & public holidays 9–11am
lunch Daily 9.30am–4.30pm
dinner Wed–Sat from 6.30pm
cards AE BC DC MC V   Bookings recommended
seats 80; outdoor area; non-smoking area 🚭
owners Rod & Robyn Maclure
chef Jenny Morgan
cost Around $76 for two, plus drinks
plus No corkage   minus No surprises
score 12/20

§

corinthian

283 MARRICKVILLE ROAD, MARRICKVILLE
PHONE 9569 7084   MAP 8

GREEK

There are times when we want to eat big.
We want juicy, slow-roasted, no-nonsense,
falling-off-the-bone lamb. Hearty beef
stews. Large creamy blocks of moussaka.
Lots of taramasalata and melitzanosalata
and hunks of bread to dunk. We want it in
the generous, congenial atmosphere of a
family-run restaurant. In short, we want the
blue-latticed ceiling and faded photos of the
Corinthian, with its 38 years' experience in
keeping customers happy. And if the
skordalia – that romance-destroying purée
of potato lashed with garlic – is a little acid,
and the dark, pungent kokoretsi, super
sausage of all things offal, could use a few
herbs, who are we to quibble? We want
bain-maries of vegetables, grilled octopus
straight off the barbecue and a fridge full of
Greek wines we've never seen before. But
most of all we want another bottle of that
retsina, please, Frank, and can you pack up
the rest of the lamb to take home?

licensed & byo
lunch Daily noon–3pm
dinner Daily 6pm–3am
cards None   Bookings recommended,
essential weekends
seats 50
owners/chefs Frank & Maria Giannakelos
cost Around $50 for two, plus drinks
plus Sheer generosity   **minus** No valet parking
score 12/20

♀

cottage point inn

2 ANDERSON PLACE, COTTAGE POINT
PHONE 9456 1011   MAP 7

MODERN AUSTRALIAN

What a joy to be sitting on the wrap-around
deck with the calm blue water of the
Hawkesbury River lapping at your feet,
whetting your appetite for a seafood
feast – only to discover that there is only
one seafood dish (salmon gravlax) for
starters. Where are the prawns, oysters,
scallops or calamari? At least the mains
feature a potato-crusted blue-eye cod on a
salad of oven-roasted tomato, lemongrass
and coriander, and pan-roasted swordfish
complemented by the subtle spicy flavours
of an Asian broth and soba noodles.
Desserts run to vanilla panna cotta with
fresh berry salad and strawberry soup, while
the passionfruit soufflé is popular with the
boaties. Situated at the junctions of Cowan
Water and Coal and Candle Creek, it's only
a short drive through the National Park
from Terrey Hills, and can also be reached
by boat, water taxi, ferry and seaplane.
So bring on the seafood, we say.

licensed; wine by the glass
lunch Daily noon–3pm
dinner Wed–Sun 6.30–9.30pm (Fri–Sat in winter)
cards AE BC DC MC V   Bookings recommended,
essential weekends
seats 95; outdoor area; non-smoking area 🚭
owners Melissa & Dan McKinnon
chef Kevin Kendall
cost Around $100 for two, plus drinks
plus Parking for boats
minus We don't have a boat
score 12/20

Have you seen our naked Goddess?

Italian mineral water. Bottled at the source in the Appennini Mountains.

SANTA VITTORIA

ACQUA MINERALE

RESERVE SOME FOR YOURSELF TODAY.

Introducing JACOB'S CREEK RESERVE SHIRAZ, CHARDONNAY and CABERNET SAUVIGNON.
These premium wines have been vintaged from specially selected grapes from South Australia's
premier winemaking regions. Reflecting the expertise that has come from more than 150
years of winemaking, these are wines of generous flavour and character that will develop
further with medium-term cellaring. Reserve some for yourself today. JACOB'S CREEK

courtney's brasserie

2 HORWOOD PLACE, PARRAMATTA
PHONE 9635 3288   MAP 6

MODERN AUSTRALIAN

It's a sad fact that, despite being nearly the demographic centre of our great city, Parramatta is a long way from the action as far as good food is concerned. So we're very thankful for Courtney's, set in the old Red Coats' Mess, built in 1830. The inside tables are sprinkled through several rooms and some around a central courtyard so you have to spy fellow diners through the blinds. Chef Paul Kuipers is one of those rare beings waving the good food flag in the west. He does a great job on the crisp-skinned duck neck sausage with duck liver and pancetta confit, and his sautéed quail fillets make an unusual but happy association with goat's cheese tortellini. But there were slips in the execution. Swimmingly fresh swordfish with baba ghanoush was perfectly cooked inside, yet acrid from the deep chargrill lines outside, while our salmon came dry. Wine buffs will find the place irresistible.

licensed; wine by the glass
lunch Mon–Fri noon–3pm
dinner Mon–Sat 6–10pm
cards AE BC DC MC V   Bookings essential
seats 120; private room; outdoor area;
wheelchair access; non-smoking area
owner Paul Creighton
chef Paul Kuipers
cost Around $90 for two, plus drinks
plus It's in Parramatta
minus Some over-cooking
score 13/20

dakhni

65 GLEBE POINT ROAD, GLEBE
PHONE 9660 4887   MAP 5B

INDIAN

It's hard to go past a dish that's prefaced with 'MUST TRY FOR OUR CHEF'S PRIDE'. Yet the entrée of spiced lamb backstrap in a deep-fried pancake is no match for the onion outhappams, delicate rice pancakes topped with onion, chilli, cumin and coriander, served with lentil, coconut and tomato sauces. The South of India is renowned for vegetarian cuisine, and a dozen such dishes successfully feature here. Those who eat meat can have their beef, chicken and lamb in an authentic Goan vindaloo and moist, tender, aromatic Telengana chicken cooked in a sealed pot with Hyderabadi spices and green chillies. Mango kulfi ice-cream and sweet, light gulab jamun dumplings will change the minds of Indian dessert doubters. With generous, well-priced banquets it's easy to return to this low-key room and its friendly service, if only for the 'amazingly interesting masala milk'.

byo
lunch Tues–Sun noon–2.30pm
dinner Daily 5.30–10.30pm
cards AE BC DC MC V   Bookings essential
seats 100; private room; no smoking
owners Nagalingam Rathnavelu
& Surenth Chelliah
chefs Meenakshisundaram Rajendra &
Tanaki Raman
cost Around $54 for two, plus drinks
plus Vegetarian friendly   **minus** The garnish
score 13/20

dante

39/23 NORTON STREET, LEICHHARDT
PHONE 9550 0062   MAP 5B

ITALIAN

Critics of Leichhardt's Italian Forum precinct
say it's too manufactured, too instant and
too full of cafés dishing out commercial
pasta, fluffy focaccia and antipasto from
a jar. But Dante is different. Admittedly,
its aged trattoria feel is simulated, yet
somehow it comes off. It especially works
on a sunny Sunday afternoon, if you can
snaffle a table outside and do some very
authentic people watching. Service is
old-style Italian, which means charming,
watchful, and pragmatic. While the menu
occasionally lapses into tourist fare, there
are some very worthwhile home-style dishes
on offer, such as pasta e fagioli, a huge
serving of hearty borlotti bean soup with
freshly made pasta, potato, pancetta and
just a touch of chilli. The capretto in terrina
(baby goat casserole) shows a subtlety one
doesn't normally associate with casseroles –
or goat, for that matter.

licensed
lunch Sun–Fri noon–3pm
dinner Daily 6–10.30pm
cards DC MC V   Bookings recommended,
essential weekends
seats 160; outdoor area; wheelchair access;
non-smoking area
owners Frank Moio & Emanuele Zerilli
chef Felice Marino
cost Around $76 for two, plus drinks
plus Piazza views   **minus** Tourist crowds
score 13/20

darling mills

134 GLEBE POINT ROAD, GLEBE
PHONE 9660 5666   MAP 5B

MODERN AUSTRALIAN

You could be forgiven for thinking that
Darling Mills actually was a mill, with its
hewn sandstone walls and trickling water.
But it's actually an old cottage that became
a dentist's folly when Dr Adey bought a
burnt-out church next door, remodelled his
surgery and named it after the family's
country property. The building is still in Adey
hands, with Sarah managing the floor, Steve
growing the hydroponic vegetables (some
on the roof), and Cynthia working in the
kitchen. New chef, Andy Davies, ex-Bondi
Sports Bard, has brought with him a vast
repertoire of bright, resonant flavours. From
a bouncingly fresh mâche and pink eye
potato salad with crisp fennel, to an
ethereal hot-smoked salmon with a perfect
poached egg, asparagus and salmon roe
pearls, his cooking has put a real spring in
the step of this Glebe favourite.

licensed (& **byo** Sun–Thurs); wine by the glass
lunch Fri noon–3pm
bar food Daily from 5pm
dinner Sun–Thurs 6–10pm; Fri & Sat 6–11pm
cards AE BC DC MC V   Bookings recommended
seats 200; private room; outdoor area;
wheelchair access; non-smoking area
owners The Adey family
chef Andy Davies
cost Around $100 for two, plus drinks
plus Freshness of flavour   **minus** Slow service
score 14/20

de beers whale beach

24B THE STRAND, WHALE BEACH
PHONE 9974 4009   MAP 7

MODERN AUSTRALIAN

Mesmeric Whale Beach is an unlikely place to find truly beautiful flavours, but there's no denying De Beers has serious class in the food department. Chef Peter Gilmore used to make boutique ice-creams, so dessert is as good a place as any to start. His technique is so sharp you can cut yourself just thinking about it, reaching its zenith in the 'five textures of Valrhona chocolate', a revelation of taste and texture. Before you get to dessert, though, you'll have to pass the rich, moist, succulent signature dish of crisp-skinned, lightly aromatic pressed duck with sesame juices, or some perfect shiitake dumplings laced with abalone. Inside is all muted tones, letting the food, in its restrained portions, take centre stage. And while the beach is barely a hop, skip and jump away, you can't see it from the inside dining room, so a walk pre- or post-dining is an absolute must.

licensed & byo; wine by the glass
lunch Fri–Sun 12.30–3.30pm; Sun noon–4pm
dinner Wed–Sat 6.30–9.30pm
cards AE BC DC MC V   Bookings recommended
seats 140; outdoor area; wheelchair access; no smoking inside
owners Rod & Jeni de Beer
chef Peter Gilmore
cost Around $93 for two, plus drinks
plus The chocolate cake   **minus** Smallish serves
score 15/20

the dolphin on crown

412 CROWN STREET, SURRY HILLS
PHONE 9331 4800   MAP 3B

MODERN AUSTRALIAN

The Dolphin sets a benchmark for modern pub conversions in the inner city. Essentially, it's three concepts: an old Sydney boozer with much of its character left intact, an adjoining bistro serving quality snacks and drinks, and an upstairs restaurant with a very likeable, eclectic menu (including an Australian 'yum cha' option). Chef Brady Ough confidently turns out food that looks smart and tastes as good as it looks. A ceviche of blue-eye cod with cucumber and Pernod is subtle and refreshing; and grilled shellfish with wild garlic and whitebait fritters is served on a very accomplished sauce nantua. Veggies will adore the kumara and spinach coulibiac with a tomato and ratatouille sauce. Some disappointments: a chocolate and honeycomb gâteau tasted commercial and the bread was dull. The wine list is a stunner, with over 60 wines available by the glass.

licensed; wine by the glass
lunch Daily 11am–3pm
dinner Daily 6–10pm
cards AE BC DC MC V   Bookings recommended, essential weekends
seats 200; wheelchair access
owners Sebastian Marsden & Lucille Marsden
chef Brady Ough
cost Around $92 for two, plus drinks
plus The wine list   **minus** Bread bored
score 14/20

$

domo sushi kitchen

SHOP 5, 207 BEN BOYD ROAD, NEUTRAL BAY
PHONE 9909 3100   MAP 5A

JAPANESE

There were great debates as to whether this
sweet little Japanese restaurant should be
included. After all, it looks like your average
yen-a-dozen Neutral Bay sushi cafe, it's
under-serviced and it takes no cards. Nor
is it air-conditioned, which, on a heatwave
summer's night, makes you long to be a
finger of sushi so you could lie in
refrigerated comfort instead of sweating
it out at the table. But, and this is why it
made it, the tiny kitchen is very, very good.
Sushi is slow and not cheap, just as it
should be (never trust sushi that is fast
and cheap). It will arrive long after your
sweetly tender grilled chicken in miso,
and refreshing seaweed salad, so fill the
gap with a platter of perfectly cooked,
fresh-tasting gyoza pork dumplings with a
must-have-more vinegar dressing. Domo is
BYO, but sits directly opposite the very
accommodating Oaks Hotel bottle shop.

byo
dinner Tues–Sun 6–10pm
cards AE BC DC MC V   Bookings recommended
seats 28; wheelchair access
owners/chefs Takashi Sano & Hidehiro Sunouchi
cost Around $54 for two, plus drinks
plus Serious sushi   **minus** No air-con
score 12/20

doyle's on the beach

11 MARINE PARADE, WATSON'S BAY
PHONE 9337 2007   MAP 9

SEAFOOD

Twenty out of twenty for location, of
course – Doyle's literally walks on water,
boldly striding out to meet the sails in
Watson's Bay. And everybody feels well-
disposed to a family business that's been
in operation on the same spot since 1885.
While the food has not always matched
the remarkable views in the past, things
seem to have improved a lot in recent
times. Apart from the odd paella or bowl
of chowder, Doyle's celebrates fish simply
by grilling or frying it. Go for something
straightforward, such as the chargrilled
Eden tuna steaks served rare with mash,
or the wild-caught barramundi fillets
golden fried. Go, too, for the decidedly
unfancy garden salad which at least has
snap, and you're guaranteed a good,
hearty meal in a top spot.

licensed
lunch Mon–Sat noon–3pm; Sun 11.30am–3pm
dinner Mon–Sat 6–9.30pm; Sun 6–9pm
cards BC DC MC V   Bookings recommended
seats 400; outdoor area; wheelchair access;
non-smoking area ⚒
owners The Doyle family
chef Peter Doyle Jr
cost Around $97 for two, plus drinks
plus Harbour views   **minus** House white
score 13/20

dragon sharkfin and seafood

445 VICTORIA AVENUE, CHATSWOOD
PHONE 9415 2785   MAP 7

CHINESE/SEAFOOD

You wouldn't be surprised if you were shown to your table by Jackie Chan in a 1930s suit. The restaurant has an old Chinese filmset quality about it, with its rounded, almost Art Deco central service islands, wood panelling, dark chairs with carved dragon backs, glowing green fish tanks, and a curving bar with a complicated darkwood mirror. Chinese families occupy most of the tables, attacking mounds of tantalising Singapore crab or salt-and-pepper lobster. Forget the menu here. Just let Leon make his recommendations. By day, the lunchtime dim sum rates among Sydney's finest. At night, the mountain of live salt-and-pepper chilli school prawns are sweet and crunchy. Duck in fluffy yam batter is complemented by Chinese spinach in fermented beancurd. But try the live coral trout steamed with soy and spring onions, a simple dish prepared simply superbly.

licensed & byo
lunch Daily 10.30am–3pm
dinner Daily 6–11pm
cards AE BC DC MC V   Bookings recommended
seats 250; private room; wheelchair access; non-smoking area ⊁
owners Connie & Leon Lau
chef Peter Lee
cost Around $86 for two, plus drinks
plus Red-paper specials   **minus** The menu
score 14/20

dragonfly

478 BOURKE STREET, SURRY HILLS
PHONE 9380 7333   MAP 3B

MODERN ASIAN

Not wanting to be pigeon-holed, this newish addition to the Sydney food scene describes itself as a sushi deli noodle bar, which just about covers all bases. Its young and energetic owners, Anthea Wright and Yuey Then, also provide a takeaway service and run a catering business. From the typeface on the menus to the restrained, clean lines of the dining space, everything screams care and attention to detail. Anthea is a joy as she meets and greets, while Yuey's sushi is a delight, and his family recipe for jasmine tea-smoked roasted chicken with fragrant rice is an exercise in delicate flavour. Whatever else you have, always, always, always order the rocket and snowpea leaves with wasabi mayonnaise, topped with the crunch of deep-fried wonton pastry skins. There is a small selection of ready-made desserts, all on show in the small front-of-house counter, which are worth a look if you can find room.

byo
lunch Wed–Fri 11am–6pm; Sat noon–6pm
dinner Mon–Sat 6–9pm
cards AE BC MC V   Bookings recommended
seats 50; outdoor area; wheelchair access; no smoking inside ⊁
owners Yuey Then & Anthea Wright
chef Yuey Then
cost Around $60 for two, plus drinks
plus Zen den   **minus** Early to bed
score 13/20

coffee
hot, sweet, strong

bar coluzzi An old-timer still going hot, black and strong, with sporty décor and a highly irregular crowd of regulars. 322 VICTORIA STREET, DARLINGHURST 9380 5420

bills A big communal table, good mags, Grinders coffee, and fresh-from-the-oven muffins make bills the benchmark café. 433 LIVERPOOL STREET, DARLINGHURST 9360 9631

concrete Bare concrete and big glass windows set the scene for sunny mornings of good coffee, groovy music, and nice-as-pie staff. 224 HARRIS STREET, PYRMONT 9518 9523

caffe italia Tucked into a corner of Sydney's International terminal, this Milanese café makes sure you leave the country with a good taste in your mouth. SYDNEY INTERNATIONAL AIRPORT, MASCOT 9669 6434

le petit crème An honest, hardworking Darlo café with good coffee (in huge French bowls), good people and fresh, warm baguettes full of eggs and bacon. 118 DARLINGHURST ROAD, DARLINGHURST 9361 4738

latteria The heart of Darlinghurst café style, from the wooden street stools to the Segafredo espresso. 320 VICTORIA STREET, DARLINGHURST 9331 2914

spring espresso *(right)* Babies, dogs and even media are welcome to lounge in, out and around this tiny white street café. CNR MACLEAY STREET AND CHALLIS AVENUE, POTTS POINT 9331 0190

north sydney primavera A little pocket of Italian charm, coffee, cake and atmosphere in North Sydney's heartless commercial district. SHOP 3, LITTLE SPRING STREET, NORTH SYDNEY 9955 2492

il baretto Great pasta and perfect risotto make it tough to stick to just coffee. And then there's the gelati as well. 496 BOURKE STREET, SURRY HILLS 9361 6163

south dowling sandwiches Rich, mellow coffee consumed on rolling cubes by street babes tucking into organically filled sandwiches bigger than they are. 377 SOUTH DOWLING STREET, DARLINGHURST 9360 9355

ebisu

22 ROCKWALL CRESCENT, POTTS POINT
PHONE 9326 9500   MAP 2

JAPANESE/SEAFOOD

You rarely see seafood treated with the reverence and respect that it receives at this reliable Potts Point Japanese eatery. Sit at the raised centre-of-attraction sushi bar (specify when booking) and watch how the chefs cradle each fillet as if they are holding something rare and precious. Once they have finished slicing, the remaining fish is gently and carefully returned to the refrigerated cabinet with all the care and concern of a parent tucking in a child at bedtime. The seafood isn't so much cooked as coddled. The care shines through in a light, crisp tempura of fresh oysters enshrouded in sticky rice; perfect, glistening scampi sushi followed by a delicate miso soup made with the scampi heads; and luscious, pearly white grilled snapper marinated in miso. Service is well-intentioned, if erratic. The room lacks any real buzz to speak of, but the sushi bar is always fun, and the Go-Shu Australian sake or Yebisu malt beer goes down a treat.

licensed
dinner Mon–Sat 6–10pm
cards AE BC DC MC V   Bookings recommended
seats 96; private room; non-smoking area
owner Saneyuki Tabata
chef Shintaro Oka
cost Around $108 for two, plus drinks
plus Sushi bar   **minus** Thick wine glasses
score 14/20

ecco

DRUMMOYNE SAILING CLUB,
ST GEORGES CRESCENT, DRUMMOYNE
PHONE 9719 9394   MAP 8

ITALIAN

It is always difficult for restaurants when they up sticks and move to a new home, especially when they have worked hard for many years to establish a reputation as good as Ecco's at the Five Dock Hotel. The new venue on the top floor of the Drummoyne Sailing Club, however, provides an added dimension with magnificent views across Iron Cove and the Parramatta River. Their next trick had to be to provide food to match the scenery, and it's one they just pull off. While the main courses were excellent, entrées fell a little flat. The plentiful beef carpaccio with rocket and parmesan, for instance, was overpowered by the intensity of the accompanying truffle oil and lemon juice. That said, the simply grilled West Australian scampi and herb-crusted rack of lamb more than made up. In fact, the lamb made us abandon all decorum, along with cutlery, to tuck into the ribs. You get bits in your eyebrows, but it's worth it.

licensed; wine by the glass
lunch Wed–Fri & Sun noon–3pm
dinner Tues–Sat 6–10pm
cards AE BC DC MC V   Bookings essential
seats 120
owners Claudio & Carmel Carnevale
chef Antonio Di Santo
cost Around $86 for two, plus drinks
plus Family atmosphere   **minus** Bit pricey
score 13/20

ecco mosman

LEVEL 1, 707 MILITARY ROAD, MOSMAN
PHONE 9969 6222   MAP 7

MODERN AUSTRALIAN/FRENCH

New chef Meyjitte Boughenout has brought some real finesse to this popular Mosman eatery. Shelled Balmain bug tails are served translucently tender in a ginger and tomato dressing. An ambitious entrée of a large ricotta and spinach purée ravioli sits simply enough in a neat bed of salad, the dish lifted by a barely cooked truffled egg yolk on top of the pasta. Good quality rouget (red mullet) fillets are unfussed and well handled, served in a pool of orange, lemon oil and fish stock reduction. Orange, cinnamon and coriander-glazed confit duck (not too salty) and grilled breast (nicely pink) work well, and a passionfruit soufflé is perfectly executed. Latter-day Clapton, Van Morrison and Sinatra (sadly, duets) attempt to fill the cavernous room, which would look better in any colour other than 1980s pastel salmon. Service is warm, and the wine list is well balanced and well priced.

licensed & byo; wine by the glass
lunch Wed–Fri noon–3pm
dinner Tues–Sat 6.30–10.30pm
cards AE BC DC MC V   Bookings recommended
seats 60; outdoor area; no smoking until 10.30pm ✻✖
owner Heydeon Young
chef Meyjitte Boughenout
cost Around $120 for two, plus drinks
plus The soufflés   **minus** The menus
score 14/20

edna's table

204 CLARENCE STREET, SYDNEY
PHONE 9267 3933   MAP 1

AUSTRALIAN

Jennice Kersh runs Edna's as if it were one of those eighteenth-century Parisian salons that attracted the brightest minds, the sharpest wits and the most entertaining personalities of their time. Media mighties, TV stars, entertainers and pollies rank among her nearest and dearest friends. And so will you, just by walking through the door of this elegant, yet comfortable, split-level restaurant. Brother Raymond tends the stoves, and while there is a fair scattering of native ingredients in his repertoire, they are used more for their natural flavour and characteristics than for their novelty or tourist attraction. So a fresh, jewel-like carpaccio of tuna is enlivened with native aniseed; corn-fed chicken breast wrapped in banana leaves gets the tang of desert lime; and Balmain bug ravioli is teamed with a soupy pepperberry sauce. Some flavours cancel each other out, and sauces can be thin, but the effort to domesticate Australian ingredients is heroic.

licensed; wine by the glass
lunch Mon–Fri noon–3pm
dinner Tues–Sat 6–10pm
cards AE BC DC MC V   Bookings recommended
seats 135; private room; outdoor area; non-smoking area ✻✖
owners Jennice & Raymond Kersh
chef Raymond Kersh
cost Around $97 for two, plus drinks
plus Warm welcome   **minus** Pricey wines
score 14/20

eleni's

185A BOURKE STREET, EAST SYDNEY
PHONE 9331 5306   MAP 2

MODERN GREEK

So, what makes people come back time and time again to a tiny, but intimate, hole in the wall overlooking Sydney's dubious William Street? It can only be the food – and the food it is. Peter Conistis keeps on producing hit after hit from his small kitchen post. Mum Eleni is there too, but it's Peter's honed skill we see in the huge helpings. Regulars debate over which entrée deserves top billing: the enduringly mighty modern Greek moussaka of eggplant, scallop and taramasalata, or the delicately creamy prawn and haloumi tartlet served with witlof, avocado and cucumber (we think the tartlet steals the show). Service is solid and very well paced – a good thing, considering the richly substantial portions. The best can be had in a pente of lamb – a mini dégustation meal in itself with sweetbreads, brains, mince and a vine-leaf-wrapped fillet all making an appearance, accompanied by a perfect baby spinach and feta tart. Luscious desserts are well worth holding out for.

byo
lunch Fri noon–2.30pm
dinner Mon–Sat 6.30pm–late
cards AE BC MC V   Bookings essential
seats 30; no smoking
owners Peter Conistis & Eleni Conistis
chef Peter Conistis
cost Around $97 for two, plus drinks
plus Nicely paced   **minus** Back-lane bathroom
score 15/20

elio

159 NORTON STREET, LEICHHARDT
PHONE 9560 9129   MAP 5B

MODERN ITALIAN

Even if the food wasn't so marvellously fresh, the service so flirtatiously delightful and the atmosphere so much fun, you'd go to Elio just for the passeggiata. The whole of Leichhardt strolls past the picture window, floodlit by a wittily positioned exterior light, like extras in a Fellini movie. Food is nuovo Italiano, with nice little twists on Italian classics here and there. Carpaccio of seared tuna with a braised leek and lemon dressing is a perfectly yielding and melding mixture of tender tastes that goes all too fast, especially when mopped up with some excellent Italian bread. Grilled calamari with asparagus and oven-dried cherry tomatoes is another very good idea – bursts of flavour and different textures, and quite the best thing to happen to cherry tomatoes to date. Linguine with Tasmanian baby clams, chilli, garlic and lemon has the ideal balance of piquant tastes and rich oil. Only the saffron and chive risotto failed to thrill.

licensed & byo; wine by the glass
lunch Sun noon–3pm
dinner Mon–Sat 6–11pm
cards AE BC DC MC V   Bookings essential
seats 100; private room; outdoor area; no smoking until 10.30pm
owner Elio Cordaro
chef Helen Konstantinidis
cost Around $80 for two, plus drinks
plus Cheeky service   **minus** Noisy surfaces
score 15/20

Ṣ

emperor's garden bbq

213–15 THOMAS STREET, HAYMARKET
PHONE 9281 9899   MAP 3A

CHINESE/NOODLES

This is probably the last authentic, big,
street-level dining room in Chinatown
where you don't have to pay a fortune
for a decent meal of whole steamed fish
and rice. The best Chinese roast meats in
Sydney hang in the take-home stall on the
street, and obviously feature heavily on the
menu of this huge, barn-like restaurant. If
you're in a hurry, there is roast duck on rice;
if you're not, there is plenty of variety. But
they can take the home-style feeling a bit
too far, with very junior service unable to
translate the specials written on the wall,
and some faded, lacklustre dishes appearing
among the genuine, honest stuff. Noodle
soups are terrific, plump with sui gow or
wonton dumplings, although fried noodle
dishes can be too wet. There is evidence
of upgrading going on – indoor neon,
new tiles and new plastic red roses to
match the Coca-Cola signs – but we still
wouldn't dress up too much.

licensed & byo
hours Daily 9.30am–11pm
cards AE BC DC MC V   Bookings recommended
seats 120; wheelchair access
owner Stanley Yee
chef Bill Chan
cost Around $54 for two, plus drinks
plus Roast meats   **minus** Junior service
score 12/20

emperor's garden seafood

96–100 HAY STREET, HAYMARKET
PHONE 9211 2135   MAP 3A

CHINESE/SEAFOOD

Sit down at this 21-year-old Chinese veteran
and you will be given an English menu
containing all the things non-Chinese
people are supposed to like. If you really
do want chicken and almonds, sizzling beef,
and sweet and sour pork, then fine. But if
you want a spanking fresh whole steamed
fish with ginger and soy, a mossy mess of
sautéed pea sprouts, a steaming, bubbling
home-style claypot, or any of the authentic
home-style dishes the restaurant turns on
for the Chinese tables, you'll have to talk
fast and point a lot. You will be repaid
handsomely for your efforts, however, as
this rambling barn of a restaurant, with its
wall of fish tanks and glittering chandeliers,
is capable of turning out some of the best,
most honest food in Chinatown. The daily
yum cha is also highly recommended, as is
anything with beancurd, especially the
sweet beancurd in ginger syrup at the
end of the meal.

licensed
hours Daily 8–2am
cards AE BC DC MC V   Bookings essential
seats 350; wheelchair access
owner Stanley Yee
chef Ma Sung
cost Around $76 for two, plus drinks
plus Beancurd   **minus** Antiseptic hand towels
score 13/20

emporio armani caffe

LEVEL 1, CHALLIS HOUSE,
4 MARTIN PLACE, SYDNEY
PHONE 9231 3655   MAP 1

ITALIAN

A trattoria inside a high fashion store?
Bound to be pretentious and expensive and
have servings designed for anorexics. Wrong
three times. The customer next to us at a
recent visit was wearing baggy shorts and
thongs, and tucking into a substantial bowl
of pumpkin gnocchi for $16, undeterred by
the perpetual fashion parade on the
overhanging TV sets. Over the past year,
chef Annabel Savill has extended her range,
introducing new dishes more frequently.
There's now a small antipasto table to
choose from (with a bargain set price for
five dishes). A true Italian would follow with
pasta (such as spaghetti with squid ink) or
risotto (zucchini is one of our favourites),
then some grilled fish (salmon, served with
a spinach and crab salad), making sure to
leave space for an impeccably gooey
tiramisu or a fig tart. With all wines
available by the glass, lunch would have no
problem stretching into afternoon tea.

licensed; wine by the glass
hours Mon–Fri 9am–5.30pm
cards AE BC DC MC V   Bookings recommended
seats 52; non-smoking area ⅹ̵
owner Giorgio Armani Australia Pty Ltd
chef Annabel Savill
cost Around $80 for two, plus drinks
plus Affordable quality
minus Unaffordable surroundings
score 14/20

epic foods

444 ELIZABETH STREET, SURRY HILLS
PHONE 9319 4748   MAP 3B

MODERN AUSTRALIAN

In an earlier Surry Hills life this was Chianti
(and later Gastronomia Chianti), a much-
loved lunching spot for newspaper execs,
opera administrators and frockmakers.
Doreen Orsatti finally retired from the fray,
handing the baton to a group of five who
continue the site's traditions for wholesome
hospitality and lashings of fresh, feel-good
food. The cold larder display has gone,
making room for more tables of gossiping
journos who plough with relish into
generous portions of simple, healthy
offerings. There's spinach 'pastirma';
soy-glazed chicken and noodle salad; and
big leek, feta and couscous rissoles. For
more serious celebrations, try the rare
sirloin with field mushies, and crisp-roast
duck with brandied pears. Excellent coffee,
homemade ice-creams and a good value
wine selection should ensure a long and
successful life for Epic's reincarnation.
And if you fall for the Caesar dressing or
butterscotch sauce, it's available in handy
take-home packs.

licensed; wine by the glass
lunch Mon–Fri noon–3pm
dinner Wed–Sat 6–10pm
cards AE BC DC MC V   Bookings recommended
seats 92; private room; no smoking ⅹ̵
owner Epic Foods
chefs Bronwyn Thompson & Adam Wilcox
cost Around $70 for two, plus drinks
plus Friendly hospitality   **minus** Parking
score 13/20

epoque

429 MILLER STREET, CAMMERAY
PHONE 9954 3811   MAP 5A

BELGIAN

Is this very jolly mussels-and-beer joint the
Belgian answer to the Irish pub? Certainly,
it's all a bit themed, with its period wooden
interior, carefully placed memorabilia and
marble-topped, zinc-edged bar. Everything
has been imported from Belgium, including
the best range of draught and bottled
Belgian beers you'll find in Sydney. We're
particularly fond of the Hoergaarden wheat
beer and the medium-bodied Leffe Blonde,
but be a little wary of the Rocherfors Abbey
beer with its 10 per cent alcohol kick. The
menu, put together by former Gekko chef
Olivier Massart, keeps pretty much to
traditional Belgian dishes such as a creamy
chicken waterzoi, and a nicely fall-apart
Flemish beef stew cooked in beer. But the
stars of the show are undoubtedly the
mussels, plump and succulent, served in a
handsome black pot with delectable soupy
juices. On the side come solid, potatoey-
flavoured chips with a mayo so irresistible
it's narcotic. If it's not careful, Epoque could
give themed restaurants a good name.

licensed; wine by the glass
hours Mon–Sat noon–10.30pm
cards AE BC DC MC V   Bookings recommended
seats 100; wheelchair access;
non-smoking area ⅔✕
owners Olivier Massart & Diane Scarr
chef Olivier Massart
cost About $60 for two, plus drinks
plus The mussels   **minus** The frites aren't thin
score 13/20

et cetra

780 PACIFIC HIGHWAY, GORDON
PHONE 9499 6600   MAP 7

FRENCH

Gordon is reaching new heights these days,
thanks to the brave souls who set up Et
Cetra. It's a tough area in which to make
quality the focus instead of quantity, so all
power to them. The restaurant has the look
of a very smart, very modern city bistro,
with its curvaceous open bar, aubergine-
coloured carpet and chairs of subdued
green and red. It's filled with a mainly local
crowd celebrating, shooting the breeze or
just eating well, and with prices nicely
below those you'll find in the CBD. Chef
Dan Brukarz's simplest dishes work the
best. Perhaps a rich and crisp potato and
leek tart, or a sensationally moist and
tender corn-fed chicken breast on cabbage
and bacon. Sometimes the flavours are too
bold; for example, the chicken's perfect
cooking was overwhelmed by a heavy hand
with the bacon. Less can be more.

licensed & byo; wine by the glass
lunch Mon–Fri noon–2.30pm
dinner Mon–Sat from 6.30pm
cards AE BC DC MC V   Bookings recommended
seats 75; wheelchair access; no smoking until
2.30pm & 10.30pm ⅔✕
owner Dan Brukarz
chefs Dan Brukarz & Simon Bestley
cost Around $82 for two, plus drinks
plus Good produce   **minus** Overly complex
score 13/20

fare go gourmet

69 UNION STREET, NORTH SYDNEY
PHONE 9922 2965   MAP 5A

AMERICAN

The gradient of the street and the hint of
ironwork tracery on the terrace opposite
help: yes, we could be in San Francisco or
an implausibly steep bit of New Orleans.
Not that America is forced on you like a
swamp of blue cheese or a plague of
blackened fish – Forrest Moebes (born in
Alabama, bred as a chef in such centres of
Francophile classicism as New York's La
Côte Basque) is too subtle for that. Instead,
America turns up in the excellent house-
made cornbread, the corn meal that coats
the oysters (a much better idea than it
sounds), the maple glaze on the quail and
the black-eyed pea salad that's served with
it. Then there's the very can-do front-of-
house staff, ready and able to answer any
question you might have about a menu
that, eschewing local fashion, does what it
wants to do and does it very well.

byo
dinner Tues–Sat from 6.30pm
cards AE BC DC MC V   Bookings essential
seats 38; private room; no smoking
owners Forrest Moebes & Cris Parker
chef Forrest Moebes
cost Around $97 for two, plus drinks
plus Star-spangled food   **minus** The loo
score 13/20

fez cafe

247 VICTORIA STREET, DARLINGHURST
PHONE 9360 9581   MAP 2

MIDDLE EASTERN/NORTH AFRICAN

Where else can you breakfast on sweet
couscous served with cardamom milk,
fruit compote, yoghurt and nuts? Or on
merguez sausage with spinach, pepper and
tomatoes on couscous while watching the
Darlinghurst tribes trip by past the vast
open windows? Apart from breakfast, it is
almost de rigueur to start your meal with
one of the mezze plates chock-full of
yummy hummus, baba ghannouj,
taramasalata and felafel, wiped up with
thick Turkish bread. At lunchtime, the beef,
mushroom and wild gherkin pie was the go.
Sadly, recent times have seen a marked
drop in the standard of service, with the
odd meal not only going astray, but
disappearing altogether. And where else
could you find a cherry and liquorice
bavarois, strange combination that it is?

licensed & byo; wine by the glass
breakfast Daily 8am–2.45pm
lunch Mon–Fri 11.30am–2.45pm;
Sat–Sun 11.30am–6pm
dinner Daily 6–10.30pm
cards AE BC MC V   No bookings
seats 120; private room; outdoor area;
no smoking until 10.30pm
owners Bruce Kaldor & Hugh Foster
chefs Daniel Radocaj & Ahmed Essafi
cost Around $60 for two, plus drinks
plus Adventurous eating   **minus** Patchy service
score 12/20

fifi's

158 ENMORE ROAD, ENMORE
PHONE 9550 4665 MAP 8

LEBANESE

There are no thick velvet drapes at Fifi's,
no brass artefacts, no embroidered floor
cushions and no belly dancer on Fridays and
Saturdays. With its polished boards, bistro
chairs, paper over cloth tables, and recessed
spotlights it looks like a hot little Sydney
BYO, circa 2000. But instead of Caesar
salad, it's tabbouli; and instead of sticky
date pudding, it's mamoula, a light semolina
pie filled with date purée. Fifi Fudda, who
has been cooking Lebanese food for 35
years, divides her menu equally between
vegetarian and meat. For the undecided,
there are bargain-priced banquets of either
gender. The dips are rich and moreish –
especially the labne yoghurt/cheese; the
felafel (chickpea and broad bean balls) are
crunchy handmade miracles; and the kafta
(minced lamb kebabs) are tender and lightly
spiced. Go if you like Lebanese food, and if
you can cope without the belly dancing.
Unless, of course, it's your own.

byo
dinner Tues–Sun 5.30pm–midnight
cards AE BC DC MC V   Bookings recommended,
essential weekends
seats 50
owners Fifi Fudda & Garry El Hassan
chef Fifi Fudda
cost Around $43 for two, plus drinks
plus The felafel   **minus** No seafood
score 13/20

figs

332 PENSHURST STREET, WILLOUGHBY
PHONE 9417 6204   MAP 7

MODERN AUSTRALIAN

This place is so warm and welcoming, you
could be forgiven for thinking you were in
owners Patrick Southon and Julie Hogg's
home. With its beautifully appointed tables,
art for sale, and a mainly Mediterranean
menu, Figs is clearly a favourite big and
medium night out for restaurant-going
locals. A tea-smoked quail entrée was a
little cool, but the flavour was good. A
gentle-tasting scallop and mussel ravioli
was nicely crafted, while oven-roasted
rudder fish with cold panzanella was all
freshness and light. By contrast, the slow-
roasted duck legs needed more than a
blandish mushroom and spinach risotto to
make a lasting impression. Desserts are easy
and comforting, enticing locals to linger
over coffee. While some dishes are one-
dimensional, this popular neighbourhood
eatery has plenty to recommend it. Service
is friendly, presentation appealing and the
dining experience polished and professional.

licensed & byo
lunch Thurs–Fri noon–3pm
dinner Tues–Thurs 6–10pm; Fri–Sat 6–10.30pm
cards AE BC DC MC V   Bookings essential
seats 56; wheelchair access;
non-smoking area
owners Patrick Southon & Julie Hogg
chef Patrick Southon
cost Around $80 for two, plus drinks
plus Warm service   **minus** Few wines by
the glass
score 13/20

fishbowl

580 DARLING STREET, ROZELLE
PHONE 9555 7302   MAP 5B

MODERN AUSTRALIAN

Busy. It's the only word to describe this tiny seafood BYO, with two sittings per night, and tables and chairs sprawled over the Darling Street pavement. Floor staff glide between tables like fish, while the cooking staff bustle about in an open kitchen that seems to take up as much space as the dining area. Despite the sardine-like conditions, locals seem to find it a very comfortable experience, attracted by the friendly service, reasonable prices and accessible food. King prawns served tempura-style are large, sweet and fresh; fish fillets fried in beer batter are about as good as fish 'n' chips can be; and a juicy, whole baked barramundi is nicely lifted by spicy tabbouli and pesto. On the downside, delicate, rare scallops were completely overwhelmed by a smoky baba ghannouj and a large Moreton Bay bug ravioli had trouble coping with a hefty kalamata olive and roast tomato sauce. Desserts are worth leaving room for – internally, that is.

byo
dinner Tues–Sat 6.30–8pm; 8.30–10.30pm sittings
cards AE BC DC MC V   Bookings essential
seats 50; outdoor area; no smoking ⌦✖
owners George Souris & Steven Tranxidis
chef Xavier Deslis
cost Around $76 for two, plus drinks
plus Friendly service   **minus** Cramped inside
score 13/20

fishface

132 DARLINGHURST ROAD, DARLINGHURST
PHONE 9332 4803   MAP 2

SEAFOOD

No bookings, no credit cards, uninviting chairs and it's bring your own. Yet the crowds still flock in. It's really just a fish-and-chip shop with tables, and a small one at that. Fishface does serve fish and chips, and they are very good, but it's the rest of the seafood that's the big draw. Oysters are opened to order, and a small variety of the freshest fish is cooked with the flair and competence you would expect in a fancy city restaurant, but for a fraction of the cost. Try a big serve of local mussels cooked with white wine and chilli; whiting cooked in magically light tempura batter; or thick mahi mahi fillets, crisply grilled, served with parmesan polenta and mushrooms. The chef knows his fish, and whatever country he turns to for style, the seafood remains the star attraction, with the flavours always in balance. Plan to arrive early, or settle for takeaway.

byo
dinner Mon–Sat 6–11pm; Sun 6–10pm
cards None   No bookings
seats 40; outdoor area; wheelchair access; non-smoking area ⌦✖
owner/chef Paul Wrightson
cost Around $54 for two, plus drinks
plus The inviting smell of frying fish
minus High chairs
score 13/20

$

flavour of india edgecliff

120–28 NEW SOUTH HEAD ROAD, EDGECLIFF
PHONE 9326 2659   MAP 4A

INDIAN

You can tell this place is good just by looking at it – it's packed to the rafters pretty much every night of the week, and has been for years. Despite the inconvenience of trying to find a park on or near New South Head Road, the sexy décor and lighting set the scene for a very enjoyable night out. At its best the service is faultless, and the multi-award winning food does its best to measure up. A mixed entrée plate featured a standard combo of tandoori lamb cutlet (delicious), pakora (ditto), chicken tikka and vegetable samosa – the only criticism being that they weren't terribly hot temperature-wise. Lamb saag lived up to its promise of 'succulent' meat in a hearty spinach and fenugreek stew, while Malabari prawn masala was a typically coconut-rich indulgence. All the dishes are presented with care and there's even a decent, please-all wine list.

licensed; wine by the glass
lunch Fri noon–2.30pm
dinner Daily from 6pm
cards AE BC DC MC V   Bookings essential
seats 100; wheelchair access;
non-smoking area ⭤
owner Lola Crossingham
chefs Shahab Uddin & Mahafuzur Rahman
cost Around $60 for two, plus drinks
plus The interior   **minus** The location
score 14/20

$

flavour of india glebe

142A GLEBE POINT ROAD, GLEBE
PHONE 9692 0662   MAP 5B

INDIAN

After last year's criticism of the décor in this Glebe staple, the owners have done it over in rich purple and orange, tastefully lit a few statues in alcoves, and put in a sisal floor to give it a more contemporary feel. And it works a treat. This is now a very pleasant dining room, a little on the noisy side when full, but offering picture-window views over Glebe Point Road and some winning flavours on the menu. A mixed entrée of samosa, tandoori lamb cutlet, chicken tikka and onion pakora contained all the right flavours but both the lamb and the pakora were overcooked and dry. The saag (palak) paneer, however, was lovely, with the spinach base a masterpiece of spicing. Channa masala, a chickpea curry, was drier than usual, but again skilfully prepared. Servings are smaller than average but for some that's probably a blessing – you can fit in more of that lovely, hot, pillowy naan.

licensed & byo; wine by the glass
hours Daily 6–11pm
cards AE BC DC MC V   Bookings recommended, essential weekends
seats 95; private room;
non-smoking area ⭤
owner Artoosh Voskanian
chefs Deepak Kumar & Artoosh Voskanian
cost Around $60 for two, plus drinks
plus The new look   **minus** Patchy menu
score 13/20

$

flavours of peking

SHOP 7, 100 EDINBURGH ROAD, CASTLECRAG
PHONE 9958 3288   MAP 7

CHINESE/NORTHERN

You'll find two types of restaurants in Beijing: dumps in hutongs (alleyways) that serve great noodles and pastry, and huge palaces specialising in the famous Peking duck. Flavour of Peking is neither a dump nor a palace, but it does manage to cook the entire range of Northern Chinese food, from duck to dumplings, exceedingly well. Always start with 'shallot' cakes, deep-fried pancakes bursting with green onions. Dumplings come in vegetable, fish, pork or pot-sticker varieties, and all are hutong stars. Peking shredded beef is crisp and nicely chewy; Shangtung chicken (steamed, then flash fried and served with a soy-based sauce) is delicious, if not delicate; and fiery ma po bean curd from the Sichuan province gives a satisfying chilli hit. While Peking duck is the undeniable star of the menu, don't overlook the crisp, aromatic duck with pancakes. The waiters are helpful, but service can be a little slow on a busy night.

licensed & byo
lunch Daily noon–3pm
dinner Sun–Thurs 5.30–10.30pm;
Fri–Sat 5.30–11.30pm
cards AE BC DC MC V   Bookings essential
seats 150; private room; wheelchair access;
non-smoking area ♿✖
owner Zhi Feng Chen (Skinny Chen)
chefs Skinny Chen & Fatty Cheung
cost Around $54 for two, plus drinks
plus Beijing food   **minus** Beijing service
score 14/20

fook yuen

LEVEL 1, 7 HELP STREET, CHATSWOOD
PHONE 9413 2688   MAP 7

CHINESE/SEAFOOD

The Fookie was one of the first restaurants to introduce the Hong Kong-style eating palace (some would say barn) concept to Sydney, and has done it well for years. Nothing has changed after the renovations, and fresh seafood in tanks still competes with an encyclopedic menu of almost every known Southern Chinese dish along with lists of daily specials. Ordering is difficult, because only a captain will take it, and they seem to be very elusive. Once captured, however, he will offer excellent advice on what the kitchen can serve and the food will then arrive quickly – in whatever order the kitchen chooses. The live seafood is always good (and priced accordingly), but many of the simplest dishes like cold sliced pork knuckle or e-fu noodles will also give you a taste of the simple and dramatic flavours that make Cantonese one of the great world cuisines. Lunchtime dim sum is up there with Chinatown's best.

licensed
yum cha & lunch Mon–Fri 10.30am–3pm;
Sat–Sun 10am–3pm
dinner Daily 5.30–11pm
cards AE BC DC MC V   Bookings essential
seats 380; private room
owner Allfx Pty Ltd
chefs Chiu Leung & Mr Au
cost Around $108 for two, plus drinks
plus Yum cha   **minus** Great wall of waiters
score 13/20

forty one

LEVEL 41, CHIFLEY TOWER,
2 CHIFLEY SQUARE, SYDNEY
PHONE 9221 2500   MAP 1

MODERN AUSTRALIAN

Some real thrills await at Forty One. Those heady views of a great harbour, the tasteful private dining rooms, and a wine list of remarkable depth lead to some very civilised corporate lunches or big nights out. Forty One's signature dishes – the majestic crown of hare and delicious caviar-scrambled eggs – are as much in demand as ever. On our last visit, scampi tails in kataifi pastry with ratatouille chutney lacked finesse; and a grilled venison cutlet, 'cromesqui' of witlof, foie gras and onion with balsamic jus didn't really work. Chef Dietmar Sawyere has since renegotiated the kitchen talent, while new staff uniforms, Christofle cutlery and Wedgwood china raise the tone. We look forward to further restructuring in late 2000, which will see the lower floor turn into a celebratory Krug room.

licensed; wine by the glass
lunch Mon–Fri noon–2.30pm
dinner Mon–Sat 6.30–10pm
cards AE BC DC MC V   Bookings essential
seats 140; private room; wheelchair access; no smoking until 2.30pm & 10.30pm
owner MID Sydney Pty Ltd
chef Dietmar Sawyere
fixed price From $90 p.p., plus drinks
plus Krug at your fingertips   **minus** The bread
score 17/20

frattini

122 MARION STREET, LEICHHARDT
PHONE 9569 2997   MAP 5B

ITALIAN

There is much to recommend Frattini: genial service, a convivial vibe and a spacious dining room that affords a measure of privacy unlike many other Leichhardt tratts. But, for the most part, it is a middle-of-the-road Italian dining experience, watered down for the new country. Diners are handed an extensive list of specials with their menus. Unfortunately many of these are unavailable, which means no osso buco for you. Everybody orders the neonata (whitebait fritters) as a starter, and you can see why – these delectable cakes of tiny cooked fish are almost perfectly formed. What follows does not always live up to the promise of this dish. A spaghetti marinara was disappointing, and lamb cutlets with lemon and olive oil were a bit overcooked, although fettuccine with a veal ragù had much more going for it. The Frattini magic, however, is such that in spite of the flaws, you still can't help but have fun.

byo
lunch Mon–Fri & Sun noon–3pm
dinner Daily 6–10pm
cards AE BC DC MC V   Bookings recommended
seats 120; wheelchair access
owner Tony Sama
chef Anita Sama
cost Around $65 for two, plus drinks
plus Family vibe   **minus** Lacklustre flavours
score 12/20

freshwater

ON THE BEACH, MOORE ROAD, HARBORD
PHONE 9938 5575   MAP 7

MODERN AUSTRALIAN

Built in 1908, this weatherboard beach house is a local landmark commanding superb views of Freshwater beach. The menu is dominated by seafood typical of beachside restaurants. Crisp, fried prawns with fresh peach and mint salad are as fresh as the sea breezes, and the colourful antipasto platter is an artist's palette of salmon frittata, prosciutto, ripe green figs, huge kalamatas, artichokes and yummy goat's cheese toasts. Main courses are less exciting and overly garnished. The beer-battered flathead with roast pine nut mayo and fries is the big order with the regulars, but irregulars might enjoy the liveliness of baked snapper fillets with a herb crust and lemon butter. Fresh fruit salad with soft nougat and toffee shards is a happy combination of nature and artifice. The well-priced wine list is a good match for the food. Do whatever is necessary to score a table on the verandah and perve on the passing beach parade.

licensed; wine by the glass
lunch Daily noon–6pm
dinner Daily 6pm–midnight
cards AE BC DC MC V   Bookings recommended
seats 130; private room; outdoor area;
no smoking
owner Kathy Maclean
chef Liz Willis-Smith
cost Around $97 for two, plus drinks
plus Position   **minus** Parking when the surf's up
score 13/20

friendship oriental

477–79 KING GEORGES ROAD, BEVERLY HILLS
PHONE 9586 3288 MAP 6

CHINESE/SEAFOOD

Friendship is a big, friendly, fish-tanked restaurant set in the midst of Beverly Hills' multicultural eating drag. Unusually, it has a huge, open kitchen, shielded only by sparkling clear panels, providing an impromptu floor show every night, as the chefs wrestle with woks and guide cleavers that look like extensions of their hands. Roast chickens and ducks hang like a golden curtain, as waiters bustle by with salmon sashimi, big steamers of pancakes for Peking Duck, and coral trout draped over squares of creamy beancurd. Hong Kong-style chicken, roasted in a spaceship of an oven, is glistening and crisp, while wilted pea shoots (dau miu) flavoured with chilli and garlic are a mossy delight. Tablecloths are pink, chairs are black, flowers are fake, staff are genuinely helpful, paintings are of goldfish and spring blossoms, and the buzz is warm and noisy even on a so-called 'quiet' night early in the week.

licensed & byo
dinner Daily 5pm–1am
cards AE BC V   Bookings recommended
seats 150; wheelchair access;
non-smoking area
owner Simon Tang
chef Mr Tang
cost Around $65 for two, plus drinks
plus See-through kitchen
minus Limited English menu
score 13/20

fuel

476–88 CROWN STREET, SURRY HILLS
PHONE 9383 9388   MAP 3B

MODERN AUSTRALIAN

Given the way Sydney restaurant prices are going, you can feel the need to pinch yourself at Fuel. Here you can pay around half the freight of more serious restaurants for food that's way up there. Under the significant influence of Janni Kyritsis, chef Jacob Brown produced simple, uncluttered food with clean, robust flavours. The richness of sautéed rabbit confit and crisp, salty bacon lardons was offset by bitter greens and a sharp seed mustard vinaigrette. Roasted fillet of john dory was lifted by a spoonful of gremolata and a rustic ratatouille. Brown's place has now been taken by Perry Hill, another tributary from London's River Café. Floor staff are bright and eager, and weekend breakfasts are special, if crowded. There are sports cars to one side of the restaurant if you like that sort of thing, and Fuel Foods to the other, selling fine fruit, veg, cheeses and breads.

licensed; wine by the glass
breakfast Sat–Sun 8am–noon
lunch Daily noon–3pm
dinner Mon–Sat 6.30–10pm; Sun 6.30–9.30pm
cards AE BC DC MC V   No bookings
seats 70; outdoor area; wheelchair access;
no smoking ✲✖
owners Janni Kyritsis, Greg Duncan & Ian Pagent
chefs Perry Hill & Janni Kyritsis
cost Around $70 for two, plus drinks
plus Sunday brunch   **minus** Eco-trek loo
score 14/20

fu-manchu

249 VICTORIA STREET, DARLINGHURST
PHONE 9360 9424   MAP 2

CHINESE

With its sleek stainless-steel communal tables, red vinyl toadstool seating and whiteboard menu, Fu-manchu was a modern world happy girl revelation when it first opened – Chinatown food in a Darlinghurst interior. These days the décor is starting to look rumpled round the edges, and service too often comes without a smile, yet we can't help but go back. After all, we're addicted to the wonton noodle soup with char sieu and slippery silky little dumplings, wonderfully al dente noodles and chrysanthemum tea overload. The food can be a little up and down, and waiting for a seat on a Friday night can try the patience of a Chinese god, but the Shanghai lamb dumplings are the real thing, the duck wraps (a cool groove on Peking duck) are good more often than not, and tofu with soy and spring onions is gentle and soothing.

byo
lunch Daily noon–3pm
dinner Daily 5.30–10.30pm
cards None
seats 36; no smoking ✲✖
owner Annie Lee
chef Wu Bing Cai
cost Around $43 for two
plus Funky vibe, baby   **minus** Fixed stools
score 13/20

fu-manchu bondi

LEVEL 1, 80 CAMPBELL PARADE, BONDI BEACH
PHONE 9300 0416   MAP 9

CHINESE

Yes, folks, Fu-manchu has hit Campbell
Parade. After bringing a little Chinese
culture to Darlinghurst, Annie Lee is now
bringing a little Darlinghurst culture to
Bondi. Walk upstairs, past the formal private
room with its Chinese rosewood chairs and
silk cushions, and come to a sleek, narrow
dining room with polished wooden floors,
red-cushioned benches, solid wooden chairs
and snappy tables that are a fusion of
white marble and dark wood. Keep walking,
and you're on a sunny terrace with killer
beach views. Darlinghurst favourites such
as the char sieu, wonton and noodle
soup, and the instant-gratification Peking
duck wraps feature, along with more
adventurous dishes from a daily specials
board. A whole deep-fried silver perch,
with a sour, hot, salty, sweet 'four-flavour'
sauce is particularly good. If Darlinghurst
had surf and sea views, this is what it
would feel like.

licensed (beer only) **& byo**
lunch Daily noon–3pm
dinner Daily 5.30–10.30pm
cards AE   Bookings recommended
seats 62; private room; outdoor area;
no smoking inside ✗
owner Annie Lee
chefs Wu Gang & Sun Jin Xin
cost Around $43 for two, plus drinks
plus The terrace   **minus** The wait for a table
score 13/20

galileo

THE OBSERVATORY HOTEL,
89–113 KENT STREET, SYDNEY
PHONE 9256 2215   MAP 1

MODERN AUSTRALIAN/ITALIAN

In a city of bare walls and hard edges,
Galileo continues to offer an old-world
Venetian fantasy of gilt mouldings, plush
furniture and a hushed atmosphere. It
wouldn't work, of course, if they didn't do
it very well, which fortunately they do. The
cooking of Randal St Clair does little to
echo the lushness of its surroundings but
that's no bad thing. Dishes like a risotto of
white asparagus and scallops or a confit
of Saskia Beer's Barossa lamb with herbed
fregola and smoked pimento purée, though
occasionally erring just a little on the
toweringly architectural side, remind us
that we are not in old Europe. This is
Modern Australian food with an Italian
accent – fresh and unfussy. The service
strikes a pleasant middle note: traditionally
attentive but equally unfussy (though never,
of course, fresh).

licensed; wine by the glass
breakfast Daily 6.30–10.30am
lunch Mon–Fri noon–2.30pm
dinner Daily 6–10pm
cards AE BC DC MC V   Bookings essential
seats 64; private room; wheelchair access;
no smoking ✗
owner Orient Express Hotels
chefs Randal St Clair & Steven Gein
cost Around $120 for two, plus drinks
plus Baroque and lush   **minus** Too much hush
score 14/20

gekko

LEVEL 1, SHERATON ON THE PARK,
161 ELIZABETH STREET, SYDNEY
PHONE 9286 6669   MAP 1

MODERN AUSTRALIAN

Gekko is back on track with new chef Mark Nicholls firmly behind the stoves. Hailing from the Michelin-starred 'Ubiquitous Chip' in Scotland, he has retained the popular signature dishes at Gekko, while introducing his own. These are thankfully unfussy, assured and produce-driven. So truffles appear as a seasonal special, in a house-made pappardelle with duck egg. Harissa-spiced prawns are spiked but not dominated by the harissa and offset with a fig and asparagus salad. Salmon is cured in mustard, crisp-skinned yet pink and finished with a kipfler potato and quail egg salad. End on strawberries simply oven-roasted yet served with a homely almond crumble and ginger ice-cream. Service is as confident as the food; attentive, informed but never pushy. Wine matches are offered for each dish.

licensed; wine by the glass
lunch Mon–Fri noon–2.30pm
dinner Mon–Sat 6–10.30pm
cards AE BC DC MC V   Bookings essential
seats 100; private room; wheelchair access; no smoking ⅋✗
owner Sheraton on the Park, Sydney
chef Mark Nicholls
cost Around $110 for two, plus drinks
plus The wine list   **minus** Uniforms
score 13/20

ginza isomura

CNR MARKET & CLARENCE STREETS, SYDNEY
PHONE 9267 4552   MAP 1

JAPANESE

Tucked away in a mid-city office block, Ginza Isomura has an intriguing split personality. In the larger of two dining rooms, white-jacketed chefs work behind a long sushi counter, slashing, slicing, moulding and pressing their way through an impressive array of sashimi, nigiri (finger) sushi and nori rolls. In the second, more intimate, room you'll find the kushiage bar where the deep-frying chef threads morsels of meat, fish and vegetables onto skewers, batters and crumbs them, then deep-fries them until crisp and golden. Most people opt for a combination sushi/kushiage lunchbox at lunchtime, complete with miso soup, pickles and fruit. At night, settle into a comfy padded booth and select any three dishes from a special list that also includes tempura, teriyaki chicken and udon noodles. It's not fancy, but the food is fun, fresh and fast.

licensed & byo
lunch Mon–Fri noon–2.30pm
dinner Daily 6–9.30pm
cards AE BC DC MC V   Bookings essential
seats 100; outdoor area
owner Yoshihiro Yura
chef Shigemi Takeoa
cost Around $86 for two, plus drinks
plus Fast kushiage   **minus** Slow bills
score 13/20

golden century

393–99 SUSSEX STREET, HAYMARKET
PHONE 9212 3901   MAP 3A

CHINESE/SEAFOOD

Sydney loves the Golden Century. Mid-week dinner crowds here can be as chaotic as the crush at weekend Chinatown yum cha. Nevertheless, try to snatch a table near the wall of tanks and watch the army of waiters dish out the freshest seafood in town. Baby abalone doused in ginger and soy is a good, clean start, and while mussels in black bean sauce may sound ordinary, they are far from it. This is also the place for steamed rice purists to rebel and order (gasp) fried rice – wickedly good and a dish in itself. Salt-and-pepper-crusted mud crab is quite simply the best in town, as evidenced by its constant appearance on tables. You won't get much help from the waiters, but if you're after something new that doesn't swim, try the soft and silky duck with crabmeat sauce. But you're better off sticking with what the Century knows best: seafood, with a good Aussie riesling on the side. Hearty post-midnight congees are a Sydney institution.

licensed & byo
hours Daily noon–4am
cards AE BC DC MC V   Bookings recommended
seats 600; private room; non-smoking area ✖
owner Eric Wong
chef Lee Ho
cost Around $97 for two, plus drinks
plus Late-night dining   **minus** Reservation chaos
score 16/20

golden kingdom beijing house

147 ANZAC PARADE, KENSINGTON
PHONE 9662 1616   MAP 9

CHINESE

Golden Kingdom is curiously situated in a block of serviced apartments. From the outside, it looks like the sort of place in which you would set a scene from one of those TV emergency service sitcoms. Inside, there are scenes of happy families, banquets for two, and university students away from home making up for it with a slap-up feed. This is a likeable and trustworthy suburban Chinese restaurant, with a readable menu that points you in a northern direction, toward a very good dry-fried shredded beef, picnic chicken with garlic and chilli, and – the biggest order – crisp fried duck shredded at the table into pancakes. As well, there are dumplings, shallot pancakes and a heavenly Shanghai dumpling soup in clear chicken broth. Service is good, fast and no-worries, and there are lots of sizzling platters for those who like them.

licensed & byo
lunch Daily 11am–3pm
dinner Daily 5–11pm
cards AE BC DC MC V   Bookings recommended
seats 200; private room
owner Catherine Yip
chef So Ting Fat
cost Around $70 for two, plus drinks
plus Dumpling soup   **minus** Boring wine glasses
score 13/20

Only one automatic kettle ↻es with a whistle.

Sunbeam

The whistle lets you know that your cuppa's ready, then the kettle turns itself off before the whistle drives you crazy. **Our cordless kettle comes with an additional 60 day guarantee. If you are overrun by dogs we will give you your money back.**

Reclining Nude

PETER LEHMANN WINES

Barossa born and bred

grace

LEVEL 3, GRACE BROS SYDNEY CITY,
436 GEORGE STREET, SYDNEY
PHONE 9238 9460   MAP 1

ITALIAN

Dining in a department store has its
challenges. But once you've navigated your
way past the fragrance counters, uplift bras
and trendy teapots you come across the
Manfredi family's hidden gem, a corner of
calm in sea of aspirational homeware. It's
a most unlikely location for such delectable
Italian-inspired creations as the terrina –
a triangular stack of asparagus and scallops
in a saffron pasta wrap – or corn-fed,
sage-spiked pigeon. Which is a pity, because
too many people are missing out on the
nicely crafted food of chef Heath Disher and
the tempting wine list. Shopaholics should
go without that extra pair of shoes, trading
them for a soft slab of poached tuna on
caponata or porcini pasta with freshly
plucked orange fly caps, along with spirited
conversation, attentive service and a stiff
short black.

licensed; wine by the glass
lunch Mon–Fri noon–3pm; Bar menu
Mon–Fri 11am–4pm
cards AE BC DC MC V   Bookings recommended
seats 110; wheelchair access; no smoking
owners Stefano Manfredi, Franca Manfredi,
Julie Manfredi-Hughes & Franck Crouvezier
chef Heath Disher
cost Around $108 for two, plus drinks
plus View of QVB   **minus** Not on view
score 14/20

grand national

161 UNDERWOOD STREET, PADDINGTON
PHONE 9363 4557   MAP 4B

MODERN AUSTRALIAN

The 'Nash' is much more than a
neighbourhood pub. Peaceful at lunch and
noisy at night, it pleases all, from casual
drop-ins to on-location business meetings.
The dining room is pleasantly buzzy, the
service relaxed and informed, and the menu
concise yet appealing. An approachable
wine list is littered with quite interesting
offerings by the glass. Chef Samantha Joel
is an adventurous cook without being silly.
Salmon almost 'melts' into pieces on top
of a warm risotto cake, its richness cut by
radicchio and sauce gribiche. Sticky pork
cabbage roll with crisp duck, water
chestnuts and tatsoi show a deft
understanding of Asian techniques on an
otherwise more Western menu. Pink lobes
of duck liver on garlic bruschetta with baby
spinach and sweet potato skordalia have
flavours that linger, until whisked away by
the brûléed figs in a slightly dry tart shell
with luscious fig ice-cream.

licensed; wine by the glass
lunch Tues–Sun noon–2.30pm
dinner Tues–Sat 6–10.30pm
cards AE BC DC MC V   Bookings recommended
seats 84; wheelchair access;
non-smoking area
owner Alexander Avramides
chef Samantha Joel
cost Around $73 for two, plus drinks
plus Value for money   **minus** It's still a pub
score 14/20

grand pacific blue room

CNR OXFORD & SOUTH DOWLING STREETS, PADDINGTON
PHONE 9331 7108   MAP 2

MODERN AUSTRALIAN

Over the past year, a host of groovy bar/restaurants has arrived on the scene. Before them, there was the Blue Room. Lavishly designed by Peter Kemp, it still looks stylish and modern, and has a new liquor licence, making it possible to drink without dining. While most of those who flock here appear to have just graduated from Beverly Hills 90210, don't let that put you off the food, which is serious and grown-up. The mixed bruschetta entrée is anything but rustic, with three little Kate Moss-thin wafers of bread topped with finely diced tomato, while the potato pancake with smoked salmon and horseradish cream is as light as air. Hearty mains include roast breast of corn-fed chicken with peas and bacon. While spaghetti might not feature on the menu, spaghetti-strap tops are the daily special for the *crazysexycool* crowd.

licensed; wine by the glass
dinner Tues–Sat 6–11pm; Bar open late
cards AE BC DC MC V   Bookings recommended
seats 100; private room; non-smoking area
owners Peter Kemp, Rob Laurie & Vladimir Cherepanoff
chef Del Francis
cost Around $80 for two, plus drinks
plus Sexy banquettes   **minus** Looksism rules
score 14/20

grappa

SHOP 1, 267–77 NORTON STREET, LEICHHARDT
PHONE 9560 6090   MAP 5B

ITALIAN

Just when we were about to give up on Leichhardt, along comes Grappa, a breakaway restaurant opened by Charlie Colosi, formerly of La Perla, a much-liked Norton Street staple. Grappa might be located down the wrong end of Norton Street (that is, the non-café end), but it is fast turning it into the right end. It's a huge rambling place full of happily Italian families, a roaring wood-fired pizza oven and a snappy bar scene. This is one of the few Italian restaurants in town where you can order a huge, baked, salt-crusted snapper from the menu, and it's a beauty. Throw in some good house-made pasta, risotto of the day, pizza of the day and carpaccio of the day (the pale and tender swordfish carpaccio is very good) and you could be in Sardinia, Rome or Naples – or down the right end of Norton Street.

licensed & byo; wine by the glass
lunch Tues–Fri & Sun noon–3pm
dinner Daily 6–10pm
cards AE BC DC MC V   Bookings recommended
seats 150; outdoor area; wheelchair access
owners Charlie Colosi, Tony Colosi & John O'Riordan
chef John O'Riordan
cost Around $80 for two, plus drinks
plus Salt-crusted snapper   **minus** Carpark views
score 15/20

greenwood chinese

SHOP G8, GREENWOOD LEVEL, GREENWOOD
PLAZA, 101 MILLER STREET, NORTH SYDNEY
PHONE 9956 8368 MAP 5A

CHINESE

This one-time sister restaurant to the
much-missed Cleveland has once again
started firing on all wok burners. With its
built-in fish tanks, cared-for appearance and
good, attentive floor staff, you can feel a
new sense of purpose about the place. The
menu lists several Northern and Western
dishes among Cantonese staples such as
steamed whole fish and roast barbecued
meats. There's also a little inventiveness at
play, as seen in the mustard chicken – deep-
fried battered chicken served with a wasabi
dipping sauce. A bamboo pith and crabmeat
soup is a subtle but satisfying beginning,
and vegetables get the VIP treatment in
dishes such as gai laan with ginger sauce
and beancurd layered with pickled
vegetables and Chinese mushroom. The
yum cha here is a more sedate version of
the Chinatown bunfight.

licensed
lunch Daily noon–3pm
dinner Daily 5.30–11pm
cards AE BC DC MC V   Bookings recommended
seats 180; private room; non-smoking area ✥
owner T.Y. Ng
chef Ted Lau
cost Around $76 for two
plus Caring service   **minus** Tricky to find
score 13/20

harbour kitchen & bar

7 HICKSON ROAD, THE ROCKS
PHONE 9256 1660   MAP 1

MODERN AUSTRALIAN

Massive changes have swept through the
Park Hyatt's premier restaurant. As No. 7
at the Park, it was formal, tizzy and
international. Now the harbour kitchen &
bar has swallowed up much of the ground
floor of the hotel in one broad curve,
and the in-your-face harbour views are
democratically shared by a one-size-fits-all
restaurant and its attendant bars. What a
relief Ross Lusted's modern but rustic
menu is. There are no Caesar salads, no
east-meets-west hybrids, no copycat stuff
and no hotel silliness. Just good food from
a wood-fired oven, a big rotisserie and a
charcoal grill. Succulent, smoky mussels
emerge from the oven, Thirlmere baby
chickens are turned to a treat on the spit,
and aged beef rib is grilled over coals and
teamed with eschallot confit. This is a
multi-functional space for anything from a
post-office drink to a big celebration. Staff
are young and eager, but an older, wiser
head is sorely needed.

licensed; wine by the glass
hours Daily 6am–10.30pm
cards AE BC DC MC V   Bookings recommended
seats 180; private room; outdoor area;
wheelchair access; no smoking ✥
owner Park Hyatt Sydney
chef Ross Lusted
cost Around $108 for two, plus drinks
plus Open windows   **minus** Confusing entrances
score 15/20

views

aria *(left)* Fine wining and dining in Sydney's dining dress circle: if you were any closer to the Opera House, you'd be in the audience. 1 MACQUARIE STREET, EAST CIRCULAR QUAY 9252 2555

the wharf Watch the ferries, Luna Park and the bridge from your table, or just concentrate on the good, honest bistro food. PIER 4, HICKSON ROAD, WALSH BAY 9250 1761

catalina rose bay Grab a table on Sydney society's verandah, sip sauvignon blanc and scoff sushi and oysters. 1 SUNDERLAND AVENUE, LYNE PARK, ROSE BAY 9371 0555

unkai Add a bird's eye view of Sydney to your kaiseki banquet. LEVEL 36, ANA HOTEL SYDNEY, 176 CUMBERLAND STREET, THE ROCKS 9250 6123

any closer to the opera house and you'd be in the audience

forty one Even the loos have views at this peak perving point, but for the full big-night-out experience you'd better go back to your table. LEVEL 41, 2 CHIFLEY SQUARE, SYDNEY 9221 2500

bathers' pavilion The gorgeous water views stretch from the easy-going café at one end to the stylish upmarket restaurant at the other. 4 THE ESPLANADE, BALMORAL 9969 5050

fu-manchu bondi A hip little noodle scene flourishes on an open-air balcony overlooking Bondi Beach, complete with Peking duck wraps and Chinese beer. LEVEL 1, 80 CAMPBELL PARADE, BONDI BEACH 9300 0416

harbour kitchen & bar Score front-row seats to the harbour in this democratic dining room, complete with spit-roasted Mediterranean flavours. 7 HICKSON ROAD, THE ROCKS 9256 1660

hugo's Cool, blond and lightly tanned, with sweeping beach views and breezy Sydney bistro food, this is the spirit of the new Bondi. 70 CAMPBELL PARADE, BONDI BEACH 9300 0900

mca café Catch up on artistic culture inside, then café culture outside with views of harbour and House. MUSEUM OF CONTEMPORARY ART, 140 GEORGE STREET, THE ROCKS 9241 4253

$

harry's fish cafe

LEVEL 1, 81 PARRAWI ROAD, THE SPIT, MOSMAN
PHONE 9960 3229 MAP 7
ALSO AT SHOP A, 235 SPIT ROAD,
THE SPIT, MOSMAN
PHONE 9968 3049 MAP 7

SEAFOOD

When the original Harry's, a tiny BYO fish caf, started to overspill, the partners checked out the old I Cannotieri site, a short stroll up the road. It came not only with pretty whooshy views of Middle Harbour, but also with a bar. So they put on a wine list, with prices that most bottle shops would be hard pressed to match. There's an honest single-mindedness here that recalls Sydney's great fish cafs. Nobody brushes crumbs from under your elbows, douses your chips with truffle oil or thinks serving ravioli with fish is a good idea. But you can start with crisp, deep-fried local whitebait, and go on to perfectly grilled whole snapper, or sweet, fleshy, wild barramundi cutlet. Harry's has the bones of a good fish caf, with simply cooked fresh fish, salad and chips, a bobbing-boat view and old-fashioned hustle-and-bustle hospitality.

licensed & byo; wine by the glass
lunch Mon–Fri 11am–2.30pm;
Sat–Sun from 11am
dinner Daily 6–9pm
cards AE BC DC MC V Bookings essential
seats 80; no smoking
owners Harry Bedikian & Harry Keoroghlanyan
chef Tahir Shaik
cost Around $60 for two, plus drinks
plus The simplicity **minus** So-so desserts
score 13/20

house of guangzhou

LEVEL 1, 76 ULTIMO ROAD, HAYMARKET
PHONE 9281 2205 MAP 3A

CHINESE

There are compelling reasons why so many customers followed Maureen Chan from the city to her corner of Chinatown. They're comfortable with the well-spaced tables and cheerful red-and-black décor, with her service and with the food. Those who stick to the classic Aussie Chinese menu will find the simple roast Guangzhou chicken crisp and succulent, Sichuan beef tasty but without any real chilli bite, and salt-and-pepper king prawns big and meaty. But ask Maureen for her recommendations, and a beautifully calligraphed Chinese menu magically appears. Pork in vinegar is succulent chunks of meat in a dark, malty, sticky glaze while a chicken hotpot with fungus is a fine muddle of flavours, including wood fungus, straw mushrooms, pickled vegetables, herbs and tiny, sweet, preserved plums. Tsing Tao beers are cold and Maureen is ever at hand: 'I talk, my husband cooks'. Get hold of that Chinese-language menu and see how well he can.

licensed
lunch Daily 11.30am–3pm
dinner Daily 5.30pm–midnight
cards AE BC DC MC V Bookings recommended
seats 180; non-smoking area
owners Maureen Chan & Kwok Wah Chan
chef Kwok Wah Chan
cost Around $65 for two, plus drinks
plus Mrs Chan **minus** When she isn't there
score 13/20

hugo's

70 CAMPBELL PARADE, BONDI BEACH
PHONE 9300 0900   MAP 9

MODERN AUSTRALIAN

Somehow, you don't think of somewhere so idyllically placed at a world-famous tourist destination as having great food. Yet Hugo's has all the wit and style of a truly grown-up restaurant. From the amuse-gueule of smoked eel and salmon roe on rose petal and crouton, to the sophisticated cocktails and the iconic prawn and avocado stack, Hugo's is all class. Service is a dream, with the young, hip staff friendly and efficient from the first phone contact. (And no, you're not allowed to take them home.) The food seems to be getting better and better. Duck comes Sichuan roasted and wrapped in two thin, Thai-style omelettes with shiitake mushrooms and Asian greens, while a feather-light goat's cheese gnocchi accompanies roasted sage-infused chicken breast with crisp pancetta. Portions are generous, desserts amazing, and coffee and petits fours excellent. An outside table at weekend brunch provides first-rate perving opportunities.

licensed; wine by the glass
breakfast/lunch Sat–Sun 9am–4pm
dinner Daily 6.30pm–midnight
cards AE BC DC MC V   Bookings essential
seats 60; outdoor area; non-smoking area 🚭
owners David Evans, Peter Evans & David Corsi
chef Peter Evans
cost Around $100 for two, plus drinks
plus Great view   **minus** The parking
score 15/20

iku

25A GLEBE POINT ROAD, GLEBE
PHONE 9692 8720   MAPS 5A, 5B, 9

VEGETARIAN/VEGAN

This is definitely guilt-free eating. No meat. No dairy. No animal products. Just vegetarian at its macrobiotic best. Service is homely friendly in an across-the-counter-pay-now-thank-you sort of way. Business is brisk, with people ducking in to pick up wheat linguine, sweet potato and carrot frittata, or chickpea, sweet potato and coriander casserole. Or you can make selections from the 'savoury smalls', which include Iku's famous rice balls, nori rolls, couscous slices and tofu rolls. And the 'smalls' definitely aren't. A lime leaf, tofu and coconut milk laksa is very good, and after the macro burger you'll think twice before you tackle a traditional burger again. Try the lemon tart or the dense bancha slice, bulging with fruit and nuts. The enticing display behind the glass counter makes it hard to resist taking something home for later. Or take it all home, from Iku Neutral Bay (168 Military Road, phone 9953 1964), or Iku Waverley (279 Bronte Road, phone 9369 5022).

byo
hours Mon–Fri 11am–9pm; Sat 11am–8.30pm; Sun 12.30–8pm
cards None   No bookings
seats 20; outdoor area; no smoking 🚭
owner Ken Israel
chef Martin Hamann
cost Around $38 for two, plus drinks
plus It's BYO   **minus** The guilt of BYO
score 12/20

il baretto

496 BOURKE STREET, SURRY HILLS
PHONE 9361 6163   MAP 3B

CAFÉ/ITALIAN

With its funky on-a-budget décor, full-steam-ahead espresso machine, and pavement tables, Il Baretto looks pretty much like your run-of-the-mill groovy Surry Hills café. But inside, you'll find something you won't find anywhere else. His name is Antonio Facchinetti, and he is quite possibly Sydney's best pasta chef. If you want spag bol, his is an absolute blinder, but check out the daily specials and you might be rewarded with the cutest, puffiest, tiniest gnocchi, teamed with an intense Roman pork-rib sauce made by co-owner Gabriella Fedeli. The house-made ravioli filled with wild nettles is a subtle delight; tortelloni filled with pumpkin and amaretti are lush and lovely; while Facchinetti's own pappardelle (broad pasta) with duck ragù is a relaxed, slippery treat. Heartier appetites should try osso buco on saffron risotto, but even picky eaters could hoover down the delicate wafers of vitello tonnato. Just bear in mind Il Baretto means a little bar, and don't wear the pearls.

byo
hours Sun–Tues 8am–4pm; Wed–Sat 8am–10pm
cards None   No bookings
seats 40; non-smoking area
owners Rose Cara & Gabriella Fedeli
chef Antonio Facchinetti
cost Around $60 for two
plus The pasta   **minus** The bus fumes
score 14/20

il perugino

171 AVENUE ROAD, MOSMAN
PHONE 9969 9756   MAP 7

ITALIAN

There should be a restaurant like this in every suburb: a friendly, local Italian with food that is thoughtful, full of flavour and well priced. In fact, judging by the crowds on a Saturday night, there should be more than one of them in Mosman. Tables are set so close together you could barely slide a stick of dried fettuccine between them, which makes things very difficult for the waiting staff, who have to spend a lot of time by each table reciting the menu, which is entirely a matter of oral tradition. Still, you know without asking that the antipasto will be worth having. What follows – wonderfully creamy veal liver, lamb shanks dropping from the bone into a little pool of mustard sauce – is likely to be good even if you didn't catch all the details first time round, and ended up bluffing your order in case they thought you were hard of hearing.

byo
lunch Wed–Fri noon–2.30pm
dinner Mon–Sat 6–10pm
cards BC DC MC V   Bookings essential
seats 80; private room; wheelchair access; no smoking until 10.30pm
owners Maurizio & Lesley Mencio
chef Lesley Mencio
cost Around $86 for two, plus drinks
plus Very friendly   **minus** A bit too friendly on a Saturday night
score 13/20

il trattoraro

10 ELIZABETH STREET, PADDINGTON
PHONE 9331 2962   MAP 4B

ITALIAN

For years now, Il Trattoraro has been one of Paddington's worst-kept secrets, with its groaning table of antipasti and family Italian blackboard specials. Tucked away down the back of a nondescript commercial block, it's a friendly, loud and neighbourly restaurant that Paddington can count itself lucky to have. While the cooked vegetable antipasto is close to irresistible, try to leave room for a pasta, especially the tomatoey, chilli-laden penne Siciliana or the spaghetti granchio with blue swimmer crab. Main courses can be a little overwrought, or as simple as a nicely plump quail with pesto, or perhaps a homely fegato alla Veneziana of seared calves' liver with white wine and onion. Il Tratt is no big-nighter, but a come-as-you-are neighbourhood drop-in spot, filled with bottle-clutching locals who lounge around as if they live here. From what we've seen, a few of them actually do.

byo
dinner Mon–Sat 6.30–10.30pm
cards AE BC DC MC V   Bookings recommended
seats 120
owners Roberto Viscontini & Giampiero Di Donato
chef Andrea Di Donato
cost Around $70 for two, plus drinks
plus The antipasto   **minus** Noisy when full
score 13/20

il trattoraro pizzeria

108–10 MAJORS BAY ROAD, CONCORD
PHONE 8765 8866   MAP 6

ITALIAN/PIZZA

When the owners of Paddington's popular Il Trattoraro opened in the west, they took the same family-run formula and added a wood-fired pizza oven to the mix. Thin-crusted pizza replaces the more complex main courses of the eastern suburbs' older sibling, but once again, the antipasto table forms much of the décor, and the pasta is the real thing, including a balanced linguine with chilli, prawns and rocket. Pizza first-timers should definitely try the 'Trattoraro', a freshly baked pizza base with tomato paste and mozzarella, topped post-oven with fresh rocket and prosciutto. Il Trattoraro neatly shows us the difference between a pizzeria and a pizza joint. Correctly made pizza is sparingly topped, cooked with care and served with family-style friendliness in a pleasant, no-fuss shop-front series of rooms. So now we know how the West was won. Pretty much the same way the East was.

byo
dinner Daily 6–10.30pm
cards AE BC DC MC V   Bookings recommended
seats 120; private room; outdoor area; non-smoking area
owners Roberto Viscontini & Giampiero Di Donato
chef Rita Viscontini
cost Around $70 for two, plus drinks
plus The pizza   **minus** The puds
score 13/20

imperial peking blakehurst

979 KING GEORGES ROAD, BLAKEHURST
PHONE 9546 6122   MAP 8

CHINESE

Pray that you have to wait for a table at the Imperial Peking, as the raised central pavilion that doubles as bar and waiting room is quite charming, with its formal, straight-backed rosewood chairs. Pray also that you don't get seated by the King Georges Road window, with a clear view of an outdoor pond arrangement that falls far short of its lily-clad lake ambitions. Then stop praying and tuck into some interesting northern Chinese food, from the big-night-out Peking duck, to a good picnic chicken from Shantung, a whole bird finely sliced and cold-dressed with an almost Thai-tasting garlic and chilli dressing. Floor staff are amiable, but the kitchen seems to have lost its drive. Our steamed rice was clumpy and the steamed dumplings really thick-skinned. Only the fried shallot (in truth, green onion) pancakes – crisp outside, lush inside – were reminiscent of former glories. Weekend yum cha is still a hoot.

licensed
lunch Mon–Sat 11am–3pm; Sun 10am–3pm
dinner Daily from 5.30pm
cards AE BC DC MC V   Bookings recommended
seats 300; private room; non-smoking area
owners Benson Lee, Richard Wong & Peter Pang
chef Hon Chung Ng
cost Around $70 for two, plus drinks
plus Chinese Pavilion bar   **minus** Lily pond
score 12/20

indian palace

235 DARLING STREET, BALMAIN
PHONE 9818 3272   MAP 5B

INDIAN

Balmain now rivals Glebe for Indian eateries, and Indian Palace is one of its most confident performers. Set over two levels, with balcony views over Gladstone Park at the front and the city skyline at the rear, it makes for a very pleasant night out. Cream walls feature dreamy frescoes, including a striking rendering of the Taj Mahal, and the entrance features a shrine – complete with incense – to the elephant god Ganesh. Much effort is put into the food here – the three chefs are expert in north Indian, south Indian and tandoori cuisine respectively. An onion bhaji is a textbook version of the popular Indian snack with its more-ish chickpea batter, and a clay oven-grilled tilli prawn complements it well. But mango chicken is a please-all experience that lacks the complexity of, say, the Goan fish curry with its high notes of tamarind and ginger. Service can be perfunctory when busy, but generally the Palace turns on the hospitality.

licensed & byo; wine by the glass
lunch Wed–Fri noon–2.30pm
dinner Daily 5.30–11pm
cards AE BC DC MC V   Bookings recommended
seats 200; private room; outdoor area; wheelchair access; non-smoking area
owners Narinder & Sarita Rahal
chefs Tika Ramsharma, Shivial Arriyial & Pavreen Soni
cost Around $52 for two, plus drinks
plus Bhaji on the balcony   **minus** Street traffic
score 12/20

international

LEVEL 14, TOP OF THE TOWN HOTEL,
227 VICTORIA STREET, KINGS CROSS
PHONE 9360 9080   MAP 2

MODERN EUROPEAN

We don't know if it's still groovy to say
groovy, but if it is, then that's exactly what
the International happens to be. The
boothed and beautiful cocktail bar may
be the haunt of choice for the young,
bare-shouldered set, but the restaurant
is a serious big-night-out-with-a-view
experience. Surprisingly for such a groovy
(or whatever) restaurant, there is
meticulous attention to detail. The wine
list is thoughtfully constructed, with an
exceptional Champagne list and a good
selection by the glass. The menu showcases
great produce, sympathetically and
intelligently handled, as in an entrecôte of
grained beef, a roasted supreme of salmon
and roasted breast of Thirlmere chicken.
Beetroot-cured Atlantic salmon was suitably
silky, but a tian of poached yabbies and
confit tomato lacked balance and cut-
through. A lemon soufflé left us a little flat,
but the trio of chocolate was, well, groovy.

licensed; wine by the glass
dinner Daily 6–11pm
cards AE BC DC MC V   Bookings essential
seats 75; private room; no smoking until
11.30pm
owners James Ingram & Bo Hanna
chef Jocelyn Riviére
cost Around $106 for two, plus drinks
plus The view
minus The crowd is too good-looking
score 15/20

jackies

CNR WARNERS & WAIROA AVENUES,
BONDI BEACH
PHONE 9300 9812   MAP 9

MODERN AUSTRALIAN

Watching the sun set over North Bondi
through Jackies' louvred glass windows is
an exquisite reminder of Sydney's splendour.
The eatery itself is fast and frenetic, a whitewashed whirl of activity anchored by a giant
wooden eight-seater surf scull propped
against a wall. A recently expanded bar area
allows for even more locals sipping Sea
Breezes. The food is unpretentious and
scrumptious, with a natty selection of pasta,
risotto and seafood as safe as swimming
between the flags. Chicken schnitzel on a
bed of mash is a crowd favourite, while
spaghetti bolognese is a must-have for its
divine sauce. Desserts are less impressive –
grab a gelato by the beach instead – but
the service is so snappy you almost forgive
this. For lunch you can trip up from the
beach in your Zimmermann bikini and
sarong. Dinner is a dressier affair, but not
that dressy. It is Bondi, after all.

licensed; wine by the glass
breakfast Sat–Sun 9am–2pm
lunch Daily from noon
dinner Daily 6–11pm
cards AE BC DC MC V   Bookings recommended
seats 120; outdoor area; non-smoking area
owner Jackie Milijash
chef Bryan Boshier
cost Around $65 for two, plus drinks
plus Cool setting   **minus** Bland bread
score 12/20

jaspers

54 ALEXANDRA STREET, HUNTERS HILL
PHONE 9879 3200   MAP 7

MODERN AUSTRALIAN

Having established Jaspers as one of Sydney's finest suburban restaurants, executive chef Hugh Whitehouse and head chef Lee Kwiez are now devoting all their energies to the owners' sister restaurant, Milsons. Stepping into their shoes is Carl Ellis, who has trained in Michelin-starred restaurants in the UK, and cooked his way around Sydney and country New South Wales. Jaspers is in a leafy street, and an unlikely corner of town to find flavours this refined, brought to the table in an upbeat manner. Part of the building (the best part) is an old sandstone cottage, which became a corner store years ago. It's serene, yet not stuffy – the perfect setting for Ellis's delicate escabeche of scallops with avocado tian, lush rillettes of duck on a warm bean and shallot salad, and hearty pot-roasted pheasant with sweet potato dumplings.

licensed & byo; wine by the glass
lunch Tues–Fri noon–3pm
dinner Tues–Sat 6–10pm
cards AE BC DC MC V   Bookings recommended
seats 60; private room; outdoor area; no smoking until 10pm ⚒✗
owners Mark Dickey & Mark Scanlan
chef Carl Ellis
cost Around $90 for two, plus drinks
plus Chocolate décor   **minus** Easy to miss
score 14/20

the jersey cow

152 JERSEY ROAD, WOOLLAHRA
PHONE 9328 1600   MAP 4B

BRITISH/FRENCH

Tucked away on the Woollahra/Paddington border, the Cow is fast becoming a minor mecca among local foodies. They like the bright splash of clean white walls decorated with jolly Jersey cow drawings, the pleasant atmosphere, and the exemplary and friendly service. And then there is the food – much of it made with the freshest of ingredients from co-owner Robert Broadbent's family property at Collector. Daryll Taylor is like a next-generation country cook. You can almost taste the fresh air in his provençale black olive, anchovy and onion tart, and hillside lamb with spinach and burnt garlic. There is a delicate side too, which shows in a subtle scallop salad with exquisite salmon crackling and linguine with new season zucchini blossoms. At the time of writing, the Cow was planning to change its menu format to a single three-course set dinner, changing daily, in the style of the great Chez Panisse of Berkeley, California.

licensed; wine by the glass
dinner Tues–Sat 6.30–10.30pm
cards AE BC DC MC V   Bookings essential
seats 58; private room; wheelchair access; non-smoking area ⚒✗
owners Robert Broadbent & Daryll Taylor
chef Daryll Taylor
cost Around $108 for two, plus drinks
plus The house red   **minus** Small tables
score 14/20

jonah's

69 BYNYA ROAD, PALM BEACH
PHONE 9974 5599   MAP 7

MODERN AUSTRALIAN

In style, the interior is early 1980s motel –
big on pastel colours and painted
metalwork – so it's just as well somebody
has put a very large ocean right outside to
take your mind off it. Fortunately, the food is
nowhere near as busy on the plate as on
the menu, although sauces of teriyaki butter
with Tasmanian salmon, spinach purée with
tempura zucchini flowers, and crab
'bouillabaisse' with sautéed baby snapper
and a leek fondue suggest a kitchen that's
trying just a little too hard. At its best the
food is simple and unforced, as in potato
gnocchi with cèpes and summer black
truffles, and pepper-coated Angus beef with
wild mushroom ragoût. Everybody does
crème brûlée these days, but it seems
typical of Jonah's to offer a whole trio of
them (pistachio, raspberry and hazelnut),
a very French idea. The service aims to
please, too, and scores every time: it's
friendly, informative and welcoming.

licensed; wine by the glass
breakfast Sat–Sun 8–10am
lunch Daily noon–2.30pm
dinner Sun–Fri 6.30–9pm; Sat 7–9pm
cards AE BC DC MC V   Bookings essential
seats 130; private room; outdoor area;
non-smoking area
manager Ali Pinnington
chef Frederic Naud
cost Around $108 for two, plus drinks
plus Distant views   **minus** Close-up décor
score 13/20

ju-ju

SHOP 320, KINGSGATE SHOPPING CENTRE,
KINGS CROSS
PHONE 9357 7100   MAP 2

JAPANESE

Ju-Ju is what the Japanese call an izakaya,
a cheerful tavern where one can eat and
drink cheaply. Once you get used to taking
off your shoes, padding across the wooden
boardwalks (even Liz Hurley would look
unprovocative carrying her stilettos in a
plastic bag) and lowering yourself into a
sunken rodeo-like corral, you can't help but
have fun. For entertainment you can watch
the young, hip, outgoing waiters, or wait
until 10.30pm, when it's karaoke time. The
huge menu manages to pack in practically
every dish from the Japanese repertoire.
Communal cook-at-the-table feasts such as
sukiyaki and shabu-shabu are fairly reliable.
The sushi, however, felt a bit production
line, and seafood dishes were sabotaged
by the presence of seafood extender. It's
not elegant, but it's a great insight into
the flipside of Japanese dining.

licensed
dinner Tues–Thurs & Sun 6.30pm–1am;
Fri–Sat 6.30pm–3am
cards None   Bookings essential
seats 140
manager Hong Saeng Lee
chef Kemichiro Mizusawa
cost Around $38 for two, plus drinks
plus Hysterical variety   **minus** Getting up from
a sunken table
score 12/20

kable's

THE REGENT SYDNEY,
199 GEORGE STREET, SYDNEY
PHONE 9250 3226   MAP 1

MODERN AUSTRALIAN

Is there life after Serge Dansereau? The former French-Canadian executive chef cast a long and influential shadow over Sydney's most famous hotel fine dining restaurant. Life has a way of moving on, however, and the new Kable's has had a glamorous makeover; still luxe in a richly conservative way, but more open and approachable. The food is highly detailed, with lots of wow appeal in dishes such as oysters prepared six ways (Asian, salmon caviar, Med etc.) and an eye-popping mould of chopped chicken confit topped with a slash of lobster tail. Some things feel too busy, a little rich and over-seasoned, but the bittersweet molten-hearted Venezuelan chocolate cake is irresistible. Kable's looks set to become the sort of high quality international hotel dining room that high quality international hotel diners love.

licensed; wine by the glass
breakfast Daily 6.30–10am
lunch Mon–Fri noon–2.30pm
dinner Mon–Sat 6–10.30pm
cards AE BC DC MC V   Bookings recommended
seats 155; private room; wheelchair access; non-smoking area
owners The Regent Sydney
chef Jerome Tremoulet
cost Around $108 for two, plus drinks
plus The luxe   **minus** Bar music
score 13/20

kam fook

LEVEL 3, MARKET CITY,
9–13 HAY STREET, HAYMARKET
PHONE 9211 8988   MAP 3A

CHINESE

Those who only know Kam Fook for the take-a-number queue for the marvellous yum cha should come at night. It's surprisingly tranquil, giving you pause to fully appreciate the classic Cantonese menu, with its side trips into regional specialities. But where the sheer delicacy of Cantonese cooking can sometimes hover close to blandness, Kam Fook stays on the side of the subtle. Start with some quickly steamed live prawns, sweet and yielding – say half a kilo for four people – and then maybe some broccoli in crabmeat sauce. Follow up with deep-fried salt-and-pepper tofu, then move on to a comforting hotpot. Perhaps some little, plump, crisp honey beans and the soft bite of scallops with a correct hint of normally assertive XO sauce. Then, rested and fortified, resolve to come back and brave lunch. (Note: no credit cards.)

licensed
lunch Mon–Fri 10am–4.30pm; Sat–Sun & public holidays 9am–4.30pm
dinner Sun–Thurs 4.30–11pm; Fri–Sat 4.30pm–midnight
cards None   Bookings recommended for dinner
seats 800; private room
owners Eddie Ng & Paul Lai
chef John Yau
cost Around $65 for two, plus drinks
plus Yum cha   **minus** Yum cha queues
score 15/20

kam fook hurstville

127–37 FOREST ROAD, HURSTVILLE
PHONE 9586 1668   MAP 8

CHINESE

Kam Fook's Hurstville outpost is a huge
barn of a restaurant, with Hong Kong
marble-and-column décor, a wall of fish
tanks and 350 people of Chinese descent
munching their sociable way through glossy
roast pigeon, whole-steamed coral trout
and deep-green bok choy and gai laan
cabbages. There is the same edgy feeling
of barely controlled chaos as at the big
brother 800-seat Market City Kam Fook
restaurant. Non-Chinese may have problems
clambering over the great wall of Chinese
waiters to get to the real, family-style
Chinese dishes, but persevere. Yum cha
here is a ripper, with trolleys of exquisitely
fresh pastries and braised dishes in a great
gastronomic merry-go-round. Be prepared
to grab a number and wait up to 30
minutes for a table on weekends. It's worth
it for the char sieu bau (steamed pork bun)
and daan (egg) tart alone.

licensed
lunch Mon–Fri 10am–4pm; Sat–Sun & public
holidays 9am–4pm
dinner Daily 5.30–10.30pm
cards None   Bookings recommended
seats 300
owner Eddie Ng
chef John Yau
cost Around $76 for two, plus drinks
plus Yum cha   **minus** Specials are in Chinese
score 13/20

kamogawa

LEVEL 1, CORN EXCHANGE BUILDING,
177 SUSSEX STREET, SYDNEY
PHONE 9299 5533   MAP 1

JAPANESE

Your first plate of sashimi says it all. The
freshest of fish, beautifully presented. No
wonder, for Kamogawa is known for its
kaiseki banquets, eight or more small
dishes exquisitely constructed and art
directed, with serving sequence determined
by the cooking method. The comprehensive
menu lists plenty of sushi, sashimi, table-
cooking and banquet options, including
lunchboxes to satisfy the expectant stream
of guests from the hotel next door. Fillet of
steak in teriyaki sauce, and ocean trout in
miso are of the expected high quality,
simple and subtle. Kamogawa sits with
cheerful incongruity in the old Corn
Exchange, complete with a disarming (and
potentially disfooting) pebbled floor. Two
large dining rooms are offset by discreet,
serene private rooms. Until 9.30pm that is,
when the karaoke caterwauls in.

licensed; wine by the glass
breakfast Daily 6.30–9am
lunch Tues–Fri noon–2pm
dinner Daily 6–9.30pm
cards AE BC DC MC V   Bookings recommended
seats 132; private room; non-smoking area ⃠✕
owner The Kamogawa Grand Hotel
manager Takaharu Miyatake
chef Akihiro Endo
cost Around $120 for two, plus drinks (kaiseki
from $103 per person)
plus The fish   **minus** Air-conditioning ducts
score 14/20

kingsleys steakhouse

29A KING STREET, SYDNEY
PHONE 9262 4155   MAP 1
ALSO AT 20 BERRY STREET, NORTH SYDNEY
PHONE 9922 5775   MAP 5A

STEAK/SEAFOOD

As you enter the historic courtyard leading
to Kingsleys, you'll see a sign, decorated
with the silhouette of a naked lady, directing
you upstairs to an establishment promising
'the corporate touch'. That's not it. If you're
into the satisfaction of basic urges,
Kingsleys' red meat – Angus beef from
Wagga, lamb from Walcha – and the fine
array of red wines should be quite enough
to send you back to the office in a mellow
mood. For wimps, there are garlic prawns,
while health freaks who need fibre with
their protein can fill up on damper or a
floury baked potato. The wooden floors
and sandstone walls enhance the effect
of a journey back to the 1920s, when
nobody had heard of pasta, chilli or
cholesterol. We congratulate Kingsleys
on doing its own thing, but hope for more
consistency in its beef, which is tender
most, but not all, of the time.

licensed
lunch Mon–Fri noon–3pm
dinner Mon–Sat 6–10.30pm
cards AE BC DC MC V   Bookings recommended
seats 170; outdoor area; wheelchair access;
non-smoking area ✣
owner Kingsley Smith
chef Jayson Parker
cost Around $86 for two, plus drinks
plus Serious steak   **minus** It's a boys' club
score 12/20

kök (shirk)

143 ENMORE ROAD, ENMORE
PHONE 9519 0555   MAP 8

MODERN AUSTRALIAN

Kök (Swedish for kitchen, pronounced
'shirk') is a welcome sleek sanctuary in the
midst of its casual BYO neighbours. Here
you will find one of the best medium-sized
nights out Sydney has to offer. More
restaurateurs should take heed of Kök's
practice of choosing wines by the Riedel
glass to match each and every course.
Nothing is meant to be hard here, and
Andrew Doyle's outstanding and exciting
wine list makes it easy. To begin, Yamba
prawns are paired with red-braised pork.
It's a salty dish, but flavours are intense
and excite the palate. The duck is all
comfort and bigness, with kipfler potatoes
and cherry sauce giving a much-needed
edge. Some dishes could do with a little
toning down, but overall, chef Lasse
Skalman shows a good understanding of
balance and texture. Air-conditioning is
now in place and the overall glow is as
warm and relaxed as Sydney itself.

licensed; wine by the glass
dinner Daily 6pm–midnight
cards AE BC DC MC V   Bookings essential
seats 50; wheelchair access; no smoking until
11pm ✣
owners Katherine Sullivan, Lasse Skalman
& Andrew Doyle
chef Lasse Skalman
cost Around $92 for two, plus drinks; six-course
dégustation menu, fixed price $90 p.p.
plus Riedel glassware   **minus** Pacing too swift
score 14/20

$

kokum – taste of goa

2 SCOTT STREET, PYRMONT
PHONE 9566 1311   MAP 5B

GOAN/INDIAN

There's a little piece of 'Goa-by-the-sea' at this pleasantly gentrified tip of the Pyrmont Peninsula. The menu shows the influence of the Portuguese, especially in the various crab, prawn and fish dishes. Fillets of fish are delicately marinated in clove and chilli, and served in a crisp, crumbed semolina coating, while okra and new potatoes are tossed with cashew, fresh coconut and green mango. All clean, lifted flavours in a clean, split-level space of polished wood and clinker brick, with a big sunny courtyard. And, at last, an authentic vindaloo whose vibrant, vinegary sauce is liberally infused with garlic, making it the real 'wine of garlic' – vin d'alho in Portuguese – thus, vindaloo. Kokum, by the way, is a dark purple Indian fruit that stars in a chilled yoghurt drink and a simmered prawn and coconut dish. Do leave room for a signature papaya and ginger sorbet. Then you'll have a fine meal from Goa to whoa.

byo
lunch Mon–Fri noon–3pm
dinner Daily 6–10pm
cards AE BC DC MC V
seats 56; outdoor area; no smoking inside ✕
owners Anil Ashokan & Walter Fernandes
chefs Walter Fernandes & Augustine Desouza
cost Around $60 for two, plus drinks
plus Fresh, true tastes   **minus** Hard to get in some evenings
score 14/20

$

la disfida

109 RAMSAY STREET, HABERFIELD
PHONE 9798 8299   MAP 8

ITALIAN/PIZZA

In many ways, Ramsay Street is indistinguishable from other suburban high streets with its corner chemist, bottle shop and pizza joint. Ah, but this is no ordinary pizza joint. La Disfida delivers traditional Italian wood-fired pizzas of the most sublime taste and subtlety, the toppings flicked with a deft hand onto a thin crust of supreme lightness. Ruggiero Lattanzio seems to have made it his life's ambition to make the best, most authentic pizza in the country. Try the eponymous La Disfida, a juicy combination of tomatoes, olives, smoked mozzarella, ham, capers and anchovies. A warning, though: after this, all other pizzas will be as ham sandwiches to a pork roast. Entrées include hardy perennials such as bruschetta and insalata caprese as well as a bubbling bocconcini speck and a chunky prosciutto dish. But really, it's the pizza you're here for. And the homemade tiramisu, if there's any left.

byo
dinner Tues–Sun 6–10.30pm
cards AE BC MC V   No bookings
seats 40
owner/chef Ruggiero Lattanzio
cost Around $54 for two, plus drinks
plus The pizza   **minus** No bookings
score 13/20

la goulue

17 ALEXANDER STREET, CROWS NEST
PHONE 9439 1640   MAP 5A

FRENCH

For all that La Goulue's exterior is blank and gruff, the interior is understated pastel elegance – all crisp white tablecloths and crisp and friendly service. And it's about as French as they come, from the staff accents to the intensely Gallic menu that celebrates the country's love affair with anything recently deceased, and stuff you have to root out of the ground. Witness the terrine of roasted tomatoes with truffle oil vinaigrette, and the white rabbit with broad beans. As an entrée, it would be hard to pass up the sautéed sea scallops with leek and miso butter sauce, or the duck sausage and seared duck livers. The fish of the day comes as it should, with little adornment and a side of perfectly crunchy snowpeas and the lightest of croquette potatoes. The signature braised and stuffed pig's trotter is a sight to behold, incredibly rich, and should only be attempted by those too young to have heard of gout.

byo
dinner Tues–Sat 6.30–11pm
cards AE BC DC MC V   Bookings recommended, essential weekends
seats 55; private room; no smoking ⊁
owners Wayne Smith & Emmanuelle Delaunay
chef Wayne Smith
cost Around $108 for two, plus drinks
plus Outstanding entrées
minus Modest exterior
score 14/20

♀

la grillade

CNR ALBANY & ALEXANDER STREETS, CROWS NEST
PHONE 9439 3707   MAP 5A

MODERN FRENCH/STEAKHOUSE

Entering 'The Grill' is like entering a restaurant put together from memories of other pleasant and comforting restaurant experiences. This is probably why north-side film and television people have eaten here for almost two decades, although we suspect the mighty fine steaks also have a lot to do with it. From the top-end grain-fed Angus eye fillet through to a choice of five other prime cuts, they're always cooked precisely to the degree you have specified. But La Grillade is more than just a steakhouse, as evidenced by a mouth-watering grilled swordfish on mash with salsa, and breast of Muscovy duck and confit leg with muscat grapes and verjuice. Entrées such as roasted tomato and leek terrine with sage and sorrel vinaigrette make an appetising preamble, while, for a finale, the caramelised mango tart with lime zest syrup makes you wish you hadn't promised to share.

licensed; wine by the glass
lunch Mon–Fri noon–4pm
dinner Mon–Sat 6–10.30pm
cards AE BC DC MC V   Bookings recommended
seats 140; private room; outdoor area; non-smoking area ⊁
owner Peter Hammerschmidt
chef Robert Davis
cost Around $103 for two, plus drinks
plus Lingering in the bar   **minus** See Plus
score 14/20

la mensa

257 OXFORD STREET, PADDINGTON
PHONE 9332 2963   MAP 4B

ITALIAN

Like all the best stayers along this hip
stretch of Oxford Street, La Mensa has
made the tricky transition from of-the-
moment fashion statement to comfortable
Paddington fixture. Kids in smart Italian
prams, footsore shoppers and pre- and
post-moviegoers all seem happy to break
pane together at the newly configured
communal tables or out in the covered
courtyard. Chef Mark Kay offers simple,
always seasonal Med–Oz cooking. For
lunch, a Campari Crush (Campari, lime,
grapefruit and orange juice, crushed ice)
and La Mensa's antipasto might be all
you need. At night, perhaps the gnocchi
with burnt butter and spring onions or
a bowl of Tuscan tomato and bread soup,
then a lightly smoked NZ king salmon
fillet with cauliflower purée. If you take
the kids (and in the true Italian sense,
it's child friendly), sneak a heaped spoonful
of the great house gelati while the little
monsters aren't looking.

licensed; wine by the glass
hours Sun–Thurs 11am–10pm; Fri 11am–11pm;
Sat 10am–11pm
cards AE BC DC MC V   Bookings recommended
seats 80; private room; outdoor area; wheelchair
access; non-smoking area ☗✖
owners Stefano Manfredi & Barry McDonald
chefs Mark Kay & Stefano Manfredi
cost Around $70 for two, plus drinks
plus Smart aperitivi   **minus** Bit cool
score 13/20

la toque

91 RILEY STREET, EAST SYDNEY
PHONE 9356 8377   MAP 2

FRENCH

The French bistro revival rolls on as Arthur
Vanson – who helped get it moving at Surry
Hills' Tabou – opens his latest venture in
deepest, darkest East Sydney. The décor is a
mass of contradictions, from the industrial
roller door at the front and the heavy-duty
concrete floors to the tizzy provençale
lounge, upright piano and rural French
murals. The food is hard-core bistro with
a gang's-all-here list that includes
andouillette sausages, boudin blanc (black
pudding), salad Niçoise, pork rillettes (rough
pâté) and jambon persille (ham in aspic).
Daily specials might include a hearty if
homely braise of guinea fowl and cabbage,
while desserts run from a streamlined
crème brûlée to a novel apple gratin served
in its own copper pot. Although the steak
in the steak frites could have done with a
bit less chew and a bit more character, it's
all pretty authentic stuff.

licensed; wine by the glass
lunch Mon–Fri noon–3pm
dinner Mon–Sat from 6pm
cards AE BC DC MC V   Bookings recommended
seats 85; outdoor area; non-smoking area ☗✖
owners Arthur & John Vanson
chef Frederic Plat
cost Around $65 for two, plus drinks
plus The boudin noir   **minus** Tizzy décor
score 12/20

lavender blue

165 BLUES POINT ROAD, McMAHONS POINT
PHONE 9955 7596   MAP 5A

MODERN AUSTRALIAN

You could be by the sea at Lavender Blue.
This cleanly decorated room has an
outdoorsy feel. Large windows are thrown
open to the breeze, while clouds scud over
the skylight by the (lavender blue) end wall.
It's very Sydney: relaxed, casual and friendly.
Real thought has gone into the food. A cold
summer soup of yoghurt and mint is graced
by a brace of warm king prawns and
enlivened with chilli. The perfectly poached,
not grilled, rainbow trout, flesh melting
and moist, is strewn with basil and
coriander. Every dish is imaginatively
matched with a suggested wine – a risotto
of roast pumpkin, peas and chives with a
Tucks Ridge Pinot Noir – while just about
all the list is available by the glass. All-day
opening can stretch a restaurant, but
Lavender Blue appears to cope admirably.
And those opening hours do give you longer
to explore the wines.

licensed & byo; wine by the glass
breakfast Daily 8–11.30am
lunch Daily noon–5pm
dinner Daily 5–10pm
cards AE BC MC V   Bookings recommended
seats 80; wheelchair access; no smoking until
2.30pm & 10.30pm
owner Wayne Davis
chef Nicholas Page
cost Around $70 for two, plus drinks
plus The wines by the glass
minus It's not by the sea
score 13/20

le kiosk

1 MARINE PARADE, SHELLY BEACH, MANLY
PHONE 9977 4122   MAP 7

MODERN AUSTRALIAN

Le Kiosk is another of those Sydney
restaurants where the view is so glorious
that you wonder whether they have left the
food to take care of itself. Happily, they've
done better than that. Fish, not surprisingly,
dominates the menu and you can set
sail with a gentle, balanced entrée of
ocean trout (sugar-cured on the premises)
with artichoke, kipfler potatoes and a soft
poached egg. Then hit the surf with pan-
fried blue-eye cod and sautéed prawns
with baby corn, shiitake and snowpea.
Truffles turn up in the mash and there's
salsa verde with the swordfish, but nobody's
trying too hard to be groovy here. Chef
Richard Latham does a fine line in warm,
sunny Sydney flavours, both Asian and
Mediterranean. If you're wondering about
the 'minus', it's because the view gets a
bit crowded at times with men in wetsuits
padding on flippered feet down to the
water's edge. Some people might, however,
consider that a plus.

licensed; wine by the glass
lunch Mon–Sat noon–2.30pm; Sun noon–3.30pm
dinner Daily from 6.30pm
cards AE BC DC MC V   Bookings essential
seats 300; private room; outdoor area;
wheelchair access; non-smoking area
owners Robert Morris & Allan Maddalena
chef Richard Latham
cost Around $92 for two, plus drinks
plus The view's terrific   **minus** Scuba divers
score 13/20

lennons

105 VICTORIA ROAD (CNR CHURCH STREET),
DRUMMOYNE
PHONE 9819 7511   MAP 5B

MODERN AUSTRALIAN

Every district deserves its steakhouse, or
at least a restaurant such as this with a
well-aged, well-marbled piece of rump
served in a light red wine jus, and a wine
list you can really chew over. But there is
more to Lennons than feed-the-man-and-
woman meat and red wine. There might
be chargrilled crocodile, crisp-skinned duck,
a whole baby snapper or an imaginative
chicken breast marinated in lime and chilli,
grilled and served on hummus with salsa
verde. To match, there is a fairly priced wine
list. Adding to the appeal of the place are
lunchtime specials of fish and chips, steak
and vegetable pie and Thai green curry that
weigh in at little more than takeaway prices.
There's a nice welcome and a good feel
throughout the three rooms and courtyard.
Décor may be ho-hum, but it fades into the
background behind a hot, fluffy raspberry
soufflé and a glass of Giesen Noble School
Road Late Harvest.

licensed; wine by the glass
lunch Tues–Fri noon–3.30pm
dinner Tues–Sat 6pm–midnight
cards AE BC DC MC V   Bookings recommended
seats 100; private room; outdoor area;
non-smoking area ✣
owners Scott & Ruth Macfadyen
chef Scott Macfadyen
cost Around $76 for two, plus drinks
plus TLC   **minus** That disco muzak
score 14/20

les trois freres

16 PRINCES HIGHWAY, SYLVANIA
PHONE 9544 7609   MAP 8

MODERN AUSTRALIAN

The trois brothers are down to un these
days but that hasn't stopped Tod Laurence
from providing perhaps the brightest and
best dining experience in the area. Facing
on to the highway, it doesn't have the most
exciting of views, and parking can be a
nightmare, but the food and cheery
ambience of the small blue-and-yellow
dining room more than make up for that.
As do the heavenly braised ham hocks with
mashed potato, rocket and aïoli. If you are
not a local – and there are plenty of them
in evidence – this dish alone makes the
visit worthwhile. Pair this with an Atlantic
salmon fillet on a bed of creamed spinach,
or the chargrilled pork fillet, and life takes
on a wholly rosy glow. It really doesn't get
much better than this. On Saturday nights
there is a three-course, $45-a-head menu
that includes seafood choices from the
blackboard and, from a large dessert
selection, an almost perfect English summer
pudding with crème Anglaise.

byo
dinner Tues–Sat 6.30–10.30pm
cards AE BC DC MC V   Bookings essential
seats 45; wheelchair access; no smoking until
10.30pm ✣
owner/chef Tod Laurence
cost Around $97 for two, plus drinks
plus Braised ham hocks   **minus** Parking
score 14/20

liago

73 STANLEY STREET, EAST SYDNEY
PHONE 9380 4503   MAP 2

ITALIAN

Restaurants open and close easily and quickly in this dedicated caffeine village, but Liago has hung in as a firm stayer. A good thing, too, with its open bar spilling out onto the street, offering cocktails to break the latte monotony. Inside, take your pick from the extensive menu of antipasto, pasta (entrée or main size), meat and fish. There is also a good list of sides. The fettuccine with salmon confit, zucchini flowers, olives, lemon and mustard seeds was recommended but is as messy as it sounds, tiring very quickly and – sin of Italian sins – not al dente. However, a crisp-skinned duck breast special, while not crisp-skinned, is triumphantly partnered with braised savoy cabbage and glazed peaches. Mustard mash is yummy. Service is a little sluggish when the pace picks up, but persist and ye shall be rewarded. Lush desserts, best shared, should not be missed.

licensed & byo; wine by the glass
breakfast Mon–Sat 7–11am
lunch Mon–Sat noon–3pm
dinner Mon–Sat 6–11pm
cards AE BC DC MC V   Bookings recommended
seats 100; outdoor area; wheelchair access; non-smoking area ☒
owners Peter Melick & David Lambert
chef Michael von Stom
cost Around $76 for two, plus drinks
plus Cocktail haven
minus Paying for our daily bread
score 13/20

limoncello

29 BAY STREET, DOUBLE BAY
PHONE 9363 3656   MAP 4A

ITALIAN

There are fewer Gucci sunglasses on the front terrace than there were when this was home to Area, and fewer wheelers and dealers in the back courtyard than during its Eliza's heyday. Nevertheless, Limoncello's bistroish good looks still pull in a fairly typical DB crowd. Overheard chatter revolves around recent shopping expeditions and tennis lessons, against a background buzzing of mobile phones. The chefs may be from Milan but the huge, far-reaching menu tours the whole country, zig-zagging between touristica staples (scaloppine al marsala) and authentic regional specialities (swordfish with salmoriglio sauce). Gnocchi alla Genovese with pesto, potato and beans is hearty and homely, while a rolled-up wood-fired pizza arrotolata filled with mozzarella, olives and anchovies makes a nice change from the flat variety. Be warned: servings are huge.

licensed; wine by the glass
lunch Mon–Sat noon–3pm; Sun from noon
dinner Mon–Thurs 6–10pm; Fri–Sun 6–11pm
cards AE BC DC MC V   Bookings essential
seats 180; outdoor area; non-smoking area ☒
owners Frank & Giselle Angilletta & Daniela Giardina
chefs Marco Gabbia & Andrea Amendolara
cost Around $97 for two, plus drinks
plus Woodfired oven
minus Slow table clearing
score 12/20

the lobby restaurant

413 BOURKE STREET, TAYLOR SQUARE
PHONE 9361 5744   MAP 2

MODERN EUROPEAN

The great thing about those new snazzy
boutique hotels that have started springing
up in Sydney is that they often come with
new, equally snazzy restaurants. The seven-
room Villa Hotel, just off Taylor Square, is no
exception. Housed in the front of a grand
old 1880s terrace (try for a table on the
front verandah), the Lobby has a smart,
modern, yet intimate feel, enhanced by
metal-shaded votive candles. The service,
headed by co-owner Franco Braico, is
smooth and personal, while the food from
chefs Blair Davison (ex-Darling Mills) and
Bill Cotis (ex-Bistro Moncur) is refined,
reinvented European fare that revolves
around good, big, honest flavours. A pavé
of roasted calves' liver with polenta and
muscat sauce is full of intense classy tastes,
while lemon and thyme roasted spatchcock
sits handsomely golden on a deliciously
messy 'bouillabaisse' of vegetables.
Chocolate alert: the bittersweet chocolate,
espresso and honeycomb tart is a force 10
of sweetness.

licensed & byo; wine by the glass
lunch Fri noon–3pm
dinner Mon–Sat 6.30–11pm
cards AE BC DC MC V   Bookings recommended
seats 70; outdoor area; non-smoking area
owners Bill Cotis, Franco Braico & Blair Davison
chefs Blair Davison & Bill Cotis
cost Around $97 for two, plus drinks
plus Balcony tables   **minus** Wonky floorboards
score 14/20

longrain

85 COMMONWEALTH STREET, SURRY HILLS
PHONE 9280 2888   MAP 3A

MODERN ASIAN/THAI

Longrain is an irresistible mix of disparate
ingredients that come together in one
glorious whole. The kitchen is a gleaming
wall of stainless steel; the bar is glossy and
dim-lit, with low-line modish furniture; and
the dining room, with its long communal
tables and woody feel, is very Philippe
Starck meets Oktoberfest. Everything is
good-looking – the room, the people, and
the food. Ex-Darley Streeter Martin Boetz
cooks the freshest, classiest Thai food in
Sydney, and his menu is one of those rarities
where nearly every dish is a favourite. A
pomelo and cashew nut salad is beautifully
balanced; grilled duck with cucumber,
shallot and loquats is one burst of flavour
after another; and a lacy eggnet filled with
pork, prawn, bean sprouts and sweet
vinegar is a must. Desserts are a little hit or
miss, but the lemongrass tea makes a good
finale if you're off the cocktails by then.

licensed; wine by the glass
lunch Tues–Fri noon–2.30pm
dinner Tues–Sat 6–11pm; Sun 6–10pm
cards AE BC DC MC V   Bookings lunch only
seats 77; private room; wheelchair access;
non-smoking area
owners Rob Sample & Sam Christie
chef Martin Boetz
cost Around $80 for two, plus drinks
plus Table length   **minus** Table width
score 16/20

l'otel

114 DARLINGHURST ROAD, DARLINGHURST
PHONE 9360 7958   MAP 2

MODERN AUSTRALIAN

It has been called everything from a swimming pool to a urinary tract, but still, the newly revamped blue-tiled passageway of linked dining rooms and bars at l'otel redefine Darlinghurst style as firmly as the original l'otel did all those years ago. Local martini babes perch on designer stools at one end while men in black fork up grilled Queensland scallops and confit chicken salad with daikon at the other. Ex-Regent chef Terence Rego hasn't moved too far away from signature hotel-style dishes. An early meal showed a light hand with pan-fried boned spatchcock on risotto sweetened with caramelised shallots, and a preference for prettiness in a tall salad of tofu and cured salmon with cucumber and wakame seaweed. The tract-like nature of the place makes it possible to walk through from Victoria Street to Darlinghurst Road and have two cocktails, zucchini flowers, mango crème brûlée and a Preece Merlot on the way.

licensed; wine by the glass
hours Mon–Fri 7.30–3am; Sat 8.30–3 am; Sun 8.30–1am
cards AE BC DC MC V   Bookings recommended
seats 96; outdoor area; non-smoking area ⚡
owners Arik & Mimi Shifroni
chef Terence Rego
cost Around $86 for two, plus drinks
plus Two street entrances   **minus** Traffic noise
score 13/20

lothar's on pymble hill

1039 PACIFIC HIGHWAY, PYMBLE
PHONE 9449 4686   MAP 7

MODERN AUSTRALIAN

The first impression on entering Lothar's is that of a comfortable North Shore home but once inside, you'll find the walls lined with awards acclaiming Lothar Winkler's culinary skills, and his commitment to showcasing Australia's best food. Upholstered chairs, crisp white linen and piped music set the tone. Waiting staff in crisp white shirts and black ties glide efficiently between tables offering professional, friendly service. Fresh Yamba prawns marinated in ginger and coriander served on a mint and mango salsa are possibly the pick of the menu. Seared Hawkesbury River calamari and Eden mussel salad with a tapenade dressing is also recommended, while grain-fed Ranger Valley beef fillet with wood mushrooms and bordelaise sauce emphasises Lothar's classic background. Game, in season, is treated with respect and care. This is cooking of real finesse and craft, combined with the kind of dining experience that big nights out are made of.

licensed; wine by the glass
lunch Wed–Fri noon–3pm
dinner Mon–Sat 6–10.30pm
cards AE BC DC MC V   Bookings recommended
seats 90; private room; outdoor area; wheelchair access; non-smoking area ⚡
owner/chef Lothar Winkler
cost Around $113 for two, plus drinks
plus Smart bar   **minus** Too many good entrées to choose from
score 15/20

"The olive is blessed by God", says one Greek farmer from Crete. "Greek olive [oi]l is the best in the world", says another. The [G]reeks are very passionate and proud of their [ol]ive oil. And why shouldn't they be? Greek [ol]ive oil came from the goddess Athena. In [he]r wisdom, she gave them a gift that would [be]come the basis of their civilisation. Their [di]et, their medicine and their trade. She gave [th]em an olive tree, which Thomas Jefferson [ca]lled "the richest gift of heaven". Over 6,000 [ye]ars ago they cultivated it on the island of [Cr]ete. For centuries they have traded olive oil, rubbed it in their skin before competing in Olympic events and poured it on their bread. Hippocrates saw it as 'the great therapeutic'. It was used to heal everything from insomnia to cholera. It was even thought to delay the aging process of internal organs and tissues. Nowadays, health experts have discovered that the Mediterranean diet is much better than the western diet simply because they eat 'healthy' fat. They use "extra virgin olive oil". It's good for arteries, as it gets rid of 'bad' cholesterol. And the Greeks don't just eat it - they drown everything in it. Their vegetables,

Το Πολιτισμένο Ελαιόλαδο*

Civilised Olive Oil

[sal]ad, fish, bread, even their cheese. Some use it as a hair conditioner. No wonder they're [he]althy. And no wonder they love it. The Greeks produce the finest in the world. They've [be]en blessed with the best soil, climate and olive trees to produce what the Greek poet [Ho]mer called "liquid gold". Next time you have a dinner party, start with crusty white [br]ead and plenty of extra virgin Greek olive oil to dip in. And if you're serious about the [he]alth benefits, start substituting extra virgin Greek olive oil for butter and all other oils.

[Lo]ok for the stamp. Greek olive oil is available where great food is sold.

If you can't get a table at Forty One, Salt, MG, Quay, Aria, or bel mondo, you can still eat the food.

We deliver the finest ingredients to Australia's top restaurants. Now you can have the same quality produce delivered to your home, at supermarket prices.

 GreenGrocer.com.au

lotus pond

LEVEL 2, STAR CITY,
80 PYRMONT STREET, PYRMONT
PHONE 9657 8275   MAP 5B

CHINESE

After some time parking and navigating
lifts, doors and escalators in Casino-land,
the pseudo-rustic Chinese pavilion setting of
the Lotus Garden is a reassuring sight. The
menu, like the décor, has something from all
over China: a wide range of regional
peasant dishes, an entire page devoted to
shark's fin, another to abalone dishes, and
many selections from the seafood tanks.
A cold dish of Sichuan ducks' web had the
correct crunchy texture but the bed of diced
carrot, pepper, celery and cashews in chilli
oil and vinegar got in the way. However,
steamed tofu with shredded calamari and
dried shrimp paste has the extreme fishy
flavour the dish demands, and eel in XO
sauce features plump, boned eel in a subtle
chilli and dried scallop sauce. Watch for
chef's specials like braised fishcakes and
bitter melon, but don't over-order – Casino
policy prohibits taking home leftovers.

licensed; wine by the glass
lunch Daily noon–3pm; yum cha Sat–Sun
11am–3pm
dinner Daily 5.30–11.30pm
cards AE BC DC MC V   Bookings essential
seats 300; private room; wheelchair access;
non-smoking area
owner Star City
chef Liu Yan Tan
cost Around $108 for two, plus drinks
plus Wins on variety
minus Loses on consistency
score 12/20

lucio's

47 WINDSOR STREET, PADDINGTON
PHONE 9380 5996   MAP 4B

ITALIAN

We enter Lucio's with high expectations.
The welcome is warm, as usual. The familiar
brûlée walls, glowing with local art, lift the
spirits. Service is brisk, smiling and wholly
professional. But the dining experience, if
anything, is better than ever. In the hands
of 26-year-old Timothy Fisher the cooking
has moved up a notch. Restraint, craft and
balance shine through in a simple dish of
scallops and wilted zucchini flowers. Sweet,
complex tastes are coaxed from a properly
cooked duck, while veal stuffed with cheese
and rolled in prosciutto with marinated
grilled figs is aptly termed a 'special'. The
wine list could use a little excitement, but
that's a minor sniff, when compared to all
the things the place is doing right. Hardly
surprising that Lucio's continues its love
affair with the media mighty and A-list
faithful, as well as a steadily swelling
contingent of mere mortals.

licensed; wine by the glass
lunch Mon–Sat 12.30–3pm
dinner Mon–Sat 6.30–11pm
cards AE BC DC MC V   Bookings recommended
seats 75; private room; non-smoking area
owners Lucio & Sally Galletto
chef Timothy Fisher
cost Around $108 for two, plus drinks
plus Salt-baked snapper   **minus** Paddo parking
score 16/20

vege

banc Heaven is a vegetarian dégustation menu at Banc, from a lush tomato terrine to a classy pithivier tart of Jerusalem artichoke and truffle. 53 MARTIN PLACE, SYDNEY 9233 5300

bodhi *(left)* Yum cha for vegans – and for everyone – all day and night, gets a well-mixed crowd all steamed-up. CAPITOL SQUARE, 730–42 GEORGE STREET, SYDNEY 9212 2828

emu tek Elektro mutants unite, and log on to this computer café complete with tofu burgers and soy smoothies. 149 ENMORE ROAD, ENMORE 9557 4577

fez café A magic carpet ride to a feast of veg options: Turkish bread and hummus, beetroot salad, fattoush salad, and of course course, spiced vegetable couscous. 247 VICTORIA STREET, DARLINGHURST 9360 9581

mg garage You don't have to be a vegetarian restaurant to offer great vegetarian food. Dress up for MG's special veg menu of deep-fried gnocchi and coulibiac of fennel. 490 CROWN STREET, SURRY HILLS 9383 9383

fifi's Cover the table with the veg Lebanese banquet in this modest BYO, and feast on tabbouli, hummus and the lightest, crispest felafel in town. 158 ENMORE ROAD, ENMORE 9550 4665

iku Tuck into the big macro burger in or out (courtyard) of Sydney's oldest vegan/macrobiotic café, or take it home. 25A GLEBE POINT ROAD, GLEBE 9692 8720

macro café Soul food for the soulful in a cute corner café that's big on fresh musubi, kumera pies and high energy juices. 31–5 OXFORD STREET, BONDI JUNCTION 9389 7611

laurie's For fill-me-up post-surf nori rolls, cheese burgers, baked potatoes, lentil hotpots, chickpea salads and soy smoothies to take away. 286 BONDI ROAD, BONDI 9365 0134

oh! calcutta! Plenty of veg options, from pumpkin kootu in coconut milk, to samosa, ashak, daal and the gang, in zoomy designer surroundings. 251 VICTORIA STREET, DARLINGHURST 9360 3650

arian

soul food and soy smoothies

lunch

5/100 EDINBURGH ROAD, CASTLECRAG
PHONE 9958 8441   MAP 7

MODERN AUSTRALIAN

When we reviewed this gem of a lunch spot in the not so gastronomically renowned suburb of Castlecrag last year, we were inundated with complaints from locals that we had ruined their little secret. Sorry folks, but Annie Parmentier's tantalising crab and green mango salad, her saffron angelhair pasta with brook trout and her feather-light gnocchi with peas and cream belong to the world, not just Castlecrag. The same goes for Susan Doran's miraculous cakes, especially the fresh date with warm praline sauce and the nicely sticky Greek lemon syrup cake with yoghurt. If you can't get a booking, go for breakfast instead, for the café bacon, poached eggs and croissants. Now for the good news: in summer months, Lunch does dinner two nights a week with tea-time favourites such as roast chicken with bread sauce. But don't say we told you – we promised not to tell.

byo
breakfast Daily from 9am
lunch Mon–Fri 11.30am–3pm;
Sat–Sun noon–3pm
dinner Thurs–Fri 6–10pm in summer
cards BC MC V   Bookings recommended
seats 91; outdoor area; wheelchair access;
no smoking inside ⅹ
owner Annie Parmentier
chefs Annie Parmentier & Susan Doran
cost Around $76 for two at dinner, $54 at lunch
plus The cakes   **minus** Trying to get in
score 14/20

l'unico

79 ELLIOTT STREET, BALMAIN
PHONE 9810 5466   MAP 5B

ITALIAN

Perched just off Darling Street, this beautifully restored terrace certainly looks the goods with shiny polished floors, high-tech fittings, and a cosy, intimate, very un-Balmain bar downstairs. Servings are enormous, the kitchen's timing is good and the breezy serving staff are super-friendly. Not all the food, however, shares their bright disposition. An entrée of king prawns cooked with garlic, chilli and baby spinach was let down by a thin, unspectacular tomato sauce, while a special of penne with crabmeat erred on the bland side. Far better was a dish of nicely tender veal on a neat arrangement of fried zucchini slices and a tomato sauce that was just what the prawns needed. Grilled, deboned quail stuffed with pancetta, fennel seeds and bread are cleverly teamed with wilted radicchio and a fennel-flavoured jus. Most notable of the desserts was an eggy crème brûlée presented with a 1970s lava-lamp swirl of fruit coulis.

licensed & byo; wine by the glass
lunch Wed–Fri & Sun–Mon noon–3pm
dinner Wed–Mon 6–10.30pm
cards AE BC DC MC V   Bookings essential
seats 140; private room; outdoor area;
non-smoking area ⅹ
owners Jennifer & Joseph Santoro
chef Paul Della Marta
cost Around $78 for two, plus drinks
plus Happy customers   **minus** Whipped cream
score 13/20

machiavelli

123 CLARENCE STREET, SYDNEY
PHONE 9299 3748   MAP 1

ITALIAN

It's an interesting conceit to call your restaurant Machiavelli and then plaster the walls with huge mug shots of politicians. Tucking into wonderful food while a young Bob Carr gazes down at you can be a little off-putting. The solution is to watch the ballet that goes on in the middle of the restaurant as salads are assembled from a huge table bursting with the freshest and most colourful of ingredients. Here lies the secret of this bustling, friendly restaurant's success – keeping everything fresh and simple. There is nothing tricksy, for instance, in the caprese salad starter, a huge plate of mozzarella, the juiciest of tomatoes and peppery basil leaves. Ditto the calamari fritti, which comes as an entrée or a main course. The signature dish of spaghetti Machiavelli is quite simply a satisfying and likeable mix of king prawns, mushrooms, basil, chilli, garlic and butter, while the fish of the day – john dory on our visit – is simple and terrific.

licensed; wine by the glass
lunch Mon–Fri noon–2.30pm
dinner Mon–Fri 6–9.30pm
cards AE BC DC MC V   Bookings essential
seats 250; private room; non-smoking area ⅀✖
owners Caterina & Giovanna Toppi
chefs Laurent Cambon & Paola Toppi
cost Around $97 for two, plus drinks
plus Little Italy   **minus** Politician overload
score 13/20

macleay street bistro

73A MACLEAY STREET, POTTS POINT
PHONE 9358 4891   MAP 2

MODERN AUSTRALIAN

Constancy rates high marks in a city whose kitchens are prone to kaleidoscopic change. Herein lies one of the reasons why this stalwart Potts Point neighbourhood bistro pumps every dinnertime. Market researchers, accountants, TV presenters, retired chefs and waiters with their flames troop in clutching favourite bottles to pair with blackboard tempters like braised farmed bunny, a generous yabby and trout salad or a mouth-melter of goose and tarragon boudin blanc with red cabbage. Meat-eaters will delight in the rarely listed DIY steak tartare, and sweet-tooths the bottom calorific third of the daily board. Tables are tight and the service haphazard, but no-one minds, as long as they admire themselves and check out the action in the wrap-round slim-line strip mirrors. Besides, you might just pick up a hot share tip or some restaurant goss from the table at your elbow, or at least a clue as to which main course to order.

byo
dinner Daily 6–11pm
cards AE BC DC MC V   Bookings recommended
seats 46; outdoor area
owner Carole Becka
chef Mark Livingstone
cost Around $86 for two, plus drinks
plus Peekaboo mirrors
minus No answering machine
score 13/20

$

malabar

332 PACIFIC HIGHWAY, CROWS NEST
PHONE 9906 7343   MAP 5A

SOUTHERN INDIAN

Squashed in the middle of a strip of
restaurants, you could easily think Malabar
is just another Indian restaurant, if you
notice it at all. But don't let the nondescript
appearance fool you. Inside, the distinctive
aromas of Southern Indian cooking –
tamarind, vinegar, mustard seeds and fresh
coconut – are enticing. Waiters swing by
with oversized masala dosai, crisp brown
rice and lentil pancakes wrapped around
spicy potato and served with homemade
chutney. These should not be missed. Try
the spinach chat – crisp, fried spinach,
chickpeas and chilli, perfect after the spicy
Mysore chilli chops. Butter chicken or lamb
khorma are dependable choices for the less
adventurous. The alloo baingan – baby
potatoes and eggplant blended with herbs
and spices – goes wonderfully with
everything. But it's the Goan fish and prawn
curries that'll send you into raptures. And
guaranteed to have you Goan back again.
(Saw that coming, didn't you?)

byo
lunch Sun–Fri noon–2.30pm
dinner Mon–Sat from 6pm
cards AE BC DC MC V   Bookings recommended
seats 150; private room; wheelchair access;
no smoking until 10pm
owner Wilson Varghese
chef Mohammed P. Sali
cost Around $50 for two, plus drinks
plus The specials   **minus** Sunday-only biryani
score 14/20

$

malaya on george

761 GEORGE STREET, SYDNEY
PHONE 9211 0946   MAP 3A

MALAYSIAN

There are no clues to the nature of the
cuisine in the clean lines and neutral tones
of aubergine, puce and blue, save for the
name and the spicy aromas in the air. Yet
while purists may lament the good old
days, a whole new generation has been
encouraged to try the Malaya's spicy
charms. The menu covers the Malaysian
peninsula, with all its Chinese and Indian
influences, from hot sambal to satay, curry,
meal-in-a-bowl noodle soup, laksa and
Sichuan specialities. Otak-otak, the dense
fish mousse cooked in banana leaves, has a
nice prickle of chilli, and a touch of garlic is
evident in the smooth sauce cloaking blue-
eye cod in the Kwan Su fish. Nothing excels,
but most please. Traditional rendang, that
long-cooked, dry, coconutty beef curry, is
known here as new rendang while the
contemporary tomato-sauced version is
known as old rendang. Confused? Then
come back and try both.

licensed; wine by the glass
lunch Mon–Fri noon–3pm
dinner Mon–Sat 5.30–10pm
cards AE BC DC MC V   Bookings recommended
seats 200; private room; wheelchair access;
non-smoking area
owners Lance & Givie Wong
chef Mustafa Kamal Jaffar
cost Around $50 for two, plus drinks
plus Looks good   **minus** Sounds loud
score 13/20

Y

manta ray

7 THE WHARF WOOLLOOMOOLOO,
6 COWPER WHARF ROAD, WOOLLOOMOOLOO
PHONE 9332 3822   MAP 2

SEAFOOD

Melbourne-based owners Frank Wilden and
Tim Connell have employed pretty much the
same formula that made their first Sydney
venture, Coast, such a runaway success at
Cockle Bay. Certainly, there is a similar feel
to the place, with its bright open spaces,
brasserie-style banquette seating, outdoor
area and breezy Sydney bistro-style menu.
General manager Terry Higgins oversees
proceedings with her usual flair and eye for
detail, and chef Phillip Waddington, formerly
of Dish in Crows Nest, brings some nicely
honed skills to the kitchen. While the menu
makes concessions to meat-eaters in the
form of a good, grilled rib eye with pepper
sauce, and roast spatchcock, Manta Ray is
basically seafood-driven. Flavours have real
definition here, from a lemon-spiked oyster
soup and good-as-it-gets flathead and
chips, right up to the roast lobster with
garlic brown butter, and a daily special of
pan-fried jewfish.

licensed & byo; wine by the glass
hours Mon–Sat noon–2.30pm, 6–10.30pm;
Sun noon–10.30pm
cards AE BC DC MC V   Bookings recommended
seats 160; outdoor area; wheelchair access;
no smoking ⊁
owners Tim Connell & Frank Wilden
chef Phillip Waddington
cost Around $92 for two, plus drinks
plus Absence of garnish
minus Absence of parking
score 14/20

marigold

299–305 SUSSEX STREET, SYDNEY
PHONE 9264 6744   MAP 3A

CHINESE

The 'gold' bit has disappeared from the big
neon name outside, but there are still plenty
of treasures coming from the kitchen. In
fact, Sum Kit Kwan and his team turn out
food that is superior to the cooking of the
flashier, younger Marigold Citymark down
the other end of Chinatown. Steamed fish
fillets, beautifully presented in traditional
banquet style, layered with Yunan-style
ham, luxurious black mushrooms and
glossy green gai laan cabbage are a
glistening, clear-flavoured delight. Also
worthy is the mossy water spinach (ong
choy) stir-fried with ginger, and a complex,
if dry, marinated duck (not the more usual
goose) cooked in the Chiu Chow style
and served with a vinegar dipping sauce.
Only the beancurd stuffed with minced
prawn was bland. Décor is reminiscent of
a faded palace ballroom with tall columns,
pattern-upon pattern, and glittering
chandeliers. Service can be good or dodgy,
depending on the night.

licensed
lunch Daily 10am–3pm
dinner Daily 5.30pm–midnight
cards AE BC DC MC V   Bookings recommended
seats 500; private room; non-smoking area ⊁
owner Nedosu Pty Ltd
chef Sum Kit Kwan
cost Around $76 for two, plus drinks
plus Steamed fish with ham   **minus** Killer air-con
score 14/20

marigold citymark

LEVELS 4 & 5, CITYMARK BUILDING,
683–89 GEORGE STREET, SYDNEY
PHONE 9281 3388   MAP 3A

CHINESE

Marigold Citymark has called in an interior designer. There are gold motif marigolds on the crimson walls, and discreet silver napkin rings on the tables. It's very handy to the Capitol Theatre, too, so negotiate yourself a pre- or post-theatre Peking duck, crisp and rich, or a simple meal of glossy, juicy soyed spring chicken (deserving of being called a speciality). Or go for the big banquet with plenty of seafood from the wall of tanks. Avoid the pipa duck, however, which was showily presented in its flattened, roasted state, but not very interesting to eat. And what sort of high-class Cantonese restaurant would ruin a dish of gai laan in oyster sauce by serving the Chinese broccoli too crunchy and the sauce too gluggy? Staff are by turns helpful and ineffectual, although the gorgeous gold jackets on the waitresses are a great improvement on the black cardies of yore. Midday yum cha is a bunfight, as you would hope and expect.

licensed
lunch Daily 10am–3pm
dinner Daily 5.30pm–midnight
cards AE BC DC MC V   Bookings recommended
seats 800; private room
owner Nedosu Pty Ltd
chef Hung Lai
cost Around $86 for two, plus drinks
plus Good for pre & post   **minus** Kitchen lapses
score 13/20

marque

355 CROWN STREET, SURRY HILLS
PHONE 9332 2225   MAP 3B

FRENCH

Mark Best may lack the self-promotional skills of some other inner eastern celebrity panhandlers, but he matches almost every chef in town with the precision of his cooking and attention to detail. The chocolate brown room feels like an understated version of Paris' red-hot Spoon; the wine list is competent and mildly eccentric with a good smattering of French options; and the service is silky. A goat's cheese soufflé is perfectly formed and (unlike the normal overkill) is subtly flavoured, complemented by an equally subtle roast tomato sauce. A salad of red mullet and baby calamari 'Niçoise' is a magnificent showcase for first-rate produce, while Barossa Valley milk-fed lamb loin with a tortellini of new onion and fresh peas is nothing less than extraordinary. If you didn't have the goat's cheese soufflé to start, congratulations. That means you're allowed to have the wonderful pear and Poire William soufflé to end.

licensed; wine by the glass
dinner Mon–Sat 6.30–10.30pm   Bookings essential
seats 50; wheelchair access; no smoking
owners Mark & Valerie Best
chef Mark Best
cost Around $112 for two, plus drinks
plus Noise levels   **minus** Hushed ambience
score 17/20

$

masuya

BASEMENT LEVEL,
12–14 O'CONNELL STREET, SYDNEY
PHONE 9235 2717, 9231 0038   MAP 1
ALSO AT 261 HARRIS STREET, PYRMONT
PHONE 9566 2866   MAP 5B

JAPANESE

The lunchbox is Japan's ingenious,
pragmatic solution to the quick, nutritious,
business and play lunch, offering a complete
meal tastefully presented in lacquered bento
boxes. Masuya boxes clever combos of miso
soup, sushi and sashimi, maybe tempura,
noodles, fish or meat, side dishes of pickles,
dessert and the West's contribution to Asian
cuisine, that ubiquitous, boring, lettuce-led
side salad with mayo. The assertively fishy
flavour of grilled eel in the unagi set is
nicely tamed by a dark, sticky-sweet soy
mirin marinade, and the rich sukiyaki beef
set with sushi will have you snoozing the
afternoon away like a Kobe bull. The lunch
and dinner boxes are the main reason so
many people descend to this large city
basement with its curious salmon pink,
metal-backed chairs, or go to ground in
Pyrmont, but both locations have a full
menu and buffet as well.

licensed
lunch Mon–Fri noon–2.30pm
dinner Daily 6–10pm
cards AE BC DC MC V   Bookings recommended
seats 120; wheelchair access
owner Ken Sadamatsu
chef Matai Saito
cost Around $27 for two, plus drinks
plus Lunch boxes   **minus** Boring salad
score 12/20

mca cafe

MUSEUM OF CONTEMPORARY ART,
140 GEORGE STREET, THE ROCKS
PHONE 9241 4253   MAP 1

MEDITERRANEAN

If there is one lunch spot you should
recommend to overseas visitors, this is it.
If they missed out on the Olympics, suggest
a front-row seat on the terrace of the
Museum of Contemporary Art instead –
the quintessential Sydney harbour view
and roasted red emperor will be ample
compensation. While not as cutting edge
as other venues in the Neil Perry empire,
MCA consistently dishes up great value in
the form of supremely fresh and satisfying
plates of prime produce. Whether it's the
tiger prawn salad and aïoli, slippery
spaghettini with chilli clams, succulent
swordfish steak with lemon mayo, or AC
Butchery's very fine Italian pork and fennel
snags, this is totally likeable food, full of
good, robust flavours. Throw in a sunny
day and a chilled glass of Rockpool riesling,
and you have the peak Sydney experience
without breaking the bank.

licensed; wine by the glass
breakfast Mon–Fri 11am–noon;
Sat–Sun 9–11.30am
lunch Daily noon–3.30pm
cards AE BC DC MC V   Bookings essential
seats 120; outdoor area; wheelchair access;
non-smoking area ⅔✖
owners Neil Perry & Trish Richards
chef Janor Goddard
cost Around $86 for two, plus drinks
plus Tables outside   **minus** Tables inside
score 14/20

mezzaluna

123 VICTORIA STREET, POTTS POINT
PHONE 9357 1988   MAP 2

ITALIAN

There's a sense of occasion as you glide, post-Campari, down the timber stairs from the neat bar to the dining room below. If you're headed for the verandah, with Sydney sprawled out in all its glory at arm's length, then the occasion need only be dinner. The smart, rakishly Italian dining room is full of life, as part-owner Marc Polese guides, and his eager staff beam, carting signature dishes of spaghetti with seafood baked in paper, or penne with cotechino ragù. While the mixed grilled seafood platter still draws oohs and aahs, there were some inconsistencies in the cooking on our last visit. Homemade pappardelle felt overcooked, while grilled polenta came overly salted with gritty porcini on the side. Still, the place drips with Italian style and there's always the white chocolate and licorice semifreddo to send you back up the stairs in a good mood.

licensed; wine by the glass
lunch Mon–Fri noon–3pm
dinner Mon–Sat 6–11pm
cards AE BC DC MC V   Bookings recommended
seats 120; outdoor area; wheelchair access
owners Norma, Marc & Beppi Polese
chef Brett Deverall
cost Around $106 for two, plus drinks
plus City views   **minus** Vague smoking rules
score 15/20

mg garage

490 CROWN STREET, SURRY HILLS
PHONE 9383 9383   MAP 3B

MODERN AUSTRALIAN

This is bold. This is a big night out. If there's one thing that MG does really, really well (and it does most things well), it's to make you feel as if lunch or dinner is an occasion. Staff are so upbeat they make normal upbeat look asleep. The menu promises serious foodies more thrills and spills than they could hope for in an average lifetime. And the décor, while boasting a token MG car or two, is smart without being a theme park. Chef Janni Kyritsis is something of a local legend, cooking as much from the heart as he does from his head. An entrancing garlic broth with sorrel purée and poached egg is goosebump material, while offal and game lovers will swoon over his tripe with merguez sausage, or squab with white polenta. Things can and do occasionally go awry on the floor, but when the service staff get their act together, the experience is joyful.

licensed; wine by the glass
lunch Mon–Fri noon–3pm
dinner Mon–Sat 6.30–10pm
cards AE BC DC MC V   Bookings recommended
seats 150; private room; wheelchair access; non-smoking area at lunch; no smoking until 10.30pm
owners Janni Kyritsis, Greg Duncan & Ian Pagent
chef Janni Kyritsis
cost Around $125 for two, plus drinks
plus The food   **minus** The coffee
score 18/20

milsons

17 WILLOUGHBY STREET, KIRRIBILLI
PHONE 9955 7075   MAP 5A

MODERN AUSTRALIAN

The amuse-gueule of luscious green olives
and a freshly made chickpea purée
immediately flags this as a quality
restaurant. The menu has evolved, now
staying mainly in Europe (ravioli of confit
duck, seafood in bouillabaisse sauce) with
occasional forays into Asia (tempura, duck
with Mandarin sauce). Dishes are cooked
with a balanced and mature style, and while
there might not be any taste surprises, they
are nonetheless clean and highly satisfying.
It is obvious that the chefs use top-quality
produce and let the flavours speak for
themselves. Double-cooked chips aren't
prepped in traditional French style as you
might expect, but disappointingly arrived
as large chunks of deep-fried potato. The
mid-sized wine list succeeds in offering
some excellent choices for the businesslike
local crowd, and the serves are family-size
big, making it difficult to fit in a pud.
Milsons fits precisely the criteria for a
Modern Australian restaurant.

licensed; wine by the glass
lunch Mon–Fri noon–3pm
dinner Mon–Sat from 6pm
cards AE BC DC MC V   Bookings recommended
seats 90; private room; non-smoking area ⊁
owners Mark Dickey & Mark Scanlan
chefs Hugh Whitehouse & Lee Kwiez
cost Around $97 for two, plus drinks
plus Stylish room   **minus** The spuds
score 15/20

minh

506 MARRICKVILLE ROAD, DULWICH HILL
PHONE 9560 0465   MAP 8

VIETNAMESE

You can't miss Minh from the street. Light,
bright, cheap and cheerful, it looks almost
canteen-like. Inside, the tables are full, the
atmosphere friendly and service fast under
Mrs Truong's benevolent eye. The extensive
menu has summer and winter variations
and the staff will cheerfully help you to
choose. Do try the mouth-watering grilled
beef wrapped in betel leaves, or the minced
prawn grilled on sugarcane, complete with
accompaniments, including do-it-yourself
rice-paper wrappings and a yummy dipping
sauce. The fried chilli quail shows terrific
spice balance, while a crisp pancake with
bean sprouts, prawns, onion and mung
beans is a textural treat. Then there's the
almost obligatory hot plate, of such treats
as five-spice-marinated kangaroo sizzled
with lemongrass and peanuts and wrapped
in rice paper with mint, lettuce and bean
sprouts. If roo doesn't sound Vietnamese
enough for you, there's also beef, prawn,
venison or chicken.

licensed & byo
hours Daily 10am–10pm
cards AE BC DC MC V   Bookings essential
seats 150; private room; outdoor area;
roof garden; wheelchair access;
non-smoking area ⊁
owner/chef Bich Thuy Truong
cost Around $43 for two, plus drinks
plus Mrs Truong   **minus** Bit too light and bright
score 13/20

the mixing pot

178 ST JOHNS ROAD, GLEBE
PHONE 9660 7449, 9692 9424   MAP 5B

ITALIAN

It's over two decades since the Zuzza family brought their special Italian touch to Glebe. That's twenty years of saltimbocca, of real (mostly northern) Italian food and passion. Now, with the next generation taking over the restaurant, the food still tastes of the old country, though it has a more modern, sensitive touch. So the veal with white wine and porcini is cooked to melt-away medium, not well done. Sautéed chicken livers with green olives and sage are similarly pink and moist, and seafood risotto is so fresh you can almost smell the ocean. On warm evenings, you could do far worse things in life than sit underneath the famous grape vines in the bacchanalian covered courtyard. What's more, the floor staff are as flamboyant, personable and professional as you'll find in the Veneto. All you need now is some opera, and a small glass of Limoncello, and life is beautiful.

licensed & byo; wine by the glass
lunch Mon–Fri noon–2.30pm
dinner Mon–Sat 6–10pm
cards AE BC DC MC V   Bookings recommended, essential weekends
seats 85; private room; outdoor area
owners Giuseppe Zuzza & family
chef Carlo Lombardo
cost Around $70 for two, plus drinks
plus Good Italian wines
minus Loud Italian noise
score 14/20

mohr fish

202 DEVONSHIRE STREET, SURRY HILLS
PHONE 9318 1326   MAP 3B

SEAFOOD

This café doesn't just buzz, it pulsates. There are no bookings, so check in, put your BYO in the fridge and hop across the lane to the pub for a beer, until summoned by the staff. The meal can be taken at the stainless-steel bar or from the few barrels that form tables in this tiny ex-butcher's shop, so be prepared for some close personal encounters. Beer-battered flathead is fresh and crisp, and calamari with coriander comes in the same light batter. Both the fishcakes and the accompanying sauce lacked real flavour, so we suggest you order a huge bowl of tender, steamed mussels as a starter instead. Worth trying is an unusual dish of groper with cherry tomato, soybeans and shallots, while rock ling with asparagus and hollandaise is a spring-like combination of flavours. Chips are hot and plentiful, and you get a pretty ordinary salad piled on the same plate as your fish. Take-home is as popular as eat-here at this new-generation Sydney fish café.

byo
hours Daily 10am–10pm
cards None   No bookings
seats 28
owner/chef Hans Mohr
cost Around $65 for two, plus drinks
plus Good take-away   **minus** The waits
score 12/20

mos cafe

MUSEUM OF SYDNEY,
CNR BRIDGE & PHILLIP STREETS, SYDNEY
PHONE 9241 3636   MAP 1

MODERN AUSTRALIAN

Perched on one side of the big open square
in front of the Museum of Sydney, MoS Cafe
is a regular haunt of CBD office workers
and tourists who need something more
soul-enriching than a takeaway sandwich.
It's a modern, professional and relaxed
restaurant boasting an adventurous menu
and an extensive wine list, although regular
patrons have been known to complain of
slow service when it gets seriously busy.
Entrées such as marinated buffalo
mozzarella and grilled summer vegetables
on bruschetta, and a sandcrab and crisp
wonton salad that includes snowpea leaf
and snake beans, are fresh and exciting.
Main courses were less so. Pan-seared
warehou fillet was slightly overdone, and a
beautifully cooked roast fillet of salmon on
parsley potato was knocked about by its
chilli and walnut oil dressing. Still beats
the hell out of a sandwich, though.

licensed; wine by the glass
hours Mon–Fri 7am–10pm;
Sat–Sun 8.30am–6pm
cards AE BC DC MC V   Bookings recommended
seats 160; outdoor area; wheelchair access;
non-smoking area ⸘✖
owners Natalie Conti, Paul Lockrey
& Ramy Shelhot
chef Jeff Turnbull
cost Around $97 for two, plus drinks
plus Central location   **minus** Slow when busy
score 12/20

𝒴 mosaic

LEVEL 1, NO. 1 MARTIN PLACE, SYDNEY
PHONE 8223 1110   MAP 1

MODERN AUSTRALIAN

There is no shortage of concepts at Mosaic,
the sleekly elegant new atrium balcony
restaurant tucked into The Westin Sydney.
Aged German wine vinegars are served to
refresh the palate and seafood cocktails are
served in zigzag-stemmed martini glasses.
At lunch, a number of lighter selections are
served bento-box style, while at dinner, the
menu is a one-size-fits-all selection divided
into Cocktails & Salads, Fish & Seafood,
Meat & Game, and From the Garden. In
spite of the gimmicky feel, some of the
food works very well indeed. A Jerusalem
artichoke soup, complete with sweet, soft
baby pencil leeks, is textbook stuff, while
a veal fillet 'tonnato style' draped with a
warm, creamy tuna sauce is graceful and
satisfying. It's an unusual space that works
best at lunch as daylight floods the atrium.

licensed; wine by the glass
breakfast Daily 6.30–10.30am
brunch Sat–Sun 11.30am–2.30pm
lunch Mon–Fri noon–2.30pm
dinner Daily 6.30–10.30pm
cards AE BC DC MC V   Bookings essential
seats 50; wheelchair access;
non-smoking area ⸘✖
owners No. 1 Martin Place Pty Ltd
chefs Todd Cheaving, Scott A. Webster
& Massimo Bianchi
cost Around $150 for two, plus drinks
plus Sleek cutlery   **minus** Patterned plates
score 13/20

♛

nelsons brasserie

LORD NELSON BREWERY HOTEL,
CNR KENT & ARGYLE STREETS, THE ROCKS
PHONE 9251 4044   MAP 1

MODERN AUSTRALIAN

'Praise the Lord,' says owner Blair Hayden,
meaning, we assume, Lord Nelson. And we
do have praise, for the on-site boutique
brewery, for the continuous licensing of this
oldest Sydney pub and for its idiosyncratic
décor, complete with wall clocks that show
the time at breweries all over the world.
There's a hopping bar downstairs and a
calmer dining room upstairs. While the
menu descriptions sound fussy, the flavours
impress, as in crisp, seasoned Queensland
calamari with marinated roma tomatoes,
rocket and avocado lime mousse. Chicken
maryland is boneless and moist, stuffed
with oregano, feta and spinach, while
seafood specials could include swordfish
with skordalia and deep-fried beetroot
julienne. Have the flourless orange and
almond cake with a drizzle of orange syrup
for dessert if it's on. The wine list is
excellent and well laid out, and service is
friendly, cheerful and efficient.

licensed; wine by the glass
breakfast Daily 7.30–9.30am
lunch Mon–Fri noon–3pm
dinner Mon–Sat from 6.30pm
cards AE BC DC MC V   Bookings essential
seats 90; private room; non-smoking area ⊁
owners Blair R. Hayden & Partners
chef Phillip Ford
cost Around $78 for two, plus drinks
plus The wine list   **minus** Noisy bar
score 13/20

neptune palace

LEVEL 1, GATEWAY BUILDING,
CNR PITT & ALFRED STREETS, CIRCULAR QUAY
PHONE 9241 3338   MAP 1

CHINESE/MALAYSIAN

No. 42 on the menu, 'fried salmon cutlet
with spicy Carnation milk sauce', appears to
strike an authentic note, as does the décor,
which eschews Asian cliché in preference to
the sort of Western cliché favoured in Asia.
Elaborately patterned, dark blue wallpaper
and classical statuary, including a beefy
likeness of the eponymous sea god himself,
complete with trident, preside over the
tanks of live seafood. It gets better: this
must be one of the few places in town to
serve mutton (very good it is too, in sup
kambing, a rich, meaty soup). Roti canai,
or handkerchief bread, one of the great
glories of the Malaysian peninsula, was
a bit heavy and doughy, but the
accompanying dishes – beef rendang, say,
or fish curry – were all very reliable, though
not terribly hot. We hope they're not
dumbing down the chilli on our behalf,
because we'd rather they didn't.

licensed; wine by the glass
lunch Daily noon–3pm
dinner Daily 5–10.30pm
cards AE BC DC MC V   Bookings recommended
seats 220; private room; non-smoking area ⊁
owners Derek Lim & Lee Ngann Ly
chefs Lam Kim Fai & Tan Fom Sau
cost Around $80 for two, plus drinks
plus Good flavours   **minus** Tragic décor
score 13/20

newsbar

MEZZANINE LEVEL, GRACE BROS SYDNEY,
436 GEORGE STREET, SYDNEY
PHONE 9238 9200   MAP 1

ITALIAN

The antipasto at Newsbar is called a
'mezzanine plate', a reference to the floor
of Grace Bros where the restaurant is
located (next to ladies' shoes). You might
think the platter's a complete meal, but
then you'd miss out on mains. There's a
good mushroom risotto (with preserved
lemon to lift it from the pack), butterfly
pasta with fish, capers and cream, or hearty
braised chicken leg with a stew of potato,
leek and garlic. If you've tucked into the
Italian and Australian offerings on the wine
list, you're also unlikely to have room for
dessert, which is no loss: the tiramisu
doesn't make Sydney's top 10. The room,
with wonderful tall windows, is a heritage
space from the pre-war days when Grace
Bros was called Farmer's, and often look
as if they need a good dusting. That's the
trouble with history.

licensed; wine by the glass
lunch Mon–Sat 9–5pm; Sun 11–4pm
dinner Thurs 5–8pm
cards AE BC DC MC V   Bookings recommended
seats 90; wheelchair access; no smoking ✸
owners Stefano Manfredi, Franca Manfredi,
Julie Manfredi-Hughes & Franck Crouvezier
chefs Heath Disher & Todd Palmer
cost Around $70 for two, plus drinks
plus Brisk service   **minus** Ladies' shoes
score 13/20

niche dining house

469 KING GEORGES ROAD, BEVERLY HILLS
PHONE 9579 1100   MAP 6

MODERN AUSTRALIAN

Tucked between the Friendship Chinese and
Asahi Teppanyaki, Niche tries to carve a
big-night-out niche for itself in the southern
suburbs. Here is a serious attempt at fine,
modern dining with a full designer
makeover of timber-panelled walls, frosted
glass peekaboo windows, table lamps and
smiling, shirt-and-tied floor staff. The wine
list is a corker – 23 pages of bottles, with
22 wines by the glass and a specially
chosen glass to accompany each dish. The
menu, however, comes from a different
head space to the wine list, and some of
the flavour combinations can only be
described as silly.

NOTE: Niche Dining House closed as we went
to press.

licensed; wine by the glass
dinner Tues–Sat from 6pm
cards AE BC DC MC V   Bookings recommended
seats 80; private room; wheelchair access;
no smoking until 10pm ✸
owners CY Group Pty Ltd
chef Danny Lai
cost Around $80 for two, plus drinks
plus The wine list   **minus** The menu
score 11/20

nielsen park kiosk

GREYCLIFF AVENUE, VAUCLUSE (INSIDE PARK)
PHONE 9337 1574   MAP 9

ITALIAN

Swimmers, joggers, lovers, picnickers – they all find their place in the sun at this popular eastern suburbs harbourside beach and park. If you're a diner, there's a spot for you too, on the lovely terrace of Nielsen Park Kiosk, a restored Federation-style bungalow no more than a frisbee's throw from the water. The Kiosk is actually a comfortable restaurant serving Lucia Lieto's endearing take on simple cucina casalinga, including a sformato of marinated tuna; lamb with a prune sauce; and fagiolini con pancetta. The food is always honest, but occasionally it can feel clunky. On our last visit, the pumpkin and porcini mushroom tortelli looked great but the sweetness was a little trampled by an over-enthusiasm of pungent marjoram. Service is mature and professional but the cultivated Italian-style formality sometimes seems out of kilter with the location. (That means don't wander in here with just your togs on.)

byo
breakfast Sun 8.30–11am
lunch Wed–Sun noon–4pm
dinner Thurs–Sat 6–10pm
cards AE BC DC MC V   Bookings essential
seats 200; private room; outdoor area; no smoking ⌇
owners Lucia & Sergio Lieto
chef Lucia Lieto
cost Around $97 for two, plus drinks
plus The location   **minus** 10pm curfew
score 13/20

obar

156–58 DEVONSHIRE STREET, SURRY HILLS
PHONE 9319 6881   MAP 3B

MODERN AUSTRALIAN

In a city where tall food is fashionable, the Obar goes highest. The 'antipasto' arrives in a teetering stack that is not so much assembled as architecturally engineered: eggplant, topped with octopus, topped with goat's cheese, topped with capsicum, topped with salami, each individual bit pleasant, but uneasy as a blend. You eat in an umbrella'd courtyard or in a small dining room adjoining a circular bar (the Obar, we assume) that buzzes at night and echoes at lunchtime. The menu is small, but more ambitious than low-priced pub food needs to be to pull in the punters. There's real effort on show in a beetroot and ricotta ravioli, tapenade-encrusted lamb cutlets (stacked teepee-style, of course), and chicken breast on paella. But the ambition stops at the desserts, which tend towards last-century clichés such as sticky date pudding and mango brûlée.

licensed; wine by the glass
lunch Mon–Fri noon–3pm
dinner Mon–Sat from 6pm
cards AE BC DC MC V   Bookings recommended
seats 36; outdoor area
owner Joe Saleh
chef Daryle Schlierke
cost Around $60 for two, plus drinks
plus Friendly service   **minus** Dull desserts
score 12/20

§

ocean king house

247 PRINCES HIGHWAY, KOGARAH
PHONE 9587 3511   MAP 8

CHINESE

Sydney has seen the emergence of a
number of restaurants specialising in the
spicy, hearty flavours of Northern Chinese
cooking in recent years. So it's a refreshing
change to find a resolutely Southern
Chinese specialist located, suitably enough,
in Sydney's south. Ocean King House
faithfully reproduces the subtle tastes and
textures of Cantonese cooking in dishes
such as a perfectly crisp and golden roast
chicken, a simply steamed whole fish
with soy and ginger, and snapping fresh
gai laan (Chinese broccoli) stir-fried with
ginger sauce. At lunchtime, the daily yum
cha is something of a local legend. The
décor is nothing to write home about, with
its cream walls, red-paper specials and
scattering of rosewood chairs, but Albert
and Eleanor Chan treat their customers like
guests in their own home. One of them is
always on hand to suggest a dish or fill a
glass. Magically, they're also at the door, to
say goodbye when you leave.

licensed & byo
lunch Mon–Fri 11am–3pm; Sat–Sun 10am–3pm
dinner Daily 5.30–11pm
cards AE BC DC MC V   Bookings recommended
seats 300; private room; wheelchair access;
non-smoking area ✣
owners Albert & Eleanor Chan
chef Yun Sang Chian
cost Around $54 for two, plus drinks
plus Happy families   **minus** Dull upstairs
score 13/20

§

odeon

32 ORWELL STREET, POTTS POINT
PHONE 9331 0172   MAP 2

MODERN AUSTRALIAN

Located in the shell of an old 1940s club,
Odeon retains the air of a swank private
boîte, with polished floorboards, padded
doors and possibly the sexiest booths in
Sydney. Lining one half of the restaurant,
the plum-coloured booths are also the plum
seating in the space, providing a valuable
cone of silence for the crowd of mostly
lawyers, stockbrokers and chic fashion
apparatchiks. You half-expect a corset-
wearing, flash-bulb-wielding door bitch to
screen potential diners as they enter but
Odeon isn't that pretentious. Neither is the
food, which veers on the cautious side with
its colour-by-numbers approach to dining.
Salads, pasta, risotto, chicken and red meat
are well covered in a menu that changes
seasonally. The T-bone with Montpellier
butter and fries is the Odeon's Armani
leather jacket – it never goes out of fashion.
Odeon is also a great breakfast option if
you find the notion of squatting on a
streetside milk crate anathema.

licensed; wine by the glass
hours Mon–Fri from 6.30pm;
Sat–Sun 8.30am–late
cards AE BC DC MC V   Bookings recommended
seats 75; private room
owner Brian Keirnan
chef Nick Cummins
cost Around $60 for two
plus Comfy booths   **minus** Awkward tables
score 14/20

oh! calcutta!

251 VICTORIA STREET, DARLINGHURST
PHONE 9360 3650   MAP 2

INDIAN

Now sporting a very cool, very Darlinghurst new look courtesy of design heavy Iain Halliday, it's pleasing to report that Oh! Calcutta! hasn't lost its sense of priority. The food is still the thing here. Common menu items such as chettinad tikka manage to rise above the everyday through skilful spicing and perfect preparation (try the lime pickle with it – magic). From the superb mantu – juicy and beautifully spiced lamb parcels – to the searingly hot beef mirsang with its tamarind tang and coriander zing, there's very little on the menu that could possibly disappoint. The coolest tables are on the tiny balcony overhanging Victoria Street, where light breezes can take some of the heat off sweating brows. Service is generally efficient, which is sometimes a wonder, given how frantic Oh! Calcutta! can be, especially at weekends. Still the most satisfying and surprising Indian food to be found in town.

licensed & byo; wine by the glass
lunch Fri noon–4pm
dinner Daily 6–10.30pm
cards AE BC MC V   Bookings recommended
seats 60; outdoor area; no smoking until 9.30pm
owner Basil Daniell
chefs Attaur Rahman & Abul Basher
cost Around $65 for two, plus drinks
plus Fabulous food   **minus** Noise levels
score 14/20

olympic hotel

308 MOORE PARK ROAD, PADDINGTON
PHONE 9361 6315   MAP 4B

MODERN AUSTRALIAN/FRENCH

On nights when the sporting types gather in the bar to celebrate after the footy or the cricket in the stadiums across the road, the Olympic dining room, now ensconced in a larger, nicer room, is an oasis of peace and taste. Of course, footy fans are capable of finer feelings, but they shouldn't try Mark Jensen's food on the day of a big match because they are unlikely to be able to give it the dedication it deserves. Under low, intimate lighting, he offers delicate interpretations of such hearty dishes as goat's cheese tortellini with green olives and rosemary, whitebait fritters with tartare sauce, herb-crusted rudderfish with prosciutto and sage, and chicken breast with parmesan polenta and green pepper caponata. The desserts are seasonally adjusted knockouts, especially a lemon and lime sponge with raspberry topping, and the fig and honey ice-cream. Now if they'd only move the stadium, diners could take over the bar as well.

licensed & byo; wine by the glass
dinner Tues–Sat 6.30–11pm
cards AE BC DC MC V   Bookings recommended
seats 110; private room; no smoking until 10.30pm
owner Paul W. Duggan
chef Mark Jensen
cost Around $70 for two, plus drinks
plus Strong on food   **minus** Weak wine list
score 14/20

$

onde

346 LIVERPOOL STREET, DARLINGHURST
PHONE 9331 8749   MAP 2

MODERN AUSTRALIAN/FRENCH

Onde is a reminder of how well Sydney does
Smart Casual. A funky neighbourhood bistro
in a funky neighbourhood, it serves up
uncomplicated but beyond basic food to a
broad customer base, from fish-and-chip-
eating families to Darlo coolsters, grazing
on mussels, radicchio and potato. All the
starters are fresh and interesting, especially
a warm salad of potato and anchovies
tarted up with the slightly bitter tang of
saffron. Mains are, in the main, hearty
affairs, running from big chunky slashes
of grilled liver served with red cabbage
to a plate-covering T-bone steak, cooked
way beyond the medium-rare requested.
Still, when you consider the surprisingly
reasonable prices, Victoire bread and neat
selection of wines all available by the glass,
it seems churlish to be too picky. Especially
when you get to eat in such a pleasant
modern space, with service you'd be happy
to find in some of our money's-no-object
establishments.

licensed; wine by the glass
dinner Mon–Thurs 5.30–11pm;
Fri–Sat 5.30–11.30pm; Sun 5.30–10pm
cards AE BC DC MC V   No bookings
seats 38
owner/chef Laif Etournaud
cost Around $60 for two, plus drinks
plus Honest prices   **minus** No bookings
score 14/20

$

original peking vip

LOWER GROUND FLOOR,
149 CASTLEREAGH STREET, SYDNEY
PHONE 9264 2693, 9264 6210   MAP 1

CHINESE

Why is it so difficult, even in these days of
savvy dining, to prise the specialities off a
Chinese-language-only menu? 'You won't
like it,' says Mrs Lo, drawing an expressive
finger across her throat. 'You're not
Chinese.' As if a perfectly innocuous, subtly
smoky bowl of steamed and fried beancurd
with seafood and vegetables might offend
the dull Anglo palate. However, there are
more than enough real Peking specialities
on the regular 179-dish English-language
menu – pages of big, slithery noodles, and
robust dumplings in their doughy casings,
enlivened with herbs. This is a northern,
wheat-oriented cuisine with steamed or
fried silver thread bread (a sort of Chinese
damper) to mop up the fragrant juices of
Shantung chicken. And where better to try
authentic and well-priced Peking Duck than
in this basement outpost of Beijing, with its
cheerfully tacky Chinese décor? (Be careful
not to over-order – servings are VIP-sized.)

licensed & byo
lunch Daily noon–3pm
dinner Sun–Thurs 6–10.30pm; Fri–Sat 6–11.30pm
cards AE BC DC MC V No bookings
seats 120; private room; non-smoking area ⊹✗
owners Allan Cheung, Mabel Lo & Tony Wong
chefs Alan Cheung & Tony Wong
cost Around $54 for two, plus drinks
plus The Peking duck   **minus** Language barrier
score 13/20

otto

8 THE WHARF WOOLLOOMOOLOO,
6 COWPER WHARF ROAD, WOOLLOOMOOLOO
PHONE 9368 7488   MAP 2

ITALIAN

Melbourne meets the Italian Riviera at
what has to be the most stylish restaurant
in Sydney's most stylish eating precinct.
Outside on the walkway, Philippe Starck
all-weather chairs line up like Portofino
tourists. Inside, the place drips with
darkwood-trimmed class from its eye-
popping bare bulb chandelier and subtle
David Band graphics to Sydney's most
desirable private dining room. The food, too,
is a cut above the Sydney–Italian norm,
including a lush taleggio and cauliflower
panna cotta, silky homemade pappardelle
pasta with rabbit, and fall-about wine-
braised beef shin with black cabbage.
Desserts include a must-try Campari and
grenadine poached pear with vanilla
mascarpone or an exquisitely nutty
Extra Testa Parmigiano Reggiano. Maurizio
Terzini is renowned for giving Melbourne
a new sense of Italian chic with Caffe e
Cucina and the Melbourne Wine Room.
Now it's Sydney's turn.

licensed; wine by the glass
hours Mon–Sat noon–midnight; Sun noon–10pm
cards AE BC DC MC V   Bookings recommended
seats 140; private room; outdoor area;
wheelchair access; non-smoking area
owners Maurizio Terzini & Burkitt Australia
chefs Nino Joseph Zoccali & Maurizio Esposito
cost Around $120 for two, plus drinks
plus Italian style   **minus** Getting in
score 15/20

out of africa

43–5 EAST ESPLANADE, MANLY
PHONE 9977 0055   MAP 7

NORTH AFRICAN

Morocco meets Manly at this breezy just-
below street-level space, and the locals love
it. This is a fun night out and a genuinely
good feed to boot. Flavour and style are
not overwhelming, so don't be afraid to
explore a little. An excellent chicken tagine
bubbles dramatically in its claypot, its
long flavours soaked up with a side of
the fluffiest, butteriest couscous around.
Lamb with roasted almonds and raisins is
served with orange and saffron sauce,
and doesn't disappoint with its cargo of
plump dates and delicious white berries –
exotic little fig-like thingies – although its
accompanying couscous wants to loosen up
and be let out of its mould. Dishes manage
to hold their own and not fight with each
other, but desserts need work – have crème
brûlée and profiteroles become all the rage
in North Africa, or is this just more proof
of Morocco meeting Manly?

licensed & byo
lunch Thurs–Sun noon–3pm
dinner Daily 6–10pm
cards AE BC DC MC V   Bookings recommended,
essential weekends
seats 120; outdoor area; non-smoking area
owners Hassan M'Souli & Omar Majdi
chefs Hassan M'Souli & Fuad Mahboub
cost Around $50 for two, plus drinks
plus Fluffy couscous
minus Non-African desserts
score 13/20

§

paddington inn

338 OXFORD STREET, PADDINGTON
PHONE 9380 5913   MAP 4B

MODERN AUSTRALIAN

The old airless back dining room that
incubated the talents of such chefs as
Matthew Moran and Paul Merrony is no
more. Instead, the dining area has been
incorporated into the pub proper, now
sporting a bold new look, complete with
sculpted glass lighting, in-demand booths
and boudoir-like themed rooms. The food
here is more a modern expansion of the
good, honest, counter-lunch theme than
haute cuisine. Fish and chips comes as
crisply battered whiting with hand-cut
thickish chips, while fall-off-the-bone pork
ribs with jasmine rice are sweet, sticky and
thoroughly likeable. Yet a duck omelette
with bean shoots felt untogether and
fishcakes were bland-tasting. On balance,
the food is fine, if somewhat ambitious and
uneven. You're either comfortable ordering
from the bar, carrying your own drinks
and cutlery and sitting in a noisy, smoky
pub environment, or you're not. Judging by
the crowds, many are.

licensed; wine by the glass
lunch Mon–Fri noon–3pm; Sat–Sun noon–4pm
dinner Mon–Thurs & Sun 6–10pm;
Fri–Sat 6–9pm
cards AE BC DC MC V   No bookings
seats 120; private rooms; wheelchair access
owner Ukena Pty Ltd
chef Marcus Mano
cost Around $43 for two, plus drinks
plus Real food in a pub   **minus** The smoke
score 12/20

palisade

PALISADE HOTEL,
35 BETTINGTON STREET, MILLERS POINT
PHONE 9251 7225   MAP 1

MODERN AUSTRALIAN

The English who colonised Sydney were a
funny lot. They get a nice piece of prime
high ground overlooking the harbour, and
they build a lovely looking pub on it which
has fabulous fireplaces, lots of character,
and such high windows you forget there is a
view. Perhaps they foresaw that one day the
talented Brian Sudek would move in and
produce food interesting enough to make
views unnecessary. The modern Sydney
cooking in the old Aussie pub is
40 per cent Italian-influenced (ravioli with
potato, ricotta and capsicum essence);
20 per cent Asian-influenced (sand lobster
wontons in lime and lemongrass broth);
10 per cent French (lemon tart); and only
5 per cent English (roast chicken with
sage and bread stuffing). The rest is
Sudek's individual inspiration. So who
needs picture windows?

licensed; wine by the glass
lunch Mon–Fri noon–3pm
dinner Mon–Sat 6–10pm
cards AE BC MC V   Bookings recommended
seats 60; private room; non-smoking area ✝✖
owners Palisade Properties
chef Brian Sudek
cost Around $80 for two, plus drinks
plus Cosy comfort   **minus** Where's the harbour?
score 14/20

paramount

73 MACLEAY STREET, POTTS POINT
PHONE 9358 1652   MAP 2

MODERN AUSTRALIAN

Christine Manfield mixes Indian spices,
Chinese veggies, Italian tastes and French
technique like every other chef doing
modern Sydney cuisine, but the result is
unique. There is nothing predictable about
the bold, structured tastes, nor do they
follow the usual fusion themes. Manfield's
duck salad epitomises the style, with a
seemingly overwhelming number of
European, Indian and Asian ingredients
brought together to create satisfying
complex taste sensations. Desserts are
perhaps less surprising, but they still
produce real highlights, including a blood
plum brioche beautifully crafted and
bursting with supercharged flavours. The
remarkable wine list is full of hard-to-find
gems, and has been carefully chosen to
complement the dishes. The staff understand
the philosophy of kitchen, and bring food,
wine and advice at the right moments.

licensed; wine by the glass
dinner Tues–Sun 6.30–11pm
cards AE BC DC MC V   Bookings recommended
seats 60; no smoking except in bar
owners Christine Manfield & Margie Harris
chef Christine Manfield
cost About $150 for two, plus drinks; six-course
tasting menu $110 p.p.
plus Highly inventive   **minus** Noisy when full
score 17/20

pavilion on the park

1 ART GALLERY ROAD, SYDNEY
PHONE 9232 1322   MAP 1

MODERN AUSTRALIAN

While the Pavilion's regular à la carte
dinners are, alas, no more, there's still lunch
to get excited about. Sit outside on a balmy
day, with the Domain at your feet, and
you'll get a sense of Sydney minus the
urban grittiness. What's more, you'll eat
exceptionally well, thanks to the talents of
Christopher Millar. Imam bayildi is a gently
aromatic, stuffed half eggplant; boned
spatchcock, wrapped in prosciutto and
stuffed with walnuts is a tender joy; while
nicely rested roast lamb rump served
with artichokes is lifted by a wobbly,
Japanese-influenced rosemary custard.
Even if you're inside on a rainy day, with
the louvred windows and palm trees as
the view, the service, food and day all slide
by with consummate ease (gosh, is that
the time already?) More low-key food can
be found at the adjoining café – perfect
after a walk through the gardens, or to get
your strength up for an assault on the Art
Gallery of NSW over the road.

licensed; wine by the glass
lunch Sun–Fri noon–5pm (Café open daily
9am–5pm)
cards AE BC DC MC V   Bookings recommended
seats 150; private room; outdoor area;
wheelchair access; non-smoking area
owners Robert & Linda Biancardi
chef Christopher Millar
cost Set price $55 p.p. for two courses;
$70 p.p. for three courses, plus drinks
plus Sylvan setting   **minus** Traffic noise
score 15/20

pazzo

583 CROWN STREET, SURRY HILLS
PHONE 9319 4387   MAP 3B

ITALIAN

Inner-city road rage and parking poos are instantly forgotten upon entering this warm, intimate cocoon at the drabbish end of Crown Street. Candles lend themselves well to the easy and relaxed atmosphere (and service), which in turn is reflected in Bruno Mazzoni's honest Italian cooking. 'Mamma's' ravioli of potato, pecorino and mint started the night off well, but pork layered with oregano and tomato polenta needed a little help. Soothing familiarity returned in a lovely dish of chicken with porcini and leek; and guinea fowl with peaches and cabbage showed a careful hand at work. Generous helpings, comfortably sized and well-appointed tables, reasonable noise levels and an airy courtyard are a relief for those who suffer permanent where-to-take-the-oldies dilemmas. There is good flavour here but more focus on balance wouldn't hurt. We need more places like Pazzo in takeaway land.

byo
dinner Mon–Sat 6–10pm
cards AE BC MC V   Bookings recommended
seats 90; private room; outdoor area; non-smoking area; no smoking until 10.30pm ✕
owner Raffaele Faro
chef Bruno Mazzoni
cost Around $76 for two
plus Candles   **minus** Fussy plates
score 13/20

peking inn

390 PACIFIC HIGHWAY, LINDFIELD
PHONE 9416 3509   MAP 7

CHINESE

Thousand-layered wind is Sydney's most curious starter, a pig's ear terrine that is at once crunchy and gelatinous. This anything but suburban Chinese restaurant is northern by nature and by physical law. That means chilli-laden specialities; hearty claypots; hot, sour sauces; and plump, bulging dumplings. On the site of an old-fashioned Aussie tea house, the wood panelling, mirrored columns, service bar and interconnecting rooms seem born to serve the cause of Chinese dining. Specialities include double-boiled belly pork; marinated and fried 'smoked' Shanghai fish and the exquisite steamed and deep-fried aromatic crispy duck, shredded at the table and served in pancakes. The motto here seems to be why cook it once, if you can cook it twice? Hot and sour soup with homemade dumplings is a real lip tingler, and spring onion pancakes are crisp and flaky. The service may look equally flaky, but somehow your whole meal comes together in a rush.

licensed & byo
lunch Tues–Sun noon–3pm
dinner Daily 5.30–11pm
cards AE BC MC V   Bookings recommended
seats 110; no smoking ✕
owner Teresa Lo
chef Yun-Kong Lo
cost Around $70 for two, plus drinks
plus Duck with pancakes
minus Distracted service
score 13/20

pre &

eat, drink and on with the show

arena Eat before or after the flicks in the come-as-you-are bar and bistro downstairs, or go more upscale upstairs. 212 BENT STREET, FOX STUDIOS AUSTRALIA, MOORE PARK 9361 3833 (RES) 9361 3930 (BISTRO)

aria A classy harbourside restaurant with show-friendly hours, from 5.30 to 7pm, and supper until 11.30pm. 1 MACQUARIE STREET, EAST CIRCULAR QUAY 9252 2555

bbq king No-frills Cantonese noodles and roast duck – just the thing pre or post the latest Jackie Chan movie. 18–20 GOULBURN STREET, SYDNEY 9267 2433

casa asturiana Nip in for Spanish tapas and a sherry and you'll still make it to the Entertainment Centre in time for the show. Open from 5.30pm. 77 LIVERPOOL STREET, SYDNEY 9264 1010

eastbank Open all day, everyday, this popular, buzzy bistro can get you fed, watered and off to the show before you can say gnocchi with fresh ricotta. 61–9 MACQUARIE STREET, CIRCULAR QUAY 9241 6722

golden century Whole steamed fish and prawns, hearty congee, roast duck. If you're still there at 3am, you should be in bed. 393–99 SUSSEX STREET, HAYMARKET 9212 3901

la mensa For pre and post cinema, cricket, football and just shopping, La Mensa serves up fast and friendly Italianate food. 257 OXFORD STREET, PADDINGTON 9332 2963

otto *(left)* Head down to the waterside wharf for a glammed-up post-show supper of linguine and seafood, Italian style. 8 THE WHARF WOOLLOOMOOLOO, 6 COWPER WHARF ROAD, WOOLLOOMOOLOO 9368 7488

rockpool An early (6pm) opening gives you time for fresh oysters, Champagne, pigeon and lobster before the concert, show or opera. 107 GEORGE STREET, THE ROCKS 9252 1888

the wharf The kitchen here is sympathetic to the adjacent Sydney Theatre Company program – they even ring a bell so you don't miss the show. PIER 4, HICKSON ROAD, WALSH BAY 9250 1761

post

perama

88 AUDLEY STREET, PETERSHAM
PHONE 9569 7534   MAP 8

MODERN GREEK

The ancient Greeks used to believe that the gods could feast merely on the aroma of slaughtered animals as it ascended heavenward from the sacrificial pyre. Judging by the greasy fumes emerging from the kitchens and smoke stacks of many a local Acropolis or Olympus, this belief is still going strong among the Greek restaurateurs of Sydney. Not at Perama, though. At this rightly popular and very charming neighbourhood restaurant, the lamb skaras has been cooked with divine thoroughness, so that what emerges is not a blackened horror but something soft and delicate in texture. They have a nice way, too, with unHellenic ingredients such as Tasmanian salmon, and the mezze plate, though short on surprises, is astutely managed. In fact, the nearest thing to a Greek tragedy in the whole experience is the news that there seems just now to be a nationwide shortage of Metaxas brandy.

licensed & byo; wine by the glass
dinner Tues–Sat 6.30–11pm
cards AE BC MC V   Bookings essential
seats 100; private room; wheelchair access; no smoking until 10.30pm ⚞✗
owners Harry Tamvakeras & David Tsirekas
chef David Tsirekas
cost Around $65 for two, plus drinks
plus Charcoal-free food
minus Metaxas-free bar
score 14/20

phatboys

118 CROWN STREET, EAST SYDNEY
PHONE 9332 3284   MAP 2

THAI

Whoa! Walking into the clean, severely modern lines of Phatboys for the first time and encountering the full-length wall mirrors is a bizarre experience, so take someone to hang on to. The chilli-shy needn't worry, because the menu is well sign-posted with icons to alert you to the presence of heat or vegetarian dishes. Novices can start with the ahahn wang, a selection of five starters that includes crisp deep-fried spring rolls, your common or garden chicken/beef satay and some of the fishiest fishcakes around. Pla neu, a main course of spicy grilled beef salad with ground chilli, is shot through with the tang of lemongrass and lime leaf, and is just hot enough to make your eyeballs quiver. Only the kai jiew poo, a crabmeat omelette with sweet tomato sauce was forgettable. While there was plenty of omelette and plenty of sauce, we would like to have seen a bit more crab.

licensed & byo; wine by the glass
lunch Mon–Fri from noon
dinner Daily from 6pm
cards AE BC DC MC V   Bookings recommended, essential weekends
seats 80; outdoor area; wheelchair access; non-smoking area ⚞✗
owner/chef Pen Townsend
cost Around $76 for two, plus drinks
plus The cheery crowd   **minus** Self-image
score 12/20

philip's

LEVEL 1, 46 MORTS ROAD
(CNR VICTORIA AVENUE), MORTDALE
PHONE 9570 3670   MAP 6

MODERN AUSTRALIAN

If you'd never been to Mortdale before, this hard-to-find gem located on the first floor above a dress shop would shimmer like an oasis in the desert. For fifteen years, chef–proprietor Philip Challis and his wife Kath have plied their loyal patrons with carefully crafted contemporary dishes like a warm fluffy slice of lobster terrine ringed with salsa verde and crowned with a prawn; pink quail breast salad with tomato onion jam; or tender lamb fillets with spiced ratatouille. Local businessfolk know the secret and shout their clients Friday lunch, an immensely good value three-course set choice selection that even includes a generous plate of ripe Australian farmhouse cheeses, or maybe a wobbly pure white panna cotta with cognac-drowned dates. Challis's food shows effort and dedication that sadly is not matched by the décor. But a lick of paint, new chairs and Havana blinds to block out the supermarket view would soon change all that.

byo
lunch Fri noon–2pm
dinner Tues–Sat 6–9.30pm
cards AE BC MC V   Bookings recommended
seats 50; no smoking ⅍
owner/chef Philip Challis
cost Around $80 for two, plus drinks
plus Friday lunch   **minus** Hideaway location
score 12/20

pier

594 NEW SOUTH HEAD ROAD, ROSE BAY
PHONE 9327 6561   MAP 9

MODERN AUSTRALIAN/SEAFOOD

You don't have to be a fiscally flush fish fanatic to like Pier, but it helps. A suave waiter presents you with a guide to where today's fish were caught, and a menu asks you to decide between a 200-gram or 140-gram serving. The descriptions probably exceed normal need-to-know requirements. For example, lobster medallions come with caramelised pork hock, cucumber and citrus sauce, and crisp-skin snapper with 'beanettes' and black truffle and honey sauce. With desserts come dissertations on the history of Valrhona chocolate (used in a cake with cherry ice-cream) and the provenance of every element on the cheese plate. But the tastes make up for the excess details. The cooking is sophisticated, the wine list diverse, and the service well-informed and somewhat formal. Surrounded by bobbing boats and soaring seaplanes, Pier is the ideal place to take rich rellies and so-this-is-Sydney visitors.

licensed; wine by the glass
lunch Daily noon–3pm
dinner Mon–Sat 6–10pm; Sun 6–9pm
cards AE BC DC MC V   Bookings essential
seats 120; private room; no smoking
until 10pm ⅍
owner The Pier Restaurant Pty Ltd
chefs Greg Doyle & Stephen Hodges
cost Around $120 for two, plus drinks
plus Wraparound harbour views
minus Not much internal atmosphere
score 17/20

the pool caffe

94 MARINE PARADE, MAROUBRA
PHONE 9314 0364   MAP 9

MEDITERRANEAN

This is relaxed dining, Sydney-style –
dusting off a day's worth of sand and
heading straight to the local foodie haunt.
Situated opposite the Mahon pool, the café
attracts not only water lovers, but flavour
chasers. When you first glimpse the blue
hanging flowerpots, spot the jars of
preserved watermelon skin on the counter,
and notice the laid-back beach-house feel of
the dining room, you can't help but warm to
the place. With a menu that darts deliciously
from Italy to Asia, it can be hard to choose.
It could be a perfectly refreshing scallop,
papaya, tatsoi and glass noodle salad, or
maybe a rich lemon and fennel risotto with
ocean-sweet Balmain bugs. Sometimes
flavours can be a little intense, and not
quite hit the mark, but there is always
something interesting to eat (Sicilian stuffed
small fish with parsley and preserved
lemon) and something sweet to finish with
(raspberry jelly with vanilla custard).

byo
breakfast Sat–Sun 9–11.45am
lunch Fri–Sun from noon
dinner Wed–Sun 6–10pm
cards AE BC DC MC V   Bookings recommended
seats 90; private room; outdoor area;
non-smoking area; no smoking until 9.30pm
owners Elizabeth & Karen Fines
chef Elizabeth Fines
cost Around $73 for two, plus drinks
plus Wave to the ocean   **minus** The back room
score 13/20

port

LEVEL 2, HARBOURSIDE,
DARLING HARBOUR, SYDNEY
PHONE 9211 7226   MAP 5B

MODERN AUSTRALIAN

Plush and businesslike, Port is one of several
new ventures hell-bent on giving the
harbourside side of Darling Harbour a
serious dining image. With its dark wood
trim, dapper chairs and in-your-face views,
it feels like a restaurant with a purpose.
Although situated deep in touristland, chef
Lawry Gordon puts on an ambitious menu
that's anything but visitors' fare. His
whipped oyster and clam soup is a creamy,
frothy treat that would have been even
better with a couple of whole oysters or
clams in it. A red snapper fillet with
saffron-buttered squid rings and saffron
risotto featured first-class ingredients, if too
many, while an iced honeycomb brioche
parfait – a kind of frozen, nude Violet
Crumble – has an effect that outstrips its
bitsy presentation. The signature 'Essential
Sydney Plate' of Balmain bugs, oysters, beer-
battered fish, smoked kangaroo and prawn
wontons is more of a buffet than a plate.

licensed; wine by the glass
lunch Daily noon–3pm
dinner Daily 6–10pm
cards AE BC DC MC V   Bookings essential
seats 150; outdoor area; wheelchair access;
no smoking until 10pm
owners Paul & Allyson Sarkis
chef Lawry Gordon
cost Around $97 for two, plus drinks
plus Darling Harbour views   **minus** Plate waits
score 12/20

post

LOWER GROUND FLOOR, GPO,
NO. 1 MARTIN PLACE, SYDNEY
PHONE 9229 7744   MAP 1

MODERN AUSTRALIAN

Don't you just love places that do more
than they have to? It seems to be the
rule for a Stan Sarris establishment, and
never is it more in evidence than at a
busy, buzzy CBD lunch at Post in the GPO
gastrobasement. Post didn't have to have
such good glasses, nor did it have to do the
whole crustacea bar thing, although with
the fresh fish shop next door, it would have
been mad not to. This same feeling of 'doing
that little bit extra' shows in the cooking.
A lobster salad is delicate, sweet, sea-fresh
and comes in the shell; fish soup with
saffron rouille is a lesson in flawless
provençale cookery; and roast rump of
Tuscan lamb is full of old-fashioned flavours,
if a little heavy on the meat. Without a
doubt, this is the quintessential city lunch,
charging fair prices for more-than-you-
bargained-for food and swift city service.

licensed; wine by the glass
lunch Mon–Fri noon–3pm; Sat (crustacea bar
only) noon–3pm
dinner Mon–Fri 6–10pm
cards AE BC DC MC V   Bookings recommended
seats 135; wheelchair access;
non-smoking area
owners Stan Sarris & Rodney Adler
chef Darrell Felstead
cost Around $80 for two, plus drinks
plus Crustacea bar   **minus** Basement blues
score 14/20

prasit's northside on crown

415 CROWN STREET, SURRY HILLS
PHONE 9319 0748   MAP 3B

THAI

Rice tells you a great deal about a Thai
restaurant, and at Prasit's it is exemplary:
fluffy, individual grains, dished from a
burnished bronze bowl. Treat yourself to
such startling beauties as puya ko samet –
a whole blue swimmer crab stuffed with a
scrummy farce of pork, water chestnuts and
crab; the smoky, crisp fish salad with green
mango; or an unusual pumpkin and chicken
stir-fry. Generous serves arrive promptly on
Prasit's signature plates, bursting with
colour and complex flavours but moderate
chilli levels. Service comes from helpful,
friendly staff in monogrammed shirts that
match the prevailing purple and gold design
theme and whimsical branding. Prasit,
arguably the first Thai to tickle Sydney's
palates with searingly authentic flavours,
has certainly come a long way since those
early Erskineville days, and we're glad he
took us with him.

byo
lunch Thurs–Fri noon–3pm
dinner Mon–Sat 6–10pm
cards AE BC MC V   Bookings essential
seats 98; private room; no smoking
until 10pm
owners Hugh Barry & Prasit Prateeprasen
chef Prasit Prateeprasen
cost Around $86 for two, plus drinks
plus Finger bowls   **minus** No ice buckets
score 14/20

prasit's northside thai

77 MOUNT STREET, NORTH SYDNEY
PHONE 9957 2271   MAP 5A

THAI

Weekday lunches can be frantic affairs at this upmarket Thai eatery in the heart of the North Sydney business district. So if you want to hear yourself think, perhaps dinner is a more civilised option. Service is friendly, if casual, while the wine list is adequate and reasonably priced. All dishes arrive at the table authentically presented with the colourful carved vegetable garnishes one would expect in the heart of Bangkok. Steamed scallops with ginger, tomato and chilli sauce are plump, spicy and tasty, while an oyster salad of freshly shucked Tasmanian oysters is topped with a well-balanced salad of green mango, lemongrass and fresh turmeric dressing. Give the tough chicken green curry a miss, and head for the galangal, chilli, lemongrass and kaffir lime stirfry of king prawns or a yellow curry of beef with sweet potato and turmeric, accompanied by fragrant jasmine rice. If the weather is kind, try for a table on the leafy outdoor balcony.

licensed; wine by the glass
lunch Mon–Fri noon–3pm
dinner Tues–Sat 6–10pm
cards AE BC DC MC V   Bookings recommended
seats 140; private room; outdoor area; wheelchair access; no smoking until 10pm
owner Eric Sudardja
chef Prasit Prateeprasen
cost Around $65 for two, plus drinks
plus The balcony   **minus** The air-con
score 13/20

prasit's northside thai takeaway

395 CROWN STREET, SURRY HILLS
PHONE 9332 1792   MAP 3B

THAI

The most expensive thing on the menu, a mango and crabmeat salad, is only $17. How do they do it? Well, for one, they do it by not having any décor. This is lino and lemongrass land, with a smattering of tatty high tables and stools downstairs and proper tables upstairs should you feel the need to linger. Not many do, mainly because the food appears almost before you order it. There is an extensive menu of basic Thai staples but it is under chef's suggestions that things begin to shine. A deep-fried king prawn fritter tossed in coconut strips is a light and subtle entrée, as is marinated chicken in banana leaf. The deep-fried deboned quail with a chilli jam dressing is quite rightly legendary but more than matched by the Heaven Beef, a BBQ scotch fillet with a sprightly kaffir lime, chilli, peanut and lemongrass dressing. Never has a dish been more appropriately named.

byo
lunch Tues–Sun noon–3pm
dinner Tues–Sun 5.30–10pm
cards AE BC MC V   No bookings
seats 43; no smoking
owner Prasit Prateeprasen
chef Aree Kilsby
cost Around $43 for two, plus drinks
plus The prices   **minus** The battle for tables
score 13/20

The classic Trilogy.

Three classic Champagne grape varieties, brought together in an elegant, bottle
fermented sparkling wine. Premium white and red table wines, created by
uniting three classic Bordeaux grape varieties. Now the trilogy is complete.

TRILOGY.

**⧓ at GPO
Produce**

GPO Table
Fresh GPO
produce and
wine at
GPO Table

GPO Store
Cellar
Cheese
Juice
Greengrocer
Baker
Chocolates
Delicatessen
Butcher
Fishmonger
Organics
GPO Produce
Urban Wares

GPO
No1 Martin Place
Lower ground floor
Sydney Australia
Telephone
02 9229 7700
Facsimile
02 9229 7734
Email
eat@gpobox.com.au

Trading hour
Monday to F
8am to 7.30
Saturday
9am to 6pm

prime

LOWER GROUND FLOOR, GPO,
NO. 1 MARTIN PLACE, SYDNEY
PHONE 9229 7777   MAP 1

FRENCH

Welcome to the new steakhouse. They
may call it a 'grill room', but we live in
euphemistic times, when a beauty salon is
an urban wellness day spa. One of three
new Stan Sarris eateries in the basement
of the revamped GPO, Prime comes with a
discreetly luxurious atmosphere, high on
detail and comfort. Attentive floor staff skim
around a coolly clubby room. The solid walls
expose the beauty and strength of Sydney
sandstone, and a monumental fireplace is
a sleek reference to earlier methods of
meat cooking. There are five steak options,
running from a 300-gram prime fillet to
chateaubriand for two. Choose your sauce
(red wine, bearnaise, café de Paris or wild
mushroom) and your potato (parsleyed,
purée, gratinated or French-fried), and you're
done. Beyond steak, chef Darrell Felstead
delivers lush, classy seafood tortellini, oxtail
raviolo and roasted barramundi with clams
and capers.

licensed; wine by the glass
lunch Mon–Fri noon–2.30pm
dinner Mon–Sat 6.30–10pm
cards AE BC DC MC V   Bookings recommended
seats 94; private room; wheelchair access;
no smoking until 2.30pm & 10.30pm
owners Stan Sarris & Rodney Adler
chef Darrell Felstead
cost Around $140 for two, plus drinks
plus Steak scalpels   **minus** Give us more potato
score 15/20

pruniers

65 OCEAN STREET, WOOLLAHRA
PHONE 9363 1974   MAP 4B

EUROPEAN/FRENCH/ITALIAN

Pruniers has seamlessly insinuated itself
back into Woollahra's lifestyle by giving
people what they want: beautifully cooked
New Conservative food and butler service in
a pretty series of rooms with garden views,
and creamed spinach on the side. After his
flurry with Modern British food in London's
Bluebird restaurant, and Modern Australian
at the Bennelong, owner/chef Michael
Moore claims he's just cooking all the
dishes he learnt as a young chef in London
some years ago. The – how shall we put
this? – older crowd love the plump,
crumbed fishcakes with sauce gribiche and
simple poached cod with parsley sauce.
And yes, the dessert trolley is back,
complete with a Valrhona chocolate
mousse, rice pudding and prunes. Add a
separate list of order-ahead dinners for
two, including coq au vin, roast leg of
lamb and whole roast chicken, and
Pruniers starts to feel awfully like a comfy,
welcome-home club of which anyone with
a credit card can become a member.

licensed; wine by the glass
lunch Daily noon–3pm
dinner Mon–Sat 6–10pm
cards AE BC DC MC V   Bookings recommended
seats 120; private room; outdoor area;
wheelchair access
owner/chef Michael Moore
cost Around $108 for two, plus drinks
plus The gardens   **minus** Dim lighting by night
score 15/20

quay

OVERSEAS PASSENGER TERMINAL,
CIRCULAR QUAY
PHONE 9251 5600   MAP 1

FRENCH

The harbour view is a killer, and for many,
so are the prices, which could even manage
to raise an eyebrow in New York. The
cooking is concise and confident, from the
French-influenced pea purée that surrounds
handsome poached king prawns, through to
the perfect blend of Asian flavours in a
Peking duck pancake. The slow-roasted veal
tongue with bok choy is pure pleasure,
while an Italian risotto with carnaroli rice
teamed with the freshest vegetables
achieves an ethereal balance.
The service matches the refinement of the
food. While Quay was the winner of three
hats last year for the quality of its dining
experience, it has been closed for renovation
for much of 2000. At the time of going to
press, the future of star chef Guillaume
Brahimi's tenure is in doubt, so this year's
experience must remain unscored.

licensed; wine by the glass
lunch Mon–Fri noon–3pm
dinner Daily 6–10pm
cards AE BC DC MC V   Bookings essential
seats 110; private room; outdoor area;
wheelchair access; no smoking until 10pm
owner Leon Fink
cost Around $194 for two, plus drinks
plus World-class view   **minus** World-class prices
score unscored

radio cairo

CNR MILITARY ROAD & SPOFFORTH STREET,
CREMORNE
PHONE 9908 2649   MAP 7

AFRICAN

Radio Cairo has one of those electrically
charged atmospheres, full of movement,
music and people. It once relied on doing
bar trade for the now defunct original Radio
Cairo restaurant across the road, though it's
now a regular café haunt for the Cremorne
crowd. They're here for what the menu
promises to be fascinating tastes of the
Caribbean and Africa, and cheap, well-
chosen wines. Favourite orders are the
buzzard (it's actually chicken) and sweet
potato curry and the Portuguese-influenced
Mozambiquan king prawns piri piri. After
the typically Caribbean pork jerk was sold
out, the waiter voted in a Kenyan curry as
the most interesting on the menu, but apart
from a few red chillies thrown on top to
spice it up, the dish lacked real depth and
character. The same went for the pale Cajun
popcorn shrimp. The feeling of adventure is
still there, but it doesn't always translate to
the plate.

licensed (byo Sundays only); wine by the glass
dinner Daily 6–10pm
cards AE BC DC MC V   Bookings recommended
seats 70; wheelchair access; non-smoking
area
owner/chef Sriân Perera
cost Around $60 for two, plus drinks
plus Affordable wines   **minus** No great depth
score 11/20

rattlesnake grill

130 MILITARY ROAD, NEUTRAL BAY
PHONE 9953 4789   MAP 5A

SOUTHWEST AMERICAN

Every night is party night at the Rattlesnake Grill, especially Saturday night, when a band adds a little musical harmony to the Tex-Mex vibes. If you like margaritas, you're going to love it. Actually, the food's not bad either, rising above the usual Mexican and south-west suspects, and adding a frisson of the unexpected with dishes such as a Yucatan lamb salad, and a grilled calamari salad rubbed with pumpkin seed recado (herbs and spices). For the main courses we eschewed dishes such as Jamaican jerk chicken for adequate and hardy perennials such as their version of paella, and margarita-friendly chicken fajitas. But it's the whole package that puts a shake in the Rattlesnake's tail. The service is fast and friendly and the atmosphere is electric. Go there, eat nice food, listen to the band and drink until the wee hours. Be careful of the dessert sampler, though. You might well explode.

licensed & byo; wine by the glass
dinner Sun–Wed 6–10pm; Thurs–Sat 6–11pm
cards AE BC DC MC V   Bookings recommended, essential weekends
seats 140; private room; non-smoking area Sun–Thurs; no smoking Fri–Sat until 10pm ⊁
owners Victor Pisapia & Jim Bahr
chefs Victor Pisapia & Michael Burgess
cost Around $86 for two, plus drinks
plus Yeee-haw atmosphere   **minus** Hard to park
score 13/20

ravesi's

LEVEL 1, CNR CAMPBELL PARADE & HALL STREET, BONDI BEACH
PHONE 9365 4422   MAP 9

MODERN AUSTRALIAN

While Ravesi's has been in and out more times than the Bondi tide, it's still a worthwhile player in the local eat scene. The food is Modern Aussie workable, occasionally managing to rise above the beachfront's mean average bistro fare. Asian-inspired dishes are the go here, including steamed Eden mussels poached in a Thai-influenced stock, and fleshy snapper served with Hokkien noodles. Regular fish and chips aren't bad either, while the small wine list manages to have a bottle to satisfy everyone. But the position, along with the Bondi-casual yet efficient service, is what this place is all about. It's informal and friendly, and on some nights the atmosphere is close to a beach party. Go ahead and join in. If it's a good day try to get an outdoor balcony table. Even if the food doesn't thrill, the view will.

licensed; wine by the glass
hours Daily 7.30–11.30am; noon–10pm
cards AE BC DC MC V   Bookings recommended, essential weekends
seats 190; private room; outdoor area; wheelchair access; non-smoking area ⊁
owner Debilu Pty Ltd
chef Pierre L'Huillier
cost Around $86 for two, plus drinks
plus Great view   **minus** Noisy crowd
score 13/20

raw bar

CNR WARNERS & WAIROA AVENUES,
BONDI BEACH
PHONE 9365 7200   MAP 9

JAPANESE

Sushi by the sea is an alluring concept.
Here you can chow down on a California or
Tokyo roll or a pork and ramen noodle soup
as you watch the waves roll in at Bondi, or
just take shelter from the heat before you
start to resemble a giant serving of
vegetarian tempura. Raw Bar is not so
much an extraordinary dining experience
as a convenient pit stop between the beach
and the bar, a popular eatery with a place
in the sun and seats that spill out onto the
street. You're so close to the water's edge
that a side of flying fish roe could almost
come from the Pacific Ocean itself. Say yes
to nasu no dengaku, an almost sinful
starter of fried eggplant with sweet miso
sauce, or avoid decisions and go for a
bento lunch or dinner box that covers
every food group imaginable.

byo
hours Daily noon–11pm
cards AE BC DC MC V   No bookings
seats 50; outdoor area; no smoking until
10pm
owner Jackie Milijash
chef Kuniaki Konda
cost Around $50 for two, plus drinks
plus Bondi sunset   **minus** Kite-flying winds
score 12/20

reds

12 ARGYLE STREET, THE ROCKS
PHONE 9247 1011   MAP 1

MODERN AUSTRALIAN

Step from The Rocks' tourist mayhem into
Reds and you immediately feel de-stressed
by the bold colours and the subdued
lighting. The bar curves from inside the door,
leading you invitingly into dining areas that
have been divided into sections to make
this large nineteenth-century woolstore
less cavernous. The tables are generously
spaced – a good thing too, considering
that most are occupied by groups of
four or more. Older family groups mix it
with business suits with loosened ties
and tourists bravely trying the 'Outback
Adventure' of chargrilled kangaroo, emu
prosciutto and fillet of crocodile. Most
dishes on the menu include a fruit or a
nut of some kind, such as Muscovy duck
terrine with pistachio and muscatel, and
quail breast with caramelised eschallot and
cider apple. The sirloin on colcannon is
delicious, but the roasted jewfish fillet is
less inspiring. Some dishes might try too
hard, but at least they're trying.

licensed; wine by the glass
dinner Daily from 5pm
cards AE BC DC MC V   Bookings recommended
seats 300; private room; outdoor area;
wheelchair access; no smoking
owner John Szangolies
chef Paul McGrath
cost Around $108 for two, plus drinks
plus Generous spaces   **minus** Pricey wines
score 13/20

the regal

347–53 SUSSEX STREET, SYDNEY
PHONE 9261 8988   MAP 3A

CHINESE

Bright and, well, regal, the Regal is a welcoming sight at the city end of Chinatown. Marbled and mirrored, it's the quintessential Cantonese banquet palace. Even the menu reads well, with most of the things you could possibly want. But once again (what is it with Chinatown these days?) the resulting meal can be a disappointment. Crisp-skin chicken with secret sauce was served Peking duck style, in two courses, but the meat felt tired, and the pancakes lifeless. The second course of stir-fried chicken was tender, if a bit gluggy – so tender, in fact, we wondered if it was the same chicken. Prawn dumplings in special broth were homely, while an eight-treasure soup was interesting only after we asked for red vinegar. A glossy but vacuous red-cooked beancurd and mushroom dish finished a lacklustre meal. By day, the place comes alive for midday yum cha, which is great fun and as cheap as chips.

licensed
lunch Daily 10am–3pm
dinner Daily 5.30pm–midnight
cards AE BC DC MC V   Bookings recommended
seats 600; private room
owner Nedosu Pty Ltd
chef Pui So
cost Around $76 for two, plus drinks
plus The buzz at yum cha
minus No buzz at night
score 12/20

rengaya

73 MILLER STREET, NORTH SYDNEY
PHONE 9929 6169, 9929 6290   MAP 5A

JAPANESE

Rengaya's entrance would be hard to find if it weren't for all the neon. Tucked under a skyscraper, more off Blue Street than Miller Street, you'll find an exotic kimono display fighting it out with scrappy flyers. Inside, the food can be fantastic, if you order what all the tables of Japanese are eating, and grill your own meat. It's like an Aussie steakhouse, only more refined. The grills are submerged in the centre of each table, with built-in fans so you don't notice the smoke. Taste real marbled beef with the premium rib (cook it medium rare at least to melt the marbling). Try sashimi of beef heart and lobster, or grill the negi shio (tongue), dressed with green onion, and finish with an unlikely yet delectable spinach and soy salad, laced with tuna and flaked almonds. If you're one of those surviving Internet millionaires, go for the Japanese crab.

licensed
lunch Mon–Fri noon–2.30pm
dinner Daily 6–9.30pm
cards AE BC DC MC V   Bookings recommended
seats 100; private room; non-smoking area
owner Yoshiro Inoue
chef Kiyotaka Kono
cost Around $86 for two, plus drinks
plus High-grade beef   **minus** Low-grade menus
score 14/20

revielle

79 DARLING STREET, EAST BALMAIN
PHONE 9555 8874   MAP 5B

MODERN AUSTRALIAN

Gentrification and urban four-wheel drives
notwithstanding, Darling Street has never
made it as one of Sydney's major eat
streets. Revielle, however, bucks the Balmain
trend of pretension and predictability, and
does so without any vulgar fanfare. This is
a sandstone terrace quietly made over into
a restaurant, with large windows thrown
open to the streets on warm nights. Locals
arrive in large and noisy parties to enjoy the
simple confidence of Robert O'Callaghan's
food: a chargrilled New York steak, for
example, with a port wine jus and a potato
and marrow pie or (a relatively rare Asian
touch) pork fillet with an Asian marinade,
soy butter sauce and jasmine rice. The
dessert menu is rich in traditional delights
like crème brûlée and bread and butter
pudding. As is the way with popular local
eateries, the service is friendly but
informative, too, and efficient.

byo
dinner Tues–Sat from 7pm
cards AE BC MC V   Bookings recommended
seats 60; private room; wheelchair access;
no smoking until 10.30pm ⅹ
owners Robert & Jennifer O'Callaghan
chef Robert O'Callaghan
cost Around $92 for two, plus drinks
plus No hassles   **minus** No wine list
score 13/20

ristorante mario

38 YURONG STREET, EAST SYDNEY
PHONE 9331 4945   MAP 2

ITALIAN

Although Mario's is still the place for a
little media-mogul spotting and serious
air-kissing, the crowd isn't quite as star-
studded as it once was. And wouldn't that
be right – because the food is better than
it has been for some time. David and Katia
Cowdrill have abandoned the eccentric
carpaccio bar concept and replaced it with
a wood-fired pizza oven which is nowhere
near as gimmicky as it sounds. David
Cowdrill plays maestro at the hearth,
producing a suitably rustic, nicely crusty
pizza marinara (the real one – not seafood,
just tomato, garlic and oregano), and a
whole swag of pizze classiche and pizze
bianche (no tomato) made to the strict
specifications of the Associazione Vera Pizza
Napoletana. The antipasto selection is now
seriously good, and stand-bys such as whole
grilled fish never disappoint. And don't
worry if you can't see the legendary pasta
Mario on the menu. Ask and you will most
certainly receive.

licensed; wine by the glass
lunch Mon–Fri noon–3pm
dinner Mon–Sat 6–11pm
cards AE BC DC MC V   Bookings recommended
seats 148; non-smoking area ⅹ
owners David & Katia Cowdrill
chef Roberto Pezzotti
cost Around $95 for two, plus drinks
plus The pizza oven   **minus** Front tables
score 14/20

ristorante riva

379 LIVERPOOL STREET, DARLINGHURST
PHONE 9380 5318   MAP 2

ITALIAN

Where are the great mid-priced restaurants in Sydney that offer true hospitality and real food? Well, here is a model for them. For three years, Eugenio Riva and partner Beverley Wood have been attracting a loyal local crowd to this narrow, unpretentious restaurant in the heart of Darlinghurst. Eugenio's sophisticated interpretation of southern cucina casalinga gets murmurs of appreciation from every table. Swordfish carpaccio with fennel and rocket salad, herb and green olive dressing is brilliant; spiced pigeon on potatoes with Ligurian olives a rustic triumph; and a chocolate and amaretti custard with poached peaches is classically Italian in spirit. The wine list is small and thoughtful, with a smart blend of food-friendly Italian wines, and a couple of Australian wines that showcase Italian grape varieties, such as Primo Estate's 'Il Briccone' Shiraz Sangiovese. This restaurant is an absolute gem.

licensed; wine by the glass
lunch Fri 12.30–3pm
dinner Mon–Sat 6.30–10.30pm
cards AE BC MC V   Bookings recommended
seats 50; no smoking until 10.15pm ⌖
owners Eugenio Riva & Beverley Wood
chef Eugenio Riva
cost Around $92 for two, plus drinks
plus The service   **minus** The tiny space
score 15/20

riverview dining room

LEVEL 1, RIVERVIEW HOTEL,
29 BIRCHGROVE ROAD, BALMAIN
PHONE 9555 9889   MAP 5B

MODERN BRITISH

Let's hear it for local pubs like the Riverview. The gastronomically inclined can climb the wooden stairs to the restaurant, leaving behind the downstairs bar-room chat, music and noise, and be looked after with consummate skill and humour. Upstairs, the decor is light and bright, with original artwork and cartoons adorning the walls, and a menu that is pleasantly original. The food is Modern British with French influences, so the famous beef and Guinness pie has light flaky pastry, and a smoked river trout is in fact two discs of trout mousse, separated by a celeriac, caper and cucumber salad rich with mayonnaise. The cooking skills in a grilled quail entrée, perfectly balanced with a fig and blue cheese salad, are precise and assured. Save room for dessert and enjoy the incredibly well-priced wine list.

licensed; wine by the glass
lunch Fri noon–2.30pm; Sun (winter only) noon–2.30pm
dinner Tues–Sat 6.30–10pm
cards AE BC DC MC V   Bookings recommended, essential weekends
seats 65; private room; non-smoking area ⌖
owners Richard Moyser & Ian Moyser
chef Richard Moyser
cost Around $70 for two, plus drinks
plus Personality   **minus** Parking
score 14/20

rockpool

107 GEORGE STREET, THE ROCKS
PHONE 9252 1888   MAP 1

MODERN AUSTRALIAN

As the birthplace of modern Australian cooking, this still glamorous eleven-year-old is something of a sacred site to Sydney foodies. Last year, we felt that the strain of an ever-booming culinary empire was starting to show. However, by moving out of Bistro Mars, Café Fish, Star Bar & Grill and the various Wockpool noodle bars, Neil Perry can now concentrate on his core business. Consequently, Rockpool has begun to evolve once again, with Perry and chef Khan Danis playing tag in the kitchen. Newer dishes, including a sweet lobster salad with figs and duck confit, and a sweetbread tarte tatin reinvent the distinctive Rockpool edge, while the much-loved stir-fried blue swimmer crab omelette, and blue-eye cod in garam masala and coconut milk, win new admirers on a daily basis. Entrées and mains are starting to blur in prices and size – a little more definition would make ordering easier. The good-looking young staff have never been keener.

licensed; wine by the glass
lunch Mon–Fri noon–2.30pm
dinner Mon–Sat 6–11pm
cards AE BC DC MC V   Bookings essential
seats 120; private room; no smoking until 11pm ⚒✗
owners Neil Perry & Trish Richards
chef Khan Danis
cost Around $157 for two, plus drinks
plus Lower lunch prices   **minus** Meaty entrées
score 18/20

the rocks teppanyaki

176 CUMBERLAND STREET, THE ROCKS
PHONE 9250 6020   MAP 1

JAPANESE

If it weren't for the stainless steel grill plates and the generous bar, you'd think you'd strayed into a Rocks' cottage of decades ago. But The Rocks Teppenyaki is not just warm, muted colours and comfy sofas, it's a place for serious teppanyaki, with set menus designed to showcase four different cuts of high quality steak, pink belly of tuna and the freshest fillets of sea perch. You can indulge in generous serves of sashimi, sushi or just-battered tempura, or gorge on platters of big, creamy, Tasmanian oysters. Teppanyaki portions are enough for two if you can bring yourself to share the garlic rice, topped with crisp grill scrapings. But don't go expecting the usual egg-throwing, utensil-twirling teppan theatrics for tourists. Go for the clean, simple tastes of fresh food, grilled in front of you so you can see what you're eating. That way you won't end up with egg on your face.

licensed; wine by the glass
lunch Mon–Sat noon–2.30pm
dinner Mon–Sat 6–10.30pm
cards AE BC DC MC V   Bookings essential
seats 56; private room; non-smoking area ⚒✗
owner ANA Hotel Sydney
chef Manabu Nagasawa
cost Around $97 for two, plus drinks
plus Fish and seafood   **minus** Piped music
score 14/20

royal hotel restaurant

FIVEWAYS,
237 GLENMORE ROAD, PADDINGTON
PHONE 9331 5055   MAP 4B

MODERN AUSTRALIAN

Ensconced on the balcony of the Royal –
and if there's two of you, we highly
recommend it – you could be in the French
Quarter of New Orleans. In fact, you're in
the heart of the eastern suburbs with a sexy
snapshot of the Sydney skyline from some
prime seats. Situated above a rowdy pub,
the restaurant naturally attracts groups of
voracious and loquacious punters
demanding sustenance. The resultant
cacophony can be deafening but the food
is worth it. A starter of figs, goat's cheese,
mint and pine nuts demonstrates the
cooking has finesse, while mains, including
Barossa chicken with eggplant and zucchini,
and slow-cooked lamb on skordalia (since
when was garlic a dirty word?) far surpass
the notion of satisfying comfort food.
Surprise, surprise: pub food that actually
rocks. The only sad news is for sweet tooths:
desserts here are too easy to pass on.

licensed; wine by the glass
hours Mon–Sat noon–11pm; Sun noon–9pm
cards AE BC DC MC V Group   Bookings only
seats 100; outdoor area; private room;
no smoking ⊁
owner Ducester Pty Ltd
chef Keith O'Leary
cost Around $65 for two, plus drinks
plus Poetic balcony   **minus** BYO ear plugs
score 14/20

sailors thai

106 GEORGE STREET, THE ROCKS
PHONE 9251 2466   MAP 1

THAI

The waiters here aren't always full of
brightness and wellbeing, so it's just as
well the food is so full of life that it
positively beams. David Thompson, the
culinary demi-god who taught the modern
world the intricacies of royal Thai food, has
sold Darley Street Thai, his high altar, and
is spending much of his time cooking and
teaching overseas. Thankfully, the more
accessible sister restaurant is still happily
in place, serving less complex but equally
authentic dishes. There are no Thai clichés
here, just wondrous revelations of taste
and texture, such as crisp fish and sweet
pork salad or smoked pork sausage with
ginger and chilli. It's not food for the
faint-hearted, being full of fragrant lime,
forests of fresh herbs and a decent, though
not overt, amount of chilli. Forget every
suburban Thai takeaway you've ever had,
and prepare yourself for some hot, sour
and spicy revelations.

licensed; wine by the glass
lunch Mon–Fri noon–2pm
dinner Mon–Sat 6–10pm
cards AE BC DC MC V   Bookings essential
seats 85; outdoor area; smoking in bar area only
owners David Thompson, Maureen O'Keefe
& Peter Bowyer
chefs David Thompson & Max Mullins
cost Around $95 for two, plus drinks
plus Traditional Thai food
minus Traditional Australian service
score 16/20

sailors thai canteen

106 GEORGE STREET, THE ROCKS
PHONE 9251 2466   MAP 1

THAI

With its cool, dark interior, gleaming open kitchen and 50-seater stainless steel communal table running the length of the room, this is no ordinary canteen. The mood is gloriously modern and the crowd a mixed bag. Service is friendly and efficient, with menus and water supplied the minute you sit down, and orders taken a split second after you've made up your mind. From the aromas drifting over from the woks, it is obvious that this is no ordinary Thai food, either. A papaya and dried prawn salad is complex and feisty, and Chinese chive cakes are little delights. Also recommended are slippery pat Thai fried rice noodles, and perfectly textured beancurd with bean sprouts and yellow beans. Leave room for mango and sticky rice, or the egg custard cubes sprinkled with sweet crispy onion. It's a canteen that's not, with Thai food that's completely different. Come to think of it, we didn't see any sailors, either.

licensed; wine by the glass
hours Daily noon–8pm
cards AE BC DC MC V   No bookings
seats 55; private room; outdoor area; no smoking ⊱✕
owners David Thompson, Maureen O'Keefe & Peter Bowyer
chefs David Thompson & Pacharin Jantrakool
cost Around $65 for two, plus drinks
plus The tiny balcony   **minus** Early closing
score 14/20

sakana-ya

336 PACIFIC HIGHWAY, CROWS NEST
PHONE 9438 1468   MAP 5A

JAPANESE/SEAFOOD

This small, somewhat pokey Pac Highway restaurant is always full of Japanese enjoying fresh sashimi, sushi, tempura, fried seafood and a large range of home-style nabemono dishes, cooked at the table. The menu and staff explain the food clearly, making it easy for your run-of-the-mill gaijin to enjoy real Japanese tastes. The sashimi platters have a generous range and quantity of very thickly sliced fresh fish, while the deep-fries work particularly well. Every day, a large range of seafood, usually including squid, whitebait and swordfish, is cooked in a magically light and crisp coating. Flavours run from the full-on smoky, oily taste of the grilled eel to the pungent vinegary hit of the sunomono of pickled octopus. The only let-down was a lacklustre grilled beef, but it serves us right for ordering meat in a seafood restaurant.

licensed & byo; wine by the glass
lunch Mon–Fri noon–2.30pm
dinner Daily 6–10.30pm
cards AE BC DC MC V   Bookings recommended
seats 75; private room
owner Yasu Yasuoka
chef Nobuaki Matsuzawa
cost Around $76 for two, plus drinks
plus Accessible Japanese
minus All the glamour of a milkbar
score 14/20

salt

sam won garden

229 DARLINGHURST ROAD, DARLINGHURST
PHONE 9332 2566   MAP 2

62–4 BEAMISH STREET, CAMPSIE
PHONE 9718 6066   MAP 8

MODERN AUSTRALIAN

KOREAN

Slick, sleek and chic, this is without a doubt Sydney's sceniest restaurant. The crowd looks as if it's been sent by a casting agent and the mood is pure New York. As if that weren't enough, the food's pretty damn good, too. Over the past year, we've watched Luke Mangan's cooking get more together, more confident and more balanced, although we still love that starter of softly poached quail's egg coated in spiced salt. Marron tail with bouillabaisse sauce arrives in a salt-crusted pot; nicely pink squab breast is stuffed and gift-wrapped in crepinette; while the finishing touches to a lush risotto, in the form of freshly sliced truffle, are delivered at the table by Mangan himself. Throw in seamless, assured service under the unflappable Lucy Allon, and a wine list to die for, and you have a restaurant that would still be great even if it weren't so darned fashionable.

This is your basic square, barn-like Korean restaurant, complete with no-nonsense tables with paper covers. Along the side are two open-fronted, sit-on-the-floor, semi-private banquet rooms, usually occupied by no-nonsense, sit-on-the-floor Korean family groups. Lightning-fast service is obtained by pushing a button which plays a tune at the reception desk. But before you push that button we suggest you think before you order. Don't let the cheap prices fool you into thinking the servings are small. Even the kimchi and various side dishes that automatically accompany your meal make you think you've over-ordered. Bulgogi – thinly sliced beef (or pork) marinated in sesame oil, garlic, onions, soy sauce, sesame seeds and black pepper and then barbecued – is addictive. So, too, is the haemulpachon – a buckwheat pancake with spring onions and mixed seafood. Or just try any buckwheat noodle dish, and you can't go wrong.

licensed; wine by the glass
lunch Mon–Fri noon–3pm
dinner Daily 6–11pm
cards AE BC DC MC V   Bookings essential
seats 90; private room; wheelchair access; no smoking ✗
owners Luke Mangan & Lucy Allon
chef Luke Mangan
cost Around $120 for two, plus drinks, fixed price lunch from $40 p.p.
plus Smooth as silk
minus Narrow tables for two
score 17/20

licensed & byo
hours Daily 10am–10pm
cards BC MC V   Bookings recommended
seats 100; private room; wheelchair access
owner Sang Yoon Shim
chefs Don Lee & Yooneun Jong
cost Around $43 for two, plus drinks
plus Big servings   **minus** Authentic decor
score 12/20

⅌

san francisco grill

HILTON SYDNEY, 259 PITT STREET, SYDNEY
PHONE 9266 2000   MAP 1

INTERNATIONAL

Hotel fine diners are bit of a dying breed
these days, to the point where some of the
more modern hotels are going to great
pains to disassociate themselves from their
top-flight restaurants, giving them a totally
separate modern bistro personality, and
even a totally separate entrance. But the
San Francisco Grill is unashamedly a hotel
dining room, right down to its reassuringly
familiar menu, faithful retainer service and
pianist tinkling away at the ivories. The
huge slab of full-flavoured rib eye is carved
at the table, a lobster bisque is textbook in
style and substance, and tuna Rossini (yes,
with foie gras) is interesting, if not exciting.
But judging by the contented expressions,
there are enough visitors and well-heeled
business types who want to sit in chocolate
brown booths and have their Caesar salad
prepared at the table, go on to lobster
thermidor or racks of lamb, and are
prepared to pay for the experience.

licensed; wine by the glass
lunch Mon–Fri noon–2.30pm
dinner Mon–Sat from 6pm
cards AE BC DC MC V   Bookings essential
seats 120; private room; wheelchair access;
non-smoking area ⅍
owner Hilton Sydney
chefs Kurt Looser & Ludovic Poyer
cost Around $112 for two, plus drinks
plus Booths   **minus** Not getting a booth
score 13/20

$

scoozi trattoria

SHOP 9, WESTLEIGH SHOPPING CENTRE,
EUCALYPTUS DRIVE, WESTLEIGH
PHONE 9484 5165   MAP 6

ITALIAN/PIZZA

Five years on, Scoozi Trattoria is everything
a neighbourhood restaurant should be. Drop
in midweek for a quick pizza and BYO red,
or eat your way through the expanded menu
in a more leisurely fashion. Busy, buzzy and
noisy, it has an appealing warmth and
friendliness. The ever-popular wood-fired
pizzas continue to be loaded with chunky,
generous toppings like Italian sausage,
olive, artichoke, anchovy and capsicum
relish. Pasta offers similar value but it is
in the main menu that real flair can be
seen. Fish of the day may be swordfish,
deliciously moist and served with chargrilled
Mediterranean vegetables and roast
capsicum chutney while chargrilled sardines
remain a constant, served with parmesan
risotto and sun-dried tomato and olive
salsa. Special nights keep the regulars
coming back: risotto on Tuesdays, chowders
on Wednesdays and game on Thursdays.
Stay for the mango gelato and zingy citrus
sorbet layered with coconut meringue.

byo
dinner Tues–Sat from 6pm
cards BC MC V   Bookings essential
seats 80; outdoor area; wheelchair access;
non-smoking area ⅍
owners Robert & Deeanne Fonti
chef Deeanne Fonti
cost Around $58 for two, plus drinks
plus Wood-fired oven   **minus** Shopping centre
score 14/20

sealevel

2 THE KINGSWAY, CRONULLA
PHONE 9523 8888   MAP 8

SEAFOOD

At Sealevel, the waves are practically
wall-to-wall through the picture windows
of the circular split-level dining room.
The décor is textbook seaside restaurant,
complete with sky blue and sand yellow
walls, fish motifs and tables draped with
hanging ice buckets that cling like prawns
from a prawn cocktail glass. It's Baywatch
meets bedtime, as first-daters occupy
tables next to old fishing cronies with
weatherbeaten skin and all-weather
jokes. Sealevel is full of the kind of things
people like to order when they go out for
a seafood blow-out by the sea. That means
oysters three ways, fried calamari, Thai
seafood curry, fish and chips and huge
seafood and tropical fruit platters. Nothing
really excels, but everyone seems to go
home happy, and kids have their own
dishes. Overall, it's a fast, friendly and
familiar way to eat a lot of seafood.

licensed & byo; wine by the glass
lunch Daily noon–3pm
dinner Daily 5.30–10pm
cards AE BC DC MC V   Bookings essential
seats 200; outdoor area; wheelchair access;
non-smoking area
owners David & Claude Allouche
chef Rod Davison
cost Around $86 for two, plus drinks
plus Baywatch views   **minus** Awkward entrance
score 12/20

sean's panaroma

270 CAMPBELL PARADE, BONDI BEACH
PHONE 9365 4924   MAP 9

MODERN AUSTRALIAN

Simplicity and whimsy can be a winning
combination, especially when teamed with
a body-surfer view of Bondi Beach. Sean
Moran and his crew have gradually upped
the standards of what was once a quirky
seaside cafe to include damask napkins,
credit card facilities and a succinct, edgy
wine list (BYO still welcome). Moran's
passion for minimal chef intervention and
prime seasonal produce shines from the
swinging blackboard dish lists – whether
it's stuffed zucchini flowers, large warm
Kangaroo Island duck salad, pink organic
Barossa anise-infused pork, or a perfect
poached golden peach with a mammary
mound of vanilla ice-cream and thick
raspberry sauce. Portion sizes can err on
the generous, and presentation needs
more attention. Be sure to add freshly
baked rolls to your order, and BYO
cushions for long lunches, as those
kindy chairs are unforgiving.

licensed & byo; wine by the glass
lunch Sat–Sun noon–3.30pm
dinner Wed–Sat 6.30–9.30pm (daily in summer)
cards BC MC V   Bookings essential
seats 50; outdoor area; wheelchair access;
no smoking
owners Sean Moran & Michael Robertson
chefs Sean Moran & Lisa Rutherford
cost Around $108 for two, plus drinks
plus Blackboard wines   **minus** Kindy chairs
score 14/20

sea treasure

46 WILLOUGHBY ROAD, CROWS NEST
PHONE 9906 6388   MAP 5A

CHINESE

And what a treasure it is! Sparkling new
seafood tanks line the shopfront window
of Sea Treasure, where Cantonese dishes
are a speciality and the décor is mediocre.
Service is brisk but friendly and your waiter
will give you the market price for the parrot
fish, abalone, morwong and lobster cruising
in the tanks and then present them for your
inspection. Perfectly cooked Queensland
mud crab with chilli sauce and e-fu noodles
is a delicious signature dish and steamed
scallops in their shells with ginger, garlic
and shallots are presented in a delicate
sauce on a large platter. For a party of eight
to ten, the giant Tasmanian king crab is
spectacular, prepared in a choice of cooking
styles, including black bean, spiced salt and
pepper or garlic and butter sauce. Beef, pork
and chicken dishes are also available but
most patrons come here for the seafood.
The daily yum cha can be even more hectic
than Chinatown on a Sunday.

licensed & byo
lunch Mon–Fri 11am–3pm; Sat–Sun 10am–3pm
dinner Daily 6–11pm
cards AE BC DC MC V   Bookings recommended
seats 140; private room
owner Sea Treasure Pty Ltd
chef Hong Goang Liang
cost Around $80 for two, plus drinks
plus Super fresh seafood   **minus** Market prices
score 14/20

seri nonya

561 THE KINGSWAY, MIRANDA
PHONE 9525 0036   MAP 8

MALAYSIAN/SINGAPOREAN

Nonya may be the world's original fusion
cuisine. When Chinese men migrated to the
Malaysian Peninsula and married the locals,
their cooking combined Southern Chinese
dishes with the spicy tastes of the Malays.
While this pleasant, buzzy shopfront
restaurant offers laksa – the best known
Nonya dish – in four varieties (prawn,
chicken, seafood and vegetarian), it lacks
the rich, complex layers of flavour that
make the dish special. Far more successful
are the spicy but flavoursome prawns
cooked in tumis sauce, and 'top hats' –
deep-fried open spring-roll-like wrappers
stuffed with minced vegetables and belacan
(shrimp paste). Seri Nonya has weekend
specials that work around a four-week cycle,
so it's best to check if you're yearning for
nasi lemak, Hainanese chicken rice, mee
rebus or the famous Malaysian breakfast
treat bak kut teh. Nonyas can't live without
their kueh teow noodles, and fortunately
they are always on.

byo
lunch Wed–Thurs 12.30–2.30pm; Fri–Sun
11.30am–2.30pm
dinner Tues–Sun 5.30–10pm
cards AE BC DC MC V   Bookings essential
seats 55
owners Alvin Tan & Jessica Tan
chef Alvin Tan
cost Around $65 for two, plus drinks
plus Nonya favourites   **minus** Dumbing down
score 13/20

shiki

CLOCKTOWER SQUARE, CNR ARGYLE &
HARRINGTON STREETS, THE ROCKS
PHONE 9252 2431   MAP 1

JAPANESE

Love the stepping stones marking the
transition from commercial shopping plaza
to a calm, wood-panelled oasis. Love the
cheerful greeting from the sushi chefs, the
gentle, eager service, the big clothed tables
and the curious, central rockpool complete
with swimming goldfish. Love the separate
sakana menu of little dishes designed to
accompany some serious sake-drinking,
including steamed green soybeans, pickled
baby squid and chargrilled oysters. Love the
perfectly grilled wafu steak, the tempura
prawn handroll and the curious dish of
rice, chicken and mushrooms all steamed
together in a little cooker at the table.
So what's not to love? Service can be slow,
prices are high, servings are small and
they can run out of the very thing you
want to order. In one night, we were told
one wine, one spirit, two sakana dishes
and two fish dishes were unavailable.
Don't you just hate that?

licensed; wine by the glass
lunch Mon–Fri noon–2.30pm
dinner Daily 6–10pm
cards AE BC DC MC V   Bookings recommended
seats 100; private room; outdoor area;
wheelchair access; non-smoking area ⅹ
owner Tatsuya Watanabe
chef Hikaru Tomita
cost Around $108 for two, plus drinks
plus Sake-friendly snacks   **minus** 'Sorry, run out'
score 13/20

shimbashi soba

SHOP 4, 24 YOUNG STREET, NEUTRAL BAY
PHONE 9908 3820   MAP 5A

JAPANESE

If Sydney had such things as living
treasures, then we nominate Yoshi
Shibazaki. Officially recognised by the
Japanese government as a master of soba
(buckwheat) noodles, he is as much a
master craftsman as he is a master cook.
It is a pleasure to watch this wiry, dedicated
man beavering away in his little glassed-in
workroom, turning shapeless globs of flour
and water into immaculate, hand-cut
noodles. The restaurant is a large, rambling
space with stairs running here and there
like Escher drawings, amid two blurs of
activity. One is the open kitchen, and the
other is at the tables of Japanese students,
smart-suited businessmen and shopping
dollies as they natter over bowls of delicious
noodles. Noodle purists will inevitably go
for the cold soba noodles with hot duck
broth, but we have a soft spot for the thick
white udon noodles, especially in winter,
served nabeyaki style with chicken and
egg in a bubbling hotpot.

licensed & byo
lunch Tues–Sat noon–2.30pm
dinner Tues–Sat 6–9pm
cards AE BC DC MC V   Bookings recommended
seats 100; non-smoking area ⅹ
owner Yoshi Shibazaki
chefs Hiromi Iino & Yoshi Shibazaki
cost Around $54 for two, plus drinks
plus The noodles   **minus** Slow when busy
score 14/20

bars

aqua luna bar Sit out and count the ferries, or in, with a nectar crush or a frosty ale if you're too cool for harbour views. NO. 2, SHOP 18, OPERA QUAYS, EAST CIRCULAR QUAY 9251 0311

wine banc With its underground chic and clubby comfort, this is a bar scene for grown-ups, complete with terrific Frenchesque food and edgy live jazz. 53 MARTIN PLACE, SYDNEY 9233 5399

chicane Design-wise, it's eclectic – concrete bar, library shelves, comfy armchairs – but cocktail-scene-wise, it's electric. 1A BURTON STREET, DARLINGHURST 9380 2121

mint Loud, lean and just that little bit grrrooovy-baby, especially after a Wrong Wong (Suzy with currant vodka). 53 MARTIN PLACE, SYDNEY 9233 5388

international The city skyline is pure Manhattan, the booths are the hottest and the drinks the coolest. LEVEL 14, 227 VICTORIA STREET, KINGS CROSS 9360 9080

fix It's like being locked in a glossy, red-lacquered sushi box – cosy, smart and full of spicy people with vanilla martinis. THE KIRKETON, 229 DARLINGHURST ROAD, DARLINGHURST 9332 2566

grand pacific blue room GPBR still rocks, fuelled by Jackie Chans (citron vodka, apple schnapps), complete with apple chopsticks. CNR OXFORD & SOUTH DOWLING STREETS, PADDINGTON 9331 7108

lobby bar Martini-by-the-sea, shaken only by the gentle lap of water and stirred by the harbour breeze. PIER ONE PARKROYAL, 11 HICKSON ROAD, WALSH BAY 8298 9999

longrain Lounge like a lizard with unsocked urbanites scoffing Thai betel leaves and Moscow Mules. 85 COMMONWEALTH STREET, SURRY HILLS 9280 2888

joe diamond's A quirky, moody, romantic, bar-cum-dining-room where you can lounge around in style. It makes a nice change from Sydney's slick, sleek, glass-and-metal brigade. 16 WENTWORTH AVENUE, DARLINGHURST 9283 8993

spicy people and

vanilla martinis

shimbashi soba on the sea

6 THE WHARF WOOLLOOMOOLOO,
6 COWPER WHARF ROAD, WOOLLOOMOOLOO
PHONE 9357 7763   MAP 2

JAPANESE

Even in Japan, noodle bars are generally low-key, casual neighbourhood affairs. Rarely do they manage to be as good-looking as this new venture of soba-noodle master Yoshi Shibazaki. Even the glass-walled workroom where you can watch Yoshi-san making his wonderful noodles from scratch has moved up a notch with its high-tech equipment and slick water views. The upstairs/downstairs dining space sports olive banquettes and shiny stainless steel tables, while more tables cluster around market umbrellas outside on the promenade of the old finger wharf. It all looks slicker than it really is, and you may need to exercise patience with the service. Shimbashi is all about noodles – wonderful, big, fat, white udon and dusky, skinny buckwheat soba served hot, cold, in broth or out of it, as part of a set course meal, or as the star attraction.

licensed & byo
hours Daily noon–10pm
cards AE BC DC MC V   Bookings essential
seats 135; outdoor area; wheelchair access; no smoking ⚥
owner Keiko Shibazaki
chefs Kazushi Ishida & Yoshi Shibazaki
cost Around $65 for two, plus drinks
plus The noodles   **minus** The service
score 14/20

silver spring

477 PITT STREET (CNR HAY STREET), HAYMARKET
PHONE 9211 2232   MAP 3A

CHINESE

There's something irresistible about the lunchtime yum cha at this barn of a city restaurant. The boisterous chatter and clatter, the wagon trains of dim sum trolleys, the plump har gau prawn dumplings, the warming wintry rice congees and the glistening roast meats make it one of Sydney's great lunchtime joys. At night, however, the crowds thin, and the mood mellows somewhat as large family groups and couples sit down to serious banquet dishes such as Peking duck served with full ceremony, and whole mud crab with shredded dried chilli. There are more homely, hearty dishes, too, such as the sautéed chicken in hotpot, braised black mushroom with broccoli, and stir-fried king prawns with XO sauce. It can be difficult prising the real down-home Chinese favourites out of the waiters, so be prepared to point to the next table and ask to have what they're having.

licensed
lunch Daily 10am–3pm
dinner Daily 5.30–11pm
cards AE DC MC V JCB   Bookings essential
seats 550; private room; wheelchair access; non-smoking area ⚥
owner Donald Tong
chef Cheung Kong
cost Around $80 for two, plus drinks
plus Yum cha   **minus** Off-hand service
score 13/20

slip inn

111 SUSSEX STREET, SYDNEY
PHONE 9299 4777   MAP 1

MODERN ITALIAN

Many who come here do so merely to gossip and giggle. But if food is your focus, slip through the barflys and down the back staircase. Simple bistro chairs and warm terracotta tiles are reminiscent of your favourite Italian osteria, and the food is just as enjoyable. Former sous chef Tania Tauakume has taken over from Adrian Way, but is well versed in the Slip Inn's easy, modern Italian style. In the past, we've enjoyed a rosemary linguine with scallops and anchovies, and a blue swimmer crab salad with avocado; both skilfully put together and delish to eat. A rotolo of fresh pasta wound around pumpkin and mascarpone on brown sage butter was at once sweet, creamy and slippery. The only miss was a rubbery sweet potato mash that accompanied an otherwise good duck confit. Drum beats from the courtyard verge on being too loud, and it can be hard to catch a waiter's eye, but it's great to enjoy good food with a little bit of soul.

licensed; wine by the glass
lunch Mon–Fri noon–3pm
dinner Tues–Fri 6–10pm
cards AE BC DC MC V   Bookings recommended
seats 200; private room; outdoor area; wheelchair access; non-smoking area ⚥
owner Justin Hemmes
chef Tania Tauakume
cost Around $86 for two, plus drinks
plus Live music outside   **minus** Hello, waiter?
score 14/20

sorriso

LEVEL 1, 70 NORTON STREET, LEICHHARDT
PHONE 9572 9915   MAP 5B

ITALIAN

Leichhardt wasn't ready for something as adventurous as Mod Oz meets Portuguese Macau cuisine at this site. So is it ready for an eastern suburbs take on Italian food as interpreted by the highly professional team from Lucio's? Certainly, the cooking under the young and gifted executive chef Timothy Fisher is a world away from the tomato-sauced pasta and fluffy focaccia of Leichhardt tradition. The meticulously crafted, pared down food runs from delicate linguine with cuttlefish and mussels to a simple grilled, boned spatchcock smeared with mustard and served with nothing but a couple of lime segments for squeezing. We particularly like the honest, earthy flavours of rigatoni pasta with Italian sausage and a creamy pudding of arborio rice and quince. Sorriso, by the way, means smile in Italian, which is exactly what this bright, modern, inside/outside first-floor eatery has brought to Norton Street.

licensed
hours noon–11pm Mon-Sat
cards AE BC MC V   Bookings recommended
seats 80; outdoor area; wheelchair access; no smoking inside ⚥
owners Lucio Galletto, Timothy Fisher & David Conceicao
chefs Timothy Fisher & Dorothy Creenaune
cost Around $76 for two, plus drinks
plus Al dente pasta   **minus** Traffic noise
score 14/20

sosumi sushi bar

LOWER GROUND FLOOR, GPO,
NO. 1 MARTIN PLACE, SYDNEY
PHONE 9229 7788   MAP 1

JAPANESE

Conveyor-belt sushi is a gimmick. So are
automatic sushi robot machines and
counters fitted with filtered water taps and
personal pots of wasabi and pickled ginger.
But the thing about gimmicks is they're fun,
especially at the GPO, where 45 silver stools
pull up to a flash little sushi bar in the GPO
gastrobasement. It's not often you see a
French-born sushi chef of Senegalese
descent who can turn out a perfectly formed
lobster and avocado handroll without
blinking, yet Moussa Ndiaye (ex-Yo Sushi!
in London) is as fresh as the sushi rolling
out in front of him. Check out the plates
as they tootle by and pick up what you
want. Black plates are the priciest, going
down through grey and blue to white, the
cheapest. The Japanese eel lacks the
lushness and stickiness of great unagi,
but most of the sushi works well enough,
especially the hand-made, inside-out
Californian roll with salmon, avocado
and flying fish roe.

licensed
lunch Mon–Sat 11.30am–3pm
dinner Mon–Fri 5.30–8.30pm
cards AE BC DC MC V   No bookings
seats 45; wheelchair access; no smoking ⌇✖
owners Stan Sarris & Rodney Adler
chef Moussa Ndiaye
cost Around $50 for two, plus drinks
plus Personal water taps   **minus** Eel sushi
score 13/20

starfish

FOX STUDIOS, MOORE PARK
PHONE 9360 0097   MAP 4B

MODERN AUSTRALIAN

There's no shortage of showbiz glamour at
this upmarket Fox Studios dining venue.
Walk up a cool, white minimalist stairway to
emerge in La-La land with red, yellow and
green spotlights waving overhead, futuristic
grandstand views and cushy brown
banquettes, even on the covered front
terrace. David Bitton, ex-Gekko at the
Sheraton on the Park, produces suitably
glamorous food, although there is a
tendency to do more than is necessary.
A tartare of lobster, lentils and green shallot
dressing had a nice presence but felt
chopped-up and bitsy, while a sticky sweet
jus and a Mediterranean mélange of
eggplant, tomato and goat's cheese clashed
like prima donnas with perfectly trimmed
and cooked lamb cutlets. Highlight was a
crisp-skinned barramundi fillet, but we
would have gladly swapped the whoopee
cushions of potato and truffle ravioli for a
sympathetic sauce. On the upper level you
can cocktail it at the Starfish bar.

licensed; wine by the glass
lunch Wed–Sun noon–3pm
dinner Daily 6–10.30pm
cards AE BC DC MC V   Bookings recommended
seats 110; private room; outdoor area;
wheelchair access; non-smoking area ⌇✖
owners Ranko Despot & Joe Matic
chef David Bitton
cost Around $92 for two, plus drinks
plus Theatrical lighting   **minus** The views
score 13/20

summerland

LEVEL 1, 741 PUNCHBOWL ROAD,
PUNCHBOWL
PHONE 9708 5107   MAP 6

LEBANESE

Do not go hungry to Summerland – go
starving. There is no menu, just food, and
lots of it. This is a different style of dining –
you don't so much eat as graze over a good
couple of hours, with friends and family
coming and going. The onslaught arrives
within minutes of sitting down: hummus,
labne (homemade yoghurt), baba ghannouj,
fresh oregano salad, shanklish (aged
yoghurt), pickled vegetables, olives, fattoush
salad and tabbouli, all with lashings of olive
oil and mountains of bread to scoop up the
offerings – and that's just for starters. If a
very ordinary seafood platter arrives, then
pace yourself for the sausages, or the lamb
and chicken kebabs that come with a
moreish garlic paste (toum). Choose from
six different types of arak, sold by the bottle
in true Arabic form, or pay for the hookah
pipe if you can handle it. The kitchen could
do with a little more polish, but you still get
a great taste of Middle Eastern culture.

licensed & byo
lunch Tues–Fri noon–3pm
dinner Mon–Wed 6.30–10.30pm;
Thurs–Fri 6.30pm–midnight
cards AE BC MC V   Bookings recommended,
essential weekends
seats 95
owners/chefs Ali & Fouad Sayed
cost Around $54 for two, plus drinks
plus The banquets   **minus** Grungy entrance
score 13/20

summit

LEVEL 47, AUSTRALIA SQUARE,
264 GEORGE STREET, SYDNEY
PHONE 9247 9777   MAP 1

MODERN AUSTRALIAN

Not even the awesome views and
glamorous fit-out at our most famous
revolving restaurant can save what is
essentially an expensive throwback to
the 1970s dining experience. Everything
from the décor to the menu is oh-so-
groovy-retro but we would like to see just
a little more attention to detail. Service,
while well-meaning, can fall disastrously
short. Smoked salmon mousse arrived
without its promised Melba toast and a
flavoursome corn chowder with scallops
came without a spoon, and we were left for
almost 10 minutes before help arrived. The
just-okay duck with cherries was almost
finished before our pinot noir landed, and
veal wrapped in bacon and tapenade was
let down by disappointing gnocchi. In spite
of the glitches, however, we'd still go for
the martinis, for the view and for the
sheer glamour of it all.

licensed; wine by the glass
lunch Sun–Fri noon–3pm
dinner Daily 6–10.30pm
cards AE BC DC MC V   Bookings essential
seats 240; wheelchair access; no smoking until
10pm ♿✖
owner ACCOR
chef Jess Ong
cost Around $108 for two, plus drinks
plus Glamorous red carpet
minus Vanishing service
score 13/20

szechuan garden

1/56–62 CHANDOS STREET, ST LEONARDS
PHONE 9438 2568   MAP 5A

CHINESE

It's a humble-looking place in an odd location, at the St Leonards end of Chandos Street, but the Garden is well worth a look if you find yourself in the neighbourhood. The menu explains China's five regional cuisines, but the chow on offer is mainly Sichuan and Hunan. Even with that knowledge, it's best to ask your waiter for tips. Juicy fried beef dumplings arrive at the table still sizzling, while the hot and sour soup turns up the heat. Try one of the Hunan dishes with magical names such as 'Ringing Bell' (shreds of pork lightly fried in tofu) or 'Dragon Bean Fish'. And you simply must have the house speciality of Hunan-style braised pork ribs, which have been marinated in soy and cooked slowly – a melt-in-the-mouth experience. Szechuan Garden is licensed and BYO, but with a limited list, so it's best to bring your own crisp, dry white.

licensed & byo
lunch Mon–Fri noon–3pm
dinner Sun–Thurs 6–10pm; Fri–Sat 6–10.30pm
cards AE BC DC MC V   Bookings essential
seats 66; private room; non-smoking area
owner/chef Mark Deng
cost Around $43 for two, plus drinks
plus The ribs   **minus** The ceiling
score 13/20

table 48 on albion

48 ALBION STREET, SURRY HILLS
PHONE 9281 8315   MAP 3A

MODERN AUSTRALIAN

Though you can see the sponged green-and-camel coloured padded walls, open kitchen, and metal-backed chairs through the windows, there's little that lets you know how nice the food is on the inside. Even the clientele don't always look that discerning, garnered as they are from the fabulously enigmatic Surry Hills. Yet the plates they're tucking into are solidly and honestly put together, the service is attentive, and the space is pleasant if not exactly glamorous. Chef Andreas Shaldin rarely puts a foot wrong. Homemade pumpkin tortellini are gently sweet pillows in a light gorgonzola sauce. Slow-roasted duck comes on a very good risotto with meaty Swiss brown mushrooms, while a stunningly simple poached peach is graced with honey mascarpone, and a lush praline ice-cream comes wrapped in crêpes with a warm fudge sauce.

licensed & byo; wine by the glass
lunch Mon–Fri noon–2.30pm
dinner Mon–Sat 6–10pm
cards AE BC DC MC V   Bookings recommended, essential weekends
seats 65; wheelchair access
owners Tony & Jasmin Mano
chef Andreas Shaldin
cost Around $92 for two, plus drinks
plus Close to town   **minus** Deep-fried leek strips
score 13/20

tables

1047 PACIFIC HIGHWAY, PYMBLE
PHONE 9983 1047   MAP 7

MODERN AUSTRALIAN

This is one of the liveliest and most likeable of the North Shore brasseries. Floor staff are young, enthusiastic and well-trained, while the kitchen shows a commitment to seasonality and quality Australian produce. A foie gras custard is certainly a sight for sore eyes on a suburban menu and very good it is too, rich yet not heavy. Boned quail filled with pork sausage wrapped in puff pastry is a surprisingly delicate dish of pure flavours and alluring aromas, while wild barramundi on Chinese greens, roasted tomatoes, sweet soy and chilli is distinguished by some of the best and freshest fish we've eaten in recent times. Also worthy of mention is a well-rested baby guinea fowl on sautéed cabbage and bacon with verjus and fried sage leaves, which is rustic and honest. You can easily come over all Proustian after the delicious raspberry madeleines with honey-glazed figs.

licensed & byo; wine by the glass
lunch Mon–Fri noon–3pm
dinner Mon–Sat 6–11pm
cards AE BC DC MC V   Bookings recommended
seats 98; private room; no smoking until 10.30pm ⅀⅄
owners Dan Brukarz & Kim de Laive
chef Kim de Laive
cost Around $108 for two, plus drinks (fixed price between 7 & 9pm)
plus Feel the quality   **minus** Weekend parking
score 14/20

tabou

527 CROWN STREET, SURRY HILLS
PHONE 9319 5682   MAP 3B

FRENCH

There should be a by-law making it mandatory for every Sydney suburb to possess a French bistro like Tabou. Everything about the shopfront space is perfectly Gallic, from the lace half-curtains in the window to the specials announced in curly white writing on the wall mirrors. The main downstairs room is as cosy as a bowl of cassoulet, while the cheery 'bon soir' greeting from waiters in long white aprons continues the pleasant illusion. Francophiles and the plain hungry will love the homemade boudin noir, the correctly presented steak frites, the yielding slices of sautéed calves liver with lemony spinach, and a tomato and basil tart on air-light flaky pastry that could have been freshly made in Provence and sent over by Star Trek transporter. Just one thing: what is filo pastry doing with the confit duck? Desserts can pose a difficult problem, as in, what don't you order – the millefeuille, pear clafoutis or crème brûlée?

licensed & byo; wine by the glass
lunch Mon–Fri noon–3pm
dinner Daily 6–10.30pm
supper Daily 10.30pm–1am
cards AE BC DC MC V   Bookings essential
seats 80; non-smoking area ⅀⅄
owner Elie Griplas
chef Helen Ward
cost Around $108 for two, plus drinks
plus The steak frites   **minus** Hard to get tables
score 14/20

$

taqsim

210 OXFORD STREET, PADDINGTON
PHONE 9361 6001   MAP 2

NORTH AFRICAN/EGYPTIAN

Dishes such as couscous, ful medames and shorba chickpea, and tomato and saffron soup are associated more with the Middle East than Sydney's inner east. However, thanks to the enterprising efforts of Egyptian-born owner Habib Massad and chef Ash Pedro Damargi, who trained in Tunisia, some authentic and delightful Egyptian and North African cooking can now be found in deepest, darkest Oxford Street. What was once a typical Paddo terrace looks like a set from the Desert Song with its Egyptian artefacts and walls emblazoned with the opening passage from *A Thousand and One Nights*. Photographs of Cairo by Reece Scannell provide an authentic taste of Egypt, as does a meal of bungar – a divine beetroot and yoghurt dip – smoky baba ghannouj, Kamounia lamb curry and a whole baked peach stuffed with ground lamb, pine nuts and mint served with hummus and pomegranate. The plates work best when simply presented.

byo
dinner Mon–Sat 6pm till late
cards AE BC DC MC V   Bookings recommended
seats 115; private room; outdoor area; no smoking ✣✖
owner Habib Massad
chef Ash Pedro Damargi
cost Around $60 for two, plus drinks
plus The beetroot dip   **minus** Can be slow
score 12/20

tasso osteria

348 VICTORIA STREET, DARLINGHURST
PHONE 9331 1708   MAP 2

ITALIAN

Your favourite local osteria (the Italian equivalent of, but not really like, a French bistro) would, of course, use good ingredients in a simple but likeable manner. So that's what Tasso is. Darlinghursters can enjoy honest if not exactly sensational food such as grilled figs with taleggio and rocket salad, or maltagliati (roughly cut homemade pasta) with roast duck and porcini, and feel as if they're in the back blocks of Perugia. Even the tiramisu has that Italian feel, piled in an ugly heap on the plate, but tasting of everything it should, despite being a tad dry. Inside the restaurant is a smallish, loud space, so those in the know head for the covered back courtyard, where white linen graces the tables. The service is attentive, though more restrained than most Sydney restaurants, and the prices are low enough to forgive the occasional fault in the food. It's not a big night out, but then, you wouldn't go to an osteria for a big night out.

licensed & byo; wine by the glass
lunch Tues–Fri noon–5pm
dinner Mon–Sat 6–10.30pm
cards AE BC DC MC V   Bookings recommended
seats 60; outdoor area; non-smoking area ✣✖
owners Attilio & Penelope Gissi
chef Attilio Gissi
cost Around $70 for two, plus drinks
plus The prices   **minus** Outside chairs
score 11/20

temasek

THE ROXY ARCADE,
71 GEORGE STREET, PARRAMATTA
PHONE 9633 9926   MAP 6

MALAYSIAN

Every chef in Sydney cooking laksa should
be made to try the Temasek version. It's the
real McCoy, with rich multiple layers of
flavours and textures, not just stark heat.
Another remarkable dish is the beef
rendang, the meat simmered for hours until
it is meltingly tender yet full of flavour. The
humble Hainanese chicken rice is as good
here as any back alley joint in Malacca or
food centre in Singapore, with juicy white
chicken served with rice cooked in a rich
stock. If you want more unusual fare, like
otak-otak fishcakes or bak kut teh (herbal
pork stew), plan your visit for the weekend,
when an expanded menu featuring more
hawker favourites is in operation. Temasek
has all the comfort of a country bus depot,
and the food is served without ceremony on
plastic tablecloths resembling the Singapore
Girl's uniform – but any Singapore girl
would love this food.

byo
lunch Tues–Sun 11.30am–2.30pm
dinner Tues–Sun 5.30–10pm
cards AE BC DC MC V   Bookings recommended,
essential weekends
seats 120; wheelchair access; no smoking until
2.15 & 10pm
owners Susan & Mei Ling Wong
chef Susan Wong
cost Around $54 for two, plus drinks
plus Great laksa   **minus** The loo
score 14/20

tetsuya's

729 DARLING STREET, ROZELLE
PHONE 9555 1017   MAP 5B

JAPANESE/FRENCH

If we didn't know what a global success
Tetsuya's restaurant is, we'd find something
downright perverse in the edgy game he
plays. The service is good, the plain interior
perfectly pleasant, but nobody here does
any of the plush things that posh
restaurants usually do to convince you that
you're having a special time. Instead,
everything points to what's on your plate,
which is likely to be something quite small,
amounting perhaps to scarcely more than a
single mouthful: here, truffle giving just the
right edge to cold pasta; there, Kervella
goat's cheese perfectly matched with a slice
of fig. Even Tetsuya's celebrated signature
dish of slow-roasted ocean trout with a salt
and seaweed crust is modest in size but
perfect in flavour. The skill is extraordinary,
but this is dangerous cooking, without
disguise, without fall-back positions. It
could so very easily not come off. But it
always does. See page *xi* for news of
Tetsuya's move to the city.

licensed & byo; wine by the glass
lunch Tues–Sat from noon
dinner Mon–Fri from 7pm
cards AE BC DC MC V   Bookings essential
seats 55; wheelchair access; no smoking
owner/chef Tetsuya Wakuda
fixed price $143 p.p. for dinner; $93.50 p.p.
for lunch, plus drinks
plus Wine by the glass   **minus** The loos and
their signage
score 18/20

thanh binh

52A JOHN STREET, CABRAMATTA
PHONE 9727 9729   MAP 6
ALSO AT 111 KING STREET, NEWTOWN
PHONE 9557 1175   MAP 8

VIETNAMESE

The menu at this little shopfront restaurant reads like an encyclopaedia of Vietnamese cuisine – pho, common soups, salads, stews, rice noodles, rice cakes and a number of special dishes. There's such an enormous choice, it's hard to think of anything they might have left out. Thanh Binh's success can be seen in the lines of enthusiastic locals that gather outside on weekends, waiting for an elusive table. The rice-paper rolls stuffed with pork are full of supercharged flavours, nothing like the insipid versions found in city restaurants, while a 'special' dish of campfire chicken is a pyromaniac's dream of chicken fillets placed on a plate of flaming spirits (mind you don't burn your chopsticks). Some of the more Chinese offerings are less successful, with bland flavours and thickened sauces. Stick to the Vietnamese dishes, as the locals do, and all will be well.

byo
hours Daily 9am–9pm
cards AE BC MC V   Bookings recommended
seats 70
owner Angie Hong
chefs Be Le & Angie Hong
cost Around $43 for two, plus drinks
plus Anything from Vietnam
minus Anything from China
score 12/20

thomas street cafe

2 THOMAS STREET, McMAHONS POINT
PHONE 9955 4703   MAP 5A

MODERN AUSTRALIAN

Lucky McMahons Point locals have this comfortable, family-minded corner café for breakfast and lunch most days. Weekends are naturally the busiest time. Take a table in the leafy courtyard with the morning papers, poached eggs with baked beans on the side, and a zingy fruit frappe, or come for a lazy lunch with a bottle of wine from the local pub. The tiny kitchen knows its limitations but there's a commitment to quality that takes it out of the Sydney café mainstream. Flavours were clean and fresh in a spicy gazpacho with toasted olive bread while beef medallions with hollandaise, asparagus and kipflers was a thoroughly good feed. However, a dish of scallops and coriander ravioli erred on the heavy side with its sweet soy sauce. Desserts consist of the usual cakey things, but when done well, there is nothing wrong with the usual cakey things.

byo
hours Tues–Sun 8am–4pm
cards AE BC DC MC V   Bookings recommended, essential weekends
seats 60; outdoor area; no smoking inside
owner/chef Gregory Higgs
cost Around $65 for two, plus drinks
plus The courtyard   **minus** The trek to the toilet
score 13/20

391 restaurant

391 ANZAC PARADE, KINGSFORD
PHONE 9313 7663   MAP 9

MODERN AUSTRALIAN/FRENCH

Once a modest corner eatery with an interesting take on Modern Australian food, 391 has hypertrophied over the years into a huge space dominating its corner of Anzac Parade with a Vegas-proportioned neon sign. Even the food comes in generous proportions. Sadly, though, size isn't everything: a little less heartiness and a little more care would be very welcome. There is a tendency to overcook some things, while others come to the table totally outgunned by the sauce with which they're served. 'Old-fashioned mustard sauce', for example, turned out to be a good deal more interesting that the orange mound of pork fillet, roast pumpkin and sweet capsicum which floated in it. The service, though, is friendly and prompt, and not only can you bring your own grog, but if you bring your own birthday cake, they'll serve it for you with ice-cream and crème Anglaise for a small cakeage fee.

licensed & byo; wine by the glass
lunch Mon–Fri noon–2.30pm
dinner Daily 6–10pm
cards AE BC DC MC V   Bookings essential weekends
seats 120; private room; outdoor area; non-smoking area ⊁✗
owner/chef Gerard Kaiser
cost Around $108 for two, plus drinks
plus Hearty serves   **minus** Big groups
score 12/20

tre scalini

174 LIVERPOOL STREET, EAST SYDNEY
PHONE 9331 4358   MAP 2

ITALIAN

On a quiet night, Tre Scalini scarcely seems like a restaurant at all. You sit at a table covered in crisp white linen, very efficient people bring you food, you pay them money, but there's little sense of location, little sense of shared experience, little to remind you of why you've come here rather than somewhere else for your pollo alla Marengo or your vitello alla melanzana. There's no reason why the menu at an Italian restaurant should be a kaleidoscope of novelties, but after years of success at the top end of town, Tre Scalini seems to have lost a bit of pizzazz. Still, everything is professionally done and it's always a pleasure to eat in a restaurant where they understand that the Mediterranean diet doesn't just mean pine nuts and al dente veg, but also runs to penne with bacon, cream and brandy.

licensed; wine by the glass
lunch Mon–Fri noon–3pm
dinner Daily 6–10.30pm
cards AE BC DC MC V   Bookings recommended
seats 65; private room; wheelchair access
owners Antonio & Kylie Cossa
chefs Joe Maccora & Mark Carter
cost Around $86 for two, plus drinks
plus No danger   **minus** No thrills
score 12/20

tsukasa 1

200 CROWN STREET, EAST SYDNEY
PHONE 9361 3818   MAP 2
ALSO AT TSUKASA 2,
75 MILITARY ROAD, NEUTRAL BAY
PHONE 9953 7317   MAP 5A

JAPANESE

Well, there was this little Japanese restaurant in Crown Street, just down from Oxford Street, called Yutaka – been there for years – then it was so popular, it spawned Yutaka 2 up the road. Now it's Tsukasa, but it's the same owner and same chef and it's still really popular. Chairs are black and ugly and tables are covered with green plakky, so it's not a first-date restaurant, but somewhere to go with friends or the no-brainers at the office for a good loud time. All the specials are written, and occasionally drawn, on the walls. Start with Asahi beer and boiled green soybeans, then maybe tempura, gyoza dumplings, deluxe sushi and teriyaki chicken. It's perfect for when you've had too many cocktails somewhere chi-chi and just want a good feed. And guess what? They've now opened Tsukasa 2 in Neutral Bay. Here we go again.

licensed & byo
lunch Mon–Fri noon–2pm
dinner Mon–Sat 6.30–10.30pm
cards AE BC MC V   Bookings recommended
seats 70
owner Shinji Tani
chefs Ryosuke Hirano & Masami Ono
cost Around $54 for two, plus drinks
plus Wallpaper specials   **minus** Tiny glasses
score 13/20

twocan

27 BELGRAVE STREET, MANLY
PHONE 9977 1558   MAP 7

MODERN AUSTRALIAN

A glance at the menu reads like a quick trip around the globe at this Manly eatery. Popular Brazilian seafood stew hangs out with Thai lime leaf, lemongrass and chilli chicken, while veal shanks with tomato, sage and gnocchi show distinct Italian roots. To start, crab and lemongrass broth has a good long-flavoured stock, and a smoked trout salad displays a sound understanding of construction and flavour. There is a curious slight sweetness that pervades everything, however – even the highly competent fish with caper–lemon butter and watercress. Prices are a little ambitious, and we loathe paying for bread, but the polished execution of dishes from the kitchen is impressive. A dessert trio of froufrou (white chocolate sponge), bombe and pistachio sablé is a treat well worth indulging in. The café-ish interior could do with a lift.

byo
dinner Tues–Sat 6–10pm
cards AE BC DC MC V   Bookings recommended, essential weekends
seats 65; outdoor area; wheelchair access; no smoking until 10pm
owners/chefs Vicky Harris & Nadine McCristal
cost Around $76 for two, plus drinks
plus Hard-working service   **minus** Kitchen fumes
score 13/20

Y

two chefs on stanley

CNR STANLEY & RILEY STREETS, EAST SYDNEY
PHONE 9331 1559 MAP 2

MEDITERRANEAN

Two Chefs isn't chasing celebrity, although most nights there are usually one or two quietly enjoying this cosy, relaxed inner-east stalwart. The décor is simple and appealing, the well-known Ulric Steiner metalwork mirrors being the only diversion from the sober white walls. In warm months the large windows are opened onto Stanley Street and the mood is very European. We loved the nicely springy gnocchi with yabbies and asparagus. A slow-cooked lamb rump with artichokes, butter beans and aïoli is unshowy but delicious, as was a blue-eye cod served with tomato relish and pretty zucchini flowers filled with prawn mousseline. To finish, a peach and sauternes mousse millefeuille is elegant and refreshing. The wine list is brief but very smart for a restaurant of this size, showing an interesting mix of European and Australian wines. Service is friendly and attentive.

licensed; wine by the glass
lunch Mon–Fri noon–3pm
dinner Mon–Sat 6–10.30pm
cards AE BC DC MC V Bookings recommended
seats 50; private room; no smoking until 2pm & 10pm
owners Branco Cergol & Mauro Carpentieri
chef Mauro Carpentieri
cost Around $92 for two, plus drinks
plus Real hospitality
minus Can be painfully slow
score 14/20

$

uchi lounge

15 BRISBANE STREET, SURRY HILLS
PHONE 9261 3524 MAP 2

MODERN JAPANESE

Although populated by members of the cool school, you don't have to wear Gucci to dine at the Uchi, but it helps. This is traditional Japanese with a funky Darlo twist. Portions are fashion-industry small, yet the taste sensations evinced by each dish are so amazing you find yourself staring at the strange wobbly door outside the kitchen, waiting to see what's up next. Order a decadent glass of plum wine and run a manicured finger over the menu. You can't really fail. Chicken pieces wrapped with seaweed and deep-fried? Yes, please. Prawn and fish balls? Oh yes. Chrysanthemum sushi? That's mine! The newly decorated upstairs section recalls an Akira Isogawa parade, with floating pieces of diaphanous fabric forming a striking room divider, and waitresses who look like they all sprang from Peter Greenaway's film the 'Pillow Book'. Now there's even more room with a new bar area serving finger food. We're sold.

licensed & byo
dinner Mon–Sat 6–10.30pm
cards AE BC MC V No bookings
seats 50
owner Hiroshi Uchiyama
chef Joshua Adderton
cost Around $54 for two, plus drinks
plus Yummy toasty sesamey things
minus Small portions
score 14/20

union hotel
dining room

271 PACIFIC HIGHWAY (CNR WEST STREET),
NORTH SYDNEY
PHONE 8923 0658   MAP 5A

MODERN AUSTRALIAN

The smart, new dining room brings an
unexpected sophistication to this venerable
old pub. In true Sydney style, the menu
jumps all over the world. Never mind that
a Vietnamese would wonder what walnuts
were doing in the rice-paper rolls; that an
Italian might be taken aback by the chorizo
in the seafood risotto; or that an Indian
might not recognise the baby veal shank
curry – these dishes stand on their own
merits. Un-Thai crab cakes are plump with
fresh crabmeat and shredded carrot, while
the marinated, chargrilled sirloin steak is full
of sizzle and good, long flavour. Louisiana
blackened lamb loin, served with soft
polenta, fried basil and a red wine sauce is
a clash of too many strong flavours, but it
doesn't seem to worry the let's-do-lunch
business crowd.

licensed; wine by the glass
lunch Mon–Fri noon–3pm
dinner Mon–Sat 6–10pm
cards AE BC DC MC V   Bookings recommended
seats 120; private room; outdoor area;
wheelchair access; no smoking until
2 & 9pm
owners Trans Media/Michael Willesee
chef Aaron Stewart
cost Around $86 for two, plus drinks
plus Stylish comfort   **minus** A bit blokey
score 12/20

unkai

LEVEL 36, ANA HOTEL SYDNEY,
176 CUMBERLAND STREET, THE ROCKS
PHONE 9250 6123   MAP 1

JAPANESE

Among the best news we can bring you this
year is the continuing return to form of
Unkai. After a period of lacklustre service
and food, Unkai has rediscovered much of
its old magic. The floor, as personified by the
energetic and charismatic Guy Ramesh, is
caring and knowledgeable, and much of the
food has the grace and wherewithal to
match the breathtaking harbour views.
A sunomono of vinegar-pickled surf clam,
octopus, oyster and cuttlefish has real
cut-through; agedashi dofu or fried tofu is
as creamy as freshly formed curds; and the
generously sized lobster tail deep-fried with
a special soy sauce combines subtlety with
in-your-face flavour. Only the sushi box
with its curious cellophane inlay and fine
but not fabulous sushi failed to maintain
the otherwise impeccable standards. The
place still feels like a museum of Oriental
artefacts, but that only adds to the charm.

licensed; wine by the glass
breakfast Daily 6.30–10am
lunch Sun–Fri noon–2.30pm
dinner Daily 6–10pm
cards AE BC DC MC V   Bookings recommended
seats 103; private room; wheelchair access;
non-smoking area
owner ANA Hotel Sydney
chef Hiroshi Miura
cost Around $130 for two, plus drinks
plus The views   **minus** Cellophane sushi boxes
score 15/20

u-turn

36–8 SOUTH STEYNE, MANLY
PHONE 9976 3332   MAP 7

MODERN AUSTRALIAN

Fish and chips are always a treat when
you're within a whiff of sea spray. At U-Turn
you can sit on the footpath, watch the
surfers through the Norfolk pines and soak
up the beachside vibes. Inside, blond timber
furniture and dark blue suede banquettes
give the place a lively upbeat feel, carried
on by the adjoining bar with its jukebox
and young, groovy-for-Manly crowd. Good
service from charming staff adds to the
enjoyment of eating here, and the wine list
is concise with plenty of choices by the
glass. Super-fresh Moreton Bay bugs are
good and sweet, while chargrilled octopus
served with a reduced balsamic sauce had
plenty of upfront character. Desserts such
as hazelnut vanilla zucotto and warm
chocolate tartlet work well enough too.
But we're not at all sure about the roast
pumpkin, spinach and French brie risotto,
even if the local groovers seem to lap it up.

licensed & byo; wine by the glass
breakfast Sat–Sun 9am–noon
lunch Daily noon–6pm
dinner Daily 6pm–1am
cards AE BC DC MC V   No bookings
seats 118; outdoor area; wheelchair access;
non-smoking area ⊁
owners Allan Maddalena & Robert Morris
chef Owen Szeto
cost Around $37 for two, plus drinks
plus The beach   **minus** As always, the parking
score 12/20

vaucluse house tea rooms

VAUCLUSE HOUSE,
WENTWORTH ROAD, VAUCLUSE
PHONE 9388 8188   MAP 9

MODERN AUSTRALIAN

While the eclectic Modern Australian menu
seems at odds with the awfully English
surrounds of Vaucluse House, it doesn't take
away from what is a charming experience.
On a sunny day, with the crenellated
battlements of William Wentworth's
mansion peeking over the trees and a cold
riesling in your hand, all is well with the
world. A chorizo sausage, pumpkin and
smoked mozzarella pizza is thin-crusted and
nicely put together, while a smoked salmon
salad is a generous serve resting on a
delicious pile of potato salad. Vietnamese-
style chicken with lime, chilli and mint has
a good, mouth-tingling bite. For the
traditionalists among us, however, the real
attraction of the place is the all-day
morning and afternoon tea and those
delicious, freshly baked scones. (Very
modern Australian.)

licensed; wine by the glass
breakfast Sun 9–11.30am
lunch Tues–Sun 10am–5pm
cards AE BC DC MC V   Bookings essential
seats 230; private room; outdoor area;
wheelchair access; non-smoking area ⊁
owner John Guthrie
chef John James
cost Around $76 for two, plus drinks
plus The scones   **minus** The tables
score 12/20

¥

vault

135 GEORGE STREET, THE ROCKS
PHONE 9247 1920   MAP 1

MODERN AUSTRALIAN

With its moneyed name and suited clientele, Vault runs the risk of being viewed as a poor man's Banc. This would be unfair, because it has a character all its own, and is far from impoverished. Vault is tall and slightly gangly, with three small dining rooms stacked on top of each other, drenched in sunlight at lunchtime and smartly decorated in dark brown and white, with a smart (too smart?) bar at the entrance. The food is mainly Mediterranean, as in a salty pissaladière (the southern French version of pizza) with anchovies, olives and celery, or a salad of figs, crisped prosciutto and feta. But there are some northern European influences too: a seared venison with pears and parsnip, and a peach Melba from dessert chef Andrew Honeysett that would have made Escoffier smile. The menu can get a bit pompous, and the service can be a little too formal.

licensed; wine by the glass
lunch Mon–Fri noon–3pm
dinner Mon–Sat 6–10.30pm; Sun 6–9.30pm
cards AE BC DC MC V   Bookings recommended, essential weekends
seats 140; private room; outdoor area; wheelchair access; no smoking ⅹ
owners Karl & Tony Kazal
chef Simon Flanders
cost Around $108 for two, plus drinks
plus Intimate rooms   **minus** Overwrought menu
score 14/20

vera cruz

314 MILITARY ROAD, CREMORNE
PHONE 9904 5818   MAP 7

MEXICAN

There are so many true crosses (Vera Cruz) here that after a few Mexican beers, you can look up suddenly and feel like you're at a service – or a sacrifice. If it weren't so stylishly decked out, you may be tempted to make the sign of the cross yourself. But Vera Cruz IS stylish, with lots of elegant straight lines and soft candlelight. What's more, this is about as far from your run-of-the-mill junky Mexican food as Mexico is from here. Surprisingly, the chef isn't Mexican, but the owners lived there for years, and flavours are bright, fresh, intriguing and downright delish. Be astounded by the crisp pastry empanadas of hominy and corn, or feel the Latino heat of pan-seared achiote cuttlefish. Mains are just as interesting. The green pork mole and chipotle chicken are as racy and as distinct as a Santana CD.

licensed & byo; wine by the glass
lunch Fri noon–4pm
dinner Mon–Sat 6pm–late
cards AE BC MC V   Bookings recommended
seats 70; wheelchair access; non-smoking area ⅹ
owners Annette Zubani & May Clementson
chef Matthew English
cost Around $65 for two, plus drinks
plus The hide-away bar   **minus** Clinically cool
score 14/20

vieri

LEVEL 2, 433–35 HARBOURSIDE,
DARLING HARBOUR
PHONE 9212 4441   MAP 5B

ITALIAN

The Darling Harbour complex hasn't quite shaken off its tourist trap reputation, but the restaurant named after Australia's international soccer star, Christian Vieri (one of the owners), is leading the struggle to raise standards. To avoid distracting from the giant orange fish moored outside, the décor is kept white and simple, while chef Ian Draper offers an ambitious take on northern Italian cucina. Some main courses, such as john dory with potato salad, pesto and 'lobster perfume', can be too rich and too complex, but entrées such as spaghetti with shredded duck and snowpeas, and crab cakes with corn salsa, are nothing short of sumptuous. Among sophisticated desserts such as espresso mousse and chocolate and biscotti parfait, Vieri always offers a 'crumble of the day' (rhubarb being our preference), the kind of homey touch that could usefully spread to the main courses.

licensed; wine by the glass
lunch Tues–Sun noon–2.30pm
dinner Tues–Sun 6.30–10pm
cards AE BC DC MC V   Bookings recommended
seats 180; private room; outdoor area; wheelchair access; non-smoking area ☒
owners Attilio Labbozzetta & Christian Vieri
chef Ian Draper
cost Around $92 for two, plus drinks
plus The effort   **minus** The background music
score 12/20

viet nouveau

731 MILITARY ROAD, MOSMAN
PHONE 9968 3548   MAP 7

VIETNAMESE

We're always bemused by the menu at this much-loved Mosman institution. One day we'll actually try the osso buco curry. In the meantime, however, the little spring rolls are pretty well flawless, the crab and green mango salad spankingly fresh and sweet, the chicken angel's wings are, well, heavenly, and that banana sago pudding hits the spot in winter. Your host is the colourful and character-laden bon vivant, Brian Schmitzer, who is happy to steer you through the idiosyncratic menu. Sometimes it can get a bit stuffy downstairs, so seek out the comfortable, cool, upstairs level. If you have to venture forth for a bottle of wine, make the effort to walk to Vintage Cellars a block away, as the selection at the League's club next door is woeful. Service is fast and polite. There may be better Vietnamese restaurants in town, but few are as much fun.

byo
dinner Tues–Sat 6.30–11pm
cards AE BC MC V   Bookings recommended, essential weekends
seats 60; private room; outdoor area; non-smoking area ☒
owner Brian Schmitzer
chef Chi
cost Around $76 for two, plus drinks
plus Quirky charm   **minus** Some quirky dishes
score 13/20

watermark

2A THE ESPLANADE, BALMORAL BEACH
PHONE 9968 3433   MAP 7

MODERN AUSTRALIAN/SEAFOOD

At the southern end of the Balmoral Beach promenade is this smart, seasoned stayer. From the frosted nautical mural window to the sleek bar with views out through the heads, it's Sydney on a stick. Chef Kenneth Leung remains wedded to the idea of fusion cooking, which can be exciting in the hands of a gifted chef who shows restraint. This was more than evident in a delicious green asparagus agnolotti with slow-roasted tomatoes, black-eyed beans and white pepper sauce. However, there were simply too many flavours in a double-roasted Muscovy duck with couscous and polenta pancake, onion confit and sugar-cured peach, and in jewfish marinated in lemongrass with sweet curry paste, grilled lemon pickle and scallops. Service is first-class, the wine list a dream, and the feel professional and likeable.

licensed; wine by the glass
breakfast Daily 8–10.30am
lunch Mon–Fri noon–3pm; Sat–Sun 12.30–3.30pm
dinner Tues–Thurs & Sun 6.30–9.30pm; Fri–Sat 6.30–10pm
cards AE BC DC MC V   Bookings essential
seats 135; outdoor area; wheelchair access; non-smoking area
owners Mark Wilson & Kenneth Leung
chef Kenneth Leung
cost Around $140 for two, plus drinks
plus Bathing beauty   **minus** Can get windy
score 14/20

the wharf restaurant

PIER 4, HICKSON ROAD, WALSH BAY
PHONE 9250 1761   MAP 1

MODERN AUSTRALIAN/MEDITERRANEAN

Not many can lay claim to surviving Sydney's fickle dining scene for so long, and this has more than survived – it is a consistent stayer. The Wharf wears its many hats seamlessly well. Catering for the pre- and post-theatre crowd who come to see the latest from the Sydney Theatre Company can be demanding. However, those in search of the quintessential Sydney dinner experience need not buy a ticket. There's a distinct favouritism towards seafood and NSW wines here. The inevitable chargrilled octopus doesn't remotely bore with its excellent skordalia, and a fish broth with saffron and potatoes is beautifully honed. Perfectly cooked and rested lamb rump is tender as a baby's, and pan-fried cod is lifted out of the ordinary with leeks, peas and butter sauce. Desserts are even better, so take your time as you fantasise about living in airy warehouses with floorboards, high ceilings and harbour views.

licensed; wine by the glass
lunch Mon–Sat noon–3pm
dinner Mon–Sat 6pm–late
cards AE BC DC MC V   Bookings essential
seats 120; outdoor area; wheelchair access; non-smoking area
owner Dvir Sokoni
chef Kirsty Greenup
cost Around $80 for two, plus drinks
plus Lofty space   **minus** Can be speedy for non-theatre-goers
score 14/20

wine banc

ELIZABETH STREET ENTRANCE,
53 MARTIN PLACE, SYDNEY
PHONE 9233 5399   MAP 1

MODERN EUROPEAN

This is absolutely the finest location in town
for James Bond fantasies, from the relaxed
lounge chairs at the foot of the stairs (a
pre-mission martini, perhaps, or a briefing
from M), to the main body of the restaurant
(low and wide like the first-class cabin of
a flight to Jamaica). There's even a cool,
shaken-not-stirred bar. Like Bond, the food
can be pleasingly retro: prawn cocktails
or steak frites. Incidentally, when they say
frites, they mean lots and lots of frites.
The fare at Wine Banc may be simpler than
what's on offer upstairs at Banc, but it
sometimes seems to be trying to make up
in quantity what it lacks in complexity.
At its best, though, the food can have a
simple and timeless appeal, as in a soft
poached egg, say, melting deliciously with
a salt-cod risotto. And naturally, a good
wine list comes with the territory. The joint
starts jumping with live jazz on Tuesdays,
Thursdays, Fridays and Saturdays.

licensed; wine by the glass
lunch Mon–Fri from noon
dinner Mon–Sat from 6pm
cards AE BC DC MC V   Bookings recommended
seats 50
owners Stan Sarris & Rodney Adler
chef Liam Tomlin
cost Around $80 for two, plus drinks
plus Live jazz   **minus** Cigar smoke
score 14/20

wockpool

PANASONIC IMAX THEATRE,
WHEAT ROAD, DARLING HARBOUR
PHONE 9211 9888   MAP 1

MODERN ASIAN

Now that the noodle bar option has been
done away with, Wockpool's bar and three
stylish dining areas are united by one menu
and one food philosophy. As a result, the
place seems more together. Even on a
packed Saturday night, the service is close
to flawless, timing is well paced and staff
are settled and personable. The caramelised
pork hock is Neil Perry's most-copied dish,
and Claudia Dunlop's version is first-class.
Long-time lovers of Wockpool's signature
crab omelette will be pleased to know that
a) it's still on the menu and b) it's as good
as ever. A crisp-skin Barossa chicken with
coriander and chilli tea was surprisingly
subtle, but the aged beef rib, roasted pink
and served sliced on top of a luscious,
complex red peanut curry sauce was right
on the money – the meat having the flavour
to take on the glorious richness of the curry.
Desserts don't come any lighter than the
delicious fig tart.

licensed; wine by the glass
lunch Daily noon–3pm
dinner Sun–Thurs 6–10pm; Fri–Sat 6–11pm
cards AE BC DC MC V   Bookings essential
seats 200; private room; outdoor area;
wheelchair access; no smoking inside
owners Neil Perry & Trish Richards
chef Claudia Dunlop
cost Around $92 for two, plus drinks
plus Darling Harbour buzz   **minus** Getting there
score 16/20

ying's seafood restaurant

270 PACIFIC HIGHWAY, CROWS NEST
PHONE 9966 9182   MAP 5A

CHINESE

Everyone knows that good Chinese restaurants are full of kitsch Chinese motifs, glittering Chinese chandeliers, and English menus that carefully avoid the kitchen's real specialities. Fortunately, these time-honoured traditions have been thrown to the wind by local kitchen god Ying Tam. His latest venture is a huge modern restaurant featuring an intriguing range of Chiu Chow, Cantonese and home-style dishes – all mercifully listed in English. The tanks of fish and crates of mud crabs attest to the freshness of the seafood here. Try the messy cracked crab with a deep, dark delicious sauce flavoured with salted duck egg; truly luscious pipis poached in a subtle Chiu Chow broth; or gloriously crunchy seasonal vegetables with special preserved shrimp. Ying's immediately joins the upper echelon of Sydney's Chinese restaurants.

licensed & byo; wine by the glass
lunch Daily 11am–3pm
dinner Daily 5.30–11pm
cards AE BC DC MC V   Bookings essential
seats 160; private room; wheelchair access; no smoking ✖
owners Ying Tam & Ying's Seafood Pty Ltd
chef Ng Hung
cost Around $86 for two, plus drinks
plus Free parking   **minus** Small tables for two
score 15/20

yoshii

GROUND FLOOR, MERCURE GRAND HOTEL,
50 MURRAY STREET, DARLING HARBOUR
PHONE 9211 6866   MAP 5B

JAPANESE

He has produced a glamorous sushi cookbook, is spoken of in glowing terms by the great Tetsuya Wakuda, and manages to pull more than his share of famous faces through the doors of his small but elegant 50-seater restaurant. Yet Ryuichi Yoshii looks like anything but a cult figure. Young, slim and wearing a nervous smile, he only ever seems to relax with a sushi knife in one hand and an expertly trimmed fish fillet in the other. Purists insist on sitting at the sushi bar where they can see the elegance of Yoshii-san's craft close-up. Watch him sculpt garfish into something that resembles a futuristic treble clef, or fashion nigiri sushi that are so perfectly formed and settled, they seem to have grown naturally on the plate. When he ventures into more experimental realms, as with his quail leg with blue cheese and miso, or somen noodles in tomato consommé with mullet roe, things get a little muddled. But oh, that sushi!

licensed; wine by the glass
lunch Tues–Fri noon–3pm
dinner Mon–Sat 6–10.30pm
cards AE BC DC MC V   Bookings recommended
seats 50; no smoking ✖
owner Yoshii Pty Ltd
chef Ryuichi Yoshii
cost Around $97 for two, plus drinks at lunch
plus The sushi bar   **minus** The carpet
score 14/20

yulla

LEVEL 1, 38 CAMPBELL PARADE,
BONDI BEACH
PHONE 9365 1788   MAP 9

MIDDLE EASTERN/MEDITERRANEAN

Dvir Sokoni first redefined casual Sydney
eating at Dov, and later at the Wharf. Now,
he has transformed what used to be the
first-dater First Floor restaurant overlooking
Bondi Beach. The curved dining room has
been defrocked into a bright, sunny, bare
board space with shaded balcony tables
outside. The Middle Eastern-cum-Israeli
menu runs from breakfasts of fruit salad
with watermelon and minted yoghurt, and
Israeli green capsicum and goat's curd
omelette, to the house special of kibbeh,
golden crunchy deep-fried footballs of
minced lamb and cracked wheat served
with tahini. The definite must-share dish is
the mixed dip platter which might include a
delicate, smoky, white taramasalata, a
creamy, substantial hummus, a wedge of
caramelised roast pumpkin drizzled with
tahini and even some good old chopped
liver pâté. Service is as sunny as the view,
prices are low, servings are big and the
quality is present and correct. Bondi gets
lucky again.

licensed
hours Daily 7am–11pm
cards AE BC MC V   No bookings
seats 100; outdoor area; wheelchair access
owner Dvir Sokoni
chef Marianne Piotrowski
cost Around $50 for two, plus drinks
plus Bondi balcony   **minus** Skeleton wine list
score 13/20

zaaffran

LEVEL 2, 345 HARBOURSIDE,
DARLING HARBOUR
PHONE 9211 8900   MAP 5B

INDIAN

Zaaffran is a seriously sexy mix of coffee-
coloured banquettes, angled mirrors and a
panorama over Darling Harbour. By day it's
a less alluring business-suit scene, but at
night the romance of the place is palpable.
The thick white tablecloths, cutlery and
glassware all speak of a superior dining
room, but over-attentive service can let the
side down, and the food lacks the same
wow factor as the design. A seafood
sampler entrée of pan-roasted barramundi,
Tasmanian salmon in spiced yoghurt and
banana prawns glazed with fenugreek
sounded tantalising but tasted less so, while
chicken karahai was a rich blend of tomato,
cashew, curry leaf and green chilli. Lamb
joshila in its onion, cardamom and saffron
gravy was good, but not transcendental.
What is great here is the bumper wine list,
with some real gems by the glass.

licensed; wine by the glass
lunch Daily noon–2.30pm
dinner Sun–Thurs 6–9.30pm; Fri–Sat 6–10pm
cards AE BC DC MC V   Bookings essential
seats 160; outdoor area; wheelchair access; no
smoking inside
owners Freddie Zulfiqar, Rush Dossa
& Vikrant Kapoor
chef Vikrant Kapoor
cost Around $92 for two, plus drinks
plus The condiments   **minus** Over-serviced
score 14/20

country 2001

blue mountains

JILL DUPLEIX, TERRY DURACK,
PHILLIP PUTNAM & LYNNE MULLINS

Take your bread knife with you when
you go to the Blue Mountains, for the
area is blessed with some of the state's
very best bakeries. Hominy in Katoomba
(02 4782 9816), run by ex-Blackheath
Bakery team, Brent Hersee and Jenny
Ingall, Quinton's (02 4784 3125) and
The Loaves and the Dishes (see entry)
in Leura can all turn mountain picnics
into an artform.

Pick up the rest at Leura Gourmet
(02 4784 1438) or Divino Delicafe in
Katoomba (02 4782 6083) and a bottle
from the bottomless Barmans cellars
in Leura (02 4784 1951), and you'll do
extraordinarily well. Tea and coffee are
becoming more of a focus here with
newcomers such as Katoomba's The
Dancing Cup (02 4782 7911) and
The Elephant Bean (see entry) leading
the way. While Devonshire teas and pizza
abound, Asia is miserably represented,
although it's nice to see that Simon and
Keiko Kjelgaard have reopened Pins
and Noodles (02 4784 1345) – complete
with their tsukimi noodle soup – in
Leura's main drag.

café bon ton

192 THE MALL, LEURA
PHONE (02) 4782 4377   MAP 11

MODERN AUSTRALIAN

Talk about something for everyone. On
a sunny day, you can sit outside on the
terrace in Parisian fashion, under the trees.
In winter, you can sit next to the flickering
fire in the salon-like dining room with its
mottled walls, grand columns and trompe
l'oeil stairway. You can pop in for a
weekend eggs-and-all breakfast, stop by
for a quick pasta for lunch, or do the full-on
three-course dinner number. Start with
a barbecued octopus salad, then maybe
some Italian sausages with mash, and finish
with the very good macadamia tart or the
Three Sisters-tall lemon meringue pie –
assuming you can tear yourself away from
the concorde chocolate cake. Not
surprisingly, Bon Ton attracts a wide variety
of diners from family groups and romantic
couples to local business types. Don't expect
the culinary Olympics, but do expect to eat
just what you feel like.

breakfast Sat–Sun 8–11am; Mon–Fri 9–11am
lunch Daily noon–3pm
dinner Wed–Mon 6–9.30pm
cards AE BC DC MC V   Bookings recommended
seats 60; outdoor area; wheelchair access;
no smoking inside ⛄✗
owner Rosemary Milenkovic
chefs Lee Pattinson & Tony Chillemi
cost Around $65 for two, plus drinks
plus The garden terrace
minus Fluffy cappuccinos
score 12/20

cleopatra

118 CLEOPATRA STREET, BLACKHEATH
PHONE (02) 4787 8456   MAP 11

FRENCH

The abdication of Trish Hobbs and Dany
Chouet as the undisputed Queens of Blue
Mountains dining sent shockwaves through
the restaurant scene. Yet the blow was
softened considerably by the calibre of the
new trustees of this gracious guesthouse
and restaurant. You can almost hear MG
Garage's Ian Pagent and Greg Duncan, and
Bistro Moncur's Damien Pignolet, breathing
new life into the place. In the meantime,
designer Neil Bradford has brought a svelte
country cosmopolitan style to the place.
The dining rooms are visions of café au lait
and mushroom, gleaming Limoges plates
and Christofle cutlery. Echoing the décor are
the equally clean lines of a pale, perfect
rabbit terrine, a neat little plank of wild
barramundi carpeted with diced ratatouille,
and a single upright cylinder of intense,
gooey-centred chocolate pudding. The food
is French regional, the staff is country
friendly and the mood is city professional.

licensed; wine by the glass
lunch Sun from 1pm
dinner Daily from 7.30pm
cards AE BC DC MC V   Bookings essential
seats 50; private room; outdoor area;
no smoking ✹
owners Damien Pignolet, Ian Pagent
& Greg Duncan
chefs Damien Pignolet & Fabrice Boone
fixed price $95 p.p.
plus Staying overnight   **minus** Driving home
score 16/20

darley's

LILIANFELS BLUE MOUNTAINS,
LILIANFELS AVENUE, KATOOMBA
PHONE (02) 4780 1200   MAP 11

REGIONAL AUSTRALIAN

Ralph Potter believes cooking should have
a sense of place. Here, the bracing air calls
for distinct, assertive flavours. Strands of
skate are draped on a tangle of intensely
green beetroot leaves with grilled pancetta,
in a sauce perked with pickled walnuts. A
delicate mousseline of snapper with salmon
roe and crab sits in a delicious, deeply
reduced yabbie broth. Local ingredients
feature, but not slavishly: meaty strips of
forest mushroom top a perfect pile of
white polenta, rich with good parmigiano.
There's pheasant for two, and a chocolate,
marmalade and orange liqueur soufflé to
follow. It's food of rare flair and finesse,
with a suggested glass of wine for every
dish. The lights are low in this lovely,
comforting 100-year-old cottage, the
atmosphere is relaxed and don't worry, the
braised pork cheeks are still on the menu.

licensed; wine by the glass
lunch Sun noon–2.30pm
dinner Wed–Sun 6.30–9.30pm
cards AE BC DC MC V   Bookings recommended
(preference given to Lilianfels guests)
seats 57; private room; no smoking ✹
owner Lilianfels Blue Mountains
chef Ralph Potter
fixed price $71.50 p.p. for two courses;
$82.50 p.p. for three; six-course tasting menus
$99 p.p.
plus 17-page wine list   **minus** No lunch Sat
score 15/20

Works
of Art

Semillon

Shiraz

Cabernet Sauvignon

Riesling

PETER LEHMANN WINES

Barossa born and bred

Naturally refined mineral water

dry dock

54 WARATAH STREET, KATOOMBA
PHONE (02) 4782 7902   MAP 11

SEAFOOD

A fish restaurant two hours from the sea is
a brave enterprise, but the photos on the
walls confirm the Dry Dockers are used to
getting into deep waters. It's neatly nautical
with oysters, crab, calamari, lobster, prawns
and four fish-of-the-day, and pasta, chicken
and King Island beef for non-believers.
Tasty, toffee-hued Coopers beer batter is
curiously at odds with soft calamari, but
a tile of cooked-through marlin is properly
moist and a half lobster holds its texture
well under the inevitably cheesy mornay
sauce. With every item meticulously priced
down to the last king prawn ($3.25 each),
the menu is finely filleted to local likes.
After 20 years high and dry, there's a danger
this local groove could become a rut.
However, a restaurant full of happy diners
downing enormous seafood platters says
much for the skill and experience of the
restaurateurs.

licensed & byo; wine by the glass
lunch Tues–Fri noon–2pm
dinner Mon–Sat from 5.30pm
cards AE BC MC V   Bookings recommended
seats 20; no smoking
owners Randi Svensen & James Rickards
chef James Rickards
cost Around $76 for two, plus drinks
plus Mountains of fish   **minus** Turn down
the lights
score 12/20

the elephant bean

159 KATOOMBA STREET, KATOOMBA
PHONE (02) 4782 4620   MAP 11

CAFÉ/ITALIAN

In a street with no shortage of café options,
the newly opened Elephant Bean stands out
as something special. For a start, the coffee
is roasted locally, and has a nice depth,
balance and real character without excess
bitterness. The food keeps to a roughly
Italian agenda, with good bouncy gnocchi
under a sweet tomato sauce, nicely solid
pork sausages with crisp, fried polenta,
and a colourful antipasto platter. About the
only letdown of our last meal was chewy
steak in the steak sandwich – mind you,
the toast (Loaves and the Dishes bread)
was so fabulous it didn't seem to matter.
Set up in an old shopfront, it's a warm,
buzzy, if cramped space, full of wooden
tables, bright colours and a framed shrine to
Michael Leunig on the wall. The house-made
flourless chocolate cake is highly
recommended, as is the affogato of cold
vanilla ice-cream 'drowned' in hot espresso
coffee.

byo
breakfast Wed–Mon 8–11.30am
lunch Wed–Mon noon–5.30pm
dinner Fri–Sat 6–9pm
cards None   No bookings
seats 32; outdoor area; no smoking inside
owner/chef Phillip Tutt
cost Around $43 for two, plus drinks
plus The coffee   **minus** Squeezy dining room
score 12/20

loaves and the dishes

180A THE MALL, LEURA
PHONE (02) 4784 3600   MAP 11

MODERN AUSTRALIAN

This is one of those rare Blue Mountains eateries that appear to exist more for the locals than for visitors. People prop at one of the big communal tables and make themselves at home, with a low-key sense of contentment that comes from being in a totally familiar space. The house-made organic bread and cakes more than keep up with the area's abnormally high baking standards, while the rest of the fare runs from fast fillers to some nicely put together dishes. At lunchtime, most make do with burrito, a quiche or a pretty solid-looking lasagna from the refrigerated cabinet or a pie from the warmer. At night, things get a bit more serious with the likes of spatchcock with salade Niçoise and salsa verde, and sirloin steak with gorgonzola polenta. Breakfast can be as simple as toasted house-baked cob with butter and jam, or as hip as a very bills-ish stack of ricotta hot cakes with honeycomb butter.

byo
hours Daily 8am–9pm
cards BC MC V   No bookings
seats 40; no smoking 💺❌
owners Rosemary News & Anthony Graham
chef Timothy Wesley
cost Around $38 for two, plus drinks
plus The bread and cakes
minus The stolid deli counter fare
score 12/20

mount tomah botanic gardens restaurant

BELLS LINE OF ROAD, MOUNT TOMAH
PHONE (02) 4567 2060   MAP 11

MODERN AUSTRALIAN

Situated inside the Mt Tomah Botanic Gardens, the place may feel like a cafeteria, but snare a table on the terrace on a sunny day, and you're in heaven, with magnificent views of the gardens, and way beyond. Even on a misty, cloudy day, the plates from John Henriksen's kitchen leave no doubt that the 105-kilometre drive west of Sydney is worth it. Steamed asparagus with homemade light-as-air puff pastry and chervil butter is a beautifully balanced dish, while roasted king prawns with basil, lemon, garlic and chilli butter are moist and moreish. One of the true high points of the menu is the perfectly cooked seared loin of kangaroo accompanied by a delicious pearl barley and mushroom risotto and a classic demi-glace. Finish with the luscious slow-baked vanilla quince or, better still, a post-prandial walk in the beautiful gardens.

byo
hours Daily 9.45am–4.45pm
(3.45pm during winter)
cards AE BC DC MC V   Bookings recommended; essential weekends
seats 150; private room; outdoor area; wheelchair access; no smoking inside 💺❌
owners John & Lidia Henriksen
chef John Henriksen
cost Around $80 for two, plus drinks
plus Desserts to die for   **minus** Car entry fee
score 14/20

the post office restaurant

148 THE MALL, LEURA
PHONE (02) 4784 3975   MAP 11

MODERN AUSTRALIAN

If only all post offices gave off such good vibes. With its purple, yellow and orange walls, cheery staff and jazzy music, the Post Office is a friendly, inviting place that seems to attract a fair mix of local shopfolk and tourists. The paper-over-cloth tables and baseball-capped chefs glimpsed through the open kitchen give the main dining room a modern bistro feel, which is reinforced by a menu that runs from the inevitable Caesar salad to fettuccine with king prawns, snowpeas and goat's cheese. And yes, truffle oil has hit Leura – in a dish of Atlantic salmon with roasted tomatoes and poached leek. A daily special of carrot, ginger and coriander soup is just the kind of insulation needed on brisk Blue Mountains nights, while an equally hearty main course of lamb shanks with kumera mash still had a likeable homely feel to it, although it could have been hotter.

licensed; wine by the glass
lunch Mon–Fri noon–3pm; Sat–Sun noon–5.30pm
dinner Daily 5.30–10pm
cards AE BC DC MC V   Bookings recommended
seats 100; outdoor area; non-smoking area ⚡🍴
owner Jonathan Glenn
chef Craig Hunt
cost Around $60 for two, plus drinks
plus Nice service   **minus** Too-low tables
score 12/20

silk's brasserie

128 THE MALL, LEURA
PHONE (02) 4784 2534   MAP 11

MODERN AUSTRALIAN

Silk's manages to combine warm country-style hospitality with a thoroughly polished dining experience. The place looks a treat, with its distinctive black-and-cream tiled floor, French brasserie decor and atmospheric mirrored bar. Service is friendly and knowledgeable, the wine list is a beauty, and chef David Waddington's cooking is assured and honed without trying too hard. Blue swimmer crab meat on avocado with lime and ginger sauce is notable for the generous serving of fresh sweet crab and the tangy, well-balanced dressing, while an entrée of luscious ripe local figs with prosciutto and yoghurt mint salad is a simple but stunning dish. Tenderloin of Victorian veal with wild mushroom cream has a nice, country-hearty feel, and a vegetarian-friendly warm salad of Domaine deep blue cheese with roasted sweet potato and lightly steamed asparagus spears is a clever combination of flavours and textures. An affogato of hot coffee, ice-cream and Frangelico is a fantastic hot finale.

licensed; wine by the glass
lunch Daily noon–3.30pm
dinner Daily 6–11.30pm
cards AE BC DC MC V   Bookings essential
seats 55; wheelchair access; no smoking ⚡🍴
owners Graham & Erin Silk
chef David Waddington
cost Around $86 for two, plus drinks
plus The total experience   **minus** Sunday crowds
score 15/20

victory theatre cafe

17 GOVETTS LEAP ROAD, BLACKHEATH
PHONE (02) 4787 6777   MAP 11

MODERN AUSTRALIAN

Blackheath's most popular café has just as much life as we imagine each performance at the old Victory Theatre would have had. Chef Ryan Pattison puts on a live variety performance everyday of pies, schnitzels, pasta, nachos and burgers. The blackboard menu is almost as big as the enormous identifying mural on the outside wall. While basil is properly evident in a satisfying, gutsy special of roast tomato soup, we found the corn and asparagus fritters, pasta with rocket pesto, and roast chicken and pumpkin with pine nuts could have done with the flavour burst of more fresh herbs themselves. It's a minor quibble, as real care goes into the food. The Big Mountain Breakfast is available all day for those who feel the need to sleep in until the morning mists clear, and the dining space, crammed into the front of what is now a colossal antiques centre, is a pleasant place to sit and while away a mountain afternoon.

byo
breakfast & lunch Daily 9am–5pm
dinner Fri–Sat 6–9pm
cards BC MC V   Bookings essential weekends
seats 42; outdoor area; wheelchair access; non-smoking area ✖
owners Wayne Newton & Robert Tarasov
chef Ryan Pattison
cost Around $42 for two, plus drinks
plus Long menu   **minus** Rampant smoking
score 12/20

vulcans

33 GOVETTS LEAP ROAD, BLACKHEATH
PHONE (02) 4787 6899   MAP 11

WOOD-FIRED

'We're just a simple country restaurant,' says co-owner Barry Ross, and in a way, he's right. In spite of the luminous reputation of chef Phillip Searle and the manic patronage the place receives from legions of devoted diners, its basic credo is relatively simple. From an old wood-fired baker's oven, Vulcans produces interesting, uncluttered food that manages to feel country-honest in spite of the liberal use of Asian flavours. Nobody else – in the city or the country – cooks food like this. In spite of its curry leaf and tamarind aromatics, a slow-roasted shoulder of lamb has a no-frills Mum's roast feel, and pot-roasted veal with lemongrass and yellow beans gives new definition to fall-off-the-bone. While the legendary chequerboard ice-cream is still the go, a bombe of mango, praline and mocha is not far behind. Vulcans refuses to be pigeon-holed, right down to its poured concrete floor, steaming espresso machine and fogged-up windows.

byo
lunch Fri–Sun noon–3pm
dinner Fri–Sun 6–10pm (2 sittings Fri & Sat)
cards AE BC DC MC V   Bookings essential
seats 35; outdoor area; wheelchair access; no smoking ✖
owners Phillip Searle & Barry Ross
chef Phillip Searle
cost Around $76 for two, plus drinks
plus The oven   **minus** No more breakfasts
score 15/20

canberra

TERRY DURACK, JILL DUPLEIX,
MATTHEW EVANS & BRUCE ELDER

It helps to have wheels in Canberra. While there's plenty of good food around, you may have to go through a few roundabouts to find it.

Our capital city's traditional strengths (Turkish food, local produce and wines) are still greatly in evidence, but there is now more smart and casual eating, more streetwise Asian and a café/bakery culture that's rising slowly and naturally, like sourdough bread. Hardened foodies will seek out Turkish takeaway at Kismet (02 6239 5185) in Manuka, the city's Charcoal Restaurant (02 6248 8015) for a good old-fashioned steak, and the spiffy new Touch Café (02 6257 0700) for modern Asian with lashings of style. The Fisho (02 6295 3153) in Kingston raises fish and chips to a new height, while chocolate lovers will hyperventilate at Bruno's Truffels (02 6295 7584) in Narrabundah. And we love the Silo bakery (see entry) for its cheese room, its divine fruit tarts, its heavenly sourdough baguettes and its mellow Cosmorex coffee. The biggest news is at the National Gallery of Australia, with the Juniperberry team doing such smart canteen fare – organic chicken and noodle soup, beef and red wine pie, quince tart – in the NGA Café (02 6240 6669) that we are all reminded of the divine marriage between art and food.

$

abell's kopi tiam

SHOP 7, FURNEAUX STREET, MANUKA
PHONE (02) 6239 4199   MAP 10

MODERN ASIAN/MALAYSIAN

There are now so many café/restaurants in Manuka (particularly ones that sprawl onto the pavement in summer) that it requires some discrimination to realise that only the rare few are worthy of serious attention. Abell's Kopi Tiam, with its bright and breezy colours and its relaxed ambience, is ideal for diners who want fine Malaysian/Indonesian with just a tweak of modernity. If you have a weakness for perfect beef rendang, marvellously subtle Bali chicken simmered in tamarind and coconut sauce, laksa (which Abell calls 'My Mum's') or traditional Mongolian lamb, Abell Ong knows how to make you fall in love all over again with these time-honoured favourites. Be warned: the menu, particularly the chalkboard, can be deceptive. Ask yourself 'Will those flavours really work together?' because often, the eye and mind give an endorsement that is not always matched by the end result.

licensed & byo; wine by the glass
lunch Tues–Sun 11.30am–2.30pm
dinner Tues–Sat 5.30–10pm; Sun 5.30–9pm
cards AE BC MC V   Bookings essential
seats 80 (50 inside); outdoor area; wheelchair access; non-smoking area 🚭✗
owners Lorna Sim & Abell Ong
chef Abell Ong
cost Around $32–43 for two, plus drinks
plus Beef rendang   **minus** Some con-fusion
score 12/20

atlantic

20 PALMERSTON LANE, MANUKA
PHONE (02) 6232 7888   MAP 10

MODERN AUSTRALIAN

Sensibly hidden from the mass eating that
characterises Manuka's main street, Atlantic
is a simple and very classy restaurant (large,
comfortable tables and real tablecloths)
where superior service and constrained
elegance are an entrée to James Mussillon's
fine cooking. The real entrées range from
such taste thrills as the subtle basil-infused
rare tuna (which is perfectly tender) with
soy and mustard seeds and a glorious
warm salad of duck confit and foie gras
with balsamic vinegar. A main course of
Atlantic mixed fish with provençale
vegetables – a house speciality – sees the
freshest of the day's catch lying beneath a
tower of layered aubergines, seared prawns
and scallops. If you can't decide how to
finish the meal, surrender to the assiette
(platter) of desserts, which offers brief,
mouth-watering tastes of everything on
the dessert menu. This is modern Australian
cooking at its very best.

licensed & byo; wine by the glass
lunch Mon–Fri noon–2pm
dinner Mon–Sat 6–10pm
cards AE BC DC MC V   Bookings essential
seats 100; private room; outdoor area;
wheelchair access; no smoking
owners David Wood, Nik Gravias & Bill Lyristakis
chef James Mussillon
cost Around $86 for two, plus drinks
plus Superb fish   **minus** Back-lane entrance
score 15/20

the boat house by the lake

GREVILLEA PARK, MENINDEE DRIVE, BARTON
PHONE (02) 6273 5500   MAP 10

MODERN AUSTRALIAN

Set on the shores of Lake Burley Griffin,
the Boat House enjoys uninterrupted views
across the lake. Swans swim by, and the
terrace offers a pleasant retreat for a pre-
or post-meal breather. The dining room is
a large and functional space – ideal for
weddings and other large gatherings – with
floor-to-ceiling windows and outstanding
acoustics. This is a restaurant prepared to
play it safe, judging by the low-heat kick in
the wasabi vinaigrette accompanying the
sashimi entrée of sea perch, salmon and
tuna. The Queensland scallops served with
coconut risotto and champagne cream
sauce is a source of confusion, but oven-
roasted milk-fed veal with wine sauce is
right on the money. A sharp and fresh berry
sorbet is an excellent conclusion to what
can be a satisfying, if uneven, experience.

licensed & byo; wine by the glass
lunch Mon–Fri from noon
dinner Mon–Sat from 6.30pm
cards AE BC DC MC V   Bookings essential
seats 180; private room; outdoor area;
wheelchair access; no smoking
owners Dennis & Merilyn Souter
chef Daren Tetley
cost Around $97 for two, plus drinks
plus Capital location   **minus** The glare
score 13/20

byrne's mill

55 COLLETT STREET, QUEANBEYAN
PHONE (02) 6297 8283   MAP 10

MODERN AUSTRALIAN

There's a flash of white outside in the garden. It's late. So with service finished, chef Anthony Mudge is tending his quince tree, urging the dusky fruit to ripen. Mudge is almost out of his precious quince paste and has been waiting patiently for the next crop. Patience is synonymous with the Mudges' time at this almost-country restaurant. In an historic mill in Queanbeyan, they have tended their dream for 15 years – Anthony even sold his Porsche to pay for the kitchen. You enter the homey space via a lavender-lined path, with the quince tree and herb garden up one side. Locals and nearby Canberrans have fallen in love with (and fallen in love over) the duck breast with quince glaze, and the sizzling fried ginger snapper that regularly grace the blackboard menu. While the service is nothing to get excited about, this is full-flavoured food that is refreshing in its honesty.

licensed & byo; wine by the glass
lunch Tues–Fri noon–2.30pm
dinner Tues–Sat 6–10pm
cards AE BC DC MC V   Bookings recommended
seats 70; private room; outdoor area; no smoking ⚡✗
owners Anthony & Lisa Mudge, David Wood
chef Anthony Mudge
cost Around $76 for two, plus drinks
plus Honest flavours   **minus** Driving home
score 14/20

♉ the chairman & yip

108 BUNDA STREET, CIVIC
PHONE (02) 6248 7109   MAP 10

MODERN ASIAN

This is one of those rare restaurants that you can take fast or slow. You can eat from an excellent set menu at lunch, pay a very modest amount and be in and out within the hour. Or explore the marvellous modern Asian cuisine over dinner. Pig out on lightly fried mushrooms with a rose wine vinaigrette; pan-fried chicken with mustard seed dill sauce; beancurd and eggplant chilli plum pot; red curry lamb; and snowpeas and asparagus stirred with beancurd puffs. You can move between vegetarian delights such as stir-fried cucumber, pumpkin and caramelised chilli and meatier offerings such as deliciously tender King Island beef with scallops and honey-ground pepper. Service is carried out with a quiet dignity and efficiency, even when the place is alive with large groups of enthusiastically noisy diners.

licensed & byo; wine by the glass
lunch Sun–Fri noon–3.30pm
dinner Daily 6–11pm
cards AE BC DC MC V   Bookings essential
seats 180; private room; outdoor area; wheelchair access; no smoking ⚡✗
owner Josiah Li
chef William Suen
cost Around $70 for two, plus drinks
plus Lunchtime value   **minus** Large groups
score 13/20

fig

2/4 GRIFFITH SHOPS,
BARKER STREET, GRIFFITH
PHONE (02) 6295 6915   MAP 10

MODERN AUSTRALIAN

Fig stands for Food in Griffith and that is
exactly what you get. Behind a nondescript
façade in suburban Griffith are elegant
blondwood tables in the front (there is a
fashionable shared dining table holding
8–10) and a large comfortable area out
the back. Service is impeccable and the
food is full of subtlety and interest. Awaken
your tastebuds with Woodside goat's curd
with fresh honey-baked figs. It's hard to
pass up a balanced dish of ling fillets
poached in coconut cream, green ginger
wine and sweet chilli, while the simplicity
of egg noodles with semi-dried tomatoes,
English spinach and feta is a delicious
vegetarian alternative. In summer, a fruit
compote with amaretti biscuit and double
cream or a mixed berry flan with coulis
and cream completes the meal. Not
surprisingly, this has become a favourite
lunchtime watering hole for those eager
to escape the city centre.

licensed & byo; wine by the glass
breakfast Tues–Sat 8.30–11am
lunch Tues–Sat noon–2.30pm
dinner Tues–Sat 6.30–10pm
cards AE BC MC V   Bookings essential
seats 100; private room; outdoor area;
wheelchair access; non-smoking area ✵✗
owner/chef Andrew Haskins
cost Around $65 for two, plus drinks
plus Speedy service   **minus** Easy to miss
score 13/20

first floor

UNIT 21, GREEN SQUARE,
JARDINE STREET, KINGSTON
PHONE (02) 6260 6311   MAP 10

MODERN AUSTRALIAN

At ground level, suburban Canberra can
sometimes be a little overwhelming. But
climb the stairs to First Floor, take a seat
beside the huge, open, floor-to-ceiling glass
windows, gaze out through the upper
branches of the trees, and you'll feel a little
closer to heaven than Kingston. Heaven is
also what chef Darren Perryman cooks up
each day. Most of the dishes come in small
and large sizes so you can start with the
finely chargrilled baby octopus marinated in
olive oil and served on baby spinach, or you
can have it as your main. Perfectly cooked
brick-fried spatchcock (flattened in the pan),
marinated in chilli, lime juice and olive oil
and served on a warm dish of tabbouli with
delicious eggplant relish is one of the real
highlights. To finish, never ignore the
obvious: the excellent tiramisu.

licensed & byo; wine by the glass
lunch Mon–Fri noon–3pm
dinner Mon–Sat 6–10.30pm
cards AE BC DC MC V   Bookings essential
seats 130; no smoking ✵✗
owners Christopher Gallahar & Darren Perryman
chef Darren Perryman
cost Around $76 for two, plus drinks
plus The elevated position
minus The shopping precinct below
score 13/20

a foreign affair

UPSTAIRS, 8 FRANKLIN STREET, MANUKA
PHONE (02) 6239 5060   MAP 10

ITALIAN

The sign at the bottom of the stairs says
'Italian Grill', but this is no Tuscan bistecca
house. Rather, it's a Dutch chef's take on
modern Italian food. Ron den Hartog learnt
a lot of his Italian cooking from books,
and proves it's nothing to be ashamed of.
If other restaurants around town borrowed
the books, perhaps they'd be able to make
his lovely prosciutto and provolone raviolini.
Or you'd find another restaurant that can
make that Emilia-Romagna classic flat
bread, piadina. If anything, the menu is
unnecessarily long, so some dishes, like our
milk-fed veal with asparagus, feel a little
under-loved and over-charred. Since opening
over three years ago, slight changes (softer
lighting, white banquettes) have given the
space more mood, though it still gets very
noisy on busy nights. And while Italy is
the home of the slow food movement,
sometimes the slow bit is taken to
extremes service wise.

licensed & byo; wine by the glass
lunch Tues–Fri noon–2.30pm
dinner Mon–Sat 6–10pm
cards AE BC DC MC V   Bookings recommended
seats 70; no smoking
owners Ron den Hartog & Monique van Gool
chef Ron den Hartog
cost Around $70 for two, plus drinks
plus Hand-made pasta   **minus** Slow service
score 13/20

juniperberry at the NGA

NATIONAL GALLERY OF AUSTRALIA,
PARKES PLACE, PARKES
PHONE (02) 6240 6665   MAP 10

CONTEMPORARY EUROPEAN

You need one of those audio tours in order
to find what was once the Mirrabook
restaurant (go down the escalators, out the
door, through the Rodin sculptures and
around to your right). The setting is a
fairytale: an open-sided pavilion by a
reedy, fish-filled lake, suddenly enveloped
by the ghostly mist of Fujiko Nakaya's
choreographed fog sculpture. Throw in the
cooking skills of Juniperberry's Janet Jeffs
and Kelly Leonard, and it's a fairytale
with a happy ending. The food is great,
appropriately flexible, and often themed to
major exhibitions. For the Celtic Book of
Kels, for instance, there was a terrific game
pie with a white ale glaze, Trinity College
burnt cream and Van Morrison music.
Big changes are planned for the place, and
we expect the somewhat temporary-looking
structure to become more permanent.
Some decent signage will no doubt be
the first of such changes.

licensed; wine by the glass
lunch Daily from noon
cards AE BC DC MC V   Booking recommended
seats 90; outdoor area; wheelchair access;
non-smoking area
owners/chefs Janet Jeffs & Kelly Leonard
cost Around $80 for two, plus drinks
plus The fog sculpture   **minus** Finding the place
score 14/20

the lobby

KING GEORGE TERRACE, PARKES
PHONE (02) 6273 1563   MAP 10

MODERN AUSTRALIAN

While the Lobby has always been an
upmarket dining room, it's only since a refit
last year that the place has been as lovely
as the rose gardens outside its doors.
The curvaceous back wall, shimmering like
the inside of an oyster, and aubergine carpet
add depth and class. And while the food has
been hit and miss, these days it's far more
of a hit, thanks to the talents of chef
Vanessa Scanes. Her menu ranges far and
wide, perhaps too far and wide on occasion,
but is mostly founded on solid European
technique. Wild mushroom ravioli are
heady with porcini and rich with sage
butter, and a Bengali kid pie actually does
marry with its minted pea sauce. A chicken
galantine stuffed with water chestnuts,
however, just didn't work with curried Puy
lentils. The space is often booked up with
weddings and functions, which can make
a weekend booking exceedingly hard to
snare if you're still single.

licensed; wine by the glass
lunch Mon–Fri noon–3pm
dinner Tues–Sat 6.30pm–late
cards AE BC DC MC V   Bookings recommended
seats 55; outdoor area; no smoking inside ✝✖
owner Fiona Wright
chef Vanessa Scanes
cost Around $86 for two, plus drinks
plus Great wedding venue
minus Getting in on a Saturday
score 12/20

mezzalira

MELBOURNE BUILDING, CNR LONDON
CIRCUIT & WEST ROW, CANBERRA CITY
PHONE (02) 6230 0025   MAP 10

ITALIAN

The low, solid, old buildings of Civic have
a certain elegance that much of modern
Canberra lacks. Mezzalira is a happy
compromise between the old and the new,
with its gracious modern fittings and
pleasant sidewalk ambience. The
knowledgeable, efficient and friendly staff
are flexible enough to move effortlessly in
and out of restaurant, café and boutique
pizza bar mode. You might start with an
entrée of pan-fried quail breast wrapped
in extremely compatible prosciutto and
teamed with sage, fresh fig jam and
mascarpone polenta. A main course of
twice-cooked Muscovy duck breast in duck
consommé with vegetables has real depth
and body, while ravioli with ricotta and
English spinach is solid rather than
inspirational. Finish with an Amaretto torte
layered with mascarpone and roasted
almonds, and you'll drift away dreaming
of Italy rather than Civic.

licensed & byo; wine by the glass
lunch Mon–Fri noon–2.30pm
dinner Mon–Sat 6–10pm
cards AE BC DC MC V   Bookings essential
seats 200; private room; outdoor area;
wheelchair access; non-smoking area ✝✖
owners Dominic, Joe & Pasquale Trimboli
chefs Pasquale & Teresa Trimboli
cost Around $80 for two, plus drinks
plus Casual elegance **minus** Can be squeezy
score 14/20

ottoman cuisine

CNR FRANKLIN STREET & FLINDERS WAY, MANUKA
PHONE (02) 6239 6754   MAP 10

MODERN TURKISH

Here is a restaurant where the familiar becomes extraordinary. Turkish cuisine has become part of Australia's culinary landscape. Everyone knows hummus, shish kebabs, dolmas and baklava. The simple secret of Serif Kaya's kitchen, and what has earned him the reputation as Australia's best Turkish chef, is that he can do all these things so much better than anyone else. Ask for sigara borek (feta and herbs wrapped in filo pastry) and you'll gasp at the subtlety of something you have tasted a thousand times before. Try the mixed kebab (lamb, beef, chicken and mince) and you'll know what a perfect kebab can be. Try kizartma – chargrilled baby eggplant with a creamy pomegranate sauce – or milk-fed Illabo lamb marinated and chargrilled and served on kipfler potato with rosemary and tomato jus. And don't even think of not finishing on a honey and nut dessert.

licensed & byo; wine by the glass
lunch Mon–Fri noon–2.30pm
dinner Mon–Sat 6–10.30pm
cards AE BC DC MC V   Bookings essential
seats 110; wheelchair access; no smoking
owners Serif & Gülbahar Kaya
chef Serif Kaya
cost Around $86 for two, plus drinks
plus Honesty with class   **minus** Often crowded
score 15/20

the republic

20 ALLARA STREET, CANBERRA CITY
PHONE (02) 6247 1717   MAP 10

MODERN AUSTRALIAN

This isn't the kind of restaurant you'd expect in the base of an office block on a quieter edge of the city. It's all dusky colours, Aboriginal-inspired wall sculptures and a honey-coloured polished floor that curls through the carpet like a meandering brook. What was a smart (bold, in fact), contemporary brasserie eight years ago is now starting to date, and in these days of the hyper-new, that's not a completely bad thing. The food, too, isn't as cutting edge as it once was, settling back into tried-and-true favourites such as Republic fish and chips and vitello tonnato with stewed peppers. Kangaroo is invariably impeccable, although the accompanying couscous has been known to let the plate down, and a harissa hollandaise seemed misplaced. Owners Derek Lyall and Paul Smith keep the place spick and span, and the wine list is brief, delightfully quirky and reasonably priced. Chefs tend to change every year or two, but the style remains.

licensed; wine by the glass
lunch Tues–Fri noon–2pm
dinner Mon–Sat 6–10pm
cards AE BC DC MC V   Bookings essential
seats 60; wheelchair access; no smoking
owners Paul Smith & Derek Lyall
chef Annabel Pryor
cost Around $86 for two, plus drinks
plus Aged wines by glass   **minus** The carpet
score 13/20

$

silo bakery

36 GILES STREET, KINGSTON
PHONE (02) 6260 6060   MAP 10

EUROPEAN

Try not to let your chin hang too low or
your eyes glaze over as you stare at the
long lines of prune, hazelnut or stone-fruit
tarts, because that's for afters. Lucky for
you, this café/bakery's befores are just as
enjoyable. You will be more than pleased
with yourself for choosing sake-poached
blood plums on toasted brioche and you'll
drool over the tomato crostini with
provolone, basil and eggs. What's more,
you'll get the best coffee in Canberra if you
ask the barista, Andrea, for her 'really good
coffee', code for something stronger than
most locals desire. The frenetic Silo is only
open during the day, just long enough for
breakfast, brunch and play lunch, before
crawling off to sleep (Canberra still has
its quiet times). There is the occasional
down side to this whole experience on
Saturdays – because it's so busy, it's hard
not to elbow fellow diners as you jostle
your way to your table. If so, just buy the
bread and take it home.

licensed & byo; wine by the glass
hours Tues–Sat 7am–4pm
cards AE BC MC V   Bookings essential;
no bookings for Saturday morning
seats 45; outdoor area; wheelchair access;
non-smoking area ✒✗
owners Leanne Gray & Graham Hudson
chef Leanne Gray
cost Around $43 for two, plus drinks
plus Anything baked   **minus** The madding crowd
score 13/20

$

tasuke

122 ALINGA STREET, CIVIC
PHONE (02) 6257 9711   MAP 10

JAPANESE

If you can track down the expats and find
out where they're eating, particularly with
Japanese food, you know you're in with a
better than even chance of eating well. So
it is with Tasuke, a humble hole-in-the-wall
tucked into a building that faces the bus
interchange (they actually promote it as
being next to the Pancake Parlour, if that
means anything). Let's face it, you wouldn't
come here for the view. But you would
come for the sashimi, undoubtedly the
best in town. And you would most
definitely come for the sweet, glistening
Japanese-style eel, the very good miso
soup, and (if you order ahead) the
renowned hotpot banquets. And, like
most of Canberra's Japanese community,
if you live in town, you too can come
here often to sit at the sushi bar, and
watch chef Yuji Takeda deftly slicing fish.
About the only thing you can't do that
they can is get homesick.

byo
lunch Mon–Sat noon–3pm
dinner Mon–Sat from 5.30pm
cards MC V   Bookings recommended
seats 65; outdoor area; no smoking ✒✗
owner Mao Yuyan
chef Yuji Takeda
cost Around $34 for two, plus drinks
plus That it's here
minus The bus interchange outside
score 12/20

timmy's kitchen

MANUKA VILLAGE,
FURNEAUX STREET, MANUKA
PHONE (02) 6295 6537   MAP 10

MALAYSIAN/CHINESE

There'll be those who miss the old Timmy's, now that this Canberra institution has moved to a bigger space next door. The staff now have logoed shirts, the paint on the walls doesn't look like it's been there forever, and there's even a whole bunch of tables out on the pavement for warm weather days (and smokers). But not much else has changed. The best dishes are still the Malaysian options, such as the gulai ayam, a sweet, fragrant, coconut curry of tender chicken, or their smoky and delicious (if not quite absolutely flaky) roti. This is food that takes you back to the market stalls of Malaysia. In fact, when you've got your face hovering over a steaming bowl of the legendary laksa, you could almost be in Malacca – or the old Timmy's, for that matter. Sammy's, its city cousin, is bigger still, with food that's nearly as good.

byo
lunch Tues–Sun 11.30am–2.30pm
dinner Tues–Thurs 5–10pm; Fri 5–11pm; Sat 5–10.30pm; Sun 5.30–10pm
cards AE BC DC MC V   Bookings recommended
seats 75; outdoor area; wheelchair access; no smoking inside
owner/chef Hang Kwok Chui
cost Around $34 for two, plus drinks
plus The new space   **minus** The Chinese stirfries
score 12/20

tu tu tango

124 BUNDA STREET, CITY
PHONE (02) 6257 7100   MAP 10
ALSO AT 36 FRANKLIN STREET, MANUKA
PHONE (02) 6239 4322   MAP 10

SOUTHWESTERN/SANTA FE

For years it's been here, looking like a cross between a Road Runner cartoon, a café and a themed Mexican cantina. And for years they've sold so many baked potato skins with guacamole to Canberra's young diners that the city is probably partially built on them. But the thing that keeps both the original city Tu Tu, and its Manuka cousin going, is the integrity of the good ol' southwest food. Chef Scott Bryce is back overseeing both places after a few years in Queensland, and if he's in either kitchen you're in fine hands. Even when he's not, you can still look forward to sultry scrambled eggs in burritos for brunch, flame-grilled prawns with citrus risotto and red pepper essence for lunch, or tumbleweed chicken salad and tandoori chicken chimichanga at dinner. Plans are afoot to open a bar upstairs for even more serious tequila sipping.

licensed & byo; wine by the glass
hours Daily 10am–late
cards AE BC DC MC V   Bookings recommended
seats 264; outdoor area; non-smoking area
owners Peter & Adrienne Griffiths
chef Scott Bryce
cost Around $66 for two, plus drinks
plus Brunch   **minus** Finding a waiter
score 13/20

$

viva zapata

SHOP 2, MCPHERSON STREET, O'CONNOR
PHONE (02) 6257 1040   MAP 10

MEXICAN

You could be forgiven for planting a
huge kiss on the cheek of the lady who
welcomes you at Viva Zapata as you arrive.
She shuffles from kitchen to table as
though she's your favourite aunt, intent on
feeding you well. And feed you she does,
but this particular aunt happens to be
Mexican, and hers is one of the few
authentic Mexican eateries in the country.
Maria Quinteros, and her husband Jose,
hand-roll all the tortillas for their soft,
delicate tacos. They hand-chop all the
prickly pears for the nopales salad, and
generally feed you very well for very little.
The incendiary heat of the food is
dampened for the local palate, although
the flavours are still very real. Even the
coffee is scented with special brown
sugar and lots of cinnamon. The space is
modest, to put it kindly, complete with
plastic-covered tables, but the food and
the intentions are generous, and the
sense of hospitality endearing.

byo
lunch Tues–Fri 11am–2.30pm
dinner Daily 5–10pm
cards BC DC MC V   Bookings recommended
seats 40; outdoor area; no smoking inside
owners/chefs Jose & Maria Quinteros
cost Around $50 for two, plus drinks
plus Hand-rolled tortilla
minus Deep-frying smells
score 12/20

central coast

SIMON THOMSEN & BRUCE ELDER

Foodwise, things change ever so slowly on the Central Coast. At the time of going to press, Tracy and Andre Chouvin were in the process of relocating their wonderful Café de La Gallerie restaurant to Avoca Beach (to be known as Feast), where Andre's great food will be matched by equally great views. Elsewhere in the area, savvy Sydney weekenders gather at the Old Kilcare Store (02 4360 1667) to check property prices over an all-day breakfast offering kippers and grilled tomato. Avoca crowds head for the unpretentious Antonia's at Avoca (02 4382 3737) or the beach-bound grab clever fish & chips from the punny Prawn Star Cafe (02 4382 1230). Finally, a minute's silence please for Terrigal stalwart Jardines, and its stunning wine list. The Central Coast's first restaurant (opened 50 years ago) fell on the sword of redevelopment as the new millennium began. Some call it progress.

♀ feast

4/200 AVOCA DRIVE, AVOCA
PHONE (02) 4381 0707   MAP 11

FRENCH

Husband-and-wife team Tracey and Andre Chouvin have built an enviable reputation at the Café de la Gallerie. The constantly changing and evolving dégustation menu, Andre's neat spin on French cuisine in Australia and silky smooth service ensured continuing success. The decision to move to Avoca has doubled the staff, seen the arrival of a French head waiter, turned BYO into a fine cellar, and given Andre the kitchen of his dreams. The views across Avoca Beach are as spectacular as the menu where favourites like barramundi served with young spinach, lobster, ginger and port sauce and Newcastle farmed duck are matched with classic French entrées of duck confit and terrine of quail, and desserts including a peerless raspberry crème brûlée and chilled orange and chocolate mousse with Grand Marnier sauce. When they settle in, this will be the best restaurant between Sydney and Byron Bay.

licensed; wine by the glass
brunch Sun 8.30–11am
lunch Daily from noon
dinner Daily 6.30–9.30pm
cards AE BC DC MC V   Bookings recommended
seats 100; outdoor area; wheelchair access;
no smoking inside ✚✗
owners Tracey & Andre Chouvin
chef Andre Chouvin
cost Around $108 for two, plus drinks
plus Sensational views   **minus** Noisy carpark
score unscored

the galley beach house

THE HAVEN, TERRIGAL
PHONE (02) 4385 3222   MAP 11

MODERN AUSTRALIAN

There's no finer view along the gentle sweep of Terrigal beach than from the balcony of this 1970s brick waterfront diner. It has all the faded glory of a function centre, decorated with aquatic bric-a-brac and, incongruously, a silverchair band poster. But basking on the timber balcony, watching over the kids parked on the gentle waterfront below, life is laid-back. So, too, is the attention to detail from the floor. Easygoing, seafood-dominated dishes (there's beef, lamb and chicken too) slip down without turning heads from the view. Cuttlefish salad is a study in green – shaved asparagus, green onions, cucumber and avocado fan – where flavours are happy to be friends rather than going all the way. Chargrilled scallops on game chips with sweet lamb's lettuce and eggplant caviar is similarly 'nice'. Blue-eye cod with tomato salsa, however, was let down by a sweet, cheesy polenta.

byo
lunch Daily noon–3pm
dinner Daily 6–9pm
cards AE BC DC MC V   Bookings recommended
seats 90; private room; no smoking until 10pm ✝✖
owners Neil & Kelly Gay
chef Tony Dexter
cost Around $86 for two
plus The view outside   **minus** The view inside
score 12/20

la mer

HOLIDAY INN RESORT, TERRIGAL
PHONE (02) 4384 9111   MAP 11

MODERN AUSTRALIAN

Such intelligent food, wheeled past on trolleys for the full silver service shebang, served on Villeroy & Boch plates, accompanied by decanted reds poured into Riedel glasses, deserves greater respect from punters in garish Hawaiian shirts or daggy T-shirts. While dress standards have slipped, Glenn Bacon's sophisticated, elegant, global fare remains firmly high life. Big night out fine dining like this – gilt-trimmed royal blue walls, padded tables, lush banquettes, discreet but eagle-eyed service – should be National Trust classified. Make the effort. Dress up, then chill out on Redgate farm quail piled on a salted duck cake with nashi pickle or a little copper pot of veal sweetbreads and crisp pork trotter in orange and cèpes butter. Vegetarians tuck into organic vegetarian risotto with white truffle oil. Carnivores love sweetly soft tea-smoked lamb with a lotus and braised shiitake torte. Summer pudding is mother country perfect. Or loosen your belt – and tie – for the five-course tasting menu.

licensed; wine by the glass
dinner Tues–Sat 7–10pm
cards AE BC DC MC V   Bookings recommended
seats 80; wheelchair access; no smoking ✝✖
owner Bass Hotels & Resorts
chefs Glenn Bacon & Peter Smith
cost Around $97 for two, plus drinks
plus Smart food   **minus** Casual diners
score 14/20

letterbox

OLD TERRIGAL POST OFFICE,
4 ASH STREET, TERRIGAL
PHONE (02) 4385 4222   MAP 11

MODERN AUSTRALIAN

This appealing reincarnation for the sturdy 71-year-old former post office successfully blends heritage colours and older-world charm with a shining stainless-steel kitchen, lithe black-clad waiters and candle-lit tables to balance subdued downlighting. A new glassed-in garden conservatory helps sate the popularity of Letterbox's clean, simple Asian and Mediterranean flavours. Bring friends to pick over a moreish, from-scratch tapas plate, or fresh oysters with soy and mirin. There's a tendency to overcook more testing dishes, even the steamed veggies. Pan-fried calves' liver with preserved lemon, sage and balsamic jus was too dry. Flaky salmon fillet, with garlic mash and pickled cucumber, had the ocean cooked out. More joy came from two big pillows of kumara-stuffed ravioli with burnt sage butter. 'Barbecued' sticky rice was anything but sticky. A smart wine list entertains.

licensed & byo; wine by the glass
dinner Mon–Sat from 6pm
cards AE BC DC MC V   Bookings essential
seats 110; private room; outdoor area;
no smoking ⃗✖
owner Paul Button
chefs Adrian & Nick Bartholomew
cost Around $92 for two, plus drinks
plus Post-haste service   **minus** Erratic delivery
score 12/20

relish the restaurant

80 OCEAN VIEW DRIVE, TERRIGAL
PHONE (02) 4384 2044   MAP 11

MODERN AUSTRALIAN

It didn't take long for hotel-trained Michael Garske to make a splash after leaving (now late) local legend Jardines, and opening Relish (formerly Meg's Manna) in August '99. Already fans are pestering foodie mags for the recipe to street-smart dishes like Moroccan-spiced lamb with minted yoghurt on a garlic crostini. They should also get the secrets to thin, translucent, marinated scallops drizzled with chilli oil and coriander aïoli on a potato pancake. This small local of tightly packed tables hums with happy banter, although it can get a little warm and airless, despite the noticeably fragrant smells wafting from a blend of Med and Asian flavours. No wonder things quieten down with the first mouthful of spiced duck on cinnamon-sweet poached pears, or snapper fillets in a ginger and kaffir lime broth with noodles. Vegetarians smile while eating the smoked mozzarella and red pepper tart. Finish with a blissed-up baked lemon tart.

byo
dinner Tues–Sat 6–9pm
cards AE BC MC V   Bookings recommended
seats 40; outdoor area; wheelchair access;
no smoking ⃗✖
owners Kelly & Michael Garske
chef Michael Garske
cost Around $76 for two, plus drinks
plus Fragrant food   **minus** Warm and airless
score 13/20

hunter valley

SIMON THOMSEN & MATTHEW EVANS

For a small, undulating valley which – all things considered – doesn't have too many hectares under vine, the Hunter sure produces a lot of wine from 80-odd wineries. Honourable vignerons acknowledge the source of their grapes, then let their alchemy do the talking. In the Hunter kitchens, however, there's a strong focus on regionally sourced produce. The Rothbury Café (02 4998 7363) even provides a regional roadmap with the menu. The Hunter Valley Cheese Factory and adjacent Pokolbin Woodfired Bakehouse, both at McGuigan Wine Cellars, offer something home-grown to soak up the tastings, while hops fanciers can head for the Hunter Valley Brewing Co. at the Hunter Resort.

Blue (02 4991 7444), tacked on to a caravan park, is a haven for caffiends, with laid-back café fare. Alas, funky wine buffs Adam & Ros Baldwin have left the Kurrajong at the Cessnock Hotel to open Mojo's in Lovedale, home of the annual Lovedale Long Lunch.

The more things change, the more they stay the same. Little boxes are filling the hillsides as developers hunt for the heads of the million-plus visitors. Two new restaurants, Taylors Café (02 4998 7117) and Esca Bimbadgen (02 4998 7585), prove that progress can be good.

cafe max

SMALL WINEMAKERS CENTRE,
MCDONALDS ROAD, POKOLBIN
PHONE (02) 4998 7899   MAP 12

MODERN AUSTRALIAN

After working up an appetite tasting the wines from vignerons represented at the Small Winemakers Centre, pick a favourite and head for the loft. Phill Kime bustles about with a cheeky grin and a quick quip, dishing out hefty platters of bistro grub to refuel vineyard cruisers. Grab a table outside (despite the enthusiastic flies), and enjoy the view over the vineyards to the mountains. Inside, you're likely to be rubbing shoulders with winemakers picking over antipasto platters crammed with Hunter cheeses, or testing a new shiraz with a chargrilled veal cutlet and sweet potato roesti. But chef Chris Martin can offer too much of a good thing, sometimes using an excess of dynamic flavours in his Asian–Med fusions. Duck confit, for example, gets lost in a melange of preserved lemon, capers, anise-flavoured pear, cos and sunflower sprouts. The talent's there in simpler dishes, which, thankfully, can be very wine-friendly.

byo
lunch Daily 11am–4pm
dinner Sat 6.30–9.30pm
cards BC MC V   Bookings recommended
seats 68; outdoor area; non-smoking area
owners Phill & Margaret Kime
chef Chris Martin
cost Around $80 for two, plus drinks
plus The bottles   **minus** Cross-cultural clashes
score 11/20

cellar restaurant

HUNTER VALLEY GARDEN VILLAGE,
BROKE ROAD, POKOLBIN
PHONE (02) 4998 7584   MAP 12

MODERN AUSTRALIAN

With recently installed air-conditioning
and new light fittings, there is talk of more
widespread refurbishment on the way at the
Cellar. In the meantime, the decor still pretty
much revolves around the same awkward
directors' chairs and the appealing, fern-
lined room, warmed with wood fires. If and
when they do change it, let's hope that they
can retain that fabulous garden-party feel.
One sure bet is the food. Mark Hosie
continues to serve up the best tucker in the
Valley – a sensible, sometimes sensational,
blend of gutsy flavours and a restrained
hand. He makes a lush oxtail risotto with
roasted root vegetables, and a mean
soy-braised suckling pig. The signature
five-spiced roast duck scented with
sesame broth is a long-standing favourite.
Curiously, the actual cellar consists of a
single wine rack, graced with some very
good older vintages.

licensed; wine by the glass
lunch Daily noon–3pm
dinner Mon–Sat 6.30pm–midnight
cards AE BC DC MC V   Bookings essential
seats 100; outdoor area; wheelchair access;
non-smoking area
owners Ian Savage, Jan Savage, Samantha
George & Mark Hosie
chef Mark Hosie
cost Around $92 for two, plus drinks
plus The old wines   **minus** Those chairs
score 14/20

chez pok

PEPPERS GUEST HOUSE,
EKERTS ROAD, POKOLBIN
PHONE (02) 4998 7596   MAP 12

MODERN AUSTRALIAN

On a rise at the end of the long, long dusty
road (if you come the back way as we did)
you'll catch a glimpse of a splendid
guesthouse. Chez Pok is surrounded by
the lush gardens of Peppers Guest House.
The restaurant is perfectly presented – pale
blue walls, garden views, polished service
and a verandah that boasts a gorgeous
vista. This is the type of elegant dining that
the Hunter Valley needs more of, although
the cooking can be uneven at times. Sage-
roasted chicken breast was beautifully
browned, with the sage lightly perfuming
the flesh, but the accompanying gluey,
sweet potato mash and dried spiced apple
were mere passengers. Young lamb fillets
with smoked eggplant were cooked to a
lovely pink but – and you knew there would
be another but – a dish of duck livers in
pastry failed to excite.

licensed; wine by the glass
breakfast Mon–Fri 7–10am; Sat–Sun 7.30–10am
lunch Daily noon–2pm
dinner Mon–Thurs & Sun 7–9pm;
Fri–Sat 7–9.30pm
cards AE BC DC MC V   Bookings essential
seats 230; private room; outdoor area;
wheelchair access; no smoking
owner Peppers Guest House
chef Jamie Hartcher
cost Around $90 for two, plus drinks
plus The gardens   **minus** Conference groups
score 12/20

esca bimbadgen

LOT 21, McDONALDS ROAD, POKOLBIN
PHONE (02) 4998 7585   MAP 12

MODERN AUSTRALIAN

From the dirt northern section of McDonalds
Road, a massive sweep of driveway climbs to
the distinctive Bimbadgen bell tower and the
airy, blond timber and glass-clad restaurant
where linen-clad lunchers prop, enjoying
the panoramic views. The café/restaurant
was rebuilt for this modern space with Mark
Armstrong as consultant. The service is smart,
the feeling contemporary. But while the food
never stops trying, not everything is an
unqualified success. Tapenade-topped rabbit
and prune terrine needed more depth, while
a walnut, prosciutto and goat's cheese tart
seemed monotonous. Nevertheless, crumbed
lamb's brains tumbled into rocket and
artichokes on a creamy sauce gribiche were
a delight; and the sweet gamey taste of spit-
roasted duck with sesame noodles and a
kick-along eggplant relish were completely
compatible. Suggested wines for each dish
makes life easier.

licensed; wine by the glass
lunch Daily 10am–3.30pm
dinner Wed–Sat 7–10pm
cards AE BC DC MC V   Bookings recommended
seats 240; private room; outdoor area;
wheelchair access; non-smoking area ✥
owner Bimbadgen Estate
chef Bradley Teale
cost Around $76 for two, plus drinks
plus Smart, modern setting
minus Over-the-top flavours
score 12/20

mulligans brasserie

CNR McDONALDS & THOMPSONS ROADS,
POKOLBIN
PHONE (02) 4993 1835 MAP 12

MODERN AUSTRALIAN

You can't really expect too much of a
restaurant in a golf resort in the Hunter,
so Mulligans is a surprising find, with its
great outlook over the pool in the
foreground and the golf course behind.
The food tries to please everyone from
international guests to Sydney refugees,
but is mostly pretty tame fare. There is
some light amidst the prawn and avocado
salads, smoked chicken linguine and beef
fillet with garlic cream prawns. A satiny
asparagus and potato soup tastes of fresh
asparagus and the open steak sandwich,
cooked dutifully pink, comes with a decent
jus. Meanwhile a smoked chicken salad
with cucumber and semi-dried tomatoes
is an honest way to spend lunch. The
resort's pricier, more upmarket Pipette
restaurant (upstairs) is open for dinner
on Saturday and Sunday only.

licensed; wine by the glass
breakfast Daily 7–10am
lunch Daily 11am–5pm
dinner Daily 6–10pm
cards AE BC DC MC V   Bookings essential
seats 148; private room; outdoor area;
wheelchair access; non-smoking area ✥
owner Cypress Lakes Group
chef Peter Trewenack
cost Around $80 for two, plus drinks
plus The view   **minus** Holiday surcharge
score 11/20

Y

the old george
and dragon

48 MELBOURNE STREET, EAST MAITLAND
PHONE (02) 4933 7272   MAP 12

FRENCH

More power to hearty hosts Ian and Jenny
Morphy, who have run this 1837 sandstock
inn, with its heavy drapes, green felt walls
and Georgian elegance for 18 years. All
the while, they've ignored foodie fashions
to deliver top-quality, robust, seasonally
driven, artery-thickening European classics.
Where else, in a Mod Oz world, can you
tuck into foie gras on brioche, or savour
the former on beef fillet with a black truffle
sauce? Morphy is whimsical – and decadent
– enough to toss truffles in a dish just
because he fancies it. The fattest Hervey
Bay scallops lift a broad bean and fennel
risotto (with truffle). Ian's bold saucing
shines in venison loin on celeriac mash
with a rich green peppercorn sauce. A
brilliant aged wine list helps bring out the
flavours. The brave, or foolhardy, might
end with 'chocoholic indulgence'. But
you'll die happy.

licensed; wine by the glass
dinner Wed–Sat 7–11pm
cards AE BC DC MC V   Bookings recommended
seats 65; private room; outdoor area;
non-smoking area ☺✖
owners Jenny & Ian Morphy
chef Ian Morphy
cost Around $92 for two, plus drinks
plus The richness   **minus** The richness
score 14/20

Y

robert's at
pepper tree

HALLS ROAD, POKOLBIN
PHONE (02) 4998 7330   MAP 12

EUROPEAN

Crossing the little bridge, past the fruit-
laden pepper trees, walking into the 1876
iron-bark slab cottage that opens out into a
candle-lit hall of exposed beams and warm
country ambience is like stepping through
the looking glass. This is Special Occasion
land, but it comes at a Special Occasion
price – extras like a pricey bowl of veggies
(and weekend surcharge) suggest there's a
limit to country hospitality. And sometimes
beauty is only skin-deep. The food can be
sublime, but occasionally it's more wayward
than a Prince Philip aside. Strongest are
offal and honest, hearty country dishes like
crisp lamb's brains on polenta with tomato,
garlic butter and caper sauce, and veal rib
with parsnip purée and porcini ragoût.
Port-poached figs with a cinnamon hint
and double cream round things out. The
wine list is a treasure hunt.

licensed; wine by the glass
lunch Daily noon–3pm
dinner Daily 7–11pm
cards AE BC DC MC V   Bookings essential
seats 190; private room; outdoor area;
wheelchair access; no smoking ☺✖
owner Tower Lodge Pty Ltd
chef Robert Molines
cost Around $120 for two, plus drinks;
$75 set price p.p. on Saturday night
plus The beautiful room   **minus** Add-on costs
score 14/20

the table

3 WATER STREET, GRETA
PHONE (02) 4938 7799   MAP 12

EUROPEAN PROVINCIAL

If you lack the time and money for a year in Provence, then a night in Greta is a pleasurable alternative. In a blink-and-you'll-miss-it town on the New England highway, Malcolm Martin has created his own *auberge*, building a provençale farmhouse and restoring a nineteenth-century miner's cottage for up to ten weary travellers gathering for the evening's *table d'hote* set menu. If you're not staying, yet are blessed with a place at the candle-lit long heavy table, remember breaking bread is a social activity. Much comes from the fertile (with help from the chooks) gardens, including the appetiser olives. In winter, your attentive raconteur host cuts loose with rich game dishes like jugged hare. Late summer offers chilled beetroot soup with sour cream, and tender pink lamb with a basil-scented zucchini timbale, plus sultana and pine nut studded saffron pilaf. A textbook Larousse chocolate crème rounds things off. Peter Mayle should be so lucky.

byo
dinner Daily 7–9pm
cards AE BC MC V   Bookings essential
seats 24; private room; outdoor area; wheelchair access; no smoking ⅸ
owner/chef Malcolm Martin
fixed price $49.50 p.p.
plus Sharing a meal   **minus** Getting to the table
score 13/20

taylors café

MCDONALDS ROAD, POKOLBIN
PHONE (02) 4998 7117   MAP 12

MODERN AUSTRALIAN

Having boosted Newcastle's reputation at Café Albion, Lesley Taylor has returned to the valley. In a tin shed with a concrete floor (formerly Chardonnays), she's created an unexpectedly stylish, candle-lit space of blue and sandy yellow, with corrugated iron and a feature wall of rough-hewn sandstone, plus homely touches like baskets of fresh eggs. The 16-strong multinational menu, which changes every two weeks, has all the strengths of a classic Hunter semillon. There are youthful, crisp, clean, flinty flavours in a king prawn, blue swimmer crab and avocado tian with a salmon roe vinaigrette; and crunchy tempura quail on a peach, rocket and Spanish onion salad with a salty-sweet dipping sauce. More mature, golden, toasty tastes come from honey-basted spatchcock with apricot stuffing and lavender jus. Spun sugar adds theatricality to desserts and a switched-on floor staff keeps things buzzing along.

byo
hours Tues–Sun 10am–4.30pm; Fri–Sun from 6.30pm
cards AE BC DC MC V   Bookings recommended
seats 65; outdoor area; no smoking inside ⅸ
owners Lesley Taylor & Jeri Finlay
chef Lesley Taylor
cost Around $92 for two
plus Style beyond its station   **minus** The flies
score 14/20

newcastle

SIMON THOMSEN & BRUCE ELDER

All of a sudden, Newcastle's air is cleaner and the food tastes better. With the steelworks gone and the waterfront enjoying a major facelift, there is a definite spring in the step of Novocastrians. They have reason to be proud of their chefs, too, especially those dedicated souls making weekly, forced pilgrimages to Sydney, so local diners can enjoy the best the markets have to offer.

The growing momentum and style of the Newcastle food scene proves it's no longer second cousin to the more tourist-inclined Hunter wine region. Beaumont Street offers a United Nations of flavours, from the self-descriptive Al-Oi (delicious) Thai (02 4969 1434) – there's also a Terrigal sibling (02 4385 6611) – to the authentic Italian Giovanni's Deli Cafe (02 4961 1093). And while local legend Barry Meiklejohn has closed his popular Fat Olive Bistro, the good news is that that former De Burghs owner, Kevin and Margaret Bourke have moved in and opened Level 1 (02 4940 8668).

The student alternative to Beaumont Street is Darby Street, where Goldberg's Coffee House offers café life, university-style. In the meantime, the Mediterranean-influenced cooking of Peter Bryant of the Scott Street Restaurant (02 4927 0107) just keeps getting better and better.

the brewery restaurant

150 WHARF ROAD, NEWCASTLE
PHONE (02) 4929 5792   MAP 12

MODERN AUSTRALIAN

Ferries come and go, ships slide by and promenaders stroll past as you gaze through the venetians at Newcastle's 24-hour industrial waterfront. This brasserie, part of a pub complex, is the highlight of the Queen's Wharf restaurant strip. Park outside for fresh oysters (rather than the baked with bacon, tomato, pesto and goat's cheese), washed down with a home brew. Inside, corporate lunchers seal deals over crisp linen tablecloths. The kitchen serves up something for everyone, with Asian and Med crowd pleasers that neither offend nor inspire. A 'tapas' plate relied too heavily on jars for us, but a sturdy asparagus-topped beef fillet served with a generous truffle mash was good stuff. Roast spatchcock on couscous works well enough, given a kick along by chilli jam. The well-priced Hunter-strong wine list offers plenty by the glass.

licensed; wine by the glass
breakfast Sat–Sun 8–11am
lunch Sat–Sun 12.30–3pm
dinner Sat–Sun 6–9.30pm
cards AE BC DC MC V   Bookings recommended
seats 90; outdoor area; wheelchair access; no smoking ✺✖
owners Ian & Marnee Burford
chef Elizabeth Box
cost Around $76 for two, plus drinks
plus The waterfront   **minus** Oyster toppings
score 12/20

cafe albion

72 HANNELL STREET, WICKHAM
PHONE (02) 4962 2411   MAP 12

MODERN AUSTRALIAN

Tony Brown has taken over this popular
café and Ross Fairleigh has stepped up
to the pans without missing a beat. A
Novocastrian journeyman who's worked
everywhere from hotel chains to Belinda
Franks Catering, he's maintaining that clever
blend of country-wholesome with snappy
twists in this swish room in a pub along the
industrial waterfront. Little rubbles of spicy
vinegared beetroot alternate with gravlax
roses to encircle a tangy lime granita in
a clever combination of zesty flavours.
A delicate pastry pie of coq au vin rides
a cushion of emerald-green pea purée in
a sea of rich demi-glace. Hunter duckling
is sweetly succulent, roasted golden in
a marmalade glaze. Aged reds tempt on a
very seductive wine list.

licensed & byo; wine by the glass
lunch Tues–Fri noon–3pm
dinner Tues–Sat 6.30–10pm
cards AE BC DC MC V   Bookings recommended
seats 90; private room; no smoking
owner Tony Brown
chef Ross Fairleigh
cost Around $103 for two, plus drinks
plus Old Hunter reds
minus Star Trek theme music
score 14/20

civic theatre brasserie

375 HUNTER STREET, NEWCASTLE
PHONE (02) 4925 3870   MAP 12

MODERN AUSTRALIAN/FRENCH

The signed show posters cramming the
walls bear testimony to the beautiful Civic
Theatre's theatrical history. Tucked into the
corner overlooking Newcastle's date-tree-
lined Civic Square, the brasserie's black
marble tables, red timber chairs and large
bar for pre- and post-show drinks feel very
French-bistro. John Agnew moved from
Customs House to turn up the house lights
here in July 1999. But sometimes the show
goes on without the stars – tardy suppliers
stopped us trying gazpacho with blue
swimmer crab or pork sausages with
caramelised onions and mash. Never mind.
The carefully piled prawn cocktail, smeared
with truffle-oiled mayo and topped with
salmon roe had retro jive. A rough jumble
of roasted Med veg in a thin shortcrust
pastry case and littered with crumbed
goat's cheese deserved applause, as did
crisp duck confit with thyme-charged
risotto. The floor team sometimes gives
new meaning to casual dining.

licensed & byo; wine by the glass
hours Mon–Fri 9.30am–3pm
dinner Wed–Sat & theatre evenings from 6pm
cards AE BC DC MC V   Bookings recommended
seats 100; private room; outdoor area;
wheelchair access; no smoking inside
owner/chef John Agnew
cost Around $60 for two, plus drinks
plus Theatrical atmosphere
minus Missing dishes
score 13/20

style **and** substance

AUSTRALIA **ELLE** *cuisine*

More good food – monthly!

For exquisite taste,
Paris, New York and London
can't compete with Vevey.

Vevey, a small town in the foothills of the Swiss Alps is the home of
Switzerland's first chocolate factory founded by François-Louis Cailler
in 1819. Using time honoured craftsmanship, fresh Swiss milk and fine
ingredients, Cailler has been the pinnacle of taste for nearly two centuries.

FOR EXQUISITE TASTE

Palmer NES 3047

clarks

1/50 BEAUMONT STREET, HAMILTON
PHONE (02) 4969 3833   MAP 12

MODERN AUSTRALIAN

Carol and Jeremy Clark, creators of this
thin white sliver of a café spilling out onto
Beaumont Street, have returned to the big
smoke. But that clever Clark style lives on,
with the duo returning on days off to keep
things humming along. Sydney refugees
pining for bills can pop in for a Saturday
breakfast of ricotta hot cakes or scrambled
eggs. At lunch and dinner, the food gets
more serious. Try finger-thick, crisp brown
rounds of sticky twice-cooked pork belly on
a fan of creamed garlic potato with braised
cabbage. Or perhaps an earthy mushroom
risotto, roast quail with truffled polenta,
or olive-oil-braised salmon with a mussel
vinaigrette and crushed kipfler potatoes.
The trifle is an ode to grandmas past and
future. Drop by, if only to sip on Grinders
coffee and crowd watch.

byo
hours Mon–Fri 10–11am; Sat 9–11am
cards AE BC DC MC V   Bookings recommended
seats 50; outdoor area; wheelchair access;
no smoking inside ✑✖
owners Carol Clark, Lynne & Chris Mangovski
chef Clinton Drew
cost Around $76 for two, plus drinks
plus Getting a table   **minus** Trying to get
a table
score 14/20

level 1

LEVEL 1, 54 BEAUMONT STREET, HAMILTON
PHONE (02) 4940 8668   MAP 12

MODERN FRENCH

When local institution Barry Meiklejohn
decided to call it a day, De Burgh's Kevin
and Margaret Bourke moved lock, stock and
Villeroy & Boch crockery to take over the Fat
Olive space. Sydney's loss was Newcastle's
gain. The upstairs restaurant now has a
clean-lined, soft-lit, Luigi Rosselli elegance
that literally – and metaphorically – rises
above Beaumont Street's bustling restaurant
strip. Slide onto the soft bel mondo-style
chairs and savour the attention to detail –
tables scraped for crumbs and clever wine-
matching suggestions – that accompanies
Bourke's sometimes fruity, French-influenced
fare. Deep-fried leek tops roast quail on
parsnip purée with a cinnamon hint. Pan-
fried lamb's brains crowd neatly on a small
island of sage-green potato purée. A bold
salmon confit mixes it with roasted
chickpeas and asparagus with lime syrup.
Summer berries swim in sabayon, capped
by puff pastry. It's enough to make you
move north, too.

licensed & byo; wine by the glass
lunch Wed–Fri noon–2.15pm
dinner Tues–Sat from 6pm
cards AE BC DC MC V   Bookings recommended
seats 50; outdoor area; no smoking inside ✑✖
owner/chef Kevin Bourke
cost Around $76 for two, plus drinks
plus The new chairs   **minus** The old stairs
score 14/20

merrett's at peppers anchorage

CORLETTE POINT ROAD, CORLETTE
PHONE (02) 4984 2555 MAP 12

MODERN AUSTRALIAN

When is a hotel-resort neither a hotel nor a resort? When the restaurant operates on a level of easy informality and the chef is both classy and endlessly inventive. Jean-Marc Pollet has found a perfect balance between French and Asian influences and created a menu more reminiscent of Tetsuya's than the usual Peppers Hotel. Entrées such as cured salmon and seaweed terrine served with cress salad and horseradish dressing walk a clear and courageous line between Japanese and French cuisines. The menu's highlight – star-anise-scented duck broth with rice-paper parcels of duck confit – is so full of subtlety and interest you'll be tempted to ask for it all over again once you've finished eating. Equally impressive are Vanessa West's desserts. Her fresh coconut and raspberry bavarois with Malibu and mango sauces is light, and full of resonating flavours.

licensed; wine by the glass
hours Daily 7am–9.30pm
cards AE BC DC MC V   Bookings essential
seats 120; private room; outdoor area; wheelchair access; no smoking
owner Peppers Hotel Group
chef Jean-Marc Pollet
cost Around $90 for two, plus drinks
plus The duck broth
minus The conference crowds
score 14/20

rob's on the boardwalk

E10, D'ALBORA MARINAS, NELSON BAY
PHONE (02) 4984 4444 MAP 12

MODERN AUSTRALIAN

The elegant boats bob gently in the marina and the tourist crowds promenade along the boardwalk. Here, as unassuming as all the rest of the eateries in the area, is a simple gem where Glenn Thompson, with attention to detail and a sense of adventure in the kitchen, has turned a seaside café into a very pleasant restaurant. If you head for the predictable fish and chips you'll be delighted to find hand-cut, unpeeled chips and fillets of flathead lightly crumbed and served with an excellent homemade mayonnaise. Equally impressive are the salads, whether rare beef with Japanese pickled ginger or smoked rainbow trout with asparagus, baby potatoes, capers and a sherry–nut dressing. The Peking Duck salad with green pawpaw and Thai dressing is a summer beachside delight. A class act in an unassuming location.

licensed & byo; wine by the glass
breakfast Sat–Sun 7.30–11am (daily in holidays)
lunch Daily 11.30am–3pm
dinner Tues–Sat from 6pm
cards AE BC DC MC V   Bookings essential
seats 109; outdoor area; wheelchair access; non-smoking area
owner Rob Murray
chef Glenn Thompson
cost Around $97 for two, plus drinks.
plus Great location   **minus** Touristy crowds
score 12/20

scott street restaurant

19 SCOTT STREET, NEWCASTLE EAST
PHONE (02) 4927 0107   MAP 12

MODERN AUSTRALIAN

Portishead's melodic lament adds to the mysterious chic of this clean, white, spartan space in an old boarding house tucked behind the lee of Newcastle's blustery beachfront. From the small open kitchen Peter Bryant watches over partner Therese Roe's smooth, cheerful service, and sends out colourful and contemporary Med-based fare, plus some precision Asian dishes. The delicious-dozen menu makes way for tempting specials like tapenade-topped sardines on pan-fried polenta. Barbecued quail, lightly smeared with chilli paste, matches wits with a sweet-scented salad of green mango. There's a clever surf-and-turf take in crisp-skinned ocean trout, topped with a slash of aïoli, on a bed of pancetta-flecked lentils in rich brown stock. Soft pink lamb cutlets balance on a bowl of whole baby beetroot, rocket, roast garlic and crumbled-ash chèvre. Leave room for seductive desserts like buttermilk pudding with poached blood plums.

byo
dinner Tues–Sat 6–11pm
cards AE BC DC MC V   Bookings essential
seats 45; private room; wheelchair access; no smoking
owners Therese Roe & Peter Bryant
chef Peter Bryant
cost Around $76 for two, plus drinks
plus The cooking   **minus** Not open for lunch
score 15/20

north coast

SIMON THOMSEN & BRUCE ELDER

A passion for regional produce is taking hold along the North Coast, from the award-winning coffee grown in the hills around Byron Bay, to Port Macquarie's wines, Casino's beef, Lismore's macadamias, Dorrigo's potatoes, Bangalow's bushfoods, Yamba's prawns and the shimmering seafood harvested right along the coastline. Producers are rising to meet the challenge from chefs keen to cook the local tucker and now, better restaurants are bobbing up like mushrooms, stretching from Forster on the Great Lakes to Kingscliff on the Tweed Border. The postcard-pretty fishing village of Yamba has a Byron-20-years-ago feel, but with food for a new millennium from the burgeoning restaurant strip. Mullumbimby's Cafe Al Dente (02 6684 3676) puts the hip in hippy, and Lismore's The Left Bank (02 6622 2338) keeps vegetarians happy. Fish-and-chip buffs beeline for Mongers Fish Takeaway (02 6680 8080) in Byron Bay, Howie's Fisho (02 6658 8085) in Sawtell and the Coffs Harbour Fisherman's Co-op for sashimi and sushi. Organic produce shines at Byron's Wholly Smoked Gourmet Foods (02 6685 6261) and Billinudgel's Billies Thai (02 6680 3352), while Lismore's Vecchiet Smallgoods (02 6629 5227) makes *molto bene* salami and cured meats.

the beachhouse café

THE OLD ROYAL HOTEL,
1 HOUGHTON STREET, PORT MACQUARIE
PHONE (02) 6584 5692   MAP 12

MODERN AUSTRALIAN

This grand nineteenth-century pub has a stylish new life as a café/restaurant/bar/nightclub thanks to hip frontman Greg Smith (ex-Star Anise in Coffs) and kitchen journeyman John Vanderveer. Settle into a teak slat chair outside, overlooking the waterfront promenade and river, for a colourful bistro lunch, starting with local Hastings River oysters in tempura batter. Vanderveer favours clean, simple but bold flavours, plus fish-and-chip twists like swordfish draped with roast capsicum and olive paste on rosemary roasted potatoes; or thin Ebor trout fillets in a crisp and spicy batter with cucumber salad and peanut-chilli sambal. There's a lush duck and noodle salad to match Mick Morris' sparkling Durif, or panzanella salad for the locally made Cassegrain Verdelho. At night, the upstairs balcony becomes the more formal Aqua Vista restaurant for lashings of chilli mudcrab.

licensed
breakfast Mon–Fri 10am–noon;
Sat–Sun 8.30am–noon
lunch Daily noon–3pm
dinner Wed–Sat 6–9.30pm
cards BC DC MC V   Bookings for dinner only
seats 160; outdoor area; wheelchair access
owners Gregory Smith & John Vanderveer
chef John Vanderveer
cost Around $70 for two, plus drinks
plus The view   **minus** It's also a nightclub
score 13/20

beachwood

16 CLARENCE STREET, YAMBA
PHONE (02) 6646 9258   MAP 12

MEDITERRANEAN

Simplicity and a love of the casual good life drives this airy peach-coloured café at the top of Yamba hill in the growing restaurant strip. From a lingering breakfast over the papers, spread across the distressed timber tables, to energetic nights of sometimes noisy celebration, Turkish-born host Sevtap Yuce has things humming along in good spirits. Chef Stephen Ellis keeps it simple on a short blackboard menu of seasonally driven Med-bistro favourites. But in hectic heats of the moment, things can go awry. Overcooked sardines, buried under a wild scrub of lettuce, lost their link with the sea. Roast duck, plucked too late from the oven, was disappointing between a wedge of potato gratin and crunchy green beans. Joy was restored by grilled gnocchi awash in a pleasingly sweetish tomato sauce with rocket and parmesan, and a blokey rib-eye fillet with mash and bearnaise.

byo
breakfast Wed–Sun 7.30–11.30am
lunch Wed–Sun noon–3pm
dinner Wed–Sat 6–10pm; daily in summer
cards BC MC V   Bookings recommended
seats 90; outdoor area; wheelchair access; no smoking ⚒
owner Sevtap Yuce
chef Stephen Ellis
cost Around $70 for two, plus drinks
plus Easygoing   **minus** Overcooking
score 12/20

the blue fig

23 FIRST AVENUE, SAWTELL
PHONE (02) 6658 4334   MAP 12

MODERN AUSTRALIAN

Under a sprawling fig in the placid main street of this seaside village, The Blue Fig offers unexpected elegance, combined with a love of life's finer things – like the Alessi and Essential Ingredient goodies filling one wall in this petite Provence-yellow room. By gentle candlelight, diners hunch over the damask tablecloths as infectiously enthusiastic gourmand Toby Dames explains wife Korryn's eloquent French homages, like a decadent boudin of duckling on lentils with a Madeira sauce. A simplified and lighter style, with delicate saucing, lets perfect produce shine. Pan-fried bug tails tumble off a potato and tomato salad with a bay leaf vinaigrette. Pink lamb loin and chestnuts ride a bed of buttered spinach and celeriac purée. Only a winey leek coulis lets down milk-fed veal on a smoked bacon roesti with tomato confit. Leave room for the aptly named chocolate heaven with a spiced fig compote, or prime French cheeses.

byo
lunch Tues–Sat 11am–2pm
dinner Thurs–Sat from 6.30pm
cards AE BC DC MC V   Bookings essential
seats 30; outdoor area; no smoking inside ⚒
owners Toby Dames & Korryn Wodrow-Dames
chef Korryn Wodrow-Dames
cost Around $76 for two, plus drinks
plus The coffee   **minus** Busy on weekends
score 14/20

castalia

SHOP 1, 15 CLARENCE STREET, YAMBA
PHONE (02) 6646 1155   MAP 12

MODERN AUSTRALIAN

The Chatsworth Island team came to town in late 1999, reinventing themselves as Castalia in a light and bright, contemporary restaurant/café/diner, adorned by Lola de Mar's neon-coloured symbolist paintings. Lounge with a locally grown Australian Estate coffee, slide into a booth for a mixed grill breakfast or afternoon snack, or head for the damask-clothed tables for panoramic views of the Clarence River. Margaret Matthews plays cheerful host, offering a bargain-priced wine list. Adam Kaluza's flexible, brasserie-style menu is mainly Med, with Asian touches. Squid in black bean struggles against too thick homemade nori noodles, but silken Meredith Farm goat feta shines in a chargrilled eggplant stack. A crisscross squirt of lime–avocado mayo makes a mild-tasting crab and whitebait pancake look like a Pollock painting.

licensed & byo
breakfast Fri–Sun 7.30–11.30am
lunch Fri–Sun noon–2.30pm
dinner Wed–Sat from 6pm
cards AE BC MC V   Bookings recommended
seats 140; outdoor area; wheelchair access; non-smoking area ⅹ
owners Margaret Matthews, Adam Kaluza & Greg Gray-Matthews
chef Adam Kaluza
cost Around $76 for two, plus drinks
plus The booths   **minus** Excess garnishing
score 13/20

divino

SHOP 4, CENTRE ARCADE,
WHARF STREET, FORSTER
PHONE (02) 6557 5033   MAP 12

ITALIAN

Down a quiet no-through road, this sunny courtyard café of faux pine tables under large umbrellas offers water views over the parked cars. It's a treat to eat Italian that rises above spag bol dag. Divino's flavours come from the olive oil-drenched Lipari islands off the coast of Sicily, where basil, chilli, garlic and parsley add zip to simple, fresh produce. The buzz comes from snappy classics: a cornucopia-like antipasto platter with homemade cred, and tuna rolled in cracked pepper and anchovies. A thin film of virgin olive oil shimmers on beef carpaccio marinated in lemon juice. Fennel-charged Italian sausages drape across a pile of lemon-and-garlic spinach. Plan ahead for prior-warning dishes like rabbit with potato and rosemary, and whole fish baked in rock salt. Service can vary from young and scatty to older and wiser.

byo
hours Mon–Sat 9am–5pm
dinner Mon–Sat 6–11pm
cards AE BC MC V   Bookings recommended, essential weekends
seats 85; outdoor area; wheelchair access; no smoking inside ⅹ
owners Michel Curcuruto & Craig Lewin
chef Craig Lewin
cost Around $76 for two, plus drinks
plus Regional Italian flavours
minus Scatty service
score 13/20

fins

THE BEACH HOTEL, BYRON BAY
PHONE (02) 6685 5029   MAP 12

SEAFOOD

The ramshackle charm of Fins in Brunswick
Heads makes way for a more sophisticated
world of red velvety chairs and soft caramel
timber curves at the Beach Hotel, but a
relaxing casual groove remains. Margarida
Snow leads a warm, sharp floor while Steve
Snow blends Asian, African, Portuguese
and bushfood flavours into aromatic and
sublime moments like his trademark oysters
steamed with kaffir lime, ginger and tamari.
The cataplana is pure Portuguese theatre,
unveiled in a copper pot of poached
seafood, in a saffron and star-anise-charged
broth. An evocative Moroccan tagine coats
succulent fish in sweet-scented African
spices with chermoula, dates and preserved
lemon. Finish with the goat's cheese
bavarois and palm sugar berries, and dream
of your own sea change. The new packaging
means Snow's lively, seafood-based cooking
has no equal in the north coast.

licensed; wine by the glass
lunch Sun from noon
dinner Daily from 6.30pm
cards AE BC MC V   Bookings essential
seats 90; outdoor area; no smoking
owners Steven & Margarida Snow
chefs Steven Snow & Matthew Wild
cost Around $76 for two, plus drinks
plus The seafood   **minus** A hectic pub
as neighbour
score 16/20

georgie's cafe

THE VILLAGE GREEN HOTEL,
230 POUND STREET, GRAFTON
PHONE (02) 6642 6996   MAP 12

MODERN AUSTRALIAN

In the quiet backstreets of the jacaranda
city, this refurbished old-world pub has
delightful charm and style. Mark Hackett
(Macleay Street Bistro, bills) returned to his
roots to surprise the meat-and-two-veg'ers
with modern bistro twists and seductive
seafood. Grab a bottle from the bar and
slump in deckchairs on the sprawling
verandah for a sassy steak sandwich with
tomato relish, or a light, fresh Greek lamb
salad with garlic yoghurt. Adventurers
can try tender octopus tentacles in a
colourful, Asian-dressed salad of capsicum,
coriander and Chinese greens. By night
there's pizza and pasta too, along with
a butch scotch fillet with grilled field
mushrooms on red wine jus. And everyone
loves the hand-cut wedges.

licensed
lunch Tues–Sat noon–2pm
dinner Tues–Sat 6–9pm
cards AE BC MC V   Bookings essential
seats 80; private room; outdoor area;
wheelchair access; non-smoking area
owners Mark & Judy Hackett
chef Mark Hackett
cost Around $54 for two, plus drinks
plus Hand-cut potato wedges
minus Buying drinks from the bar
score 13/20

$

the little snail

26 WALLIS STREET, FORSTER
PHONE (02) 6555 6355   MAP 12

FRENCH

Sydneysiders with long memories will recall
a certain Little Snail at Bondi years ago.
This is the son of the son of the original,
although it was later adopted by new
owners. Nevertheless, French snails still
feature on the menu, and to the best of our
memory, they are just the same as they
were all those years ago – in the shell with
traditional garlic butter. There are changes
and concessions to local requirements, but
when chef Christopher Deland turns his
attentions to France, expect traditional,
slow-cooked, impossibly tender duck in
a delicious duck and mango sauce. No
French meal would be complete without
profiteroles, and the ones offered by The
Little Snail, with that wonderfully dark,
slightly bitter chocolate sauce, seem to
have miraculously flown in from the other
side of the world. If you decide to sit
outside, it's very clear, however, that
you're in Australia: beware of the mozzies.
The restaurant knows the problem and
provides suitable spray.

licensed & byo; wine by the glass
dinner Tues–Sat from 6pm
cards AE BC DC MC V   Bookings recommended
seats 91; private room; outdoor area;
no smoking ✘
owner Grant Hallinan
chef Christopher Deland
cost Around $43 for two, plus drinks
plus Traditional French   **minus** Mozzies
score 12/20

mahlbergs

58 RIDGE STREET, NAMBUCCA HEADS
PHONE (02) 6568 5533   MAP 12

EUROPEAN

In the middle of nowhere along Nambucca's
Ridge Street, you'll find this smart local
with its long, clotted-cream-coloured room,
churchy windows, eye-catching dot
paintings, and padded wrought-iron chairs.
Mahlbergs offers something-for-everyone
pizza and pasta, plus a few well-worn
favourites. English-born Oliver Mahlberg
worked for the Roux brothers before falling
in love, then landing in his wife's home
town. Stay-homers wander in for takeaway
upmarket pizzas like garlic prawns with
olives, garlic and oregano, or lasagne made
with homemade pasta. Others settle in for a
textbook chilli-oiled penne with anchovies,
garlic, parsley and lemon, a more-savoury-
than-sweet onion tart in puff pastry, or a
full-on meat hit such as fillet steak or
crumbed chicken, served with a jumble of
veggies and roast potatoes. If the osso
buco is on, order it. Mahlbergs is also kid-
friendly. It may not be big night out
territory, but it hits the spot.

byo
dinner Tues–Sat from 6pm (closed during winter)
cards BC MC V   Bookings essential
seats 45; outdoor area; non-smoking area ✘
owners Oliver & Lisa Mahlberg
chef Oliver Mahlberg
cost Around $76 for two, plus drinks
plus It's in Nambucca   **minus** Can get warm
score 11/20

misaki byron

SHOP 1, 11 FLETCHER STREET, BYRON BAY
PHONE (02) 6685 7966   MAP 12

JAPANESE

A balmy Byron night is the perfect setting
for picking at individual serves of sashimi –
salmon, eel, pickled mackerel, salmon roe,
avocado and lemon zest wrapped in nori –
in the sail-covered courtyard of this clever
Japanese café. Stylish new chairs add a
touch more class. 'Eki', as he's known to
the locals, knocks up ever-reliable standards
like cloud-light tempura and restorative
miso soup. The fun comes from funky
fusions like baked mackerel with coriander
and macadamias, and seaweed-flecked
seafood and chicken paella. Then there are
mind-blowers like a cold mound of sweetly
steamed duck in a salad with celery and
onion shards, Brunswick prawns on veg-
laden Hokkien noodles, topped with tobbiko
(flying fish roe), and a warm beef salad with
pickled plum and wasabi dressing. A glass
of translucent lemon agar, awash with
Cointreau, mangoes, lychees and
raspberries, is a tongue-twanging ending.

byo
lunch Wed–Fri 11.30am–2.30pm (closed January)
dinner Tues–Sat from 6.30pm; Mon–Sat from
6.30pm in January
cards AE BC MC V   Bookings essential weekends
seats 50; private room; outdoor area;
wheelchair access; non-smoking area ✕
owners Hideki & Mayumi Takagi
chef Hideki Takagi
cost Around $65 for two, plus drinks
plus Sushi & sashimi   **minus** Shopping arcade
score 14/20

no. 2 oak street

2 OAK STREET, BELLINGEN
PHONE (02) 6655 9000   MAP 12

MODERN AUSTRALIAN

Just around the corner from the town's
memorial to its lost sons lies the warm glow
of this pretty timber cottage. Ray and Toni
Urquhart settled in the picturesque
Bellingen valley four years ago, tracking
down the best local produce for hearty,
honest country dishes. An effervescent Toni
flits from diners in deckchairs on the
verandah to the small, soft-lit dining room,
pointing out the lesser-known lights on a
thoughtful wine list. Local farmed rabbit is
a sweet treat in a rocket salad dressed with
sesame oil. Sticky, succulent slow-braised
duck confit drapes over an earthy jumble
of potato and roast apple, while lamb cutlet
sits on a fried sweet potato cake, spurred
on by a minted jus. A big white casserole
pot holds a gumbo-like mix of chicken
strips, okra, tomato and garlic on a bed
of rice. To finish, lime and coconut pudding
is naughty and nice.

licensed & byo; wine by the glass
dinner Tues–Sat from 6.30pm
cards BC MC V Bookings essential
seats 40; outdoor area; wheelchair access;
non-smoking area ✕
owners Toni & Raymond Urquhart
chef Raymond Urquhart
cost Around $76 for two, plus drinks
plus A friendly welcome   **minus** It's small
score 14/20

§

pacific hotel bistro

16–18 PILOT STREET, YAMBA
PHONE (02) 6646 2491   MAP 12

MODERN AUSTRALIAN

This whitewashed mid-century pub, perched
over Yamba's surf beach, offers million-
dollar ocean views for a relaxed fraction of
the price. The surfboard's evolution is told
by boards mounted on the walls. A simple
left/right divide separates diners from
drinkers, so wander up and order from a
daily blackboard menu, then head to the
bar for the 50-something wine list. Grab a
window table to watch the whales and
dolphins play as the fishing fleet sets sail.
Adrian Batten made a name for himself in
Tassie's Schouten House and Plate of the
Art. He coaxes feisty flavours from
globetrotting bistro dishes, amidst half-a-
cow sirloins and fish and chip favourites.
A seafood tagine is a fragrant, chermoula-
infused hotpot with saffron yoghurt. Twice-
cooked eggplant soufflé with pesto is boldly
simple, and chilli-crusted squid on cucumber
noodles with nam jim zaps the palate. White
chocolate redeems itself (for not being
brown) with fig baked in filo.

licensed
lunch Daily noon–2.30pm
dinner Daily 6–8.30pm
cards BC MC V   No bookings
seats 120; private room; outdoor area;
wheelchair access
owners Redvat Pty Ltd & Karen Bull
chefs James Rook & Adrian Balten
cost Around $60 for two, plus drinks
plus Ocean views   **minus** No bookings
score 13/20

paupiettes

56 BALLINA STREET, LISMORE
PHONE (02) 6621 6135   MAP 12

MODERN FRENCH

Just before you hit the strip of fast-food
joints along the highway, there's a brown
brick building giving no hint of the delights
within. Paupiettes was a 1990s creation,
even if the décor is 1970s shocker – from
maroon and peach tablecloths to folk art.
But chef David Forster's talent keeps
leapfrogging ahead with deft style and
presentation that's distinctly post-
millennium. When his wife Shirley explains
the Asian and Mediterranean blackboard
menu, featuring Korean-style salmon with
wasabi mayonnaise, you'll forget the
surrounds. Pan-fried lambs' brains huddle
neatly on a slice of spinach-topped
sourdough in black butter; braised pork
hock sits in a shallow shiitake and anise-
scented pool with wilted bok choy. A wild
frizz of parsnip chips tops baked lamb loin
on eggplant and potato roesti, while
desserts such as poached summer fruit
with brioche and macaroon crumble prove
country towns have their own charms.

byo
dinner Tues–Sat 6.30–9.30pm
cards AE BC DC MC V   Bookings recommended
seats 65; no smoking ⚡
owners David Forster & Shirley Forster
chef David Forster
cost Around $76 for two, plus drinks
plus The food   **minus** The décor
score 14/20

rae's on watego's

8 MARINE PARADE,
WATEGO'S BEACH, BYRON BAY
PHONE (02) 6685 8246   MAP 12

MODERN AUSTRALIAN

Rae's is special, knows it and shows it –
from tropical touches like gorgeous orchids,
to fast and sharp, but deferential, service.
To luxuriate on the whitewashed terrace
of this exclusive guesthouse, tucked under
Cape Byron, gazing across the sparkling
ocean, is a lesson in la dolce vita. A
40-bottle wine list that kicks off with a
Cristal magnum proves this is no place for
the faint of wallet. The predominantly Asian,
seafood-focused menu shows similar class.
Big, plump Moreton Bay bugs are lightly
smeared with Thai spices; goat's cheese and
mushroom tortellini is lifted by a fragrant
apple and tomato relish and grilled prawns.
Crisp barbecued blue-eyed cod takes on
chilli caramel, sprinkled with deep-fried
bok choy; and a tangle of wakame and
salmon roe caps a delicately steamed
clean-flavoured barramundi in a small pool
of wasabi and soy dressing. But a pricey
mesclun salad is as overvalued as those
early dot.com shares.

licensed; wine by the glass
lunch Sat–Sun noon–3pm
dinner Daily from 6.30pm
cards AE BC DC MC V   Bookings recommended
seats 40; outdoor area
owner/chef Vincent Rae
cost Around $130 for two, plus drinks
plus Sunny days   **minus** Rainy nights
score 14/20

serrano beach café

1/26 MARINE PARADE, KINGSCLIFF
PHONE (02) 6674 5511   MAP 12

MODERN MEDITERRANEAN

If there's an upside to development in this
easy-going, fast-growing coastal town
below the Gold Coast, it's that enough
people can appreciate the robust talents
of multi-skilling chef/hosts like Patrick and
Kathy Hobbs. Serrano is a striking duck-egg
blue/lemon yellow/ochre red café on the
beachfront restaurant strip. You can plonk
in a deckchair with sand between your toes
and tuck into a bowl of steamed mussels
with saffron, caponata and chilli, and let
the bold Mod Med flavours flow over you
like waves. A wedge of sweet onion tart is
piled high with grilled artichokes, pesto and
splayed cotechino sausage. Dusky cumin-
roasted beetroot sits beside twice-cooked
goat's cheese soufflé topped with jammy
fennel, while succulent braised rabbit lies on
creamed parsnip coated in a spiced orange
jus. A chunky, spicy, lush venison and prune
pie also helps to explain why so many
people want to move here.

licensed & byo
breakfast Sat–Sun 9–11am
lunch Wed–Sun noon–3pm; Tues–Sun in summer
dinner Wed–Sat 6–9.30pm; Tues–Sun in summer
cards AE BC MC V   Bookings essential
seats 65; outdoor area; wheelchair access;
non-smoking area ⟡✗
owners Patrick & Kathy Hobbs
chef Kathy Hobbs
cost Around $76 for two, plus drinks
plus Gutsy flavours   **minus** Cakey desserts
score 14/20

star anise

93 GRAFTON STREET (PACIFIC HIGHWAY),
COFFS HARBOUR
PHONE (02) 6651 1033   MAP 12

MODERN AUSTRALIAN

Coffs Harbour is one town the highway
hasn't bypassed, giving you a better chance
to spot this easy-to-miss shopfront on the
southbound side of the street. Gary Tyson
runs a fast, fun and colourful ship, backed
by a country-friendly team that manages
to keep kids as happy as the grown-ups.
The no-fuss four-by-four blackboard menu is
guided by what's fresh, and could include
goodies such as tuna tartare resting on
sweetly enticing caramelised onion bread.
While Gary's deft technique shows due
deference to meat and fish, not all the
combinations work. Local sand crab in
chalk-perfect risotto was overpowered by
too much preserved lemon. Chilli-buttered
chargrilled spatchcock on braised pumpkin
is a smarter act. Leave space for truly
scrumptious desserts like the rich,
hazelnutty, chocolate semifreddo or
a cinnamon bavarois with poached
pear and shortbread.

byo
dinner Mon–Sat 6–9.30pm
cards AE BC MC V   Bookings recommended
seats 50; no smoking ⌇✗
owners Gary Tyson & Giorgio Pietralunga
chef Gary Tyson
cost Around $76 for two, plus drinks
plus On the highway   **minus** Highway noise
score 13/20

toscanis

SHOP 4, CNR JONSON & MARVEL STREETS,
BYRON BAY
PHONE (02) 6685 7320   MAP 12

MEDITERRANEAN

Day and night, things are pumping to a
funky dance beat as the groovy gather in
this yurt-like, very organic two-storey stone
and timber building. They might be upstairs
for the latest exhibition, lounging around,
picking at the half-dozen blackboard tapas.
Others prefer the bistro chairs and
butchers'-papered tables in the wedge of
a courtyard open to street life. The menu is
no less varied, offering entrée and main
options for most of the dozen-odd
African–Asian–Italian dishes that come
with a recommended tipple. Workman-like
penne with tomato, olives, asparagus and
parmesan has a distinctive lemon tarragon
twist. Fish and scallop cakes drift in a light
red curry and coconut pool. Lamb shanks
braised with tomato and chickpeas were,
however, emasculated beside a glug of egg
noodles. The showstopper is a dreamy,
fragrant Asian salad of tea-smoked salmon
with chilli dressing.

licensed & byo; wine by the glass
lunch Fri noon–5pm
dinner Sat–Thurs 4pm–late
cards AE BC DC MC V   Bookings recommended
seats 100; private room; outdoor area;
wheelchair access; non-smoking area ⌇✗
owners Ben & Belinda Kirkwood
chef Tippy Heng
cost Around $76 for two, plus drinks
plus It's so casual   **minus** It's so hectic
score 13/20

wild about food

33 BYRON STREET, BANGALOW
PHONE (02) 6687 2555   MAP 12

SEAFOOD

Fairy lights flag the delights inside this cheerful room in a pretty village 20 minutes from Byron Bay. Glenn Beaver blends older charm and quirky sass in the décor – from Fauve-vibrant landscape paintings to coloured glass-studded tables – with the same clever confidence that his kitchen mixes local bushfoods into Asian and European flavours. After cooking a gossamer-light omelette to wrap around smoked salmon, with a watercress and nectarine concassé and creamy mustard dressing, he'll stroll out to serve it. Whole deep-fried garfish in a bowl of satisfying tamarind broth with angelhair noodles and crushed macadamias is bliss, but squid stuffed with salmon and basil on roast capsicum coulis doesn't quite feel together. There's a fish and chips twist – Moroccan spiced whiting with potato and beetroot chips and wattleseed chilli jam. Desserts like lemon myrtle bavarois with finger lime and stonefruit are bonza tucker, cobber.

byo
lunch Sun noon–3pm
dinner Mon–Sat 6–9.30pm
cards AE BC MC V   Bookings recommended
seats 65; outdoor area; no smoking inside ✖
owners Glenn & Christine Beaver
chefs Shaun White & James Larkin-Taylor
cost About $65 for two, plus drinks
plus Bushfood blending
minus Rowdy crowd reverb
score 13/20

snow country

BRUCE ELDER

The New South Wales snow country – basically the two major ski resort towns of Thredbo and Perisher Valley – has undergone a dramatic culinary metamorphosis in the past five years. Crowds of well-heeled city visitors are demanding good wine lists, local produce and imaginative cooking that's a cut above steak and chips. The beauty of the region now attracts visitors all year round, so a small number of restaurants stay open through the summer months and manage to sustain continuity and maintain high quality standards. As well as the three listed here, both Altitude 1380 (02 6457 6190) and Sante (02 6457 6083 – previously Reds and now under new management) in the main shopping square in Thredbo are worth checking out. The chefs in the area all know each other, so some discreet enquiries will reveal which places have seen the winter-time arrival of a culinary genius who will stay for five months, ski between courses, and disappear with the snows. This can be part of the fun and the challenge for the winter skier.

crackenback cottage

ALPINE WAY, THREDBO VALLEY
PHONE (02) 6456 2198   MAP 11

AUSTRALIAN

The Young family has created a perfect café/restaurant on the way to the snowfields. There are plenty of activities for the children (including a maze), excellent coffee, a good gift shop and a huge range of flavoured schnapps (the apple and the peach are out of this world). The menu, with its strong emphasis on local produce, is ideal for those who want to sit in front of a log fire and stoke themselves against the winter cold. Try the wood-fired trout pizzetta with local goat's cheese and dill. Beef and burgundy pie is a winter-time favourite. Whole local trout with herbed potatoes, braised or rack of lamb, and the kangaroo fillet are all well cooked and attractively presented. Desserts are substantial and designed to warm those frozen extremities. And then, there's that peach schnapps.

licensed
lunch Daily 10am–4pm (Wed–Sun 10am–4pm in summer)
dinner Wed–Sun 6–9pm in winter and school holidays; Fri–Sat 6–10pm in summer
cards AE BC DC MC V   Bookings recommended
seats 110; outdoor area; wheelchair access; non-smoking area
owners The Young family
chefs Jason Vandenberg, Sharon Matthews & Janene Howard
cost Around $82 for two, plus drinks or three courses for $26 p.p., plus drinks
plus The schnapps   **minus** Very family orientated
score 12/20

Ψ

credo

RIVERSIDE CABINS,
DIGGINS TERRACE, THREDBO
PHONE (02) 6457 6844   MAP 11

MODERN AUSTRALIAN

The setting is outstanding: a view across
Thredbo River with the snow-capped
mountains (at least in winter) in the
background. It's a pity that this view is no
longer accessible at lunchtime, but such is
the nature of restaurants in regions where
bookings are either feast or famine.
Given Thredbo's relative inaccessibility,
the menu is a wonderland of surprises.
Where else in rural New South Wales would
the discriminating diner find that perfectly
cooked taste thrill – salt-and-pepper
whitebait with lemon mayo? The restaurant's
signature dish is double-roasted duck with
citrus glaze, a sweet and succulent main
course. In winter-time, if you are wanting a
more Alpine, Central European experience
try the excellent chorizo sausages with
a subtle beetroot and parsnip mash and a
sweet beetroot glaze. Desserts are always
worth the effort, particularly the homemade
ice-creams (a real treat for the kids) and the
lemon zest tart.

licensed; wine by the glass
dinner Daily from 6.30pm
cards AE BC DC MC V   Bookings recommended
seats 94; outdoor area; wheelchair access;
non-smoking area ✣✖
owners Ron & Noni Plewes
chefs Justin Miles & Tyler O'Brien
cost Around $70 for two, plus drinks
plus Superb setting   **minus** Can get noisy
score 14/20

stables

VALHALLA ROAD, PERISHER VALLEY
PHONE (02) 6457 5755   MAP 11

MODERN AUSTRALIAN

The clean open lines of the Stables are a
little Glenn Murcutt and a lot inner-city
chic. High arched ceilings, some mandatory
corrugated iron, windows through which
the winter sun pours and an upstairs bar
that is more like a gallery give the whole
place a crisp and inviting buzz. Mine host
Andrew Drummond is friendly, energetic,
curious and perfectly capable of making
suggestions. New chef, Marcia Branson,
fresh from Canberra, is already weaving her
spell on a new menu. Start, as we did, with
a delicate and wonderfully clean-tasting
spinach and sweetcorn broth with cubes
of feta and follow with a warm salad of
smoked trout with a poached egg and an
ever-so-subtle dill sauce. To finish – and you
always finish with dessert in snow country –
lightly grilled fresh figs served with honey
yoghurt. This restaurant will get better and
better as the year progresses.

licensed; wine by the glass
breakfast Daily 7.30–11am
lunch Café menu Daily noon–4pm
dinner A la carte daily 6.30–10pm (Tues–Sat in
summer); café menu daily 6.30–10pm
cards AE BC DC MC V   Bookings recommended
seats 90; private room; wheelchair access;
no smoking ✣✖
owner Midika Pty Ltd
chef Marcia Branson
cost Around $76 for two, plus drinks, less in café
plus Warm hospitality   **minus** Hot seats in sun
score 13/20

south

MOLLY FOSKETT, BRUCE ELDER
& JOHN PEGRUM

Slowly the South Coast is realising that
it is a region full of high-quality local
produce, and therefore one that is full of
restaurant potential. The 'weekends away'
industry, however, is growing much faster
than the number of quality restaurants,
which means that too often visitors find
great accommodation only to be
confronted with 'where do we eat?'

The ethos of the cheap, poorly cooked
fish 'n' chips to be consumed in a park
still dominates, but things are changing.
For the first time, a Kiama eatery has made
it into the *Good Food Guide*. The work
done by the tireless Donna Shannon has
helped lift Eden's game, including Donna's
own Oyster Bar at the town's harbourfront
(02 6496 1304). If you are around
Greenwell Point, check out Back Gate
Seafoods (02 4447 1231) where Michael
O'Donnell knows how to cook perfect
fish. The café at Hyams Beach is a beacon
around Jervis Bay and, for vegetarians,
the Perfect Break Cafe (02 4234 1211) at
Gerringong is an attractive option. But why
are there only two top-notch restaurants in
Wollongong, when there are at least three
times that number in Newcastle?

bianca's

AUSTRALASIA HOTEL, 60 IMLAY STREET, EDEN
PHONE (02) 6496 1600   MAP 11

MODERN AUSTRALIAN

Donna Shannon may have laid down the
ground rules – keep it simple, make sure
you get the best of the day's catch – but
new chefs Briony Armfield and Dean Love
are gently giving her old menu an ever-so-
gentle nudge. This is a very smart move.
Keep the best of the old and tickle it with
something new. Particularly impressive, and
gloriously subtle, is the fresh seafood laksa
with Thai coconut broth, chilli, lemongrass
and coriander, Hokkien noodles and bok
choy cabbage. The seafood platter, a
wonderland of fresh produce, is still
incredible value – as in, you'll think you've
died and gone to King Neptune's heaven.
As for the decor and ambience, it never
changes. It is pure Aussie country hotel
circa 1950 with exhausted carpet, fishing
nets, glass balls, large corks and a specials
blackboard in the shape of a whale. Bianca
is the mother of Eden's culinary revival.
She deserves to be loved.

licensed; wine by the glass
dinner Mon–Sat 6–8.30pm
cards BC MC V   Bookings recommended
seats 70; outdoor area
owners John Crosby & the Slater family
chefs Briony Armfield & Dean Love
cost Around $54 for two, plus drinks
plus Fresh fish   **minus** Old-style décor
score 12/20

cookaburra's

10 WASON STREET, ULLADULLA
PHONE (02) 4454 1443   MAP 11

MODERN AUSTRALIAN/SEAFOOD

The merry king of the bush is he . . . Barry
Pawsey, assisted by his wife Sylvi, reigns
supreme in the culinary limbo of the South
Coast. The moment the bread plate hits the
table, you know you're in for a treat (try
homemade exotics such as a soy, wasabi
and seaweed bread). Enjoy every mouthful
of the inventive entrées, which range from
a tender New Zealand rabbit tartlet with
caramelised leek and mustard mash to a
roasted guinea fowl salad with Japanese
tea quail eggs and a blueberry vinaigrette.
For mains, the tempura brains wrapped in
bacon with orange and mustard glaze are
beautifully cooked and deliciously piquant.
The grilled seafood sausage crammed with
the sweet meats of prawn, scallop and
octopus and wrapped in crepinette atop a
pond of lobster sauce is sheer bliss. To
finish, try the generous dessert of cassata
covered in a raspberry glace served with
honeycomb biscuit.

byo
lunch Mon–Fri noon–3pm
dinner Daily from 6pm
cards AE BC DC MC V   Bookings essential
seats 50; private room; outdoor area;
no smoking inside
owners Sylvi & Barry Pawsey
chef Barry Pawsey
cost Around $108 for two, plus drinks
plus Good music   **minus** Unpromising exterior
score 14/20

doncaster inn

WILSON STREET, BRAIDWOOD
PHONE (02) 4842 2356   MAP 11

MODERN AUSTRALIAN

Surrender to the grandeur of this converted
convent, now a gracious guesthouse.
Andrea Villinger delivers the delights of
partner–chef Daniel's creative Mod Oz
offerings in the ambience-filled dining room.
A set two- or three-course menu with a
choice of three entrées, mains and desserts
keeps it simple. Local delicacies abound,
with starters of smoked trout fillet with
horseradish cream served on a bed of fresh
salad greens, and a warm salad of kangaroo
fillet with a refreshing lime and coriander
dressing. Slow-roasted spicy duck legs in
orange sauce are delicious and the spicy
Tunisian lamb served with couscous and
harissa sauce is equally tempting. Finish
with sorbet and fresh berries marinated in
Cointreau before you collapse in one of
the charming drawing rooms or take a
stroll around the peaceful garden. This is
old-fashioned country hospitality at its best.

byo
breakfast Daily 7.30–9.30am
dinner Daily 7–10pm
cards AE BC DC MC V   Bookings essential
seats 65; private room; outdoor area;
wheelchair access; no smoking
owners Andrea & Daniel Villinger
chef Daniel Villinger
cost $31.50 p.p. for two courses; $40.50 p.p.
for three courses
plus Grand and gracious
minus Foiled butter squares
score 13/20

jameson's on the pier

OLD PUNT ROAD, BATEMANS BAY
PHONE (02) 4472 6405   MAP 11

SEAFOOD

The pier, which is on the bank of the Clyde
River, is a relaxing and unpretentious place
to kick back. Nick and Pat Jameson are very
much hands-on hosts offering warm and
friendly service. Of course fresh seafood
dominates. A seafood crêpe starter is
overloaded with fresh prawns, scallops
and catch of the day sitting in a dill cream
sauce. Not to be missed are the tempura
king prawns with plum dipping sauce, a
definite local favourite. Caesar salad with
smoked salmon is a good lunchtime option
if you can manage to pass up the tempting
fish-of-the-day selections. Crisp-skinned
seared Tasmanian salmon fillet, served on
pumpkin mash and asparagus with a
rosemary, honey and lemon dressing, is a
perfect combination of flavours. Watch the
pelicans glide in while you try Jameson's
popular crème brûlée or the luscious layered
ice-cream cake for a refreshing finale.

licensed & byo; wine by the glass
lunch Tues–Sun noon–2.30pm
dinner Tues–Sat 6–9pm
cards AE BC DC MC V   Bookings recommended
seats 80; outdoor area; wheelchair access;
no smoking inside
owners Nick & Pat Jameson
chef David Parker
cost Around $43 for two, plus drinks
plus The river   **minus** Speedboats
score 13/20

ristorante due mezzi

119 KEIRA STREET, WOLLONGONG
PHONE (02) 4229 5633   MAP 11

ITALIAN

An evening with acclaimed owner–chef
Lorenzo Pagnan and partner-in-style
Rebecca Wilford is one to remember.
Delicious deep-fried zucchini flowers
descend while you gloat over the amazing
menu and observe the local foodies tucking
in with familiar gusto. Start with a more
than generous saffron lasagne with pork,
veal and chicken filling resting on a creamy
tomato sauce or a superb dish of crisp salt-
cod croquettes with sugar peas, eggs and
crouton salad. Roasted veal loin stuffed
with silverbeet and ricotta, served with
perfectly baked parmesan polenta on a
rich tomato sauce, is sensational, as is the
lime and honey spatchcock with butternut
pumpkin, pine nuts and lime zest. This
sophisticated northern Italian experience is
not complete without a dessert. Be tempted
by the mango semifreddo with raspberry
caramel sauce and poached blueberries.
As much as we love Wollongong, this feels
more like a night in Florence.

licensed; wine by the glass
lunch Thurs–Fri noon–2.30pm
dinner Tues–Sat 7–10pm
cards AE BC DC MC V   Bookings recommended
seats 50; no smoking until 10.30pm
owners Rebecca Wilford & Lorenzo Pagnan
chef Lorenzo Pagnan
cost Around $100 for two, plus drinks
plus Sophisticated flavours
minus Closeness of tables
score 15/20

salmon & co

4/70 ALBERT STREET, BERRY
PHONE (02) 4464 3037   MAP 11

MODERN AUSTRALIAN

Bustling and busy, this casual diner is not the perfect setting for a romantic duet, although in summer you can retreat to the courtyard if the volume bothers you. Great starters include chargrilled chicken breast and bacon salad tossed with oven-roasted tomatoes, avocado and basil mayo, served on a bed of sweet potato slices, or the stone-baked pizza bread served with a fabulous range of dips, including tomato and chilli jam and roast red capsicum with pecans and pine nuts. These generous starters can be followed by stone-baked pizza of chargrilled eggplant, artichoke hearts, red capsicum, black olives, pesto and Spanish onion. More predictable are main courses of chicken, beef, lamb and veal, and a stand-out chargrilled Atlantic salmon served on potato mash with sautéed spinach and hollandaise. If you fancy something sweet, try the peach and strawberry spring rolls with a honey yoghurt dipping sauce.

byo
lunch Sun 11am–3pm
dinner Wed–Sun from 6pm
cards AE BC MC V   Bookings essential
seats 60; outdoor area; wheelchair access; no smoking inside ⅀✗
owners Julieann & Robert Salmon
chef Robert Salmon
cost Around $80 for two, plus drinks
plus The buzz   **minus** The bustle
score 12/20

the settling in

SETTLEMENT ARCADE,
PRINCES HIGHWAY, MILTON
PHONE (02) 4455 3449   MAP 11

MODERN AUSTRALIAN

A weekend spent in historic Milton is enough to de-stress and repair the most jaded worker – as is the unpretentious local eatery, The Settling In. Word is that regulars travel from far and wide for the soy-braised duck, and we gladly join that club. A blackboard menu of daily specials tempts with a vegetarian mezze plate, a deliciously interesting range of delicacies. Corn cakes with smoked salmon sit simply on a fresh-from-the-garden bundle of dressed greens, while in-the-know Miltonians devour toasted sourdough and tapenade. The highlight, of course, is that rich, succulent and generous duck. Also impressive is the fresh Tassie salmon with mashed potato and bok choy, which sit happily on a lemon myrtle cream sauce. Leave a little space for coconut ice-cream with mango sorbet terrine, or a rich chocolate lovers' truffle tart with coffee ice-cream. A fresh, simple and honest dining experience that is well worth repeating.

byo
dinner Wed–Sat from 6.30pm
cards AE BC DC MC V   Bookings essential
seats 40; wheelchair access; no smoking ⅀✗
owners Narelle & Denis Dean
chef Narelle Dean
cost Around $76 for two, plus drinks
plus Milton   **minus** Dinner only
score 12/20

the silos

B640 PRINCES HIGHWAY,
JASPERS BRUSH, BERRY
PHONE (02) 4448 6160   MAP 11

MODERN AUSTRALIAN

Old Reliable is still happily sitting on top
of the gentle hill and gazing across the
vineyards. It is, by any measure, an idyllic
setting for dinner on a warm summer's
evening or lunch on a bright and sunny day.
The service is sharp and bubbly. The meals,
solid without being really inspiring, are
predictable and satisfying. Kick off with the
excellent warm salad of seared scallops
with roasted capsicums and tarragon
dressing or very substantial servings of
Hokkien noodles with vegetables and chilli.
The locally smoked rack of lamb with mint
and rosemary glaze is still a deserved
favourite and a rare kangaroo fillet with
sweet potato purée and port glaze is cooked
perfectly. The wine list includes a good
cross-section from the local vineyards at
Camberwarra, Coolangatta Estate and from
the vines just outside the restaurant.

licensed; wine by the glass
lunch Wed–Sun noon–3pm
dinner Wed–Sat 6–11pm
cards AE BC DC MC V   Bookings recommended,
essential weekends
seats 80; outdoor area; wheelchair access;
no smoking inside ♿✖
owners Linda & Fritz Banholzer
chef Aaron Fleming
cost Around $38 for two, plus drinks
plus The setting   **minus** Predictable menu
score 11/20

the starfish deli

SHOPS 1 & 2, 2 CLYDE STREET,
BATEMANS BAY
PHONE (02) 4472 4880   MAP 11

MODERN AUSTRALIAN

Idyllically located on the banks of the Clyde
River is this busy, something-for-everyone
eatery. During the day you will be
surrounded by teenagers sharing tempting
wood-fired pizza, while couples and kids
tuck into what seem like never-ending
feasts of fish 'n' chips, fresh pasta,
mountainous salads and succulent local
Moonlight Flat oysters. Outside on a warm
summer's evening is the place to be while
deliberating over the great selection of first
courses, from king prawns chargrilled in
bacon with pesto bruschetta, feta and
Roma tomatoes; to smoked salmon parcels
with spiced scallop and avocado salad on
ginger pikelets with coriander dressing.
Fresh local fish fillets are generously coated
in macadamia and chive crumbs and served
on a cherry tomato salad with sweet
vinegar dressing. There are plenty of dessert
and coffee options before you take a stroll
along the promenade.

licensed; wine by the glass
hours Daily 9.30am–late
cards AE BC DC MC V   Bookings recommended
seats 280; private room; outdoor area;
wheelchair access; no smoking inside ♿✖
owners Brendan McClelland & Alan Imrie
chef Brendan McClelland
cost Around $65 for two, plus drinks
plus Fast and fun   **minus** School holidays
score 12/20

sweetlips cafe

SHOP 3, 50 CROWN STREET, WOLLONGONG
PHONE (02) 4225 9542   MAP 11

MODERN AUSTRALIAN

Bravo! A café environment where the floor staff are clued-up about what is about to pass your lips. Spoil your tastebuds with a stack of feta and kalamata olives drizzled with good olive oil and surrounded by bruschetta. Then move on to pillows of fresh mussels in a light batter on a crisp salad with a light citrus dressing at once delicate and full of flavour. Follow with a seared fillet of Atlantic salmon with chermoula on potatoes and roma tomatoes – a meal that is both generous and nicely cooked. There can be a tendency to be heavy-handed when it comes to the chargrill: a corn-fed chicken breast with Cajun spices was a little too dry. If you want to throw your diet out the window, sliced chocolate salami with a compote of candied orange and cream will blow you off the Richter. Please sir, may I have some more?

byo
lunch Tues–Fri noon–2pm
dinner Wed–Sat 6–9pm
cards AE BC DC MC V   Bookings recommended
seats 50; no smoking
owners Rebecca Wilford & Lorenzo Pagnan
chef Antoine Cheron
cost Around $76 for two, plus drinks
plus Chocolate salami
minus Turn down the heat
score 12/20

termeil country guesthouse

OLD PRINCES HIGHWAY, TERMEIL
PHONE (02) 4457 1188   MAP 11

MODERN AUSTRALIAN

Regulars will know this as Barry's Guesthouse. New owners Michael and Cherie Stening carry on the high standards set by the Barrys. Seated in front of an imposing fireplace, we kicked off with an entrée of aubergine and red pepper roulade with rocket and balsamic. Ours was a little too recently out of the coolroom, however. The Thai braised octopus salad had a strong chilli kick that was nicely complemented by the cool texture of green mango and lime. Baked breast of chicken cooked with preserved lemon and oregano juices and a feta risotto were pure Mediterranean heaven, and roast breast of duck with roasted plums was beautifully long-flavoured. Finish with a subtle and refreshing panna cotta flavoured with pennyroyal.

licensed; wine by the glass
breakfast Mon–Fri 8.30–9.30am;
Sat–Sun 9–10am
dinner Daily 7–9pm
cards AE BC DC MC V   Bookings essential
seats 50; no smoking
owners Michael & Cherie Stening
chef Andrew Morrow
cost Around $86 for two, plus drinks
plus Ambient dining   **minus** No prices on menu
score 13/20

theodore's brasserie

116 KINGHORNE STREET, NOWRA
PHONE (02) 4421 0300   MAP 11

MODERN AUSTRALIAN

Dining in Nowra need not be an apocalyptic experience. Sample the culinary prowess of Horst Bleuel and the smooth floor manners of Patricia Bleuel, and be pleasantly surprised. All dishes are classic and masterfully handled. An entrée of bug-tail ravioli in a light cream and tomato sauce shows layers of subtle, defined flavour. A good salad of gravlax, avocado and bitter greens is simple and refreshing. Mains are a case of 'Ah! remember when' as in a hale and hearty Lyonnaise sausage on a bed of garlic mash and onion marmalade with a rich beef demi-glace. Equally impressive is a perfectly grilled piece of eye fillet stacked on a bed of baked potato with a mushroom and red wine sauce. A lemon tart with caramelised top served on a crème Anglaise is nicely sharp, although the whipped cream looked as though it has been dropped from 30,000 feet.

licensed
dinner Mon–Sat 6–10pm
cards AE BC DC MC V   Bookings recommended
seats 70; no smoking
owners Horst & Patricia Bleuel
chef Horst Bleuel
cost Around $76 for two, plus drinks
plus Nowra nouvelle
minus Acoustically sensitive
score 13/20

the wheelhouse

MAIN WHARF, EDEN
PHONE (02) 6496 3392   MAP 11

SEAFOOD

Proof positive that a town's culinary standards can be lifted by one enthusiastic and passionate chef. Vicky Evelyn has worked with Donna Shannon, and the latter's influence is all over this excellent menu. For an entrée, it is hard to go past Mike Bamford's famous Eden mussels served with tomato and basil sauce, which is subtle, uncomplicated and delicious. Equally delightful as entrées are the Jamaican prawns and a king prawn, mango and macadamia salad. The delicious and ridiculously cheap seafood platter for two is reason enough to travel from Sydney (the produce is fresh off the fishing boats), boasting a bewildering array of perfectly cooked goodies – fish of the day, usually john dory, prawns, oysters, Eden mussels, calamari and more. The views across the harbour at sunset will make you feel as if you are eating in some exotic tropical paradise, which is not to say that Eden cannot be thought of as exotic.

licensed
dinner Daily 6pm–midnight
cards AE BC DC MC V   Bookings recommended
seats 100; outdoor area; non-smoking area
owners David & Vicky Evelyn
chef Vicky Evelyn
cost Around $36 for two, plus drinks
plus Exceptional value   **minus** Huge helpings
score 13/20

zumo – taste australia

127 TERRALONG STREET, KIAMA
PHONE (02) 4232 2222   MAP 11

MODERN AUSTRALIAN

With the ambience of a Far North
Queenslander, Zumo belies its South Coast
origins. The menu is an interesting blend of
the exotic that sometimes misses the mark.
For starters, try the great wok-fried octopus
with wilted greens and spiced yoghurt –
delicious. A pan-fried crocodile fillet on a
grilled slice of mango with curry mayo and
peach chutney is highly tropical and a touch
try-hard. Mains are more subdued, which is
probably just as well. A perfectly cooked
piece of blue-eye cod with hazelnut beurre
blanc was delicate, and baked tandoori
lamb fillet on potato with cherry tomatoes
and cucumber raita was generous, although
each dish was overloaded with starch. The
dessert of Zumo ice-cream (Midori and
chilli) was a strange concoction, which
seemed too heavy to serve with poached
pear, roasted coconut and toffee shards.

licensed & byo; wine by the glass
lunch Sun from noon
dinner Wed–Sun from 6pm
cards AE BC MC V   Bookings recommended
seats 60; private room; outdoor area;
wheelchair access; non-smoking area ⟡✘
owners Kees Timmer & Jenny Allen
chef Kees Timmer
cost Around $92 for two, plus drinks
plus Funky food   **minus** That ice-cream
score 12/20

southern highlands

ROSEMARY STANTON

The superb scenery, gardens and antique shops of the Southern Highlands are easy to find, but good food is not always where you might expect it. For example, the best coffee is served at the Bundanoon bicycle shop (02 4883 6043), the most relaxing lunch is in the garden adjoining Sturt Craft Gallery in Mittagong and the best steaks are the aged ones you cook yourself at Briars Country Inn, midway between Bowral and Moss Vale (02 4868 1734).

If you're bushwalking or picnicking, stop off in Bowral for sourdough bread from Gumnut Patisserie (02 4862 2819) and detour via the quaint village of Burrawang to pick up fruit and vegetables from Scarletts (02 4886 4209) and excellent meat from Major's Meats (02 4886 4327).

There are also berry farms dotted around the district and excellent sandwiches at the Pig and Whistle in Robertson. If you're canoeing along the delightful Kangaroo river, phone Alfresco Picnics (02 4465 1909) and ask them to pack one of their irresistible lunches. Those heading further south should leave the highway to visit the Rimbolin (02 4821 7633) in Goulburn or Lynwood Café (02 4848 0200) in Collector. The latter, particularly, is a destination in itself.

the bantam café

CNR JELLORE & BRYAN STREETS, BERRIMA
PHONE (02) 4877 1611   MAP 11

MODERN AUSTRALIAN

Once you've discovered the Bantam, tucked away down the end of a quiet street, you almost feel like keeping it all to yourself. Set in three rooms of a historic old building, it's quaint, cosy and comfortable. Daniel's superb sourdough rolls are reason enough to visit, but everything else is good too. Start with a fresh entrée of prawn spring rolls with Asian greens or scallops on excellent house-made pasta. If you don't like seafood, you'll have to skip all four entrées but you'll do well with the main courses. The duck pie with shiitake mushrooms is hard to resist, as are kangaroo with juniper berry demi-glace, roasted beetroot and caramelised shallots, and sliced rare duck breast with cassis jus, bok choy and kumera crisps. Desserts include a double crème brûlée or a choice of several tortes – the fresh fig torte with rich ice-cream is recommended, as is a long walk after the meal.

byo
hours Wed–Sun 11am–3pm
dinner Fri–Sat 6–8.30pm
cards None   Bookings essential for dinner
seats 18; private room; wheelchair access, no smoking
owners Daniel Abotomey & Susanna Schmid
chef Daniel Abotomey
cost Around $70 for two
plus The bread rolls   **minus** No credit cards
score 14/20

L'original

Just a few minutes walk from the city

centre you'll find a huge range of the world's finest wines, over 400 wine book titles, top brand glassware, gifts and accessories all under one roof. The Ultimo Wine Centre specialises in the finest wines in the world, and Australia.

Jon Osbeiston & the team, together with over 50 years in the industry, are there to help you make the right choice whether for investment or just pure pleasure.

Come in, enjoy a glass from our tasting bar and browse through the amazing selection, especially the superb range of mature wines. Or, if time is precious call, fax, or email us and we can make the selections, gift package and deliver throughout Australia and the world.

99 Jones Street, Ultimo

Telephone 9211 2380 Fax 9211 2382

ultimo
wine
centre

the catch

250 BONG BONG STREET, BOWRAL
PHONE (02) 4862 2677   MAP 11

MODERN AUSTRALIAN

Dan Touma and his family have steered this bright and airy restaurant for some years. Christian is currently at the helm in the kitchen. The menu has 'gone about' a bit, and now emphasises several varieties of lightly battered fish and chips. Tempura prawns with pickled ginger, sweet soy and preserved lemon are still on offer, thank goodness. You might also be tempted by a delicate entrée of lobster discs with avocado, witlof and a chilli and mango mayonnaise. Pan-fried john dory on a smooth mash, swimming in a small puddle of seeded mustard cream, is a thoroughly ship-shape dish. Non-fish eaters can opt for steak or chicken, or one of the very good pizzas from the domed wood-fired oven. Don't leave without trying the trio of deliciously rich ice-cream, or go for broke with a hot apple, mango and lime crumble. Lunch is cheaper and more casual.

licensed & byo; wine by the glass
lunch Fri–Sun noon–3pm
dinner Wed–Mon 6–9pm
cards AE BC DC MC V   Bookings dinner only
seats 100; wheelchair access; non-smoking area ♿✗
owner Dan Touma
chef Christian Touma
cost Around $70 for two, plus drinks
plus The ice-cream   **minus** Skinny chips
score 13/20

fitzroy inn

26 FERGUSSON CRESCENT, MITTAGONG
PHONE (02) 4872 3457   MAP 11

MODERN AUSTRALIAN

After years of loving restoration, the Fitzroy Inn offers good food and charming accommodation. Visit the original stone kitchen with its fireplace, ovens and old well, and the small stone room where prisoners were housed in the 1830s while en route south. Back in one of the welcoming, roomy dining rooms, tuck into good bread while you decide on which of the Italian-inspired dishes to choose. Saffron risotto with steamed asparagus and tomato pesto is carefully cooked and full of flavour. Chicken breast filled with ricotta and lemon thyme is deliciously moist and herby, while seared tuna with fresh greens and a crisp pastry tartlet of lime potato mash also works very well. The tartlet might seem unnecessarily fussy, but you'll wind up eating every little bit. Desserts include pannacotta with fresh fruit and a rich caramel sauce.

licensed & byo
lunch Wed–Sun noon–2.30pm,
dinner Tues–Sat 6–9.30pm
cards AE BC DC MC V   Bookings recommended
seats 56; private room; wheelchair access, no smoking inside ♿✗
owners Cosmo & Maria Aloi, Paul & Gabriella Lovell
chefs Gabriella Lovell & Richard Neale
cost Around $65 for two, plus drinks
plus Historic building   **minus** Empty cellar
score 14/20

hordern's

MILTON PARK COUNTRY HOUSE HOTEL,
HORDERN'S ROAD, BOWRAL
PHONE (02) 4861 1522   MAP 11

MODERN AUSTRALIAN/FRENCH

Make time to stroll through the wonderful
gardens before entering the gracious and
relaxed dining room of this historic property.
Try for a window table, to better enjoy the
weeping English beech trees outside. The
food, while a little old-fashioned, is well
prepared and complemented by a good
wine list and friendly service. A salad of
Moreton Bay bugs, scallops and prawns
with a walnut oil dressing is just the right
size for a good beginning. Aged beef
tenderloin with mushroom jus is long on
flavour, given Milton Park's previous
incarnation as one of Australia's leading
cattle studs, but gets stiff competition from
a perfectly cooked rare loin of lamb on
delicious haricot beans, enlivened with
pesto and tarragon jus. Desserts are quite
rich, but you could share a crème brûlée
with quince and glazed pineapple.

licensed; wine by the glass
breakfast Daily 7.30–10am
lunch Daily noon–2pm
dinner Daily 7–9pm
cards AE BC DC MC V   Bookings essential
seats 120; private room; wheelchair access;
no smoking ⚹✖
owner John & Marlene Dobler
chef Henrik Hein
cost Around $86 for two, plus drinks
plus The gardens   **minus** Few wines by the glass
score 14/20

janeks

CORBETT PLAZA,
14 WINGECARRIBEE STREET, BOWRAL
PHONE (02) 4861 4414   MAP 11

MODERN AUSTRALIAN

By day, this bustling café serves good
coffee, great snacks and good fresh lunches.
If it's a nice day, relax outside under the
trees next to the fountain and enjoy the
good-natured energy of Pascal and his staff.
Two nights a week, you get a well-prepared
French-accented dinner. The duck livers with
butter beans and an apple cider vinaigrette
are excellent; as is buckwheat blini with
roasted beetroot, smoked salmon, salmon
roe and just enough crème fraîche to bring
it all together. For mains, Puy lentils and
kipfler potatoes topped with rare lamb rump
and a splodge of aïoli works well in the
crisp Highland air. Also recommended are
the nicely rich duck confit with braised
cabbage, and roasted blue-eye cod
marinated in saffron, perched on potato
gnocchi and swimming in a delicate sea of
creamy roast capsicum. The 20-minute wait
for a thin apple tart served with cinnamon
ice-cream is worth it.

byo
hours Mon–Sat 8am–5pm; Fri–Sat 6.30–9pm
cards AE BC MC V   Bookings recommended
for dinner
seats 48; outdoor area; no smoking inside ⚹✖
owners Karina & Pascal Timores
chef Pascal Timores
cost Around $65 for two, plus drinks
plus Country cheerfulness
minus Limited dinners
score 14/20

katers

PEPPERS MANOR HOUSE,
KATER ROAD, SUTTON FOREST
PHONE (02) 4868 2355   MAP 11

MODERN AUSTRALIAN

It's hard not to feel special, sitting in the gracious dining room of this elegant country house, while nibbling on good yeasty bread and sipping from a small demitasse of well-flavoured soup. The produce and cooking techniques are beyond reproach, but some flavour combinations are less successful than others. A classy lasagne, with crisp eggplant replacing the traditional pasta, interleaved with roasted capsicum, avocado and oven-dried tomato, was total harmony, but scampi teamed with a Waldorf salad with a dill and salmon roe dressing just didn't seem to gel. Similarly, a pawpaw and lychee salad did little for a perfectly steamed fillet of salmon with ginger and spring onion, yet the fall-off-the-bone slow-roasted guinea fowl was perfect. To finish, share some excellent local berries on a shortbread lemon mascarpone flan.

licensed; wine by the glass
breakfast Daily 7–10am
lunch Daily noon–2.30pm
dinner Daily 7–9pm
cards AE BC DC MC V   Bookings essential
seats 100; private room; outdoor area;
wheelchair access; no smoking ✗
owner Peppers Leisure Limited
chef Jonas Ottoson
fixed price 2 courses $45 p.p., plus drinks
plus Vegetarian menu
minus Extra cost
for veg
score 14/20

lynwood cafe

1 MURRAY STREET, COLLECTOR
PHONE (02) 4848 0200   MAP 11

EUROPEAN

Don't even think of travelling to Canberra or beyond without making a slight detour to this rustic old settler's cottage with its log fires, 'jam' room and small vases of Robin Howard's own herbs and flowers. Vegetables are freshly picked from the organic garden at the back door, and have the flavour to prove it. Travellers might choose from the all-day menu, enjoying an excellent omelette with Heidi gruyère and bacon or indulging in scones with one of Lynwood's wonderful jams and cream. At meal times, the menu expands. Oxtail-filled pasties with beetroot and horseradish cream melt in the mouth, and mains of Atlantic salmon with cauliflower, a curry sauce and lovage, and a rack of lamb with smoky aubergine purée, tomato and marjoram are excellent. The muscat trifle is irresistible, unless you succumb to a superb pancake with home-made lemon curd and rich ice-cream. Even the memory makes the mouth water.

licensed; wine by the glass
hours Wed–Sat 10am–10pm; Sun 10am–6pm
cards AE BC MC V   Bookings recommended
seats 65; private room; outdoor area;
wheelchair access; no smoking area ✗
owners Robin & Alan Howard
chef Andy Bunn
cost Around $62 for two, plus drinks
plus The produce   **minus** Can't stay over
score 14/20

osbornes of the valley

146 MOSS VALE ROAD, KANGAROO VALLEY
PHONE (02) 4465 1314   MAP 11

MODERN AUSTRALIAN

Beautiful Kangaroo Valley is just the right
distance from Sydney for a relaxing
weekend. A good lunch is no problem,
but the dinner scene is dismal, except for
Osbornes. Here is a serious young chef,
still keen to learn, offering good food.
Some nights, his wife Jane adds tender
background singing. For entrées, try warm
goat's milk feta with pan-fried king prawns,
pine nuts, wilted sunflower sprouts and
coriander oil, or a flavour-bursting smoked
chicken and oven-dried tomato ravioli with
mushroom essence and white truffle oil.
Osbornes' way with kangaroo (with candied
sweet potato, glazed baby beetroot, roast
garlic and sautéed rocket) is well known.
Venison is equally well treated: rare slices
on a capsicum and carrot relish, under an
onion-jam-filled gnocchi, surrounded by jus
infused with lemon thyme and star anise.

licensed & byo; wine by the glass
lunch Thurs–Sun 11am–4pm
dinner Wed–Sun from 6pm; daily during
school holidays
cards AE BC MC V   Bookings essential
seats 100; outdoor area; no smoking inside
owners Jane & Luke de Ville
chefs Luke de Ville & Glenn Parkes
cost Around $76 for two, plus drinks
plus Warm and friendly
minus Between-course sorbets
score 13/20

the rimbolin

380 AUBURN STREET, GOULBURN
PHONE (02) 4821 7633   MAP 11

MODERN AUSTRALIAN

While Melvyn no longer feeds your soul
with his didgeridoo and violin-playing,
Catherine can still feed your body a hearty
meal or, if you're travelling through, a
flavourful express soup or casserole. Fresh
herbs add life to almost everything here,
including an entrée of big mushrooms
stuffed with semi-dried tomatoes, pine
nuts and Swiss cheese, made fragrant
with thyme. For mains, kingfish is crusted
with basil, and surrounded by a sea of
herbed roast tomato and capsicum sauce,
while fresh marjoram adds even more
flavour to the millet, carrot, corn and arame
seaweed loaf, piled with sautéed eggplant
and roast capsicum. Meat eaters have
plenty of choices, including a hearty beef,
bacon, red wine and mushroom pie.
All mains come with a bowl of six different
vegetables, including delicious roast kipfler
potatoes. A dessert of ice-cream with fresh
berries and lots of passionfruit tops off a
good home-cooked meal.

byo
hours Wed 11am–5.30pm;
Thurs–Sat 11am–9.30pm; Sun noon–5.30pm
cards AE BC DC MC V   Bookings recommended
seats 66; outdoor area; no smoking inside
owne/chef Catherine Cann
cost 2 courses $54 for dinner for two;
$25 for lunch for two
plus Country charm   **minus** Country timing
score 13/20

§

station street

50 STATION STREET BOWRAL
PHONE (02) 4861 7171   MAP 11

MODERN AUSTRALIAN

From the initial welcome at the door of
this converted terrace house, you get the
impression that all is right with the world.
The service is friendly but unobtrusive,
and the small carpeted rooms ensure a
peaceful meal. The menu matches the
quiet competence of the place. An entrée
of warm shredded duck salad with fresh
pear, dressed with a sweet soy and ginger
dressing is pleasant, but you wonder if the
chilled baby octopus with chilli and roast
capsicum coulis wouldn't be more
successful as a hot dish. The reliable mains
include a flavoursome lamb fillet stuffed
with spinach and served with grilled
eggplant and tomato tapenade, and their
signature kangaroo rump, accompanied by
spicy lentils and red wine glaze. Desserts
are quite rich and more suitable for winter
eating, but it's unlikely you will have room
for them anyway.

licensed & byo; wine by the glass
lunch Wed–Fri & Sun noon–2.30pm
dinner Mon–Sat from 6.30pm
cards AE BC DC MC V   Bookings essential
seats 50; outdoor area; wheelchair access;
smoking in bar area only
owners The O'Brien family
chef Jason O'Brien
cost Around $60 for two, plus drinks
plus You hear yourself speak
minus Not much joy for veggies
score 13/20

§

the sturt cafe

CNR WAVERLEY PARADE & RANGE ROAD,
MITTAGONG
PHONE (02) 4860 2086   MAP 11

MODERN AUSTRALIAN

Whatever the season, this café, craft gallery
and delightful garden combine to calm
frazzled city nerves. Locals have appreciated
Mark Chance's quest for quality food for
some years and they're not disappointed
by the simple, elegant dishes that grace
his lunch menu, accompanied by good
home-made bread. Enjoy a warm salad of
prawns, cannellini bean purée, tomato and
bruschetta or the surprisingly good marriage
of salt-and-pepper squid with aïoli,
coriander, mint, nam jing and hot mango
chutney. When pine forest mushrooms
appear, make the most of them. Otherwise
enjoy a confit of duck with Puy lentils and
rosemary-roasted potatoes or succulent
roast veal with prosciutto and pumpkin
gnocchi. Don't leave without trying the
buttermilk panna cotta with caramelised
figs and praline.

byo
breakfast Wed–Sun 10am–noon
lunch Wed–Sun noon–3pm
dinner Fri–Sat 6.30–9.30pm
cards AE BC MC V   Bookings essential
seats 88; outdoor area; wheelchair access;
no smoking inside ✘
owner Winifred West
chef Mark Chance
cost Around $36 for lunch; around $60 for dinner
plus Simple flavours   **minus** The chairs
score 14/20

§

that noodle place

279 BONG BONG STREET, BOWRAL
PHONE (02) 4861 6930   MAP 11

MODERN ASIAN

Look for the rickshaw, the welcoming orange shutters and the bright blue and yellow walls, and stop off for a quick snack or linger over a longer meal at That Noodle Place. Kids will happily hoe into tempura or mini steamed pork buns. Don't miss the Vietnamese prawn and pork rice-paper rolls (the herb inside is perilla) or fragrant Beijing dumplings served in little bamboo steamers with a coriander and peanut pesto. Continue with home-smoked ocean trout served with soba noodles, a salad of snowpea sprouts and rocket dressed with wasabi mayonnaise. Or try udon noodles which soak up the flavours of Chinese roast duck, shiitake mushrooms and Asian greens. As an alternative, opt for a full-flavoured Thai salad with green papaya or curries, noodles, soups or laksa. Vegetarians have at least six choices, including a Fijian Indian vegetable curry. Finish with an nicely sticky sago pud with coconut and palm sugar.

byo
lunch Wed–Sun noon–2.30pm
dinner Tues–Sun from 5.30pm
cards AE BC DC MC V   Bookings recommended
seats 75; private room; wheelchair access;
no smoking ⅍
owner Pamela Charity
chef Paulette Turford
cost Around $43 for two, plus drinks
plus Vietnamese rolls   **minus** Coloured glasses
score 14/20

♈

willowvale mill

LAGGAN, VIA CROOKWELL
PHONE (02) 4837 3319   MAP 11

EUROPEAN

Willowvale doesn't fit into any pigeonhole. There's no menu, no wine list and no pretensions. Go with a group of friends rather than for an intimate dining experience. The setting is charming – an old stone mill, olive trees, herbs, ducks, pigs, veggie garden and a new glass-walled pavilion among the trees for aperitifs. The place is a bit (pleasantly) run-down and you eat communally in the mill dining room under huge wooden beams, warming yourself by an enormous fire as you roast chestnuts or start on Takako's sushi or home-made bread. The rest of the food is then laid out so you can help yourself. Graham Liney cooks what's in season, and always includes several excellent local potato dishes. Dinner may include succulent quail wrapped in bacon and roasted with sliced plums; richly flavoured roast pork neck, plus big bowls of vegetables, potato frittata and gnocchi. Desserts are nostalgic offerings.

licensed
lunch Fri–Sun by appointment
dinner Fri–Sun from 7pm by appointment
cards AE BC DC MC V   Bookings essential
seats 150; private room; outdoor area;
no smoking ⅍
owners/chefs Graham & Takako Liney
fixed price Around $48 p.p., plus drinks
plus Relaxing setting   **minus** Buffet syndrome
score 12/20

west

BRUCE ELDER & LYNNE MULLINS

The challenge for country restaurants never changes. How can a place trying to make a reasonable living cater for both country and city expectations when they are so different? The answer seems to be high-quality locally sourced produce and inoffensive concessions. Some places, like Echidna in Dubbo, solve the problem by opening for up to 15 hours a day. Others, like Selkirks and Highland Heritage in Orange, present menus designed to appeal to all palates. Others just cross their fingers and pray. Eating beyond the Great Dividing Range is a different experience from eating in Sydney or in the fashionable watering holes along the coast. Still, with a careful understanding of the rationale behind a menu, a few discreet enquiries as to the best local produce and some gentle instructions (let the chef know that your definition of 'rare' may be different from that of the local farmer), discriminating diners can find themselves seduced by a freshness and honesty that the city can rarely match.

archie's on the park

MOORE PARK INN, URALLA ROAD,
SOUTH ARMIDALE
PHONE (02) 6772 2358   MAP 12

MODERN AUSTRALIAN

Piping-hot mini loaves of damper delivered to the table as soon as you are seated make a warm welcome at this friendly country restaurant. The colonial charm of the New Englander is apparent as you drive up the tree-lined gravel road to the remodelled 1860s homestead. The 120-year-old chapel is now an intimate private dining room, and the extensive wine list includes wines by the glass as well as some gems from Archie's reserve cellar. His menu is short but appealing. Cream of pumpkin soup is earthy and rich; chargrilled grain-fed local lamb with red witlof and watercress makes a hearty entrée; and Atlantic salmon fillet on mash with roast tomato and basil is recommended. Only a rack of pork with tempura fennel felt out of kilter. Still, a country restaurant that can start with good bread and end on a more-than-reasonable sticky date and butterscotch pudding has an awful lot going for it.

licensed
breakfast Daily 7–8.30am
dinner Daily 6.30pm–midnight
cards AE BC DC MC V   Bookings essential
seats 150; private room; outdoor area; wheelchair access; non-smoking area ♿✗
owner Archie Campbell
chef Glen Findley
cost Around $80 for two
plus Staying the night   **minus** No lunch
score 13/20

brooklyn on fitzroy

10–12 FITZROY STREET, TUMUT
PHONE (02) 6947 4022   MAP 11

AUSTRALIAN REGIONAL

Gazing over the paddocks towards the
willow-edged Tumut River from the grassy
terraces behind the restaurant, you could
believe you were somewhere in England's
Upper Thames Valley. This is true rural bliss.
If you ask Marianne Webb how she knows
the beef is grain-fed she'll reply, 'Because
my father breeds them and my brother,
who's a butcher, kills them.' You can't get
any more in touch with your produce than
that. There is a simplicity and honesty about
both the approach and style of Brooklyn.
Start with the locally smoked trout, which
is served with Dijon and dill mayonnaise,
and follow it with the sirloin or local lamb,
both of which are served with carefully
cooked fresh local vegetables. Check what
is currently being picked in the district –
nectarines, apples or peaches – before
ordering dessert. If the season is right, the
Sauternes-poached apples are excellent.

licensed; wine by the glass
dinner Tues–Sat from 6.30pm
cards AE BC DC MC V   Bookings recommended
seats 144; private room; outdoor area;
non-smoking area ✗
owners Ellen Webb & Marianne Webb
chef Ellen Webb
cost Around $76 for two, plus drinks
plus Superb setting   **minus** Popular with groups
score 12/20

caffe bassano

453 BANNA AVENUE, GRIFFITH
PHONE (02) 6964 4544   MAP 11

ITALIAN

Given that 60 per cent of Griffith residents
claim Italian ancestry, it would be
reasonable to expect this elegant and classy
establishment to be bulging with
enthusiastic customers. However, Griffith
Italians seem to find Sam Vico a little too
modern and classy for their tastes. His
gnocchi ai quattro formaggi (with four
cheeses) is light, subtle and arguably the
best for 500 km in any direction. Spaghettini
saporiti is exquisitely understated, with only
a few green prawns mixed with hints of
basil, parsley, garlic, carrot, celery and
onion, and a chicken salad is bursting with
Riverina goodness and freshness. As always,
it is the homemade tortes, accompanied by
excellent coffee, which set the tastebuds
racing. Locals and visitors alike will be
delighted to learn that Caffe Bassano is
now open on Friday and Saturday nights.

licensed; wine by the glass
breakfast Mon–Sat 9–11am
lunch Mon–Sat noon–3pm
dinner Fri–Sat 6–11pm
cards AE BC MC V   Bookings recommended
seats 80; outdoor area; wheelchair access;
no smoking ✗
owners Sam & Olga Vico
chef Sam Vico
cost Around $54 for two, plus drinks
plus Atmosphere   **minus** Main street setting
score 14/20

$

echidna cafe

177 MACQUARIE STREET, DUBBO
PHONE (02) 6884 9393   MAP 12

AUSTRALIAN REGIONAL

Here, in Dubbo's rather uninteresting main
street, is a café that is a triumph of tenacity,
hard work and imagination in a region of
indifference. Somehow, although he is
open for twelve hours, five days a week,
chef Stephen Neale manages to find time
to smoke local Gilgandra silver perch and
serve it surrounded by fresh avocado
and delicious local tomato slices. Ask for
the antipasto and marvel at the attention
to detail that can produce a plate of lightly
warmed and light-as-a-feather frittata with
smoked salmon, and delicate tandoori
chicken with yoghurt salsa. When it comes
to mains, it is hard to pass up four small
French-cut local organic lamb cutlets on
a bed of couscous, surrounded by a Greek
salad of local button tomatoes, feta and
cucumber. Neale claims regional produce
makes up 90 per cent of his menu, so
you're getting a real taste of regional
cuisine. The coffee is strong, and the
bottle shop is over the road.

byo
hours Tues–Sat 9am–9pm
cards BC MC V   Bookings essential
seats 90; private room; outdoor area;
wheelchair access; non-smoking area
owners Richard Harris & Stephen Neale
chef Stephen Neale
cost Around $54 for two, plus drinks
plus All-day opening   **minus** Street views
score 13/20

$

eltons cafe

81 MARKET STREET, MUDGEE
PHONE (02) 6372 0772   MAP 12

MODERN AUSTRALIAN

Eltons is like one of those resonant
metaphors in a nineteenth-century novel –
it is Mudgee's pulsing heart. Go to breakfast
around 10.30 and you'll share it with the
town's young mums. Go to a late lunch and
you'll mix with the BMW/Country Road set.
With its elegant, wooden floors and large
comfortable tables, it has become the kind
of drop-in centre that every country town
needs. At breakfast, don't miss the light
yeast pancakes with crisp pancetta and
maple syrup, or smoked salmon eggs
benedict with excellent homemade bread.
At lunch, try a vegetarian frittata or a rare
roast beef open sandwich. At weekend
dinners, choose from heartier options such
as chargrilled chicken breast with corn and
red capsicum pancake and red capsicum jus,
or Gilgandra silver perch with fennel mash.
This country café sets standards in service,
quality and friendliness that a lot of other
country cafés would do well to emulate.

byo
breakfast Daily 9–11am
lunch Daily 11am–4pm
dinner Fri–Sat 6.30–9pm
cards BC MC V   Bookings recommended
seats 70; outdoor area; wheelchair access;
no smoking inside
owner Alan Cox
chef David Cox
cost Around $34 for two, plus drinks
plus Interesting café food   **minus** Can be noisy
score 13/20

highland heritage estate

MITCHELL HIGHWAY, ORANGE
PHONE (02) 6361 3054   MAP 11

AUSTRALIAN REGIONAL

Only ten minutes east of Orange, and surrounded by vineyards and trellises of raspberries, Highland Heritage has very limited opening hours. Instead of trying to please all palates at all times, chef Paul Wilderbeek chooses to please only lunchtime diners on Friday, Saturday and Sunday. The result is three sensational meals each week, and this shows in such delicacies as smoked trout pâté with local lettuce and (nice touch) a warm, miniature old-style loaf. Mains include plump, moist Muscovy duck with forest mushrooms, glazed quince and a Highland Heritage pinot jus, and a hearty North African mix of Blayney district free-range chicken and local lamb on couscous with pumpkin. The outstanding dessert menu is a wonderland of pears, plums, raspberries and figs all appearing in season. Each course comes with wine suggestions, most from the Highland Heritage cellars.

licensed; wine by the glass
lunch Fri–Sun noon–2.30pm
dinner Thurs–Fri 6–10pm
cards BC MC V   Bookings recommended
seats 200; private room; outdoor area; wheelchair access; no smoking inside ⌖✗
owner Fernbrow Pty Ltd
chef Paul Wilderbeek
cost Around $78 for two, plus drinks
plus Great countryside   **minus** Large groups
score 14/20

inland cafe

407 PEEL STREET, TAMWORTH
PHONE (02) 6761 2882   MAP 12

MODERN AUSTRALIAN

Despite its yokel country music associations, Tamworth is a large and thriving inland city and it is entirely appropriate that it should have a really worthwhile restaurant/café such as the Inland. No matter what time of day you arrive, chef Helen Hunt will have something you feel like eating. Perhaps the bruschetta with vine-ripened tomatoes and yabbie with pesto sauce or fettuccine with tiny cubes of lemon mixed with smoked trout, cherry tomatoes, artichoke, olives and pesto. This smart café seriously tries to be all things to all people. There are kids' dishes (bow-tie pasta with cheese sauce), takeaway Mediterranean lamb burgers (local lamb, of course) and roast lamb loin and beef rib-eye, all served in the hustle and bustle of a busy café that spills out onto Peel Street. Expect excellent coffee and a bewildering array of desserts.

licensed & byo; wine by the glass
breakfast Mon–Fri 7–11am; Sat–Sun 7am–noon
lunch Mon–Wed 11am–6pm;
Thurs–Sat 11am–5pm; Sun noon–5pm
dinner Thurs–Sat 5–11pm
cards AE BC MC V   Bookings recommended
seats 70; outdoor area; wheelchair access; no smoking inside until 10pm ⌖✗
owners Paul Lockrey & Stacie Sherwin
chef Helen Hunt
cost Around $60 for two
plus Chic café decor   **minus** Pedestrian traffic
score 13/20

jenkins street guest house

85 JENKINS STREET, NUNDLE
PHONE (02) 6769 3239   MAP 12

AUSTRALIAN REGIONAL

Bedding down where you have just eaten (which is what most of us do every night anyway) has the added advantage of ensuring that you can drink without the company of a designated driver. Thus a night at Jenkins Street can be a total experience. Chef Nick Cummins is so eager to have a chat that his presence pervades this very pleasant rural experience. The menu proudly boasts that the chicken, yabbies, trout, pheasant and lamb are all 'grown in the region and sourced directly from the growers'. The service is bright and breezy and the meals, particularly the Mandalong double lamb cutlets with parsnip purée and rosemary jus and the chargrilled rib-eye fillet, are perfectly cooked and accompanied by excellent sautéed vegetables. Finish with warm berry pudding and then totter upstairs.

licensed
lunch Sat–Sun noon–3pm
dinner Daily from 7pm
cards BC DC MC V   Bookings essential
seats 40; private room; outdoor area;
no smoking ⌖✖
owner/chef Nick Cummins
cost Around $76 for two, plus drinks
plus Exceptional service
minus Not staying overnight
score 14/20

lindsay house

128 FAULKNER STREET, ARMIDALE
PHONE (02) 6771 4554   MAP 12

MODERN AUSTRALIAN

Sip on chilled champagne as you wander through the gardens before dining inside this magnificently restored country house hotel. The stunning dining room and interior are decorated with French and Victorian antiques. Service is warm, attentive and professional; a demitasse of flavoursome vichysoisse is delivered to the table to enjoy while you browse through the menu. The kitchen is in the skilled hands of French-trained Rene Pauvert, evident in a smart entrée showcasing a trio of Tasmanian salmon: salmon rillette, cured and seared salmon and roasted Chinese-style. Try tender grain-fed local lamb accompanied by a roasted garlic risotto and grilled zucchini, or local Angus beef on mascarpone polenta, the beef respectfully and perfectly cooked to order. Desserts are heavenly, and the wine list is short but well chosen. Lindsay House puts Armidale on the map in terms of serious food.

licensed; wine by the glass
lunch Sunday from noon
dinner Wed–Sat from 6.30pm
cards AE BC DC MC V   Bookings essential
seats 60 private room; outdoor area;
wheelchair access; no smoking inside ⌖✖
owner Carolyn J. Raza
chef Rene Pauvert
cost Around $80 for two, plus drinks
plus Heritage building   **minus** Only one lunch
score 14/20

l'oasis

150 YAMBIL STREET, GRIFFITH
PHONE (02) 6964 5588   MAP 11

MODERN AUSTRALIAN

L'Oasis is one of the largest quality
restaurants in regional New South Wales,
boasting a vast space with polished wooden
floors and a chic inner city brasserie feel.
L'Oasis offers an interesting mixture of
Mod Oz cuisine that leans heavily on the
rich produce of the Riverina and reliable
rural favourites such as Scotch fillet, rack
of lamb and grilled sirloin which fulfil local
expectations. Chef David Lowe is not afraid
to experiment, and consequently his entrée
of barbecued marinated octopus with
herb salad and peanut sauce (a kind of
Australian cephalopod version of Malaysian
saté) is perhaps more interesting than it
is successful. But this is a minor glitch.
Better was local chicken stuffed with
camembert and almonds on celery
jus with fresh, crisp, steamed vegetables.
Warning: the grenadine-poached pears
and honey mascarpone is practically
impossible to resist.

licensed; wine by the glass
lunch Tues–Sat 11.30am–2.30pm
dinner Tues–Sat 6–10pm
cards AE BC DC MC V   Bookings recommended
seats 150; private room; non-smoking area ⌗✖
owners Suzy & Martin O'Donnell & David Lowe
chef David Lowe
cost Around $73 for two, plus drinks
plus The space   **minus** Noisy when busy
score 12/20

nagano shinshu-mura

'GLENFINE', GILES ROAD, ORANGE
PHONE (02) 6365 4324   MAP 11

JAPANESE

For sheer cultural incongruity, the idea
of a traditional Japanese restaurant (right
down to the fact that no nails were used
in its construction) set in the heart of the
Australian bush some kilometres out of
Orange makes Nagano Shinshu-Mura very
special. It is a pity that the uniqueness of
the setting isn't matched by the menu,
which – with a few notable exceptions –
is standard Japanese. Starting with sushi,
sashimi and Californian rolls and moving
through sukiyaki (which comes with
lettuce instead of Chinese cabbage) and
shabu-shabu, it is the kind of menu one
would expect at any one of a thousand
small Japanese restaurants in the city.
This comparison extends to the lunch
boxes of sushi and tempura and the
kaiseki specials. However the attractive
décor, lowered tables, tatami mats,
pleasantly warm sake and the views
across the fields of billowing buckwheat
make it a pleasant daytime destination.

licensed & byo
lunch Fri–Sun noon–2pm
dinner Wed–Sat 6–10.30pm
cards BC MC V   Bookings essential weekends
seats 90; private room; wheelchair access;
non-smoking area ⌗✖
owner/chef Noboru Orihashi
cost Around $65 for two, plus drinks
plus Delightful setting   **minus** Standard menu
score 11/20

selkirks

179 ANSON STREET, ORANGE
PHONE (02) 6361 1179   MAP 11

AUSTRALIAN REGIONAL

Set in a charming old home that has been carefully redesigned, this is the one restaurant west of the Great Divide that can stand confidently beside anything Sydney has to offer. Michael Manners, ably assisted by Scott Want, has turned sourcing local produce into an art. His relationship with local producers is so simpatico that if you order the Bloodwood Chardonnay, his staff are under strict instructions as to how it is to be served. Every course is a celebration. An entrée of prawn custard on prawn-infused tomato sauce will take your breath away, and the chicken liver terrine is perfectly complemented by honey-pickled pears. Waverleigh Park pasture-raised chicken sautéed with herbs and lemon is like no chicken you have eaten, and Mandagery Creek roasted venison on creamy polenta is served rare and silky smooth. Don't leave without trying the mixed dessert plate, and take the menu's advice when choosing accompanying wines.

licensed; wine by the glass
dinner Tues–Sat from 6.30pm
cards AE BC DC MC V   Bookings essential
seats 50; outdoor area; wheelchair access;
no smoking 🚭
owners Michael Manners & Josephine Jagger
chefs Michael Manners & Scott Want
cost Around $92 for two, plus drinks
plus Changing menu   **minus** Street setting
score 16/20

capital dining

melbourne

FINE DINER
langton's
61 FLINDERS LANE, MELBOURNE
PHONE (03) 9663 0222
Philippe Mouchel is the kind of chef that other chefs want to be when they grow up. The gentlemanly, three-star-trained Frenchman extracts every ounce of flavour from his produce and presents it in a warm, elegant, ever-busy dining room.

PURE MELBOURNE
grossi florentino
80 BOURKE STREET, MELBOURNE
PHONE (03) 9662 1811
To sit in the thoroughly atmospheric mural room with its wood panelling and Florentine art is to touch the very heart of the Melbourne dining experience. Now that the Grossi family is in residence, not all the pleasures are nostalgic.

HOT SPOT
ezard at adelphi
ADELPHI HOTEL, 187 FLINDERS LANE, MELBOURNE   PHONE (03) 9639 6811
With its adventurous, multi-influenced food, and smart designer dining room tucked away in a funky hotel, Ezard at Adelphi is generally regarded as Melbourne's answer to Sydney's Salt. Teage Ezard's cooking is edgy, chancy and always interesting.

CAFÉ LIFE
bird cage
129 FITZROY STREET, ST KILDA
PHONE (03) 9534 0277
It's a wine bar, a sushi bar and a Japanesque café, all tucked into a deeply groovy corner of the old George building in St Kilda. The food is delicate, subtle and perfectly matched to Neil Prentice's thoughtful wine selection.

EXOTIC
flower drum
17 MARKET LANE, MELBOURNE
PHONE (03) 9662 3655
Cantonese food is refined into something pure, clear-minded and precious in this ground-breaking restaurant. The Peking duck is without peer, the wine list is far better than it has to be, and Gilbert Lau's dedication to his diners is legendary.

GASTRO TEMPLE
est est est
440 CLARENDON STREET, SOUTH MELBOURNE
PHONE (03) 9682 5688
Donovan Cooke and Philippa Sibley-Cooke brought a new work ethic to Melbourne fine dining, channelling their boundless energies into producing the most refined and honed food in Melbourne. The influences are British but the flavours are resolutely French.

FOOD WITH A VIEW
donovans
40 JACKA BOULEVARD, ST KILDA
PHONE (03) 9534 8221
Few restaurants are as professionally or as nicely run as this popular beachfront eatery. Gail and Kevin Donovan are natural, caring hosts while chef Robert Castellani has a happy knack of cooking just what you feel like eating by the sea.

hobart

FINE DINER
lebrina
155 NEW TOWN ROAD, NEW TOWN
PHONE (03) 6228 7775
More than 150 years old, the cottage
that houses this popular restaurant is
a direct link to Hobart's past. The food,
however, crafted from top notch local
produce by Scott Minervini, is light, bright
and very now.

PURE HOBART
kafe kara
119 LIVERPOOL STREET, HOBART
PHONE (03) 6231 2332
With its big city feel and Italian good looks,
Kafe Kara has the nous and the skills to be
all things to all people. Whether you're
looking for (good) coffee and (great) cake,
a satisfying no-frills breakfast, or pasta
and glass-of-red lunch, you've found it.
Sorry, no dinner.

HOT SPOT
rockerfeller's
11 MORRISON STREET, HOBART
PHONE (03) 6234 3490
Buzz, buzz, buzz. That's the scene at
Rockerfeller's, a chic young crowd-magnet
located in a renovated flour mill. The food
doesn't really have to be good here, but
thankfully it is, from nicely done tapas
dishes to an international roll call of
modern faves.

CAFÉ LIFE
jackman and mcross
59 HAMPDEN ROAD, BATTERY POINT
PHONE (03) 6223 3186
The Jackman is Chris of Mit Zitrone fame,
so you'd expect quality from this honest
bakery café. You get it in fab pies, nicely
worked pizza, old-fashioned sandwiches
and baguettes, and cakes that are so good,
it's impossible to order just a cup of coffee.

EXOTICA
orizuru
VICTORIA DOCK, HOBART
PHONE (03) 6231 1790
Somehow it seems totally appropriate to
be nibbling on such pristine, fresh sashimi
and sushi in the middle of a picturesque
and fully operational fishing port. The
agedashi (deep-fried) tofu is a delight,
and the nigiri (finger) sushi is always good,
especially the tuna.

GASTRO TEMPLE
mit zitrone
333 ELIZABETH STREET, NORTH HOBART
PHONE (03) 6234 8113
A street-friendly bistro adored by locals and
food critics alike, Mit Zitrone is Hobart at its
foodiest best, from the sea urchin custard to
the local mussels in chilli jam.

FOOD WITH A VIEW
prosser's on the beach
BEACH ROAD, LONG POINT, SANDY BAY
PHONE (03) 6225 2276
This beachside beauty is a true Hobart
stalwart. The only way you'll get closer to
the sea is to swim in it, and the only way
you'll get fresher fish and shellfish is to
catch them yourself.

adelaide

FINE DINER
nediz
170 HUTT STREET, ADELAIDE
PHONE (08) 8223 2618
The very same location that once
showcased the talents of the great Cheong
Liew and Le Tu Thai continues to provide
Adelaide with inventive, Asian-influenced
Modern Asian cooking. Genevieve Harris's
cooking manages to be both adventurous
and soundly balanced.

PURE ADELAIDE
universal wine bar
285 RUNDLE STREET, ADELAIDE
PHONE (08) 8232 5000
The wine list is a marvel and the food (think
brain timbale with aïoli and fried spinach
leaves) can be way up there, but that's not
why we love this popular wine bar. It's the
buzz, the vibe, the scene. Whatever you call
it, it's got it – in spades.

HOT SPOT
eccolo
22 GROTE STREET, ADELAIDE
PHONE (08) 8410 0102
The space is modern and look-at-me, the
bar is hot, the crowd is invariably good-
looking, and the service is silky. As for
the food, think modern Italian with
enough twists and turns to keep you
coming back for more.

CAFÉ LIFE
cibo
8 O'CONNELL STREET, NORTH ADELAIDE
PHONE (08) 8267 2444
Cibo is a pizza joint, a pasticceria, a coffee
and gossip hangout, a reliable breakfast
spot, a sunny al fresco lunch spot and an
authentic Italian restaurant. What makes it
special is not that it does a lot of things,
but that it does a lot of things really well.

EXOTICA
charlick's
EBENEZER PLACE, EAST END, ADELAIDE
PHONE (08) 8223 7566
What was once an 1850s provisions store is
now a restaurant and wine bar specialising
in more contemporary provisions. Run by
Maggie Beer and her two daughters,
Charlick's turns out honest, regional
food running from THAT pâté to wild
rabbit and kangaroo.

GASTRO TEMPLE
the grange restaurant
HILTON ADELAIDE, VICTORIA SQUARE, ADELAIDE
PHONE (08) 8217 2000
The idea of any self-respecting foodie
visiting Adelaide without visiting the home
of kitchen god Cheong Liew is close to
blasphemy. The Malaysian-born master
chef who turned fusion into an artform
continues to amaze and inspire with his
flavour harmonies.

FOOD WITH A VIEW
magill estate restaurant
78 PENFOLD ROAD, MAGILL
PHONE (08) 8301 5551
Located on the very site where Max
Schubert created Grange Hermitage, this
smart modern restaurant with its views
over vines towards the bright lights of
Adelaide is still dedicated to the enjoyment
of red wine. Chris Matuhina's cooking is
suitably wine-friendly.

perth

FINE DINER
altos
424 HAY STREET, SUBIACO
PHONE (08) 9382 3292
A moody, stylish restaurant specialising in
equally stylish Northern Italian dishes.
Throw in snappy, helpful waiters, a smooth
crowd, and the best risotto in Perth, and
you're getting an experience that rises
above the pack.

PURE PERTH
jackson's restaurant
483 BEAUFORT STREET, HIGHGATE
PHONE (08) 9328 1177
Although Neal Jackson originally made his
name in the Bunbury region, Perth diners
wasted no time making this popular, classy
restaurant a local landmark. Here is cooking
with real finesse along with a separate,
dedicated vegetarian menu.

HOT SPOT
lamont's east perth
BROWN STREET, EAST PERTH
PHONE (08) 9202 1566
Known for her award-winning Swan Valley
restaurant, Kate Lamont has been called
the Maggie Beer of the West. Her swish
new restaurant, next to Janet Holmes à
Court's new gallery, features her polished,
yet honest cooking and views over
Claisebrook Cove.

CAFÉ LIFE
44 king street
44 KING STREET, PERTH
PHONE (08) 9321 4476
The staff are super-friendly, the feeling is
relaxed, the wines-by-the-glass list is huge,
and the food goes way beyond your normal
café fare. 44 King has been doing so many
things right for so long now, it's a legend.

EXOTICA
the globe
PARMELIA HILTON, MILL STREET, PERTH
PHONE (08) 9215 2421
There's a little more West in Cheong Liew's
famous East meets West cuisine, now that
it's found its way to Perth. As consulting
chef, Adelaide's famous fusion finesser has
put together an exciting Asian-influenced
menu in a modern stylish space.

GASTRO TEMPLE
the loose box
6825 GREAT EASTERN HWY, MUNDARING
PHONE (08) 9295 1787
Not every Western Australian chef can
boast the coveted Meilleur Ouvrier de
France. The 40-minute drive from Perth to
Mundaring is well worth the effort, for
the chance to sample rich, classical gutsy
French cooking in an idyllic setting.

FOOD WITH A VIEW
fraser's restaurant
FRASER AVENUE, KING'S PARK, WEST PERTH
PHONE (08) 9481 7100
For a restaurant that does such a good
job with seafood, they don't come much
higher or drier than Chris Taylor's perfectly
positioned restaurant, perched on a hill
in Perth's King's Park. The views over the
city are stunning, and Taylor's cooking is
super-confident.

brisbane

FINE DINER
circa
483 ADELAIDE STREET, BRISBANE
PHONE (07) 3832 4722
Pay special attention to the sauces at this classy Brisbane newcomer. Chef Craig Hopson was saucier at Paris's three-starred Lucas Carton and it shows in his scallops with white radish rémoulade and barramundi with vanilla parsnip sauce.

PURE BRISBANE
arc bistro
561 BRUNSWICK STREET, NEW FARM
PHONE (07) 3358 3600
Since leaving E'cco a year or two back, Peter McMillan has built up a steady fan club of his own at this plain but pleasant bistro where easy, Mediterranean flavours predominate.

HOT SPOT
II (two)
2 EDWARD STREET, BRISBANE
PHONE (07) 3210 0600
After wowing Brisbane at Two Small Rooms, chef David Pugh and partner Michael Conrad continue to make waves at their newest restaurant near the Botanic Gardens. Two is obviously their lucky number – it's pretty lucky for Brisbane diners too.

CAFE LIFE
aix café & bistro
83 MERTHYR ROAD, NEW FARM
PHONE (07) 3358 6444
The weekend breakfasts are legendary, but this bright popular meeting spot serves up a storm every day of the week from 7am to midnight. The grills are good, the cakes are moreish, the pastas are reliable, and the prices don't hurt a bit.

EXOTICA
marco polo
LEVEL 2, TREASURY CASINO, GEORGE STREET, BRISBANE   PHONE (07) 3306 8744
Wherever there's a casino, the chances are there's also a good Asian restaurant. So it is in Brisbane, where this plush award-winning restaurant puts a fusion twist on Chinese, Japanese and Indian dishes and throws in a great wine list for good measure.

GASTRO TEMPLE
e'cco bistro
CNR BOUNDARY ROAD & ADELAIDE STREET, BRISBANE   PHONE (07) 3831 8344
After also running the Hilton's fine dining restaurant for a brief period, Philip Johnson is now back full time at his popular easy-going bistro. With its finely honed, yet relaxed Mediterranean cooking, E'cco remains the heartbeat of Brisbane dining.

FOOD WITH A VIEW
pier nine
1 EAGLE STREET, BRISBANE
PHONE (07) 3229 2194
Whoever called Queensland 'beautiful one day, perfect the next' must have lunched on Pier Nine's river-view, sunny terrace. Throw in a mudcrab, some freshly opened oysters and a glass of something chilled, and it's like eating in a tourist ad.

QLD resorts

FINE DINER
cristel's
PARKROYAL SURFER'S PARADISE,
2807 GOLD COAST HIGHWAY, SURFERS
PARADISE   PHONE (07) 5592 9972
A hotel dining room with a difference, and
that difference is talented young chef, Steve
Ritchie. Out of his always pumping open
kitchen comes a swag of bright, innovative,
contemporary dishes that are occasionally
daring, but never boring.

PURE QUEENSLAND RESORT
nautilus restaurant
17 MURPHY STREET, PORT DOUGLAS
PHONE (07) 4099 5330
Sitting outside among the jungle-like foliage
with candles flickering, dining at Nautilus is
a gloriously romantic adventure. The whole
free-standing deep-fried coral trout is still
the go here.

HOT SPOT
fellini (gold coast)
LEVEL 1, WATERFRONT, MARINA MIRAGE,
SEAWORLD DRIVE, GOLD COAST
PHONE (07) 5531 0300
The Percuoco family – relatives of Sydney's
legendary Armando Percuoco – run what is
generally regarded as the Gold Coast's
finest restaurant. The marina views are
sensational, the staff are fun, and the
Italian cooking is first rate.

CAFÉ LIFE
fez bah
SHOP 6, 46 DUKE STREET, SUNSHINE BEACH
PHONE (07) 5447 5655
Laidback and friendly in a scatter-cushion
kind of way, Fez might be on Queensland
time, but its mindset is totally Turkish.
Everything from the luscious dips to the
excellent pide bread is the real thing, with
real flavour.

EXOTICA
max's native sun
SHOP 1, ISLANDER RESORT, THOMAS STREET,
NOOSAVILLE   PHONE (07) 5447 1931
Max Porter made his name in Noosa
cooking at the multi award-winning Artis.
While less salubrious, his shopfront
Noosaville eatery is equally well-loved for
its adventurous, wide-ranging menu that
runs from ostrich to local duck.

GASTRO TEMPLE
season
30 HASTINGS STREET, NOOSA HEADS
PHONE (07) 5447 3747
Gary Skelton's savvy Sydney bistro cooking
has effortlessly melded into Noosa's culinary
landscape. Look for his new beachside
restaurant Lumini for more of his (and chef
Glenn Bowman's) classy but simple cooking.

FOOD WITH A VIEW
ricky ricardo's deck bar and grill
NOOSA WHARF, QUAMBY PLACE,
NOOSA HEADS   PHONE (07) 5447 2455
Sitting out on the back deck overlooking the
water and the odd pelican is one of those
special Noosa moments. What makes it
even more special is Leonie Palmer's famed
hospitality and the eclectic tapas selection.

index by cuisine

225

Get a taste of the restaurant before you eat out.

Just visit www.citysearch.com.au to sample the most comprehensive guide to Sydney's restaurants. Here you can read the latest reviews, visit restaurant websites, cast an eye over the menu and even email a booking. All before you've set one foot outside your house.

The key to the city.

Subscribe to The Sydney Morning Herald and you'll get more than a great read every day. With a home delivery subscription you can enjoy the convenience of tomorrow's paper delivered directly to your home.

Open the door to The Sydney Morning Herald and we'll open the door to the best of Sydney for you. Only subscribers can enjoy all the benefits of subculture – a new program that offers priority bookings, exclusive invitations, discounts and giveaways for the very best of Sydney – art and cultural events, food, movies, music and more.

subculture

12345678   12/99

John A. Brown

Subscribe today. Call (02) 9282 3800 or visit us on the web at www.smh.com.

Offer is available to home delivery subscribers of The Sydney Morning Herald in NSW and the ACT where normal home delivery exists. KSMS0354

private rooms

Abhi's (North Strathfield), 2
Al Ponte (Darling Harbour), 3
Ampersand (City), 4
Andy's (Redfern), 5
Arakawa (City), 6
Archie's on the Park (South Armidale), 211
Arena (Moore Park), 6, 109
Aria (Circular Quay), 7, 65 109
Atlantic (Manuka), 162
Azuma (Crows Nest), 9
Banc (City), 10, 87, 130
Banjo Paterson Cottage (Gladesville), 11
The Bantam Café (Berrima), 204
Bathers' Pavilion (Balmoral), 11, 65
Bathers' Pavilion Café (Balmoral), 12, 21
Bay Road Bistro (Lane Cove), 12
Bayswater Brasserie (Kings Cross), 13
BBQ King (City), 13, 109
Bennelong (City), 15
Beppi's (East Sydney), 15
The Boat House by the Lake (Barton), 162
Bonne Femme (East Sydney), 23
Brazil (Manly), 24
Brooklyn Hotel (City), 24
Brooklyn on Fitzroy (Tumut), 212
Buon Ricordo (Paddington), 26
Byrne's Mill (Queanbeyan), 163
Cafe Albion (Wickham), 180
Cafe Sydney (Circular Quay), 27
Cala Luna (Mosman), 28
Casa Asturiana (City), 29, 109
The Chairman & Yip (Civic), 163
Chequers (Chatswood), 30
Chez Pok (Pokolbin), 175
Cicada (Potts Point), 32
Civic Dining (City), 32
Civic Theatre Brasserie (Newcastle), 180
Claudes (Woollahra), 33
Claudine's (Chatswood), 34
Cleopatra (Blackheath), 156
Coast (City), 35
Cookaburra's (Ulladulla), 197
Courtney's Brasserie (Parramatta), 37
Dakhni (Glebe), 37

Darley's (Katoomba), 156
Darling Mills (Glebe), 38
Doncaster Inn (Braidwood), 197
Dragon Sharkfin and Seafood (Chatswood), 41
Ebisu (Potts Point), 44
Echidna Cafe (Dubbo), 213
Edna's Table (City), 45
Elio (Leichhardt), 46
Epic Foods (Surry Hills), 48
Esca Bimbadgen (Pokolbin), 174, 176
Fare Go Gourmet (North Sydney), 50
Fez Cafe (Darlinghurst), 50, 87
Fig (Griffith), 164
Fitzroy Inn (Mittagong), 205
Flavour of India Glebe (Glebe), 53
Flavours of Peking (Castlecrag), 54
Fook Yuen (Chatswood), 54
Forty One (City), 55, 65
Freshwater (Harbord), 56
Fu-Manchu Bondi (Bondi Beach), 58, 65
Galileo (City), 58
The Galley Beach House (Terrigal), 172
Gekko (City), 59
Georgie's Café (Grafton), 187
Golden Century (Haymarket), 60, 109
Golden Kingdom Beijing House (Kensington), 60
grand pacific blue room (Paddington), 62, 130
Greenwood Chinese (North Sydney), 63
harbour kitchen & bar (The Rocks), 63, 65
Highland Heritage Estate (Orange), 214
Hordern's (Bowral), 206
Il Perugino (Mosman), 68
Il Trattoraro Pizzeria (Concord), 69
Imperial Peking Blakehurst (Blakehurst), 70
Indian Palace (Balmain), 70
International (Kings Cross), 71, 130
Jaspers (Hunters Hill), 72
Jenkins Street Guest House (Nundle), 215
The Jersey Cow (Woollahra), 72
Jonah's (Palm Beach), 73
Kable's (City), 74
Kam Fook (Haymarket), 74

Kamogawa (City), 75
Katers (Sutton Forest), 207
La Goulue (Crows Nest), 78
La Grillade (Crows Nest), 78
La Mensa (Paddington), 79, 109
Le Kiosk (Manly), 80
Lennons (Drummoyne), 81
Letterbox (Terrigal), 172
Lindsay House (Armidale), 215
The Little Snail (Forster), 188
L'Oasis (Griffith), 216
Longrain (Surry Hills), 83, 130
Lothar's on Pymble Hill (Pymble), 84
Lotus Pond (Pyrmont), 85
Lucio's (Paddington), 85
L'Unico (Balmain), 88
Lynwood Café (Collector), 204, 207
Machiavelli (City), 89
Malabar (Crows Nest), 90
Malaya on George (City), 90
Marigold (City), 91
Marigold Citymark (City), 92
Merrett's at Peppers Anchorage (Corlette), 182
Mezzalira (Canberra City), 166
MG Garage (Surry Hills), 87, 94
Milsons (Kirribilli), 95
Minh (Dulwich Hill), 95
Misaki Byron (Byron Bay), 189
The Mixing Pot (Glebe), 96
Mount Tomah Botanic Gardens Restaurant (Mount Tomah), 158
Mulligan's Brasserie (Pokolbin), 176
Nagano Shinshu-Mura (Orange), 216
Nelsons Brasserie (The Rocks), 98
Neptune Palace (Circular Quay), 98
Niche Dining House (Beverly Hills), 99
Nielsen Park Kiosk (Vaucluse), 100
Ocean King House (Kogarah), 101
Odeon (Potts Point), 101
The Old George and Dragon (East Maitland), 177
Olympic Hotel (Paddington), 102
Original Peking VIP (City), 103
Otto (Woolloomooloo), 104, 109
Pacific Hotel Bistro (Yamba), 190
Paddington Inn (Paddington), 105
Palisade (Millers Point), 105
Pavilion on the Park (City), 106
Pazzo (Surry Hills), 107
Perama (Petersham), 110
Pier (Rose Bay), 111

outdoor eating

wheelchair access

Open on Sunday

alphabetical index

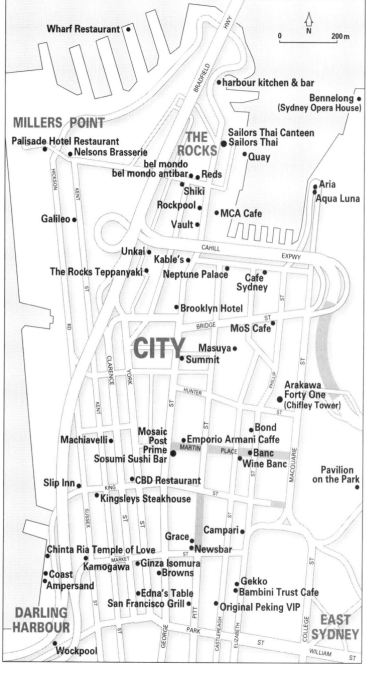

Wharf Restaurant

N

0   200 m

harbour kitchen & bar

Bennelong
(Sydney Opera House)

MILLERS POINT

Palisade Hotel Restaurant

Nelsons Brasserie

THE
ROCKS

Sailors Thai Canteen
Sailors Thai

Quay

bel mondo
bel mondo antibar   Reds

Aria
Aqua Luna

Shiki

Rockpool

MCA Cafe

Galileo

Vault

CAHILL   EXPWY

Unkai

Kable's

The Rocks Teppanyaki

Neptune Palace

Cafe
Sydney

Brooklyn Hotel

BRIDGE

MoS Cafe

CITY

Masuya

Summit

Arakawa
Forty One
(Chifley Tower)

HUNTER

Bond

Machiavelli

Mosaic
Post
Prime

Emporio Armani Caffe

MARTIN   PLACE

Banc
Wine Banc

Sosumi Sushi Bar

Slip Inn

KING

CBD Restaurant

Pavilion
on the Park

Kingsleys Steakhouse

Campari

Grace

Newsbar

Chinta Ria Temple of Love

MARKET

Ginza Isomura

Kamogawa

Browns

Coast

Gekko

Ampersand

Bambini Trust Cafe

Edna's Table

San Francisco Grill

Original Peking VIP

DARLING
HARBOUR

EAST
SYDNEY

Wockpool

GEORGE   PARK

WILLIAM   ST

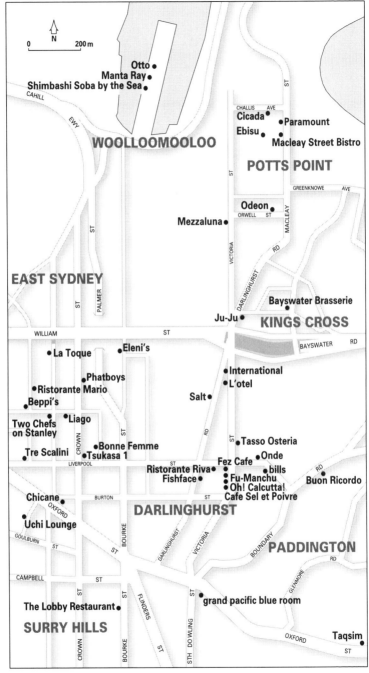

0   200 m

Otto •
Manta Ray •
Shimbashi Soba by the Sea •

CAHILL
EWY

WOOLLOOMOOLOO

CHALLIS   AVE
Cicada •
Ebisu • • Paramount
Macleay Street Bistro •

POTTS POINT

GREENKNOWE   AVE

Odeon •
ORWELL   ST
Mezzaluna •

MACLEAY
RD

EAST SYDNEY

PALMER

DARLINGHURST

Bayswater Brasserie •

Ju-Ju • •   **KINGS CROSS**

WILLIAM   ST
BAYSWATER   RD

• Eleni's
• La Toque

• International
• L'otel

• Phatboys
• Ristorante Mario
Salt •

• Beppi's
• Liago
Two Chefs
on Stanley
• Bonne Femme
• Tre Scalini   • Tsukasa 1
LIVERPOOL

CROWN

• Tasso Osteria
• Onde
Fez Cafe •   • bills
RD
Ristorante Riva •   • Fu-Manchu   Buon Ricordo •
Fishface •   • Oh! Calcutta!
Cafe Sel et Poivre •

Chicane •
BURTON
OXFORD
Uchi Lounge •
GOULBURN   ST

DARLINGHURST

BOURKE

DARLINGHURST

VICTORIA

BOUNDARY

PADDINGTON
GLENMORE   RD

CAMPBELL   ST

CROWN

BOURKE

FLINDERS

STH DOWLING

The Lobby Restaurant •

• grand pacific blue room

SURRY HILLS

OXFORD

Taqsim •
ST

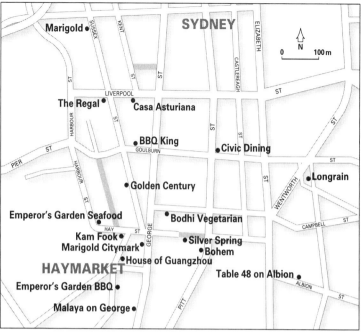

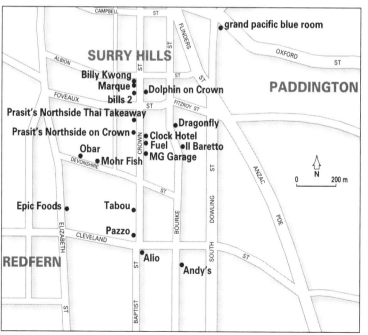

4A

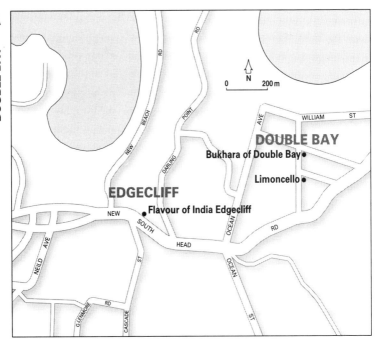

0 N 200 m

WILLIAM ST

DOUBLE BAY

Bukhara of Double Bay ●

Limoncello ●

EDGECLIFF

● Flavour of India Edgecliff

NEW SOUTH HEAD RD

OCEAN ST

4B

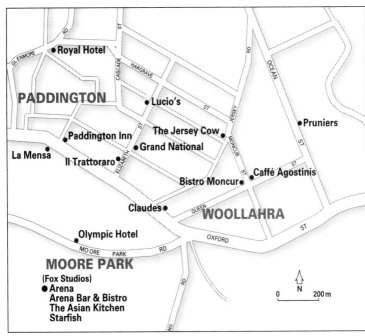

● Royal Hotel

HARGRAVE

● Lucio's

PADDINGTON

● Pruniers

● Paddington Inn   The Jersey Cow

La Mensa ●   ● Grand National

Il Trattoraro   ● Caffé Agostinis

Bistro Moncur ●

Claudes ●   **WOOLLAHRA**

● Olympic Hotel

MOORE PARK RD   OXFORD ST

MOORE PARK

(Fox Studios)
● Arena
   Arena Bar & Bistro
   The Asian Kitchen
   Starfish

0 N 200 m

244

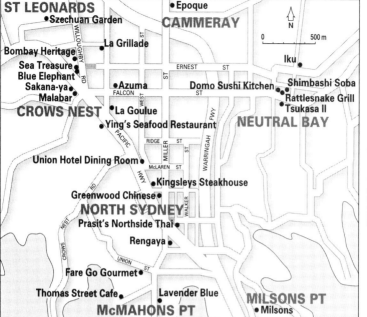

ST LEONARDS
● Epoque
● Szechuan Garden
CAMMERAY
N
0   500 m
● La Grillade
Bombay Heritage ●
● Iku
Sea Treasure ●
Blue Elephant ●
Sakana-ya ●
Malabar ●
● Azuma
FALCON
Domo Sushi Kitchen ●
Shimbashi Soba ●
Rattlesnake Grill ●
Tsukasa II ●
CROWS NEST
● La Goulue
NEUTRAL BAY
● Ying's Seafood Restaurant
RIDGE   ST
MILLER   ST
McLAREN   ST
Union Hotel Dining Room ●
● Kingsleys Steakhouse
Greenwood Chinese ●
NORTH SYDNEY
WALKER
Prasit's Northside Thai ●
Rengaya ●
UNION   ST
Fare Go Gourmet ●
Thomas Street Cafe ●
● Lavender Blue
MILSONS PT
McMAHONS PT
● Milsons

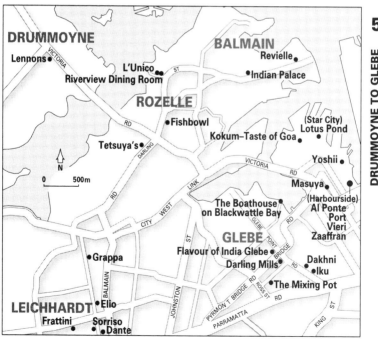

DRUMMOYNE
BALMAIN
Lennons ●
Revielle ●
● L'Unico
Riverview Dining Room ●
● Indian Palace
ROZELLE
● Fishbowl
(Star City)
Lotus Pond ●
Tetsuya's ●
Kokum–Taste of Goa ●
VICTORIA   RD
Yoshii ●
N
0   500m
Masuya ●
The Boathouse ●
on Blackwattle Bay
(Harbourside)
Al Ponte
Port
Vieri
Zaaffran
GLEBE
● Grappa
Flavour of India Glebe ●
Darling Mills ●
Dakhni ●
● Iku
LEICHHARDT
● Elio
● The Mixing Pot
Frattini ●   Sorriso ●
● Dante

WAHROONGA
The Coonanbarra Cafe

Scoozi Trattoria
WESTLEIGH

PARRAMATTA
Temasek• •Courtney's Brasserie

WESTERN

MOTORWAY

CONCORD
Il Trattoraro Pizzeria

•Abhi's
NORTH
STRATHFIELD

CABRAMATTA
Thanh Binh•

HUME   HWY

BANKSTOWN
An Restaurant•

PUNCHBOWL
•Summerland

BEVERLEY
HILLS

Niche Dining House•
Friendship Oriental

MORTDALE
•Philip's

N
0   5 km

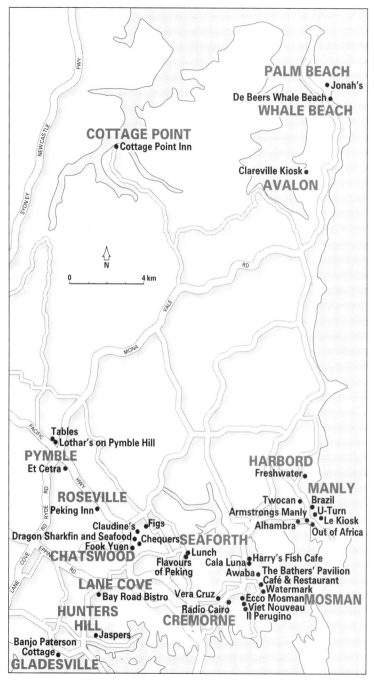

PALM BEACH
• Jonah's
De Beers Whale Beach •
WHALE BEACH

COTTAGE POINT
• Cottage Point Inn

Clareville Kiosk •
AVALON

N
0   4 km

RD

MONA VALE

Tables
• Lothar's on Pymble Hill
PYMBLE
Et Cetra •

PACIFIC

HARBORD
Freshwater •
MANLY

ROSEVILLE
Peking Inn •

RYDE RD

Claudine's • Figs
Dragon Sharkfin and Seafood •   • Chequers
Fook Yuen •
CHATSWOOD

LANE COVE

EPPING RD

Twocan •   Brazil
Armstrongs Manly •   • U-Turn
Alhambra •   • Le Kiosk
Out of Africa

SEAFORTH
• Lunch
Flavours   Cala Luna •   Harry's Fish Cafe •
of Peking   Awaba •   • The Bathers' Pavilion
Café & Restaurant
Vera Cruz •   • Watermark
• Bay Road Bistro   • Ecco Mosman
Radio Cairo •   • Viet Nouveau   MOSMAN
HUNTERS   CREMORNE   Il Perugino
HILL   • Jaspers
Banjo Paterson
Cottage •
GLADESVILLE

NEW CASTLE FWY
SYDNEY

LANE COVE RD

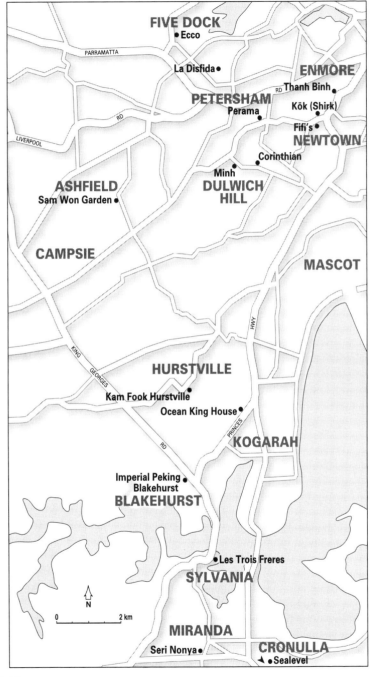

FIVE DOCK
• Ecco

PARRAMATTA

La Disfida •

ENMORE

RD Thanh Binh •

PETERSHAM
Perama •

Kök (Shirk) •

Fifi's •

LIVERPOOL

RD

NEWTOWN

Corinthian •

ASHFIELD

Minh •

DULWICH
HILL

Sam Won Garden •

CAMPSIE

MASCOT

HWY

KING

HURSTVILLE

GEORGES

Kam Fook Hurstville •

Ocean King House •

RD

PRINCES

KOGARAH

Imperial Peking •
Blakehurst

BLAKEHURST

• Les Trois Freres

SYLVANIA

↑
N

0   2 km

MIRANDA

Seri Nonya •

CRONULLA

◄ • Sealevel

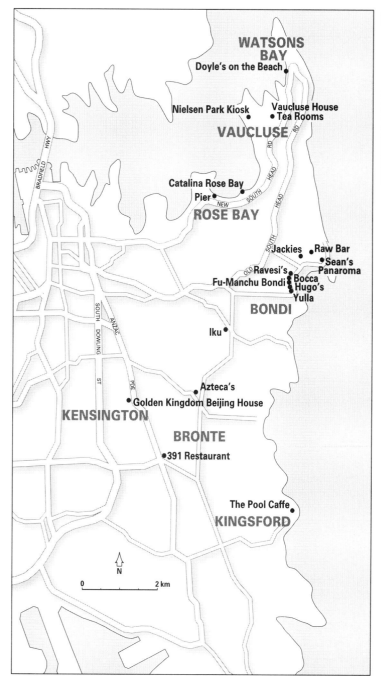

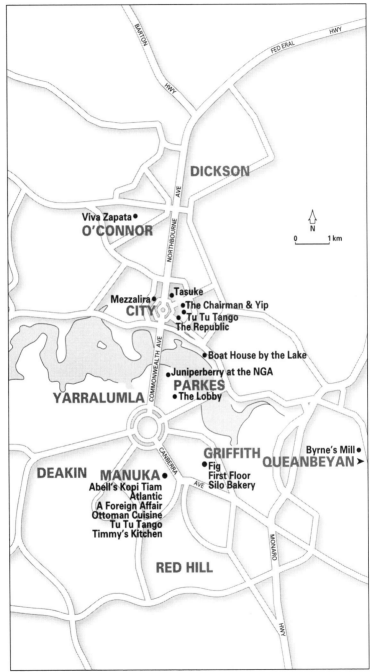

BARTON HWY

FED ERAL HWY

DICKSON

NORTHBOURNE AVE

Viva Zapata •
O'CONNOR

N
0   1 km

• Tasuke
Mezzalira •   •The Chairman & Yip
CITY   •Tu Tu Tango
              The Republic

COMMONWEALTH AVE

• Boat House by the Lake

• Juniperberry at the NGA

PARKES

YARRALUMLA   •The Lobby

CANBERRA AVE

GRIFFITH   Byrne's Mill •

QUEANBEYAN ➤

•Fig
First Floor
Silo Bakery

DEAKIN   **MANUKA** •
Abell's Kopi Tiam
Atlantic
A Foreign Affair
Ottoman Cuisine
Tu Tu Tango
Timmy's Kitchen

MONARO

RED HILL

HWY

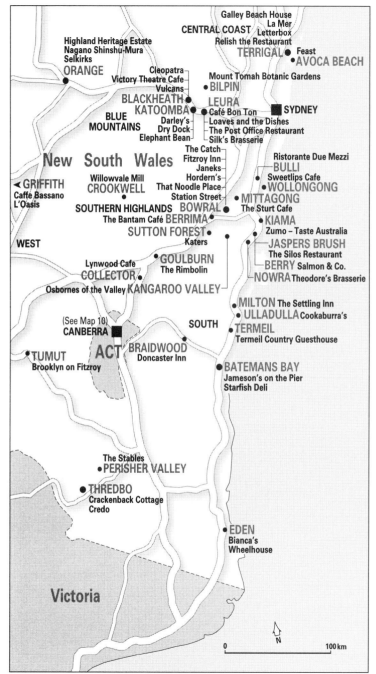

Galley Beach House
La Mer
CENTRAL COAST Letterbox
Relish the Restaurant
TERRIGAL Feast
AVOCA BEACH

Highland Heritage Estate
Nagano Shinshu-Mura
Selkirks
ORANGE

Cleopatra
Victory Theatre Cafe
Vulcans

Mount Tomah Botanic Gardens
BILPIN

BLACKHEATH
KATOOMBA
LEURA
Café Bon Ton
SYDNEY

BLUE
MOUNTAINS
Darley's
Dry Dock
Elephant Bean
Loaves and the Dishes
The Post Office Restaurant
Silk's Brasserie

New South Wales
The Catch
Fitzroy Inn
Janeks
Hordern's
That Noodle Place
Station Street

Ristorante Due Mezzi
BULLI
Sweetlips Cafe
WOLLONGONG

GRIFFITH
Caffè Bassano
L'Oasis

Willowvale Mill
CROOKWELL
SOUTHERN HIGHLANDS BOWRAL
The Bantam Café BERRIMA
SUTTON FOREST
Katers

MITTAGONG
The Sturt Cafe
KIAMA
Zumo – Taste Australia
JASPERS BRUSH
The Silos Restaurant
BERRY Salmon & Co.
NOWRA Theodore's Brasserie

WEST

Lynwood Cafe
COLLECTOR
GOULBURN
The Rimbolin
Osbornes of the Valley KANGAROO VALLEY

MILTON The Settling Inn
ULLADULLA Cookaburra's
TERMEIL
Termeil Country Guesthouse

(See Map 10)
CANBERRA

SOUTH

ACT
BRAIDWOOD
Doncaster Inn

TUMUT
Brooklyn on Fitzroy

BATEMANS BAY
Jameson's on the Pier
Starfish Deli

The Stables
PERISHER VALLEY
THREDBO
Crackenback Cottage
Credo

EDEN
Bianca's
Wheelhouse

Victoria

0   100 km

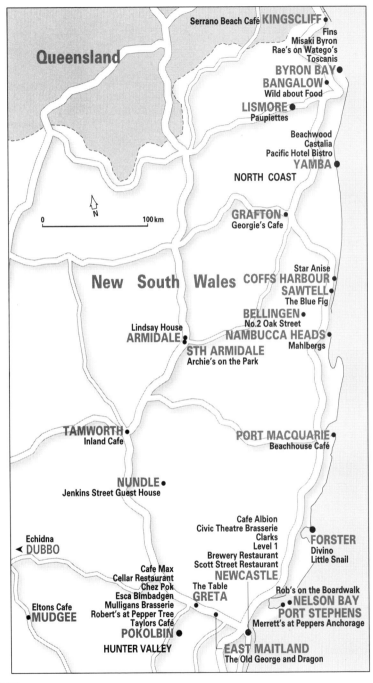

Serrano Beach Café **KINGSCLIFF**

Queensland

Fins
Misaki Byron
Rae's on Watego's
Toscanis
BYRON BAY
BANGALOW
Wild about Food

LISMORE
Paupiettes

Beachwood
Castalia
Pacific Hotel Bistro
YAMBA

NORTH COAST

0   100 km
N

GRAFTON
Georgie's Cafe

New   South   Wales

Star Anise
COFFS HARBOUR
SAWTELL
The Blue Fig

BELLINGEN
No.2 Oak Street

Lindsay House
ARMIDALE

NAMBUCCA HEADS
Mahlbergs

STH ARMIDALE
Archie's on the Park

TAMWORTH
Inland Cafe

PORT MACQUARIE
Beachhouse Café

NUNDLE
Jenkins Street Guest House

Cafe Albion
Civic Theatre Brasserie
Clarks
Level 1
Brewery Restaurant
Scott Street Restaurant

FORSTER
Divino
Little Snail

Echidna
◄ **DUBBO**

Cafe Max
Cellar Restaurant
Chez Pok
Esca Bimbadgen
Mulligans Brasserie
Robert's at Pepper Tree
Taylors Café
POKOLBIN

HUNTER VALLEY

The Table
GRETA

NEWCASTLE

Rob's on the Boardwalk
NELSON BAY
PORT STEPHENS
Merrett's at Peppers Anchorage

Eltons Cafe
MUDGEE

EAST MAITLAND
The Old George and Dragon